Dan –
In the hopes we never
tire of talking about history –
Gran
Christmas, 2007

THE AGE *of* LINCOLN

THE AGE *of* LINCOLN

Orville Vernon Burton

HILL AND WANG

A division of Farrar, Straus and Giroux

New York

HILL AND WANG

A division of Farrar, Straus and Giroux

19 Union Square West, New York 10003

ISBN-13: 978-0-8090-9513-1

Designed by Cassandra J. Pappas

Book Club Edition

For Georganne

The Kentuckian, LINCOLN, defended the Declaration of Independence against the attacks of the degenerate Vermonter, DOUGLAS, and against BRECKENRIDGE and the whole ruling class of the South. Here was a Southerner, with eloquence that would bear a comparison with HENRY CLAY'S, defending Liberty and the North against the leaders of the Border Ruffians and Doughfaces of Illinois.

—*Belleville Weekly Advocate* (Illinois), October 22, 1856

If God now wills the removal of a great wrong, and wills also that we of the North as well as you of the South, shall pay fairly for our complicity in that wrong, impartial history will find therein new cause to attest and revere the justice and goodness of God.

—Abraham Lincoln to Albert Hodges, April 4, 1864

Contents

THE AGE *of* LINCOLN

Prologue

RIVERS OF BLOOD flowed as Americans turned against each other in battle. The land was torn asunder. Four and a half months after the Battle of Gettysburg, standing in the November chill of a military cemetery still hardly half-finished, President Abraham Lincoln articulated the meaning of the battle, of the war, of the American dream. He called for a "new birth of freedom."

In Mathew Brady's famous photograph of that day, Abraham Lincoln looks ordinary, indistinct, trivial. The crowd of twenty thousand had come to hear another man, silver-tongued Edward Everett, onetime president of Harvard and former senator from Massachusetts, speak of valor and values and victory, the stuff of melodrama that the age so loved. None could have anticipated the president's confession, the benediction, and the challenge he set forth in the sweep of a few sentences. With the Gettysburg Address, Lincoln proclaimed the hopeful determination of the human spirit. That determination is, ultimately, the theme of this book, which traces the forces and events that led Lincoln to speak of liberty in a Pennsylvania graveyard in 1863, and considers the path Americans would take across the next three decades. This determination for freedom and the numerous contests it would inspire would become the legacy of the Age of Lincoln.

Lincoln began his brief remarks at Gettysburg with a grand, overreaching claim, declaring that eighty-seven years earlier "our fathers" had brought forth "a new nation." The population of the country eighty-seven years earlier was about 2.5 million men and women; the population in 1863 was about 32 million and rising. Lincoln's claim discounted the impact of these newcomers. These men and women from England, Ireland, Germany, China, and elsewhere had played no part in shaping the country's fortunes initially but were now making their presence felt on the battlefield, on the homefront, and in the broader culture.

The new nation's very name—the United States—gave lie to single-mindedness. From the start, that had been more than half the problem. Thirteen separate political entities with divergent cultural traditions and economic interests had been lashed together by the rebellious acts of a strident minority in the mid-1770s and, once the British had been expelled, assembled into a loose confederation. Even after the federal Constitution supplanted the Articles of Confederation in 1789, state power and regional differences remained strong. Most citizens considered themselves New Englanders or Virginians or derived their identities from smaller localities still. Others used occupation, religion, or ethnicity to explain who they were. Yet Lincoln in 1863 was seeking prior ratification for the revolutionary changes he was so hard at work in promoting. For America, since Fort Sumter's fall, was rapidly and irreversibly *becoming* "a new nation."

At this moment of apocalypse the nation into which Lincoln had been born had changed dramatically and was now at a crossroads. The Age of Jackson had seen the extraordinary opening of democracy and the suffrage to white men, even propertyless white men. The Age of Lincoln would see democracy fused with a millennial impulse, leading many to believe in the near attainment of Christian perfection and a patriotic certainty that America was meant to witness it. While disagreeing, often dramatically, as to particulars, a majority of Americans felt they knew how to perfect this white man's democracy and felt compelled to convince one another, even as they spread this wonderful experiment through Manifest Destiny. For reformers who knew God's will, there could be no compromises on the path to true Christian righteousness. In the North, all the reform issues of the day, from temperance to women's rights, ultimately fetched up on the shoals of the one uncompromisable issue, slavery. For abolitionist millennialists, there could be no heaven on earth with the evil of slavery embedded in the very fabric of the nation. For southern white proslavery advocates, their orderly plantation society reflected the will of God, and they worked to bring that millenarian community to the nation.

Lincoln's faith, however, precluded understanding the mind of God. Although certain that God was using him to His end in working out history, Lincoln found it presumptuous to dictate what God's intent might be. Thus, in order to ensure that democracy could work, that the republic could survive, citizens had to rely on law. And amid the horrors of a nation embroiled in civil war, Lincoln developed his own view very different from the majority's: freedom means equal rights protected by the rule of law. Only the rule of law could check the fundamentalist and fanatical impulses that stemmed from this millennial age. Born of his very southern yeoman sense of honor, Lincoln's ideas of equality of opportunity protected by the law became incorporated into the document he revered, the Constitution. Ironically, African Americans went from being the immovable obstacle to millennial attainments to being the clearest benefactors of the new nation the president proclaimed. Moreover, former slaves would become Lincoln's true heirs and the greatest champions of the republican values that Lincoln identified as crucial to the survival of the nation. And, in a further irony, in fighting the war that enabled this remarkable achievement, Lincoln inadvertently unleashed the worst as well as the best angels of democratic capitalism.

A great lie encompassed all generalizations about American freedom. The new nation, Lincoln pronounced, had been "conceived in liberty" and "dedicated to the proposition that all men are created equal." Here again lay trouble. Revolutionary America had been born of commerce, expropriation, war, and slavery. Its premises were grounded in ruthless ideas of inequality of race, class, and gender. The Founding Fathers *had* been men of high principle and breathtaking vision—Lincoln's words here, after all, merely quoted and qualified what Thomas Jefferson had written in the Declaration of Independence. Yet Patrick Henry's prerevolutionary cry for liberty or death had been the shout of a self-interested slaveholder as well as a selfless patriot. The right of property, like the wealth of thousands of other patriots from northern as well as southern colonies, had been rooted directly and indirectly in slavery.

At Gettysburg the president passed over in silence how freedom's meanings had been debated across three generations and more. That conflict had been rehearsed endlessly in newspapers, pamphlets, and speeches—and in violent acts of rebellion and repression, vigilantism and terror. Lincoln's own evolving views had been clearly set forth in debate against the Democrat Stephen Douglas for an Illinois senatorial seat, in the pleas and warnings of his inaugural address, and finally in the Emancipation Proclamation that he had delivered the previous January. Lincoln often spoke about the differences between two groups who "declare for liberty." Some, he said, used the word *liberty* to mean that each man could "do as he pleases with himself, and the product of his labor." Others used the word *liberty* meaning "for some men to do as they please with other men, and the product of other men's labor."

The problems of freedom that Lincoln and Americans wrestled with were part of a debate that stretched back centuries and that had expanded to global proportions. Regardless of color, most migrants to the American colonies before 1750 had come in chains, physical or legal. Most blacks arrived bound to labor for the one who enslaved them; they were to be enslaved for their whole lives, as were their children and children's children after them. They had been reduced to this awful fate, in most cases, by the intersection of European power and the social conditions of African life. Tribal warfare, slave raiding, indebtedness, or the fiat of kin and community meant that Africans worked hand in glove with Europeans to kidnap and enslave Africans.

Prior to 1750 most whites were also driven or drawn into conditions of unfreedom in the New World, entering servitude on a temporary and "voluntary" basis to settle a debt or a criminal conviction. They came because the old order in Britain and across Europe had been on the decline for the preceding century. There for the past one hundred years, men with the means to do it drew new lines on maps, laying individual claim to lands that had previously supported many. They enclosed their estates with walls, fences, and hedges. They deforested the lands, drained marshes and fens, and replaced unprofitable human occupants—tenants and crofters—with moneymaking sheep and cattle. Propertied interests hunted down the working people they had evicted with new statutes making poverty and homelessness a crime, changing hunting and fishing into trespass and theft, and putting forth the gallows, the workhouse, military service, or colonial servitude as the only options for many. Colonial servitude for whites, however, was never as bleak as for enslaved blacks. Whites came toward more freedom rather than less, for themselves and most definitely for their progeny.

The early republic offered whites an unparalleled freedom to be left alone by powers of church and nation-state. That citizens would not be unrepresented, mistaxed, overlorded, or involuntarily impressed into military service put the country in a New World indeed. Others did not fare as well. Lincoln made no reference to antislavery struggles; nor, in passing from "[f]our score and seven years ago" to "now," did he recount how the forefathers had mortgaged the bright promise of freedom at America's birth. The boldest words against slavery had been stricken from the Declaration of Independence as deal-breakers. The Articles of Confederation had turned a blind eye to bondage. The constitutional framers, with no hope of achieving unity to legislate its uprooting, had written racial division (though studiously avoiding the word *slavery* itself) into the fundamental law of the land. Enslaved blacks, asserted the wisest of white minds, counted as three-fifths human when it came to reckoning taxation and political representation. Statute law and simple racism ranked both free and enslaved African Americans lower still. Freedom-seeking fugitives from slavery were to be captured and reenslaved. In the early republic political unity and freedom of commerce were the more fundamental values. By 1861 Jefferson's self-evident "truth" about human equality had become to Lincoln's generation a very debatable "proposition."

Those who threatened stability with rebellion on behalf of personal rights all discovered that the government's willingness to maintain order took precedence over personal freedom. Rebellions among the enslaved were put down quickly. When slaves in New York rebelled in 1712 and in South Carolina in 1739, colonialists stiffened their laws, sure that hard punishment would end further resistance. They were wrong. Unruly whites also—the farmers who followed Daniel Shays in Massachusetts in 1786 and 1787 against the government's unfair taxation and one-sided juries, the Whiskey Rebels of western Pennsylvania in 1794 who demanded government services and protested the whiskey tax, and much later in 1841 the propertyless Rhode Islanders who demanded the right to vote and fought federal troops in the Dorr War—discovered the limits of freedom.

Individuals spoke out in pursuit of freedom for all, but they were simply ignored and marginalized. American slavery grew and thrived in the cotton South as that crop fed an industrial revolution in the North. In both North and South slavery was sanctioned by law. The slave system created a civilization in deadly opposition to—yet wholly enmeshed with—northern capitalism.

Lincoln spoke to a nationwide aspiration among yeomen for equality of opportunity under the law. That aspiration defined for many northerners a view of freedom that prompted their loyalty to the Union. Lincoln's consistent advocacy of opportunity and free labor, however, held flaws as well as promise, and Lincoln was slow to see how power and greed could subvert those ideals. Lincoln made no mention at Gettysburg of how Yankee dreams could become a nightmare. An ever-quickening market revolution brought prosperity for some, poverty for others, and an overall anxiety about the loss of personal autonomy and freedom. While most working people still labored on farms, workers in growing urban centers discovered industrialization brought them long hours, low pay, frequent layoffs, and the specter of industrial injury, sickness, or death. Meanwhile new arrivals continued to flood into the cities, seeking opportunity and undercutting wages. From the perspective of the old elite, these new people "corrupted" politics and "polluted" culture. While both sides of the Mason-Dixon Line agreed on the founders' vision of liberty, the consensus on how to maintain that vision was shattered.

That may partly explain why Lincoln's words at Gettysburg were so focused on the present—and the future. Constructing and consecrating military graveyards was—and is—far from what the revolutionary founders aimed at with their words and deeds. The ceremony, Lincoln implied, was a waste of time and effort if that was all it accomplished. "The brave men, living and dead, who struggled here," he noted, "have consecrated it, far above our poor power to add or detract." But they had left their work "unfinished." A "great task" lay ahead. The task was not simply restoration or reconstruction; it was a rebirth. Lincoln here spoke a language of love, patriotism, and piety to his listeners: honor, dedication, increased devotion, and strong resolve needed to be brought to the labor. As he stated in his first presidential address, this conflict, this task, was not about North and South, black and white. Human liberty and democracy themselves were at stake. What would victory in this awful war look like? Lincoln's vision was at once conservative and revolutionary. There would be overflowing cemeteries, vacant chairs at family tables, and men broken bodily and spiritually, but "government of the people, by the people, for the people shall not perish from the earth." More than simply preserving the liberty of the fathers, Lincoln's new nation, "under God," would have "a new birth of freedom."

One

Kindred Spirits and Double-Minded Men

FROM THE ROCKY SHORES of Maine to the Ohio Valley and beyond, men and women by the thousands rose up early on the morning of October 22, 1844. Quickly and carefully they bathed, put on spotless new clothes, and expectantly went outside. They looked up toward heaven. Before the day was through the skies were to open, the angels of the Lord were to descend, and the world they knew was to come to an end. Today was the day appointed for Christ's return to judge mankind and establish God's rule on earth.

It was not to be. Although their leader, a Baptist minister named William Miller, had promised through thirteen years of vibrant preaching that the advent of the millennium had been calculated down to that very day, their faith was disappointed. Many had abandoned farms and workshops; others had given away worldly possessions in expectation of the Second Coming. They knelt on rooftops, bowed their heads in prayer, and waited, shivering in an early winter's wind and rain, for the Savior's return. Finally they stood up in confusion, went home, and continued on with their lives. That was an act of faith of a rather different sort.

In the 1800s many Americans came to embrace a new and radical idea, that they could advance the millennium by right living. Faithfully, eagerly, defiantly, they took up cudgels against the evils they saw around and within them. They did not simply wait for the government of God. They believed they could bring on the glad day of jubilee by piety and the labors of their own hands, and they strove to make that vision real. "There is more day to dawn," Henry David Thoreau assured them even as he eschewed the growing materialism, and the best was yet to come: "The sun is but a morning star." His was an ascetic version of a faith in boundless uplift and spiritual perfection that motivated the age in count-less ways. "Make sure you are right," that rough-hewn, larger-than-life folk hero Davy Crockett told his countrymen, "then go ahead." Whether progress meant—as it did in Crockett's case—dispossessing and killing Native Americans, spreading slavery, and stealing foreign lands at gun-point was of no consequence. For the vast majority of Americans such considerations little impinged on establishing whether they, or America, were right.

Faith helped to balance the warring dualities that abounded throughout antebellum culture: East and West, wilderness and civiliza-tion, country and city, rudeness and refinement, home and market. Older patriots worried that the poles of each opposition might tear asunder the American experiment in liberty. While some worried that the moral and political contradiction of slavery would trip up progress, other men and women located the difficulty in neglect of God, corrup-tion of community, and the pursuit of mammon. Most were convinced that the American experiment was intimately interwoven with the con-cerns uppermost in their minds.

Across the antebellum era northern and southern American atti-tudes toward commerce betrayed deep ambivalence. Many enjoyed a growing prosperity and availability of goods. At the same time many considered the market a place of trickery and danger. The real riches seemed to accrue to men of commerce, like the wealthy John Jacob Astor, or to conniving "Sam Slicks" who bought cheap and sold dear, fleecing a portion of others' well-earned income for their own narrow benefit. The common farmer and his family, who might know nothing more of reading than Holy Scripture and *Pilgrim's Progress*, understood enough to give Vanity Fair a wide berth. Could the market possibly serve the new nation as the engine of freedom without engendering inequal-ity and abundant sin?

Ambiguity and contradiction grew as the nation expanded in territory. On April 30, 1803, American and French negotiators signed the deal for Louisiana—not the ownership of but the right to settle the vast territory marked on maps simply as "Indian Territory." For this Louisiana Purchase, which President Thomas Jefferson called an "Empire for Liberty," the United States government paid Napoleon $11.25 million, and they paid American merchants in the Northeast another $3.75 million to cover outstanding claims against the French. Two months after the purchase, when Jefferson commissioned an expedition to explore the territory, he told Meriwether Lewis that the object of the journey was "for the purpose of commerce." The purchase added over 800,000 square miles, territory that would become thirteen states. A disaster for Native Americans, it made American citizens of French and Spanish settlers, whether Catholic or Protestant, rich or poor, familiar or unfamiliar with U.S. history and traditions. The population of New Orleans included an influx of free black refugees from Haiti, the second independent nation in the western hemisphere and the first black-led nation. Many of these new U.S. citizens of color held slaves and worked hard to perpetuate slavery. Yet, they joined other free people of color who advocated the blessings of liberty for an educated elite such as themselves.

As the country grew, national bonds between South and North remained strong. The root of commonality was the household itself, at once an economic, familial, and political unit. Leadership over the home was the sign of personal independence, an attainment that white males worked toward across early adulthood as they acquired property, achieved skill at their trade or craft, created a network of relations with other men of property and ambition, and gained the reputation and the wherewithal to wed and begin a family of their own. Soon enough other figures would gather within the household: servants and apprentices, extended kin of all sorts. In North and South both, the market economy nourished the growth of households. Although free labor predominated in one section and slavery in the other, similarities often seemed to outweigh differences. In both the North and the South, men of property understood that their economic success, their social reputations, the legacy of their heirs, and the good of the nation itself depended on their ability to bend will and nurture skill among subordinates. They also believed this to be their right, for some even their God-given responsibility. Close supervision, words of praise and reproof, and material rewards were supplemented by physical violence within each household—as they were in the political affairs of the nation at large. Whether that meant putting the boot to a dozing apprentice, whipping a recalcitrant slave, or laying the stick on a back-talking wife, household heads considered such punishments a just and necessary defense of order and honor, a regrettable part of the educative and judicial function mastery required of them. The fitness of paternal rule seemed evident in the way it reflected God's own guidance of His people. The watchfulness of masters over their own households and their just application of discipline was required in a world without police forces or fire departments, where military force was slight, scattered, and ill coordinated. Social stability itself and the progress of the nation depended on household order.

East, West, North, and South, Americans united in a proud belief in "republicanism," the old theory handed down from Aristotle about how households formed polities. Republican liberty never implied leveling, and most antebellum Americans would have regarded such a doctrine as quite unnatural, just as they accepted the necessity of paternal rule within the household. At that time people plainly saw that the beneficence of the social order rested on hierarchies of gender, race, age, and skill. Power fell inevitably on the side of property. The sovereign people—those accorded the rights of citizenship to select their leaders or to sit in the seat of power itself—were drawn from those who belonged to the social community and cared about the common good and the maintenance of their good name. They were independent—that is, they possessed sufficient material wealth to avoid being manipulated by economic necessity or feelings of inferior status, and they held the firepower to defend their property. Yet essential to republicanism was civic responsibility. Not political "spoilsmen," who identified government with personal gain, and not "capitalists," who pursued private wealth ahead of community welfare, republicans were to be men of enlightened virtue. Armed with the certain knowledge that what they defined as virtuous and enlightened was beyond contestation, northern and southern republicans were to hold the well-being of the whole above their own narrow interests.

South and North alike shared strong nationalistic feelings. The brief, bungled, but ultimately glorious experience of war against England between 1812 and 1815 intensified nationalism. That war settled the questions of whether the United States would ever again invade Canada (no) and whether Native Americans would be able to prevent U.S. expansion to the West (again, no). While New Englanders opposed to that war spoke of states' rights and secession, they joined other Americans in applauding the improbable, one-sided victory of General Andrew Jackson's frontier army at New Orleans (after peace had already been concluded). Americans explained their great victory (or at least their great escape from defeat) as a tribute to the superiority of a free republican government, America's providential standing in a godly world, and evidence of glories to come. After the British bombardment of Fort McHenry near Baltimore, attorney Francis Scott Key wrote a poem that was put to the tune of a popular drinking song. Newspapers from New Hampshire to Georgia printed the words, and although the song did not gain the title of national anthem until 1931, "The Star-Spangled Banner" promoted nationalism both North and South.

The two-party system of Federalists and Republicans had effectively collapsed into a national consensus. Virginian John Marshall had swung the Supreme Court behind the nationalist cause, and Congress, led by John C. Calhoun of South Carolina, Henry Clay of Kentucky, and Daniel Webster of Massachusetts, provided legislative support. With such strong feelings of unity throughout the country, most hoped to avoid conflict in 1819, when the territory of Missouri offered its constitution for congressional approval as a state. How confounding then, when New York congressman James Tallmadge offered an amendment to the bill allowing Missouri's admission to the Union. The ardently antislavery Tallmadge demanded that no more slaves be allowed to emigrate to the territory and that all children of slaves residing there be emancipated at age twenty-five. An aged Thomas Jefferson regarded the Yankee's amendment as "a firebell in the night." The economic and social consequences of such meddling looked dangerous indeed. How could men dare move westward with their property—enslaved or otherwise—when the national Congress might at some future date wave a hand and without warning withdraw the right of ownership? Liberty demanded secure property rights. More than that, while western expansion seemed to confirm the rightness of America's destiny, it also uncovered underlying tensions, particularly increasing sectional divisions of legislative power.

Ultimately, and appropriately, it was a pair of westerners, Illinois senator Jesse Thomas and Kentuckian Henry Clay, who hammered out the Missouri Compromise: Missouri would be allowed to enter the Union as a slave state, but no other territory north of the line 36° 30' would be permitted to write slavery into its constitution. That concession was simply a nod toward realism: everywhere north of that line, harsh climate or harsher racism had blocked black immigration heretofore. The Northwest Ordinance of 1787 outlawed slavery in that section, and there was no reason to believe that slavery might somehow gain a foothold in Colorado or the Dakotas at some distant date. Neither was there much expectation in 1820 that those wild and rugged spaces would soon be clamoring for statehood. In return, northerners affirmed the right of citizens to organize the Arkansas Territory, below the line 36° 30', as one or two slave states. Thomas and Clay offered up statehood for chilly Maine to maintain legislative balance with the fractious slave state of Missouri. In 1821 Congress threw its weight behind Clay, in a rebuke to Tallmadge's sectional "selfishness." The nation gained a firm—if decidedly inegalitarian—basis for westward expansion.

Going west meant leaving safety and security behind, leaving webs of church, kin, and community. Pioneers had to grasp the future with both hands and wring the best meanings out of it by main force. Yeoman settlers into the Old Northwest and the Old Southwest brought with them a republican dream of independent farm ownership for all who would work. True believers thought the West was the best hope for freedom for the average white man, and a demand for squatter sovereignty often held an upper-class animosity as a subtext to equal rights principles. Northwestern settlers initiated a democratic society of citizen participation and created fairly equal land and tax laws, including laws to break up nonresident absentee holders of large tracts of land. No great landholding elite developed. But even in the seeming abundance of land in the west, people still worried that public land was expensive and of poor quality. Early in 1830, Illinois senator Elias Kent Kane spoke about "people and a great many of them without land, who want it on fair terms." Kane noted, "In such states as Illinois and Missouri, then, more than half of the persons entitled to vote are not owners of the soil."

With or without land, people continued moving into the Old Northwest. As rural settlements became towns, problems demanded solutions, and those adept at problem-solving became successful leaders in the community. This democratic texture did not take hold in the Old Southwest, where the economy was not complex enough to require innovative problem-solving. Population was smaller, and towns were fewer—five to six times fewer towns in Alabama, Mississippi, Arkansas, and upper Louisiana—than in the three states of Ohio, Illinois, and Indiana. The state of Mississippi grew from 75,448 (42,176 whites, 32,814 slaves, 458 free blacks) in 1820 to 375,651 (179,074 whites, 195,211 slaves, 1,366 free blacks, 49 others) in 1840. Illinois population in 1820 numbered 55,211 (53,788 whites, 917 slaves, 457 free blacks, 49 others); in 1840, it was 476,183 (472,254 whites, 331 slaves, 3,598 free blacks). In the Southeast, planters owned the best land and controlled many functions of local government. While democratic forms or institutions could be introduced, community leaders would continue to come from slaveholding classes.

Towns in the Northwest also drew a more diverse group of settlers. The future home of Abraham Lincoln was settled by people of the Southeast who named the town Calhoun, after Senator John C. Calhoun of South Carolina. Its incorporation in 1832 gave it the name of Springfield, Illinois. To northern Illinois came settlers from the crowded Northeast and from Europe, including various ethnic and religious groups. Beginning in the late 1830s large numbers of laborers came from Ireland to work on the canals and railroads across the Midwest. In such heterogeneous areas, local government leaders had to get along with a wide assortment of people and activities. By the middle of the nineteenth century the Midwest was a thriving and rapidly expanding region of its own.

Territorial expansion complicated relationships between settled East and frontier West, between orderly states and untidy territories. More and more the world of coastal cities, farms, and plantations came to seem at odds with the social relations of the frontier. America's western edge was younger, wilder, and more dangerous than the East. It lacked the socializing institutions of church and state. In many places the rule of law offered little or no protection to honest and decent citizens. When the children of one yeoman family in South Carolina decided to move west, the heartbroken father wrote that although his five sons needed more space, he and their mother worried that the West was too wild, that people there "were desperate in their dealings between Man and Man." Western boundlessness, summed up in heroes like Andrew Jackson, Davy Crockett, and Sam Houston, became part of an American sense of freedom from restraint tethered to raw articulation of manly virtues of stoic endurance and honor defended by rough justice. Whereas Virginia men of honor might resolve difficulties among themselves by resorting to the highly ritualized *code duello*, westerners were just as likely to seek revenge by gouging out an enemy's eye or biting off his nose. The razor edge of frontier life remained unblunted.

Although the raw, unbridled quality of the West contrasted with the stability and order of the East, national ties of sympathy and interest were abiding and strong. One of the linchpins of economy, culture, and ideology was slavery itself. In colonial times whites—both North and South—accepted slavery unthinkingly. Slavery was a part of every American colony. Such northern heroes as John Hancock and Benjamin Franklin bought, sold, and held black people. Quaker William Penn had been a slaveholder. Whites in every section of the country agreed that slavery had existed throughout history.

Blacks strove to challenge white presumptions. In June 1773 slaves sent a petition to the colonial authorities in Massachusetts "in behalf of all those who by divine permission are held in a state of slavery within the bowels of a free country." They sought, unsuccessfully, permission to be free one day a week to work to save their money to purchase their freedom. During the Revolutionary War thousands of enslaved African Americans ran away to join the British who, for reasons of expediency rather than principle, offered liberty. In the South the patriot cause was proslavery. Not so in the North, where African Americans joined the patriots, constituting one-fourth of the American forces gathered at White Plains to march on Yorktown.

During the Revolutionary War, while thinking about and fighting for freedom and independence from England, some whites acknowledged the contradiction of slave-holding republicans, and victory brought freedom to some African Americans. New York, for example, had not one free black prior to 1776; by 1790, 33 percent of African Americans in

New York were free. The Republic of Vermont outlawed slavery in 1777, becoming a free state in 1791. Yet in the early republic, slaves continued to be auctioned openly in the Market House of Philadelphia, in Boston taverns and warehouses, and at Merchant's Coffee House of New York, as well as in the southern states. For most of the enslaved, the war for American freedom only sharpened the contrast between slavery and the young nation's proclaimed aspirations and values. Stronger government and police regulations were erected to enforce enslavement. Law codified unfreedom. While legal codes were never capable of inducing a person to consent to slavery, slave codes spelled out in great detail what behavior was permissible and what was punishable. Codes forbade slaves to assemble publicly, own property, travel without a permit, own weapons, or become educated.

Despite grave risks, the slave community challenged the slave system in various ways. Because of the high incidence of arson, one Philadelphia company refused to issue fire insurance policies in slave states. Fear of slave rebellion was real. Well-known insurrections were plotted by Gabriel Prosser in 1800 and Denmark Vesey in 1822 and led by Nat Turner in 1831. All had religious underpinnings and a millennial view of bringing on Armageddon. After Gabriel's rebellion of enslaved and free blacks and local poor whites in 1800 was systematically put down, one of the conspirators declared, "We have as much right to fight for our liberty as any men." White Americans were not prepared to concede any such claim. Historians debate whether free black Denmark Vesey actually organized a rebellion in Charleston, South Carolina, but he was charged and executed for the crime, along with 46 others, including 4 whites. In Virginia, Nat Turner and his 75 followers killed about 50 white people. Not only were Turner and his men executed, but the state militia and white mobs also killed about 100 innocent enslaved persons. In the aftermath the state of Virginia debated whether to end slavery but in a close vote decided instead to institute a more repressive system against blacks, both free and enslaved. Slave rebellions stoked northern antislavery feelings, indicating to those open to the suggestion that America's enslaved people wanted liberty and did not acquiesce in their oppression. In the South they generated fear and repression.

Slavery continued in northern as well as southern states. In the years after the revolution, Rhode Island merchants controlled between 60 and

90 percent of the American trade in African slaves. New York emancipated its enslaved reluctantly, and not completely until 1827. Slavery lingered in New Jersey until the Civil War, with the state reporting 236 slaves in 1850 and 18 as late as 1860. In 1824 Illinois held a state referendum on whether to become a slave state. The issue was of great consequence to the voters; at a time when a good turnout in Illinois was typically about 5,000, 11,612 went to the polls. In the close contest, 4,972 proslavery votes lost to 6,640 to keep Illinois slave-free.

Support for slavery was often predicated on the belief that the Bible sanctioned it. While some, in the Deep South as well as in the North, maintained that the Bible did not authorize slavery, least of all racial slavery, most whites pointed out that Old Testament patriarchs held slaves. Moreover, they said, Africans had inherited the biblical curse of Ham to be "drawers of water and hewers of wood." The president of Dartmouth College, the Reverend Nathan Lord, agreed: "Slavery was incorporated into the civil institutions of Moses; it was recognized accordingly by Christ and his apostles." The Reverend Nathaniel Taylor, principal of the Theological Department of Yale College, confidently declared that "if Jesus Christ were on earth, he would, under certain circumstances, become a slaveholder."

For white southerners and northerners both, questions of interest and aspiration, of material progress and economic prosperity, rested on enslaved labor. Fortunes built on the foundation of slavery included those of Washington, Jefferson, and Madison, men who had stepped forth to steer the national course by liberty's star. Eliminate slavery and the republic itself might founder. And yet prior to 1830 in both North and South, whites shared deep anxieties about slavery and an uncertainty about the place of blacks in the republic. Immersed in such fear, Thomas Jefferson had tinkered with his perfect palace of reason, Monticello, trying to square his dreams of rationalist liberty with the material foundation of African American slavery upon which they rested. Americans held "the wolf by the ears," he pronounced; they could neither hold it nor let it go.

At the same time that most white people accepted slavery without much thought, both northerners and southerners balked at the darker commerce that slavery entailed—kidnapping men, women, and children and jamming them aboard slave ships. Between ten and fifteen million Africans were forcibly transported across the Atlantic between 1500 and 1800; at least two million Africans died in this Middle Passage. These figures grossly understate the actual number of Africans enslaved, killed, or displaced as a result of the slave trade. Upon being shipped to the New World (mostly to the Caribbean Islands), people were treated like animals and sold at auction, where children and parents, crying and clinging to each other, were pulled apart and sold separately. So jarringly did the facts of the transatlantic slave trade conflict with American notions of righteous idealism that most whites in the North and the South were very willing to eliminate the practice in 1808, as soon as the Constitution allowed.

That moral measure was supposed to be the beginning of the end of slavery in America. Curtailment of the slave trade would result in the ultimate elimination of bondage and the marginalization—if not, as some hoped, the complete removal—of the black presence in the American republic. No other enslaved population had ever grown in number without fresh imports. The theory was that ending the slave trade would raise the price of enslaved labor too high. Masters would be forced to emancipate enslaved workers grown too expensive to keep while replacing them with wage labor, or to work them to death in the drive to realize comparable profits. Either way, white men concluded, slavery would attain a gradual and natural demise over the course of a few decades.

But closing the slave trade did not send the republic's black population plummeting. Between 1800 and 1860 the enslaved African American population shot up, quadrupling by natural increase from one to four million over three generations. In total population the African American proportion went down as the United States's population, growing by annexation and immigration as well as natural reproduction, went from 5.3 million in 1800 to 31.4 million in 1860. Along the south Atlantic coast and in the lower Mississippi Valley, African Americans became the majority.

This was a turning point in American history. Instead of dying out, instead of merely hanging on, the institution of slavery flourished. The reasons are manifold and complicated, but without a doubt slavery as a commercial enterprise was extremely profitable.

Historians have usually concluded that slavery grew and became an all-pervasive system because of a remarkable new machine, that Eli

Whitney's marvelous saw gin placed King Cotton on his throne and thereby sent the republic spinning toward civil war. Revolutions, however, are seldom accomplished so simply. Whitney, a clever Yankee sojourning in Georgia, did contrive an inexpensive, hand-driven machine in 1793 to remove seeds and trash from the valuable cotton fiber. This "cotton engine" could clean fifty pounds of cotton a day, as opposed to one pound by hand. Prior to the cotton gin, cotton cultivation had been a troublesome business, hardly profitable and confined to the coastal regions of South Carolina. By 1830 cotton production had increased exponentially and showed no sign of retreat. Formerly slavery's fortunes had seemed tied to the prices and profits of tobacco, rice, indigo, and sugar, all of which, except sugar, had grown steadily gloomier. Now sensible financial considerations gave chattel bondage a new lease on life: southern white men borrowed money to buy land and slaves to grow cotton to make money to buy more land and slaves. Fortunes were made with startling ease—or so it seemed—and the only danger for whites looked to be getting in on the bonanza too late.

By 1830 the growth of cotton culture had become central to America's economic expansion—and the world's. The large and seemingly boundless supply of homegrown cotton gave incentives to New England manufacturers to upgrade mill sites to produce textiles on the basis of the factory system. Spinning and weaving had been a daily part of routine farm life for women across the region, but factories were replacing domestic production. By 1830 the textile mills of Lowell, Massachusetts, had become a magnet for more than six thousand young, unmarried New England women. Far better, many daughters decided, to go into the mills, with the prospect of a steady wage to be sent home to save the family farm (minus a percentage to build a nest egg for marriage), than to go hungry under paternal supervision at home. The chance for personal independence seemed invigorating, though six days of twelve-to-fourteen-hour shifts, Sunday church services, strict company rules, and close supervision severely limited its scope. Thousands of young women and children followed the "Lowell girls" into textile mills and shoe factories across Pennsylvania, New York, and other parts of New England. Laboring harder and longer than they ever had at home, under the steady gaze of a barking "overseer," many came to consider that they had sold themselves into a species of "wage slavery." In 1840 the United

States produced 60 percent of the world's cotton, and all hands were straining to turn out more. Cotton that year accounted for two-thirds of the total value of American exports. The world itself, declared the southern writer William Gilmore Simms, was "cotton-mad."

Producing and manufacturing the staple crop tied North and South together commercially. But in the end it was not Whitney's machine alone that had done the tying; his patent only systematized innovations that others, including enslaved African Americans, had already tinkered with for several years. The cotton gin certainly did not cause farmers to embrace the "mania" for cotton en masse by its own motive power. Nor did the spread of cotton cultivation in the South cause whirring factories to leap up in the North in a score of sleepy New England towns. Without capital funding and strong, sustained world demand, southern cotton production would not have reached such remarkable heights. It was the decision of British merchant bankers to underwrite American cotton plantations with vast infusions of credit that turned vast fields snowy white—and made the South a slaveocracy. The Bank of England, the Houses of Baring and of Brown, and a dozen more close-calculating little firms of enormous power and influence poured their sterling into cotton culture because simple cost-cutting innovations made cotton weaving more profitable just as world demand—especially in Asia—surged upward. North, South, Europe, Africa, and Asia—the whole world, it seemed—was drawn together by cotton, capital, and the black enslaved workers who produced both.

As British capital flowed to the United States, towns and cities, trade and commerce, mushroomed across the North and throughout the country. New roads and new steamboats enabled farmers to transport and sell their produce in cities like New York, Baltimore, and Charleston. By the 1830s more than seven hundred steamboats operated on the Mississippi and Ohio rivers. When the Erie Canal opened in 1825, travel time between Buffalo and New York City decreased from twenty to six days. Shorter transportation times meant lower prices; freight charges for a ton of goods fell from $100 by road to $10 by canal. Prior to canal transportation, wheat could not be shipped farther than fifty miles for profit. New markets in commodities, capital, land, and labor spread out to the near West. Rail transport—unsurprisingly, first in cotton-rich South Carolina in 1829—brought freight costs down further still.

Building and maintaining plank roads, canals, and railroads was the work of many hands—most of them drawn from impoverished Irish immigrant labor—and was funded by the pooling of fortunes or the creation of corporations. For the most part railroads did not connect North and South or even with one another. Although American financiers dreamed more grandly, states supported railroad construction to improve statewide commerce. Except in the Northeast, which developed regional railroad networks, most early railroads transported goods and people between established eastern areas and western areas within a given state.

Although some Americans called for federal support for these new enterprises, others disagreed. Southern slaveholders viewed the expansion of federal authority that would accompany such support as inimical to their liberty. As North Carolina senator Nathaniel Macon succinctly explained, "If Congress can make banks, roads, and canals under the Constitution, they can free any slave in the United States." Wealthy southerners supported some growth in industrialization and transportation but wanted limits. In the West vast fortunes were made by men who preached "private enterprise," all the while begging new, unheard-of privileges from local assemblies and state legislatures. While relying upon their own entrepreneurial spirit, they requested land grants, conveyance rights, financial loans, tax relief, and the opportunity to issue currency and create their own banks. Local farmers, seeing the chance to get higher prices for the corn and wheat they had worked so hard to raise, were happy to vote aye for each of these concessions.

As new markets in commodities, capital, land, and labor spread, some benefited and some were left behind. Losing out economically as the factory system began taking root in the budding urban areas of the Northeast were the laborers employed in workshops. Workshops were small household affairs, relying on hand power and directed by a master who had worked himself up from the hard blows of apprenticeship to the ranks of business owner. In towns and cities with expanding market opportunities, however, men of property began building fine houses on the fringes of their communities, reserved for their nuclear families alone. This was a startling change from the house that had been at once a workshop, a home, and a political entity over which the master provided just governance. As households in urban areas began to split, household heads abdicated responsibilities for which they had been taught to take pride. The split between home and work spread throughout northern urban society as bosses shucked off the domestic and community responsibilities with which republican theory saddled them and abandoned the old promises and compromises upon which urban craft labor had founded itself.

It seemed a dangerous and irresponsible choice to separate work and home, a sign that the fabric of social relations was unraveling. Instead of training apprentices and nurturing their careers, masters abandoned the traditional claims of reciprocity. Increasingly, journeymen found themselves working harder and faster, at reduced wages, with less prospect of entering the circle of mastery. For youngsters, the educative role of apprenticeship disappeared. As bosses subdivided the labor process into simple steps, children acquired no skills. In 1830, children constituted one third of the workforce in textile mills in New England; what they learned was stoic endurance to perform repetitive tasks for a dozen hours or more each day. In proud crafts like printing, mechanization abetted a de-skilling process; in other trades, such as tailoring and woodworking, the division of labor split a complex process of construction into many simple steps, each amenable to a heightened pace of work. In these environments hope of moving from manual labor to the ranks of master craftsmen grew more limited, though the need for skilled labor never ceased.

Recognizing their opportunities—and fearing the threat of competition—some bosses fired the old, slow, and incompetent, regardless of past service. Some employers, on arriving at their stores and workshops in the morning, discovered workers with bleary eyes, soiled clothing, and rough words. Bosses complained that their "hands" were too saucy, drunk, and ungrateful, and they projected onto their workers a perception of intemperance, crime, and whoring that marked a class divide. Those working under the changed spirit of the times slackened their pace wherever possible, shirked their duties, and sometimes walked angrily off the job, begging for open conflict and shouting defiance. To them, poverty and homelessness seemed a better fate than emasculation.

While manufacturing was only a small part of the economy in the 1830s and 1840s, seeds were sown and a pattern of strife and conflict was beginning to emerge. Striking shoemakers in New York in 1835 declared that they needed a union "to resist the oppressions of avarice" that was depriving them of "the means and opportunity of learning the rights and duties which they are to exercise as citizens." The New York Supreme Court, however, ruled against them, finding that unions were "injurious to trade and commerce." To some, it seemed a sham to believe that the little guy, working in a new urban job for wages, could claim to be free and independent.

To counter the grim realities for some of the white laborers in the East, many encouraged migration to the West. Southeasterners also migrated west, pouring into the Texas province of Mexico. Initial settlers in 1821 obtained permission from Mexico. In 1836 the Mexican Congress prohibited slavery and moved to limit new immigrants into the territory. In response, Texans rose up in defense of slavery and property, declaring the right of self-government. On March 2, 1836, a convention in Texas adopted a declaration of independence and a constitution. War ensued, the United States sitting on the sidelines cheering on the Texans as freedom fighters. At San Antonio 188 Texans held off three thousand Mexicans for eleven days. The battle cry "Remember the Alamo!" stirred Texans and Americans alike. Myths around this famous siege defined the battle as one for freedom. The freedom Texans died for, of course, included the freedom to enslave others. Ultimately Texan independence meant security of enslaved property and freedom from Catholicism. One of the first pieces of business in the new Republic of Texas was to expel all free blacks.

The question of whether to annex Texas to the United States as a slave state was a lengthier battle that took place over the next nine years. The simple fact that Texans wanted to annex their Republic to the United States reflected the predominance of nationalism over sectionalism at the time. Mexico naturally opposed America's annexation of Texas and announced that it would be equivalent to "a declaration of war against the Mexican Republic." In the meantime more than two hundred thousand Americans flooded into the new Lone Star Republic, the white men among them eager to reap windfall profits and establish personal fiefdoms on the basis of African American slavery. Britain and other European nations granted recognition to Texas, hoping that the independent state would act as a buffer to growing U.S. power as well as prove a source for cotton. British interference motivated the United States to proceed with annexation. Just as motivational was Texan contemplation of extending its borders through Mexican territory all the way to the Pacific Coast as a rival to U.S. expansion efforts.

Advocating annexation of Texas, newspapers spoke of America's "manifest destiny." Coining that phrase, New York journalist John L. O'Sullivan wrote about "the fulfillment of our manifest destiny to overspread the continent." Population growth was putting pressure on landholdings back east, and some cried out for an expanded agricultural base. "Our multiplying millions" needed land for "free development." Just as important was an idea that captured the national imagination: America had a destiny to spread the "great experiment of liberty." Poet Walt Whitman rhapsodized about the ever more fixed assumption that America's "great mission" was to populate "the new world with a noble race." Spreading white republican civilization and Christian religion slowly and surely became the order of the day. "Let the eagle soar!" cried one congressman, and Americans North and South united in their fervor for the great land grab.

On the presidential stage Democrat James K. Polk of Tennessee, the "dark horse" candidate in 1844, ran on a platform of economic noninterference and bold territorial expansion. Prior to Polk's candidacy, linking national politics with the future of slavery had been strictly out of bounds. The Whig candidate Henry Clay and the Democratic frontrunner Martin Van Buren agreed not to advance their campaigns by advocating war with Mexico, tied as it was to the slavery issue. As politicians since Jefferson had understood, the slavery question threatened to fragment the nation into dangerous sectional shards, destroying coalitions, parties, and compromises—dissolving the broad middle ground of moderation and common interest itself. When abolitionist societies in the North, exercising an activism that far exceeded their number or popularity, flooded Congress with petitions detailing the horrors of bondage in lurid terms, Senator John C. Calhoun introduced legislation requiring that offending appeals be laid on the table unread, unrecorded, and not open to discussion. Eager to silence the fanatics, Congress instituted this congressional "gag rule" in 1836, thus curtailing freedom of speech until 1844. It was defeated through the leadership of "Old Man Eloquent," Massachusetts representative and former president John Quincy Adams, who was driven by his unequivocal opposition to slavery and by his faith in free speech.

Polk won in 1844 because he proposed to feed the land hunger of all sections. His energetic expansionism appealed to enough voters to deny Clay the presidency. Calculating that interest would trump principle during crises, Polk propelled the northwestern frontier to the Pacific by snatching up Oregon's rich Willamette Valley and pushing British claims back beyond the forty-ninth parallel. Few seemed to care that this acquisition marked a retreat from his stump speech demand of "54° 40' or fight!"

People began moving west along an ill-defined route, the Oregon Trail. Multitudes would follow. Freedom to move west was available to those who could afford a horse and wagon and supplies. While mobility was one of the freedoms white Americans treasured, their move west took away freedom from Native Americans. Native women accustomed to traveling freely to gather food were no longer safe, as rape became one of the deliberate ways to dominate that population. Native Americans in certain areas of northern Nevada went from almost 100 percent of the population in the early 1840s to a very small minority only a decade later. A vivid example of a people who were certain they knew the will of God was the Mormons. These Latter Day Saints had been traveling slowly but surely westward as persecution drove them out of each settlement. When their leader Joseph Smith was lynched in 1844 in Nauvoo, Illinois, they continued their search for religious freedom, and, under the leadership of Brigham Young, many migrated to the Salt Lake Valley, in what later became Utah.

The nation's next major piece of territory was acquired through war. Polk wanted war with Mexico, still in the midst of economic and political turmoil after its struggle for independence from Spain. The president was convinced that war would secure for the nation vast new territory and for the Democrats political ascendancy—with all the opportunities of patronage, administration, and party control that went along with territorial gain. When Texas declared that its southern border was the Rio Grande and not the Nueces River, General Pedro de Ampudia of Mexico demanded that American forces move off Mexican land or "arms and arms alone must decide the question." After a skirmish in the disputed territory, Polk asked Congress to declare war because Mexico had "shed American blood upon the American soil." Congress did so in May 1846. As a new member of the House of Representatives in December 1847, Abraham Lincoln opposed the war.

Questioning the president in lawyerly fashion about the justification for the declaration of war, he asked "whether the particular spot of soil on which the blood of our *citizens* was so shed, was, or was not, *our own soil?*" Other representatives thought this was plain ridiculous, and for a while they mocked the junior representative as "Spotty Lincoln."

It all seemed to turn out as well as any proponent could have hoped. True, the Mexican War acquainted thousands of young Americans with the most unglamorous side of military service—killing, harsh discipline, bad food, disease, fatigue, race and ethnic prejudice, corruption, cowardice, and desertion. Yet the fighting itself was stunningly brief, battle casualties were low, and the prize magnificent. A generation of Civil War military leaders gained combat experience in Mexico: McClellan, Hooker, Meade, Grant, Thomas, Hancock, Lee, Jackson, Johnston, Bragg, Longstreet, Pickett, Pemberton, Beauregard, Davis. As volunteers returned home to national acclaim, mapmakers drew new lines extending slavery's potential domain all the way to California. For this new territory, America paid the defeated Mexico a paltry $15 million, a pathetic face-saving device that legitimized its attainment as a consequence of commerce rather than war. Five years later, in 1853, the southern politician and railroad entrepreneur James Gadsden negotiated a further sale of Mexican territory, this time accomplished without gunfire. It was all exceedingly valiant, a vindication of "Manifest Destiny's" broadest claims, taken as evidence of the superiority of the American "race."

There were a few long faces amid the jubilation. In the Northeast especially, peace advocates had rallied against "Mr. Polk's War," but their numbers were few. Oddest of all, perhaps, was young Henry David Thoreau, jailed in 1846 for refusing to pay his taxes in support of a war benefiting slavery; then, after someone else paid his taxes for him, he scuttled home—too earnest to recognize the self-mockery of his action. That sort of "civil disobedience" made for noble prose, but it worried no one of a political mindset. The worried man with the longest face was the besieged and desperate John C. Calhoun, and not just because the battlefield victories of Winfield Scott and Zachary Taylor scotched his last hopes of winning the White House. Calhoun led the political opposition to armed conflict with Mexico because he feared where that war might ultimately lead. Seizing New Mexico and California was bound to vault the slavery question back into the political sphere, defeating a decade of silence and inaction carefully contrived to prevent passionate sectionalism.

Breaking that silence, David Wilmot, a Democratic representative from Pennsylvania, proposed in 1846 an amendment to the "Two Million Bill" to fund negotiations with Mexico. Wilmot's proviso stipulated that "neither slavery nor involuntary servitude shall ever exist in any part" of the territory gained from the Mexican War. The proviso passed the House in a sectional vote, with northern Whigs and Democrats lined up in favor. Southern volunteers who fought in the Mexican War took offense that they would not be allowed to settle there with their property. As often as Wilmot introduced his amendment over the next several years, the South's senatorial majority, though slim, turned back the assault. Lincoln, who would take a seat in Congress later that year, afterward wrote his friend that "I voted for the Wilmot Proviso as good as forty times." Calhoun's fears were confirmed—the new territory reopened the issue that the Missouri Compromise and the gag rule had tried to shut off.

Issues of expansion, of slavery, of unrestrained capitalism fed an American anxiety. As the proportion of independent household heads steadily dropped, as industrialization increased and somewhat larger plants replaced smaller enterprises, many Americans came to fear they were losing out in personal freedom and control. Even as they were gaining economic opportunity, even as more moved upward in status than downward, the rocketing economy of the market revolution intensified anxiety. One might gain riches one day and lose them the next. In an article in *The American Review* titled "The Influence of the Trading Spirit upon the Social and Moral Life of America," Henry Bellows warned in 1845 about the "anxious spirit of gain." Anxiety ran high in growing cities in the Northeast as they were becoming home to the astoundingly rich and the pitifully poor. New York City grew to rival London and Paris in its spectacular scenes of "light and shadows."

Throughout the nineteenth century, people were on the move geographically, economically, and socially. While the country as a whole remained rural, the number of farm laborers continued to grow even as many left farm work to labor in factories. In 1840 only 11 percent of Americans lived in urban areas; by 1860 that percentage had doubled. Boston grew from sixty-one thousand people in 1830 to ninety-three thousand in 1840. But a growth of thirty-two thousand was only part of the story; more than half the people residing in Boston for the 1830 census were not there in 1840.

In the midst of such unsettling changes, northern and southern men of property were united in their unease about where enslaved labor would ultimately lead and in their alarm over the problems besetting the industrializing Northeast. They were united in their worry about the possibilities of linking East and West without betraying republican virtue. In this context, Asher Durand painted a landmark of nineteenth-century American culture. His masterpiece, *Kindred Spirits* (1849), portrayed his hope for a nation in stress. The canvas itself is simple: two well-dressed men, sharing each other's company, commune with nature in a sunlit glade. They were the painter's friends, the immigrant artist Thomas Cole, who made his home west of the Appalachians, and the New England poet James Russell Lowell. Durand painted the natural world as inviting and luminous—God-filled. Man and nature are kindred spirits, linked in a common, splendid, unfolding destiny. The men approach a promontory, not a precipice—there is no suggestion that the next step might tumble all into disaster. Durand expressed the idealism, the hope, and the values that were typical of antebellum culture. Just as the Millerites had believed that the millennium was only days or weeks away, most Americans in the 1840s thought that social perfection was imminently attainable, if only men and women would seek common purpose. Defining a common purpose would be a challenge, however, when Americans looked northward to the trade of Wall Street, or southward to the world of slavery. "A double-minded man," the disciple James had warned, "is unsteady in all his ways." How much worse then was a double-minded nation?

Two

"Gale of Simple Freedom"

STOMPING AND SPINNING, his coattails flying, Brother Joseph Brackett sang out in joyous tones. Rail-thin and plainly dressed, the chanting elder must have seemed to observers in the early 1840s the very personification of stiffness and repression, until he and his flock began to sing. Then, moved by a Holy Spirit which knew no bounds of race or sex or class, these humble, rejoicing "Shakers" began to shuffle and stamp and twirl, speak in tongues, and declare values and ideas that were either manifestly God-given or the ravings of dangerous lunatics. They were revolutionary either way, and their implications seemed as boundless—or as dangerous—as the simple, endless, rhythmic whirl of their dance. "In the gale of simple freedom," called out an African American leader, Laughing John, "who will drink the wine of freedom . . . Pride and bondage all forgetting."

Joseph Brackett, Laughing John, and thousands of others in upper New York and throughout the Northeast were members of a group that originally had migrated from Manchester to the American colonies in the early 1770s. That early group of eight men and women had come with the English prophet Ann Lee, "Mother Ann," to establish a new, communal form of living, purer and more devoted to God's plan than that of the Quakers from whom they split. Convinced that the Second Coming had been achieved—in female form through the spiritual awakening of Mother Ann—these religious radicals determined to build heaven on earth by embracing righteous equality and abandoning the bondage of sin they called "Old Stiff." The Shakers represent one of the most daring and comprehensive attempts to unite the best aspects of tradition, capitalism, and community in a more satisfying trinity.

Men and women in the Age of Lincoln wondered how to square the desire for individual liberty with notions of equality and the duty to be "my brother's keeper." By the 1830s the Second Great Awakening had spread eastward from its Kentucky roots in the early 1800s. Religious revivals and camp meetings of unprecedented multitudes roiled the Northeast and parts of the coastal South with its theological message of one's personal opportunity for salvation. The Reverend Charles Grandison Finney of New York preached that individuals were "free moral agents," obliged to make a choice between good and evil. The movement exalted personal responsibility, morality, and self-discipline. Free will assumed less a flowering of personal choice than the unimpeded freedom of the righteous not to err. It was up to individuals, as the Reverend Finney explained, to look within their own hearts, find the path of right conduct, and seek salvation. A rising spirit of personal enlightenment driven by a Christian faith increasingly turned on the righteous man knowing and fulfilling God's plan.

The idealism expressed a balance of certainty and pessimism, since all men and women were in need of God's grace. Along with the idea that the righteous were free to act rightly came the dread that if they did not, they alone were to blame. The project of perfecting oneself could easily become the project of perfecting the nation, of bringing forth God's will "on earth as it is in heaven." The onus was less on offering aid and opportunity to one's fellow man than on achieving the right articulation of the correct path to perfection and keeping to it at all hazards. That theme found countless permutations across the following generations, casting up the millennialism of the Millerites and the utopian projects of the Shakers, the Mormons, the Oneida community, and much else besides. The millennial dreams of the main-line Baptists, Presbyterians, and Methodists drew upon a more hierarchal structure to God's kingdom on earth. White elite planters insisted that ideas of individual equality, such as those of the Shakers and even those of the New Light Baptists and others in the South, were just plain wrong-headed. As early as 1826 wealthy white southerners instituted religious schools, such as Furman Academy in South Carolina, so preachers would learn the "proper" way to think about theology and slavery.

Regardless of creed or faction, at the center of various reforms were questions of bondage and freedom. For temperance reformers, North and South, it seemed perfectly obvious that American men had become slaves to drink, wasting their fortunes, ruining their health, and wrecking domestic happiness. Editors of the *Chicora*, a newspaper in Charleston, South Carolina, published a lengthy short story in 1842 by Harriet Beecher Stowe on the evils of drunkenness, called "Let Every Man Mind His Own Business." Many teetotalers agreed that reining in the thirst for liquor, either through moral suasion or rule of law, would improve the quality of life for ordinary citizens, would raise the moral character of the nation itself, and would advance the cause of the millennium. Just as groups aimed to purify family and community by expelling the poisons of drink and sex, reformers hoped to cool down sinful passions by eliminating stimulants like tobacco, meat, and coffee. For Christian soldiers like Presbyterian minister Sylvester Graham, the battle against sexual immorality would be won not through prayer and scripture alone but by the sustenance provided by daily draughts of cold water and a vegetarian diet, including bread without refined white flour, wafers that came to be called Graham crackers. The link between spiritual growth and bodily control launched a variety of social institutions in America—workhouses, penitentiaries, lunatic asylums, public schools— all charged with disciplining bodies and controlling conduct in hopes that the light of reason might shine forth once passion's reign was checked.

The connection of godliness and sexuality reached its acme in the social experiments of John Humphrey Noyes and his polar opposite, the Shakers. For Noyes, patriarchal nuclear families demonstrated the enslavement of women to sinful men, the devilish unleashing of selfish masculine carnality, and a troubling turn away from the love of God. Outside of traditional marriage, however, Noyes had no doubt that love found profound expression through sexual relations. Noyes's radical notions drew hundreds to the commune he founded in Putney, Vermont, in 1844 and later relocated to Oneida, New York. Based on the belief that men and women could voluntarily renounce sin and render themselves perfect, the community sought a harmonious coexistence of freedom and restraint. The polygamous ideas he sponsored spoke to deep concerns about the debilitating effects of monogamous marriage on men and women both, and flourished in other perfectionist groups like the

Mormons. For Noyes, however, they brought trouble. In 1879 he fled charges of adultery and statutory rape, dying in Canada seven years later. By that time, the Oneida experiment was well on its way toward devolving into a quaint socialist village surviving on the manufacture of flatware. The quest for stability had elbowed aside perfectionist dreams.

The Shakers never made such compromises, not least because they took such an uncompromising stance on human sexuality. Whereas Noyes's followers had focused originally on achieving millennial bliss through the mass production of female orgasms, Ann Lee's disciples took a strictly hands-off approach to the Second Coming. It seems unsurprising, given her own experience, that Mother Ann preached a message of total celibacy within marriage. She had been pressured as a young woman into an unwanted marriage, and had given birth to four children in steady succession—each of whom had died in infancy. God's judgment was readily seen in such tragedies, Shakers thought, and for Lee they pointed to the solution to the problem of gender slavery. She held that contemporary social institutions, chief among them marriage and private property, only shackled one sex to the other and plunged both into the debasement of carnal lust.

Shakers envisioned a different world, and built it in a series of villages across New York, Pennsylvania, New England, and farther afield. Each Shaker house was strictly gendered, with separate but identical male and female doorways, chairs, bedsteads, and so on. By rendering clothing, furniture, housing, food, music, dance, language—everything—simple, plain, and chaste, inequality of all sorts was banished and the godly essence within all became plainly revealed. Steady, dedicated labor and the communal worship of God promised a life of purpose, prosperity, and liberation from anxiety and sin. Shaker theology was resolutely color-blind, and for women especially the separate-but-equal arrangements that ran through every aspect of social life offered perhaps the best chance in nineteenth-century America for economic success, personal independence, and healthful longevity.

But such freedom was anything but free. Even as they carefully avoided all physical contact between men and women, Shakers could not quite dismiss sin. Indeed, when they shuffled and shook and finally fell out, writhing upon the floor in religious ecstasy, these "Shaking Quakers" looked to outsiders to be fully in the throes of sexual release.

And certainly Shaker Elders feared that carnality had not been fully banished. They carefully policed individual conduct, spying through windows to catch men and women exchanging furtive glances, brushing up against each other, or fondling material objects a little too openly. In seeking to cleanse their world of sexuality, they had eroticized it fully. The more spotless they made their millennial communities, the more prominently the stains of sin stood forth.

By the 1850s, nearly two hundred thousand Americans had come into contact with Shaker ideas and practices, though group membership never numbered more than six thousand converts at any time. The same pattern held true for nearly every variety of perfectionist reform, from vegetarianism to free love to temperance advocacy: astonishingly large numbers of Americans came in search of answers to troubling questions about the proper shape of family and community, personal and social life, but few settled long on any particular panacea.

Both North and South wrestled with contradictions arising within the millennial impulses for perfection. Deeply self-conscious about effects of the market revolution, many thought the sin of greed was vastly more pernicious than any other facing America. In 1844 lawyer and former U.S. senator from Ohio Benjamin Tappan wrote to one of his many brothers: "You are contending for great moral principles, & while you are doing this you are indifferent to the establishment of banks." While his brothers Lewis and Arthur Tappan, silk merchants in New York, felt slavery was the most blatant enemy of freedom, Benjamin predicted that it would be through the establishment of banks "that free principles are to be extinguished." Transcendentalist Ralph Waldo Emerson promised that prosperity would advance America "into a new and more excellent social state than history has ever recorded." Henry David Thoreau, on the other hand, issued warnings. Popular writers wrote about the tension between accountability on the one hand and economic prosperity on the other. One of the most popular writers of the day was George Lippard, whose novels *The Quaker City* (1844) and *New York: Its Upper Ten and Lower Million* (1853) lambasted corporations and portrayed the rich as just plain evil. Timothy Shay Arthur's *Ten Nights in a Bar-Room and What I Saw There* (1854) depicted the iniquity of drink. Reform, however, seemed unable to root out all the sins besetting the household and the social order— domestic violence, masturbation, illegitimacy, gambling, dancing, and more. In New York City before the Civil War, prostitution was second only to the garment industry in the number of women employed.

Gazing upon the filth and degradation of northern industry at mid-century, southerners recoiled in horror. "So surely as God is the ruler of the Universe," warned one planter, "this state of things must be in opposition to his will, and cannot endure. It cannot be the will of God that his creatures shall exist in hopeless degradation, toiling harder than slaves, with none of the slaves' security." Justifying the "love of gain," capitalism was "the offspring of the devil." Southern writers pointed straightforwardly at the problems of northern urbanization. They saw every sort of wild-eyed "-ism" walking the streets, and community values rotting from the inside out. Large cities seemed money-mad. Men chased the commercial humbugs of P. T. Barnum, women unsexed themselves in dress and demeanor, and lying "Confidence Men" turned virtue and reality upside down.

The South, they argued, offered a steady world of order and harmony governed by the Bible and the Constitution. The majority of Americans lived in rural settings and adamantly insisted that traditional American values and personal autonomy depended upon continuing its agrarian heritage. White southerners especially boasted that their section of the country preserved that heritage. Here white men still maintained paternal control over the households they governed, and they knew enough to respect one another's judgment. A rock-solid code of honor and a clear-eyed Christianity regulated conduct in the South, they declared. Slavery limited class conflict in the South, proslavery theorists pointed out. According to Calhoun, "With us the two great divisions of society are not the rich and the poor, but white and black; and all the former, the poor as well as the rich, belong to the upper class, and are respected and treated as equals."

Democracy in the South was never used to assault the plantation oligarchy. Rather, in areas where the cotton plantation economy expanded, slavery insulated the planter class and helped it maintain its leadership, authority, and control. While community leaders generally came from slaveholding classes, every white male was the lord of his domain. Large planters and yeoman farmers shared interests and fears. They were tied to each other in a multiple network of obligations, trade, and exchanges of labor and service. In agrarian areas people knew one another—one's word was one's bond. Whites developed camaraderie across economic lines, sharing conversation at barbecues and sitting across from one another at church. Wealthy men at the top of the social ladder were expected to show respect for poorer whites. Mutual respect among white men, the argument went, gave even the poorest whites an interest in the community.

Slavery was a powerful symbol of degradation that white yeomen contrasted with their own pride and perceived independence. As long as the mass of poor and yeoman farmers accepted that slavery provided the means to rise economically and, more important, provided a floor beneath which they could not fall, they were willing to accept and defend the slave system. Racial privilege bound whites together in a sense of community and a way of life. Even though yeomen were for the most part nonslaveholders, slavery permitted these farmers a certain degree of independence and pride. Most nonslaveholding southern whites believed that their liberty depended on the subjugation of blacks.

Complicating issues of subjugation and freedom was the situation of free blacks, who provided a daily reminder that the parameters of freedom in a slave system were complex and somewhat flexible—always of course within discernible limits. In 1830 about 142,000 free blacks lived in the North, 122,300 in the Upper South (Delaware, D.C., Maryland, Virginia), 58,792 in the rest of the South, and 1,400 in the territories. Most free black families in the early part of the nineteenth century descended from free ancestors, but some were descendants of slaves who gained their freedom during the colonial era or during that brief period of liberalization inspired by the revolution. Many free blacks derived from the manumission of mulatto children (usually the offspring of the master). After the 1820s free blacks, while they had more freedom than enslaved blacks, had their activities monitored and their economic and educational opportunities severely limited. This was true in the North as well as in the South. And yet, even though most had been enslaved just two generations earlier, by 1860 one out of five free black household heads in the South owned land. This group of 16,172 African Americans lived in all fifteen slave states and in the District of Columbia and claimed property worth $20,253,200. Always aware that perceived transgressions could call down upon them white mobs unrestrained by any rule of law, free black communities in both sections kept abreast of white politics, paid attention to shifting public opinion, and used it whenever possible to advocate for more freedom.

The absence of equality of opportunity became cause for greater ingenuity and enterprise in pursuit of any opportunity. Enslaved potters, blacksmiths, or wheelwrights sometimes made money they were allowed to keep. Some especially gifted slave women earned extra by cooking, designing cloth and clothes, and weaving baskets. Some African Americans were allowed to raise their own chickens and hogs. Robert Smalls, born in 1839, was sent to Charleston to hire himself out for pay when he was just a boy of twelve years. He worked as a waiter, lamplighter, stevedore, ship rigger, and sailor, turning in his wages each month. When he turned eighteen, he negotiated his situation with his owner and thereafter retained all but fifteen dollars per month of his pay.

The case of Harvy Pendicord of Tennessee is instructive up to a point. Enslaved by Isabella Saver and then, upon her marriage, by Columbus Pendicord, Harvy Pendicord was hired out by him to a Mr. Childs. In 1862 he was hired to Mr. O. P. Butler. While working for Butler, he leased a small tract of land from a local farmer, working it "at night and on Saturday" in tandem with young Curran Butler, O. P. Butler's slave. Pendicord "employed Curran" to help him raise four acres of corn, "and I was to give whatever part of it I saw fit to do, to him for helping me." According to Pendicord, "I then left Mr. Butler's." He returned to Childs to cut wood for the Louisville Railroad for the next three years. Because Pendicord had married one of O. P. Butler's slaves, it was at Butler's place that he "staid there every night."

Pendicord's life complicates our understanding of what slavery entailed. A slave hired for wages who leases property from a third party and hires another man's slave to be paid as he "saw fit" with a share-wage of a crop? Pendicord was a slave, a waged hireling, a tenant farmer, and a boss paying wages to another slave. One white man's human property, he lived with the black woman he called his wife (though slaves could not marry by law)—drawing comfort and value from her unpaid domestic labor on his behalf—on the property of her master, even though (it appears) he "left" that man's employment by his own decision. Pendicord's slavery was not monolithic, but his freedom had a clear end point: he did not own himself.

No matter how the master class saw their slaves, the slaves saw themselves as fully human and worthy of dignity, and within the horrendous confines of enslavement they acted accordingly. Freedom never was an either/or proposition. Within the limits of an unfree system of enslaved labor, variations existed. Despite the power of the master class, many slaves were able to find some space for themselves and create a culture and community rooted in African memories, Christianity, and family life. While the isolation on large plantations kept many enslaved workers cut off from the rest of the world, living quarters on the large plantations generally provided a buffer away from white supervision. Most enslaved men and women belonged to holders of twenty or more slaves, even though half of the total number of slaveholders held no more than five slaves each. On the larger plantations life was lived from sundown to sunup in the quarters as well as from sunup to sundown in the fields. In the quarters, enslaved people shared religious traditions, songs, and stories, and told of trickster tales. Of course, even in the quarters, slaves were never free from the threat of harsh treatment and humiliation, from sexual exploitation or degrading punishment, or the specter of a sale that might break up a family. In spite of all that, however, a slave community created a barrier behind which African American culture did grow and thrive.

Southern reformers wrestled with abuses they saw within their slave system. They were actually somewhat successful in using stigma and shame to discourage flagrant mistreatment of slaves. Southern religious reformers often focused their efforts on eliminating the worst of slave conditions. They recommended recognizing slave marriages and keeping slave families intact. Paternalism is often mistakenly construed as white kindness and black accommodation. While many paternalistic southern slaveholders may have preferred using the carrot to the stick, slaves knew that only the threat of coercion permitted resort to persuasion. Paternalism was based on careful calculation of the balance of power between master and slave, white-held presumptions of right and wrong, and economic self-interest; kindness in the abstract entered into the equation only incidentally if at all.

Protestations to goodness and godliness by white slaveholders, however, ran afoul of debt and a master's death. Economic need almost always trumped benevolence. Between 1820 and 1860 over two million slaves were sold. The largest sale of human beings in the history of the United States took place at the Savannah racetrack in Georgia in March

1857: 436 men, women, and children. White reformers admitted that there were abuses on some plantations, that masters and slaves both shirked their duties to one another, that sin and greed slipped in too easily, corrupting paternalist ties—but these were narrow human failings, they insisted, not irredeemable flaws.

Sometimes religion helped to ameliorate the worst of the system. Black Christians strove to claim a measure of equality as believers before God, and they used religion to legitimate their complaints about family separation. Many proslavery whites saw religion as essential to establishing their own goodness and that of their peculiar institution. Stressing individual piety and redemption, they encouraged the spiritual life of slaves, and some taught them to read the Bible. And while slaves had no standing in courts of law, some churches allowed complaints about unfair treatment before church disciplinary committees, where some slaves were given a hearing and some, fewer, even a ruling in their favor.

In the development and pervasiveness of paternalism, and even more so in reaction to challenges from a small group of abolitionists, the southern white viewpoint that slavery was evil changed. Proslavery theorists denied Jefferson's assertion to the contrary and declared slavery "a positive good." John C. Calhoun, who had built his fortune on slavery, announced in 1838 that southerners, goaded by abolitionist agitation, now had a new attitude toward slavery. "This agitation has produced one happy effect at least; it has compelled us to the South to look into the nature and character of this great institution, and to correct many false impressions that even we had entertained in relation to it." While southerners used to think that slavery was "a moral and political evil," he declared, they had now come to a different realization: "we see it now in its true light, and regard it as the most safe and stable basis for free institutions in the world." In South Carolina first and then elsewhere throughout the South, the note of apology was subtracted from discussion of slavery. Slavery was good, its defenders argued, because it brought Africans into civilization and into Christianity. Slavery was beneficial for America, they claimed, because only in the South had conservative values and the measured accumulation of wealth allowed men of leisure to develop a higher sense of duty toward their inferiors and an understanding of their crucial role in the advance of Western civilization. For them, slavery made possible the only sort of white man's democracy worth having.

By 1830, slavery (though not racism) had become a sectional rather than a national institution, setting the South apart from the North. While the number of northern industrial workers was about 75,000, the population of enslaved people in the United States passed two million. The slave system increasingly came to circumscribe southern life. The violence necessary to perpetuate it created a militant culture of slave patrols and local militias. Slavery affected southern politics, both substantially and stylistically. It defined the social structure and class divisions. Sensitive to outside attacks and disturbed by uncertainties within, slavery came to characterize southern identity. At this time, a minority of religious reformers in the North began to declare fervently that slavery was the worst sin facing America. Against the laws and customs of community, they posed a higher law of individual conscience and a new vision of social order.

Religion played a large role in both pro- and antislavery movements. Methodists, Presbyterians, Episcopalians, and Baptists, while strong in the belief that the Bible condoned slavery, also had important antislavery wings. Pope Gregory XVI published an apostolic letter banning Catholic participation in the slave trade, though he did not condemn slavery outright. And the Catholic Church opposed abolition because it feared liberal individualism. Protestant evangelical antislavery activists frequently denounced slavery and Catholicism as parallel despotic systems, both opposed to education, free speech, and political liberty.

Formal antislavery efforts began with the American Colonization Society, predominantly led by southerners. Its program encouraged voluntary emancipation and the colonization of freed slaves in Africa. Very few white Americans, North or South, could envision a racially egalitarian society in which black people were fully citizens of the republic. Free African Americans in the North were active and vocal opponents of colonization. In 1832, the peak year of emigration to Liberia, only about eight hundred blacks left America, most of them enslaved persons freed on condition of emigrating to Africa. A few courageous whites, such as Milton Gregg, a Whig from Indiana, disagreed with the majority: he thought that blacks were "esteemed citizens in the eye of the law" and that forced emigration "must of necessity contravene the spirit, if not the very letter, of the supreme fundamental law of the land." Gregg was, and would long remain, the exception to the rule.

African Americans, not surprisingly, were the strongest advocates for the immediate end of slavery. It was always clear to them that when whites spoke of liberty, they limited it to whites. Not accepting this limitation, virtually all free black community organizations, including schools, churches, fraternal associations, and mutual aid societies, favored abolition. African American contributions to the abolitionist movement itself began in the Northeast with several "African Societies" during the late eighteenth century. During the 1820s, organizations such as the Massachusetts General Colored Association were formed to fight southern slavery and northern segregation, and the African American newspaper *Freedom's Journal*, published in New York in 1827, provided sustained criticisms of slavery. African American abolitionists also preceded white abolitionists in their insistence that moral suasion alone would not effect an end to slavery. In 1829 David Walker, son of a free black mother and an enslaved father, published an *Appeal to the Colored Citizens of the World*. He advocated uncompromising resistance to slavery, encouraging African Americans to fight "in the glorious and heavenly cause of freedom." When Walker's pamphlets were found in the possession of African Americans in Savannah, the Georgia legislature reacted quickly, enacting legislation that imposed the death penalty for circulating publications designed to stir insurrection. Seeing danger coming from trouble-making whites as well as enslaved blacks, they also enacted severe penalties for teaching slaves to read or write. Other states followed suit.

Forces against abolition were also strong in the North. Abolitionists had to fight against the Constitution, the courts, precedent, expediency, and prejudice. The vast majority of whites blamed abolitionists for stirring up sectional trouble. At best, abolitionists were scorned and marginalized; at worst, they lost their lives. Antiabolitionist mobs were common in the North.

In Boston, Christian pacifist William Lloyd Garrison represented the radical end of the white abolitionist spectrum. While he opposed slave uprisings and violent resistance, Garrison thought that African Americans should share an equality with whites. Garrison denounced any and all who excused slavery—people, churches, political parties. He excoriated the Constitution as a proslavery document. He advocated dissolution of the Union in order to establish a true democracy without slavery. Garrison, an ascetic nonconformist, was not a popular man and was once forced to parade through Boston with a noose around his neck. While circulation of his abolitionist newspaper *The Liberator* was relatively limited, the paper and his own speaking engagements brought attention to the cause of abolition and were imputed an influence they did not yet warrant. Because Nat Turner's rebellion occurred seven months after the first publication of *The Liberator*, many blamed the insurrection on Garrison.

Among those falling under Garrison's influence was Frederick Bailey. Enslaved in Baltimore, Bailey, carrying forged papers as proof that he was a free black sailor, purchased train tickets to Philadelphia and then to New York, where he was directed to abolitionist David Ruggles. Ruggles sent Bailey and his new wife, Anna, to live with the family of Nathan Johnson, a free and well-to-do African American. To avoid slave-catchers, Bailey changed his last name to Douglass. Frederick Douglass became a mighty spokesman for abolition. By invoking his personal experiences, he was able to counter proslavery propaganda that slaves were content and had an easy life.

Douglass and Garrison came to differ on how best to seek freedom for the enslaved. Douglass would not concede that resisting slavery through violence was wrong. And unlike Garrison, Douglass thought the Constitution could "be wielded in behalf of emancipation." Like other black Americans, Douglass coupled antislavery activities with demands for justice and racial equality. Long before their white counterparts, African Americans saw equality of opportunity safeguarded by rule of law as the litmus test of any meaningful freedom. In December 1847 Douglass published the first issue of his abolitionist paper *The North Star*, a four-page weekly out of Rochester, New York. Named after the star pointing the way north to fugitive slaves, the paper printed as its motto, "Right is of no sex— Truth is of no color—God is the Father of us all, and we are all Brethren."

Although differences between Garrison and Douglass became bitter, both men were part of a radical faction that relied on changing individual conscience. Garrison, Douglass, and their allies—including female antislavery activists—pursued moral suasion, which they believed could change hearts radically and so change the world, achieving complete and immediate emancipation, wiping away racism, and advancing the government of God on earth. Another group, equally religious, clustered around two successful New York businessmen, brothers Lewis and Arthur Tappan. This evangelical faction focused on working through political institutions. Whereas the Boston contingent worked in hired lecture halls, church basements, and shabby newspaper offices, always in search of donations and petition signatures, the New York crowd took a less pie-in-the-sky approach. They were mostly lawyers and merchants, well acquainted with the levers of power and the paying of bills and as much concerned with channeling and limiting social change as initiating it. They rejected any idea that reformers should rely on a higher law than the Constitution. To them, fulfilling one's civic responsibility in a free society required working within the law. The Tappanites, organizing the political process with all the mundane labor and pitiful compromises that that entailed, worked at the precinct, local, and state level to elect antislavery men. By putting the right men in office, the Tappanites set out to transform the nation and resolve the contradictions that the Founding Fathers had institutionalized.

Fired by a conviction that the Constitution was fundamentally antislavery, Arthur and Lewis Tappan used the judicial process to defend enslaved Africans in the 1841 *Amistad* case; captive slaves had mutinied and taken over the ship of that name from Spanish slavers. The whole idea that the captives might have a right to bring a lawsuit troubled the Spanish minister. Observing the proceedings, Minister Chevalier de Argaiz was incredulous. Why, he wondered, did not the U.S. government "interpose its authority to put down the irregularity of these proceedings"? Attorney John Quincy Adams eloquently handled the defense, and the verdict ultimately went in favor of the Africans. Lewis Tappan and his associates gave thanks to God that the case established the "liberties of thirty-six fellow-men" as well as the "fundamental principles of law, justice, and human rights."

The two factions of the abolitionist movement, one working on moral suasion and the other working on political and civic processes, did not see each other as complementary. They made war with each other as well as with the forces of slavery itself. A powerful subtext of gender conflict undergirded this split. At stake, the Tappanites insisted over and over, was the sustained existence of a republic with responsible men in charge and passion held in check. Anyone attending a Garrisonian rally could understand what they meant. Black orators like Frederick Douglass, Henry Bibb, and Henry "Box" Brown told gatherings their tales of victimization and loss, breaking hearts and firing passions. White preachers and would-be preachers, like Henry Ward Beecher, Theodore Weld, and William Henry Channing, moved their worshipers with scandalous stories of whipping and rape. White women seized the podium and spoke in stentorian tones against bondage. Indeed, to many it seemed that earnest Sarah Grimké and stern Quaker Lucretia Mott behaved like men. Worst of all to these critics was the sight of Sojourner Truth, shouting and calling all categories of social order into dispute.

To many white men, such performances seemed threatening. Although they jeered Amelia Bloomer's attempts at dress reform and smirked at how Lydia Child and Angelina Grimké henpecked their husbands, the changes in gender relations they saw unfolding before them seemed genuinely frightening. To be sure, vastly more women embraced the domestic philosophy of Catharine Beecher, who, though unmarried, urged American women to change the nation by perfecting their homes, a perspective that promised strength and influence through dutiful submission. Yet even here men feared—rightly—that paternal rule was being undermined. Among white male abolitionists who turned toward the Tappanite political strategy were those who did so because it excluded leadership and participation by women activists. Neither is it surprising that a small cadre of white women, having recognized their chance to gain a greater voice in public affairs, chose to gather at Seneca Falls, New York, in the summer of 1848, to demand political rights. Their demands addressed none of the economic concerns of working-class, African American, or Native American women. Such transforming visions and practices, at once broad and narrow, revolutionary and conservative, magnificent and flawed, were among the chief characteristics of the splintering of antebellum America.

Those contradictions seemed sharper in the wake of the failed revolutions that swept across Europe in 1848. Blended with the Garrisonians were all kinds of freethinkers who came to America after their efforts to achieve representative government, better economic life, and greater civil liberties were crushed throughout Europe. Anarchists, gender revolutionaries, race-mixers, and communitarians came. Their numbers were swelled by still stranger creatures preaching sexual freedom, abolition of the family, and "red republicanism." The New York Tappanites wanted no part of this group, for its limitless and diffusive radicalism and its tendency to alienate more moderate potential support. To the

Tappans and their wealthy supporters, the elimination of slavery required hard heads, not soft hearts. Although their efforts cost them financially, the Tappans persevered. To them, mobilizing the political power of western territory that was naturally "free soil" and impelling it toward constitutional reform was a practical task destined to doom bondage and reinvigorate the nation, socially and economically.

As for the slaveholders, they had great contempt for the pious, tub-thumping Garrisonians, as well as a ready stock of coiled hemp. When Boston radicals had tried to flood Charleston with antislavery pamphlets in the 1830s, South Carolinians used the papers for a splendid bonfire. When Massachusetts congressman Samuel Hoar went south in 1844 to survey slavery's evils for himself, vigilante slaveholders waited eagerly for his boat to dock; he declined their grim welcome and hurried home, as they expected. When the abolitionist "Brutus" (actually a turncoat southerner gone north) urged nonslaveholders to rise and slay the master class in 1847, squires employed the opportunity to shore up local support, prying into the details of community life in search of those who might be "soft" on slavery and encouraging their speedy departure. And indeed, southern whites who had complaints learned to mute them. Religious opposition to bondage, especially among Quakers and Universalists, was hemmed in and rooted out. Moralists in Georgia and the Carolinas were warned to hold their tongues. In the Upper South antislavery yeomen sometimes simply pulled up stakes and established new antislavery bulwarks north of the Ohio. Men with few prospects or no desire to ascend into the planter class likewise emigrated to the Northwest. Just so did antislavery Thomas Lincoln move with his family out of Kentucky to Indiana as early as 1816 and then, early in 1830, to Illinois. Nonslaveholding racists followed in their footsteps, unwilling to live in "a Negro country" any longer, and by the mid-1830s southern sections of Illinois, Indiana, and Ohio were becoming hotbeds of religious moralism, Free-Soil ideology, and racism.

Yet none could deny that antislavery sentiment was on the increase. Southern slaveholders viewed the small but growing number of abolitionists as part of an international movement that was steadily encircling them. Mexico had abolished slavery in 1829, England in 1833. Following a gradual emancipation, by 1838 all slaves within the British Empire, including Canada, were free. Over the course of the early nineteenth century most of the new nations of the western hemisphere (with the important exceptions of Brazil and Cuba) also gradually abolished slavery when they gained their independence.

As antislavery activists grew louder, so did proslavery advocates. Proslavery writers, in addition to seeking sympathy from the North, also needed to convince nonslaveowners, particularly those in the back country and in the Upper South who had a history of animosity and friction with the lower South, and the southern evangelical groups who thought and interpreted the Bible independently. Slaveholders also had to deal with the guilt that lurked in the conscience of many southerners. Although assuredly proslavery, William A. Smith, president of Randolph Macon College, wrote as late as 1856, "There are not a few spread throughout our Southern states whose minds are in a state of great embarrassment on this subject" because of religious beliefs and "the great abstract doctrine of Mr. Jefferson on the sinfulness of slavery."

Both northerners and southerners worried about sinfulness. While ideologues of the North, however, located safety in a gospel of liberty and righteous individualism, southern thinkers saw danger lurking all around, threatening from without and within. Compared with the North, the South was fully as cosmopolitan intellectually, fully as well read. Southerners were given to a vibrant debate on a wide range of cultural issues: legal reform, Romanticism, domestic relations, and a broad range of religious topics. This activity was born not from a greater curiosity in the abstract, however, but from an overwhelming, many-sided sense of growing peril. Looking to the "free" societies of the North and England and to liberal impulses on the continent, appalled slaveholders wore out their pens in combat against each threat. In the end, all their scribbling must be considered part of a comprehensive, relentless, xenophobic defense of slavery. However much they may have cared about Karl Schlegel's philosophy of freedom and the legal theories of Hugo Grotius, ultimately it all mattered only insofar as it affected the peculiar institution and the way of life that southerners had raised upon it. In the vehemence of proslavery arguments, all branches of knowledge and learning were ransacked to buttress the defense of slavery, now an obsession in the antebellum South.

The South turned in upon itself. It struggled with emerging currents of Western thought and tried to purge itself of all dissidence. With regionwide endorsement, questioning was no longer allowed; opposition was heresy. Religious denominations in America had no North/South divide until the 1830s and 1840s when animosities developed over slavery. Presbyterian factions formally split their denomination in 1838 over the question. The Methodists in 1844 declared, "We regard the officious, and unwarranted interference of the Northern portion of the Church with the subject of slavery alone, a sufficient cause for a division of our Church." When the national Baptist Church Board refused to accept slaveholders in the missionary field, southern members withdrew from this, the largest denomination, and in 1845 formed their own Southern Baptist Convention. Calhoun and Clay both worried about the schism in religious denominations. Clay warned, "This sundering of the religious ties which have hitherto bound our people together, I consider the greater source of danger to our country."

White southerners denied themselves the Bill of Rights. Freedom of religion and freedom of speech fell victim to proslavery forces in the South. Newspapers were suppressed. Slaveholders who wanted to free their own slaves had obstacles to overcome first. The South erected an "intellectual blockade" or "cotton curtain" against antislavery sentiment. Most of the South's intellectual energy was spent explaining and rationalizing the culture of which southerners were proud. The beliefs of those mild and cultured fanatics posed a mortal danger to the nation they yet controlled—and to humanity itself. Merely sustaining slavery where it existed seemed neither desirable nor possible to these brilliant, twisted sons of Jefferson and Madison and Jackson. Their hideous dream saw chattel bondage expanding across the nation itself and then, by the laws of nature, around the world.

Most Americans remained content to imagine that fervent prayer and steady labor would be sufficient until God brought forth his government on earth. For those few who were not content to wait for the Lord, their moral choices made all the difference in driving the nation toward Civil War. It would be in the tumultuous 1850s, with the circulation of a sentimental novel about family, an unmanly attack on free speech in the U.S. Senate, a dehumanizing racial ruling by the Supreme Court, and the martyrdom of a messianic murderer, that Americans came to fear that their domestic institutions were threatened, not threatening. It was not the slavery of sin that looked to destroy the nation and confound the millennium, but the sin of slavery.

Three

To Carry Out the Lord's Vengeance

THE SENATE HAD JUST ADJOURNED for the day when a tall, slightly built man entered the chamber, walking with a slight limp. As befitted a southern gentleman, Preston Brooks marked time until all the ladies had departed into the foyer; then he acted. Marching up to Charles Sumner, Republican senator from Massachusetts, the South Carolina congressman announced his purpose: "Mr. Sumner, I have read your speech with care and as much impartiality as was possible and I feel it my duty to tell you that you have libeled my State and slandered a relative who is aged and absent and I am come to punish you for it." As the hulking Sumner peered up from his correspondence, Brooks began to rain down blows with a gutta-percha cane. In a few moments the Yankee lay stunned and bleeding on the Senate floor, his bolted-down chair torn off its grounding. The Southron withdrew, in the company of his friends, satisfied that he had performed a just and manly deed.

Few individual acts in American history have done more to change the course of national events—or proven so self-destructive to a cause. The supposed slander that triggered Brooks's assault had come in the course of a lengthy, much-heralded speech, "The Crime Against Kansas," that Sumner delivered before a packed Senate on May 19 and 20, 1856. Sumner's harangue aimed to rally the North against slavery's spread, while jabbing at southern sins and hypocrisies. Clearly Sumner expected outrage in response, but neither he nor anyone else anticipated that this little-known southern moderate would rescue the fortunes of political abolitionism. His assault, a mere forty-eight hours after the speech's conclusion, catalyzed sectional controversy, but more than that, it marked a change in tactics. Not all at once and with much variation, more abolitionists found efficacy in working through the political process, while proslavery theorists began to replace their reliance on the Constitution and legal process, and turn instead to a higher law of southern honor.

On the first day of his oration, Sumner had taunted South Carolina senator Andrew Pickens Butler as an aged imbecile, lusting for the "harlot, Slavery." Southerners winced twice under Sumner's onslaught, first for its unbounded attack upon one of their most inoffensive leaders, who at that moment was convalescing from the latest of a series of strokes. They winced again when they encountered the barb of truth within Sumner's screed: the humiliating fact was that Butler's illness had begun to unman him. Now when Butler rose to address the nation, he did drool and spit, holding forth crankily like one on the threshold of senility. But to flaunt Butler's weakness, and to expose their own by calling up the ugly sexual side of slavery in the process, seemed to southerners a cowardly thing. So Brooks had acted, as he and his supporters believed any honorable man would.

To the South, the justice was divine. Sumner had got what he deserved, a just reward for impugning southern honor. From this perspective, Brooks had had no other recourse: he was above suing, while Sumner was below dueling. "The rapier or pistol for gentlemen," explained one young gallant, "& the cudgel for dogs." The law provided no protection against spoken outrage. Against such insults to one's inviolable honor, one could appeal only to a higher law. "For your beating the Damnd Rascal liar tory & Trator Sumner you deserve all the honors your country can bestow," agreed a Georgia farmer. "Yes sir Kill the infamous Scoundrel and all such." Across the South mass meetings proclaimed Brooks a hero, and newspaper editorials heralded his selfless action.

What was a self-evident higher law to the South was to the North a self-evident threat. Northern rallies condemned Brooks's assault as well as his defenders and demanded legal justice for the fallen Sumner. Ralph Waldo Emerson, lamenting the barbarism of the South in lauding the attack, connected the violence with the slave system: "We must either get rid of slavery, or get rid of freedom." Infuriated Republicans denounced the attack, enshrining Sumner as an abolitionist martyr. Even northern Democrats helped transform the moderate Brooks into "Bully Brooks," "Bludgeoner-in-Chief of South Carolina." Brooks wrote his brother, "I have been arrested of course & there is now a resolution before the House the object of which is to result in my expulsion. This they can't do. It requires two-thirds to do it and they can't get a half. Every Southern man sustains me."

Over the two days prior to his assault, Brooks and his collaborator, fellow congressman and mess mate Laurence Keitt, had been drinking. Keitt had goaded Brooks into the assault and watched his back. Both men now resigned their seats in response to the House's failed attempt to expel them. When new elections were held in South Carolina to determine their replacements, however, their constituents with one voice returned Brooks and Keitt to Washington as their own successors, to the surprise of no one except puling Yankees.

During the 1850s no single incident did more to disrupt sectional harmony and propel the nation toward civil war than Sumner's caning and its aftermath. It revitalized Republican fortunes in 1856, and it laid the groundwork for Lincoln's election four years hence. "The Republicans ought to pension Brooks for life," an angry ex-president Millard Fillmore complained. As nothing before, the caning revealed raging differences between northern and southern perspectives on the code of honor. The parameters of personal conduct and the dynamics of social order in a free society were in question. Slaveholders for a generation and more had taken refuge from abolitionist attacks behind the shield of the Bible and the Constitution. Legalities were on their side, with court precedent and majority indifference. Brooks changed that. The extremism of the attack was surprising, for Sumner's speech had assailed A. P. Butler only in passing. Sumner had disparaged Illinois Democrat Stephen Douglas and Virginian James Mason in equally vigorous terms, yet neither had offered more than bitter words in response. Douglas, however, clearly foresaw the coming violence. Pacing in the rear of the Senate while Sumner spoke, Douglas had worried aloud, "That damn fool will get himself killed by some other damn fool."

Indeed, it was not enough that Brooks had laid out Sumner. On the following day, when Massachusetts senator Henry Wilson railed against the Carolinian's "brutal, murderous and cowardly assault," Butler, just returned to the Senate, denounced Wilson as a liar. When that outburst failed to provoke a violent response from the Yankee, Brooks sent him a challenge to duel. When Wilson demurred, Brooks challenged another Yankee, and another, and another. Finally he set his sights on Massachusetts congressman Anson Burlingame, who had reviled him in the House. Burlingame agreed to duel but facetiously fixed the Canadian side of Niagara Falls as the field of honor. Unwilling to run a "gauntlet of mobs and assassins, prisons and penitentiaries, bailiffs and constables," Brooks refused but continued to bluster impotently, demanding that Burlingame name another spot. Nothing happened, but increasingly absurd posturing made him appear more foolish and intemperate, even to moderate southerners. Hotheaded Carolinians and their fire-eating friends seemed determined to start a scrap with someone, anyone who dared speak against them. It all seemed irrational and unnecessary—though it was anything but.

The South's overwrought response to Brooks's defense of southern honor and manhood points out just how important and how threatened slaveholders believed these qualities to be. In 1856 it seemed to many white southerners that their whole world was being undermined, and Sumner's remarks only uncovered more profound anxieties over a deeper threat to honor, manhood, and social order. After almost a half-century of private turmoil and public debate over slavery's place in the nation's fabric, southerners were coming to believe that the time for talk was finished. Men who had rooted their defense of bondage in reason and interest grew steadily more convinced that violence offered the better recourse. Conversely, northerners were coming to base their opposition to slavery firmly upon the rock that southerners were abandoning. As slaveholders shouted ever louder about the moral "positive good" of their peculiar institution, as they grew ever touchier about honor besieged, antislavery northerners increasingly embraced the broad middle ground of the Constitution. Striking down an immoderate ranter like Sumner was the greatest impetus that southern solons could have given their abolitionist foes. For in his place came other men, less high flown in their oratory but clever in crafting practical legislation and determined to grasp the levers of state and national power.

Most white Americans understood that something fundamental was changing in the parameters of their social vision, that a new desperation and pessimism had set in. The millennial aspirations of the early republic, that America could fulfill God's destiny, seemed less certain. The impulse that derived from the Second Great Awakening had been at its heart emancipatory: men and women who opened their spirits to the light of love would overcome the base conflicts and human wretchedness that defined social life. For so long it had seemed that republicanism, the rod of reason, and the gentle staff of moral suasion had been leading Americans toward a higher road and a new beginning: the steamboat, the telegraph, the educative explosion of print culture and public lectures, the growth of temperance, missionary, and sabbatarian movements, the new reliance upon the softening impulse of women and the home—all these and more pointed toward the emergence of a more civilized, humane, and godly America, where freedom was in perfect balance with virtue and civic responsibility.

At heart, of course, this reform mentality had never been able to resolve its contradictory drives: Was social salvation to be accomplished by reining in and carving out man's lower propensities, or was the millennium possible only if the holy light within the human heart was allowed to shine forth in free abandon? Was the soul of the nation ultimately good or evil? Should government support unbridled release or uncompromising control? Was the project of bringing America to Christian perfection within grasp or a dangerous delusion? Those questions were played out again and again, in religious reform endeavors and in political parties. Democrats argued that government should adopt a "hands-off" policy in terms of economic development, allowing markets to flourish freely and local communities to determine the shape of their social institutions. Whigs, by contrast, believed that legislators should actively shape the direction of progress through tariffs, government-sponsored banks and railroads, and an activist national Congress.

In cultural terms, Americans idealized both nature free and nature subjugated, both the freshness of the frontier and the positive fruits of its passing. In James Fenimore Cooper's rough-hewn Natty Bumppo (Hawkeye) and in the exquisite singer Jenny Lind (the Swedish Nightingale), they recognized poles of nature and culture that they both embraced and rejected. Ultimately, in the mid-1850s, America's quandary was summed up in George Inness's pessimistic landscape *The Lack-*

awanna Valley (c. 1856). Although he and Asher Durand came from the same school of artists, here all the hopes of the latter's *Kindred Spirits* were undone. A lone figure sits huddled on a hillside, gazing down at what man's efforts to mesh nature and culture have wrought: a vista dotted with tree stumps, a smoky sky, and uncoiling from a roundhouse in the painting's center background, a locomotive hauling a long line of cars. There is nothing of epiphany or transcendence in this work. The mood is overwhelmingly one of irony, failure, and defeat.

As the millennial hopes of women and men seemed increasingly jeopardized, Americans from South and North, East and West, came to identify difference with danger. The nation appeared threatened by extremism—and by moderates who failed to take problems seriously. The only sensible course, many came to believe, was to reject the middle ground and challenge foes head-on. National and personal salvation increasingly resided in adamantly holding positions the rightness of which seemed incontrovertible. That such a challenge could end only in violence and bloodshed, as Brooks's action amply demonstrated, was a lesson most Americans missed. Steadily, unwittingly, northerners and southerners marched together toward the precipice.

Advancing that march was the question of slavery in the western territories. Southern and northern politicians faced a proximate and material threat to sectional balance: the mushrooming growth and booming economy of California. With the conclusion of the Treaty of Guadalupe Hidalgo in 1848, ceding Mexican territory to the United States, it appeared that a North-South equilibrium had been roughly established—at least in the wishful thinking of those who stared at a map. So long as sectional parity was maintained in Congress, potentially explosive mishaps like Wilmot's proviso could be defeated. There seemed little prospect of any western territory seeking statehood in the near future. Moreover, all were confident that when new lands eventually established their territorial governments, the abilities of Clay, Calhoun, and Webster to work out statesmanlike compromise and realistic deal-making would surely win out.

But then in January 1848, in constructing a sawmill for John Sutter in northern California, millwright James Marshall from New Jersey made a discovery: golden nuggets. During the following year Yankees, southerners, Irishmen, Chinese, and others flooded into California by the thousands, as these "49-ers" tried their fortunes. Just one year after the first gold strike, California sought admission to the Union as a state—without slavery. Perplexed and outraged southerners turned back to their maps in horror. Whereas western Texas and the lands of New Mexico looked unsuited to cotton culture, California, the richest prize of the Mexican War, was definitely ripe for slavery. Moreover, if California came into the nation so rapidly, other territories would soon be knocking at the door of the Union—and maybe crossing its threshold as havens of abolitionism. As foreign immigration spiraled upward in the wake of European political and agricultural disasters, westward migration increased dramatically, and clever heads were already planning to build a railroad to the Pacific. The ranks of those trekking westward would soon fill up the Great Plains. With one voice, southerners shouted against the admission of an antislavery California.

Proslavery politicians knew that slavery's expansion was necessary to maintain the sectional balance in Congress. Economics dictated the same necessity. While cotton growers had been hit hard by the worldwide depression of 1837–44, they remained in the grip of a boom mentality, sure that next year's crop would be grand beyond expectations. So they refinanced old debts, bought new lands and slaves on credit, and hoped for the best. Their situation improved with the admission of Texas to the Union in 1845, and the prospect of more slave states, welcoming markets for every kind of property, spurred the westward interstate slave trade and drove prices up. Where soil was most fertile and farms were accessible to market—as in the Yazoo-Mississippi Delta and along the Red River—planters snatched up a bonanza. On lesser lands they cinched up their belts, drove their slaves harder, and pushed aside mounting bills. If the nation admitted California as a free state, the consequence would be a further tumbling of slave prices. When cotton prices next turned downward, a harder crash would surely come. On that day the abolitionists would only need to stand by with folded arms and knowing grins while the peculiar institution and the civilization built on its foundation broke to pieces of its own accord.

So it was that when Californians threatened the southern dream of expanded slavery, southern slaveholders panicked. When Daniel Webster rose to speak on the issue, he called for "the fresh air of liberty and union" and insisted that a nonslave California be admitted without tinkering. Webster was a trusted man in the Senate and throughout the country. Only three years earlier, in 1847, when northern and southern soldiers were united in a fight against Mexico, the elite in Charleston, South Carolina, invited Webster to give a speech in their fine city. Charleston's St. Andrew's Hall displayed banners welcoming the "Bright Star of the East" and celebrating "Our Country, Our Whole Country, and Nothing But Our Country." Honoring Webster were such South Carolina luminaries as Robert Barnwell Rhett, William J. Grayson, and William Aiken, as well as a host of others devoted to states' rights and slavery. They toasted Webster, and they toasted the Constitution because it bound "all parts of our country in one great and glorious Republic." But that sense of unity had deteriorated over the short three years since then.

The spokesman for slavery, John C. Calhoun, was no longer interested in binding together. Too ill to speak, Calhoun was carried on a stretcher into the Senate chamber to make plain his opposition. As a colleague read his dying warnings, the Carolinian feebly pointed his finger heavenward. Calhoun urged southerners to consider their own course, to meet in sectional conference, and to decide what steps to take if the North would not bend. What made this impasse most alarming was that both men were confirmed nationalists. Both had constructed and sustained a system of compromise and conflict-avoidance throughout their years in office.

Calhoun was particularly alarmed by the breakdown of compromise, the abandonment of the middle for the extremes, and the willingness of political radicals, North and South, to inflame public opinion in pursuit of their own narrow advantage. As Calhoun understood better than anyone, the South could simply be outnumbered and outmaneuvered. Intending to construct a new middle ground, he pondered what, in a nation where majorities ruled, was to prevent the self-interest of the many from tyrannizing over and abrogating the rights of the minority. As a leader and political theorist, Calhoun struggled with the problem of how the South could continue to exist and the nation remain whole. He concluded that the only way that the two areas could live together would be to create a "concurrent majority" of both.

Ever in pursuit of his own ambitions, Calhoun never abandoned his ideals of national unity, even when he led South Carolina in the nullification crisis some two decades earlier. The South and other rural areas preferred the lower costs that came with foreign competition and so opposed high tariffs. Calhoun's defense of free trade (which, many knew, was actually a covert defense of slavery itself) brought South Carolina to the brink of civil war when the state declared in 1832 that the federal tariff acts were "null and void." In response to the nullification challenge, Senator Daniel Webster of Massachusetts proclaimed that the sovereignty of the United States lay in the people and not in the states. Americans could not have "Liberty first and Union afterwards," Webster declared. "Liberty and Union, now and forever, one and inseparable." President Andrew Jackson had already put Calhoun on notice at a dinner celebrating Jefferson Day (April 13, 1830). He toasted, "Our Union: It must be preserved." On that occasion, Calhoun responded to Jackson's challenge and offered the next toast: "The Union, next to our liberty, most dear." Privately, Jackson threatened to hang Calhoun. When Jackson dispatched a fleet of eight ships and a shipment of five thousand muskets, South Carolina responded by organizing militia regiments. Calhoun's brinksmanship paid off when Congress worked out a lower tariff. No other state had supported South Carolina's dare, and the moderate middle held.

As secretary of state in 1844, Calhoun had championed the annexation of Texas, always with one eye on his presidential prospects. Yet he had led the political opposition to armed conflict with Mexico, fearing where that war might ultimately lead. His solution to sectional conflict, which he hammered out in his *Disquisition on Government* (1849), was ironically a strange and strong defense of affirmative action. He rooted political ideology firmly in material interest, demanding for the minority a limited veto power over the decisions of the whole. Treating a sectional minority as a majority in its own right simply provided for the effective protection of such rights as the national covenant already allowed, whether those rights concerned security of property, relief from unfair taxation, or civil liberties. Without such safeguards, Calhoun asked, what defense did a state or community have against the power of Washington and the prejudice of outsiders? Slaveholders, understandably, lauded the clever twist that Calhoun gave constitutional debate. Only much later did they understand his argument's fatal flaw: however well southerners checked the aggressions of abolitionist Yankees, what could sustain the master class if its own nonslaveholding majority sold them out?

California proved that political parity was essential. A compromise was needed, and compromise, as usual, called for pragmatism. In the upper house Henry Clay, the aged yet still powerful Whig who had saved the Union a generation earlier with the Missouri Compromise, promoted a basket of legislation based on quid pro quo. In the lower house a shrewd young dynamo from Illinois, close-calculating Stephen Douglas, helped put together the measures that became known as the Compromise of 1850. On the one hand, Clay and Douglas promised to abolish the slave trade—though not slavery—in the District of Columbia. On the other, they proposed a more effective law to recapture fugitive slaves. On one side, they sponsored the immediate organization of territorial government in New Mexico—a potential windfall for slavery's forces. On the other, California would join the union under an antislavery state constitution.

Antislavery extremists as well as extremists for slavery refused to support the Compromise of 1850. Parsing sin or hedging honor was to them nonsensical on its face. More practical men, however, prevailed. Breaking the measures into separate pieces of legislation, Douglas and Clay effected a triumph of political horse-trading. Various and shifting coalitions in Congress tempered their animosities, held their noses, and voted for enough of the proposals to prevent secession and keep the Union together. Calhoun, however, saw disaster in the making: "Crying 'Union, Union, the glorious Union!' can no more prevent disunion than the cry of 'Health, health, glorious health!' on the part of the physician can save a patient lying dangerously ill." Rather than working with Douglas, Clay, and Webster to orchestrate a compromise, Calhoun blamed antislavery protests for putting the Union in jeopardy. His remarks forecast doom: "The agitation [on slavery] has been permitted to proceed with almost no attempt to resist it, until it has reached a point when it can no longer be disguised or denied that the Union is in danger. You have thus had forced upon you the greatest and gravest question that can ever come under your consideration: How can the Union be preserved?" Within weeks Calhoun was dead, and Webster and Clay two years after him. Men certain of their own righteous position, and therefore less willing to compromise, would stride forward to take their places.

While issues of the compromise were still under debate, delegates from all over the South met in Nashville that June of 1850. They shouted defiance at the North and passed voluminous declarations. They resolved "that Congress has no power to exclude from the territory of the United States any property lawfully held," and that in the territories the government should secure "full enjoyment of religion, the freedom of the press, the trial by jury, and all other rights of person and property." They resolved that the federal government had to "recognize and defend" what a state recognized as property. Although they did not like the compromise forbidding slavery north of the 36° 30' latitude specified in the Missouri Compromise, they were willing to abide by it "as an extreme concession." They found the Wilmot Proviso to be "disparaging," "dishonorable," and "degrading." While they thought they had the right to petition Congress for a redress of grievances, they thought others should not be allowed to do so because those others were "inflicting injury" and "jeopardizing" rights.

Determined to secede independently if need be, hotheaded South Carolina radicals worked in the convention to promote disunion. Their efforts fizzled. Long-talking "cooperationists," who vastly outnumbered hard-line single-state separatists, dragged out debates. Moderates won the day as tempers cooled. The time for secession was not yet right, the moderates announced, secure in the belief that in any future crisis it would be possible to deflate secessionists like Robert Barnwell Rhett of South Carolina simply by running out the clock. Block immediate action, keep all parties talking, and fiery plans would die out of their own accord. That had been a lesson learned over two decades and more.

When passed, the Compromise of 1850 was no model of righteousness. Although it brought California into the Union as a free state, other territory ceded from Mexico was unspecified as to whether it would be free or slave. Slave trade between states was excluded from federal interstate jurisdiction and the slave trade was abolished in the District of Columbia, but the institution of slavery was specifically allowed in that district, the first of any such guarantees. Among the most controversial issues was the passage of an aggressive fugitive slave act.

African American runaways had been a problem for slaveowners for as long as slavery existed. While escape from slavery was rarely an option, those enslaved in a border state had somewhat better prospects of success. Those who managed to escape had powerful stories to tell. In 1830 Josiah Henson of Maryland earned enough money on the side to pay his slaveholder the $350 price of freedom. The owner pocketed the money and then told Henson that the price had gone up to $1,000. Soon thereafter, Henson and his wife and four children escaped to Canada. Whether writing their own passes while pretending they could not read or write, traveling in a coffin, or stowing aboard vessels, these fugitives intensified debate over slavery and inspired an emerging abolition movement. Although potent symbols for freedom, challenges and resistance amounted to little in the vastness of the system. Yet those able to escape infuriated slaveholders.

Slaves in the lower South fled to freedom in Mexico or to areas of Florida still outside jurisdictional control. In Florida they joined other fugitives in Maroon communities of Indians, blacks, and some whites. Frustrated that the Seminoles harbored fugitive slaves, the United States attacked Florida several times. Chief Osceola, married to a fugitive slave, made clear his own appeal to a higher law when he plunged his dagger into the treaty he was asked to sign that would move his people from their swamplands. This action precipitated the Second Seminole War, 1835–42. (Some say it lasted until 1858.) Ostensibly waged over the question of whether Seminoles should be moved westward across the Mississippi River into what is now Oklahoma, it was also about the refusal of the Seminoles to give up fugitives from slavery. Invited to a meeting to discuss peace, Osceola was captured in 1837 while carrying a white flag of truce. He died in prison and was beheaded.

Slaves in the Upper South looked northward. Free African Americans, along with some whites, helped deliver fugitives to Canada. Antislavery people worked informally with others they trusted to provide a network of safe places for fugitive slaves. In 1844 an abolitionist newspaper in Chicago printed a cartoon of fugitives happily riding to Canada on a train called "Liberty Line." Neither underground nor a railroad, the so-called "Underground Railroad" is hard to document due to its informal nature and the need of secrecy. Records on how many fugitives used this network are understandably scarce. Runaway slave Harriet Tubman became heavily involved in the Railroad in the 1850s and eventually accepted the most dangerous of roles, a "conductor" who would travel into slave territory and actively help liberate slaves. One of her friends in Wilmington, Delaware, wrote in 1854, "We made arrangements last night, and sent away Harriet Tubman, with six men and one woman to Allen Agnew's, to be forwarded across the country to the city. Harriet, and one of the men had worn the shoes off their feet, and I gave them two dollars to help fit them out, and directed a carriage to be hired at my expense, to take them out, but do not yet know the expense." Barely five feet tall, Tubman was a strong and impassioned leader who knew how to encourage a runaway who was suffering from trepidation or regret. Knowing the disastrous consequences that would follow upon exposure of the inner workings of the Railroad, she would show him her gun and say that "a live runaway could do great harm by going back, but that a dead one could tell no secrets."

To reclaim footloose property, not to mention to justify owning it, slaveholders could turn to the Constitution. Article IV states: "No Person held to Service or Labour in one State, under the Laws thereof, escaping into another, shall, in Consequence of any Law or Regulation therein, be discharged from such Service or Labour, but shall be delivered up on Claim of the Party to whom such Service or Labour may be due."

Part of the Compromise of 1850, the Fugitive Slave Law brought much harsher enforcement than any previous fugitive law. Federal commissioners helped slaveholders capture escapees, who had no right to a trial or to testify before a judge. An affidavit by the slaveholder was all that was necessary to reclaim a slave. Anyone obstructing recapture could get a $1,000 fine, six months jail, and $1,000 civil damages for each slave that such interference left at liberty. Moreover, citizens whether willing or not were obliged to help with the law enforcement: "All good citizens are hereby commanded to aid and assist in the prompt and efficient execution of this law." As bounty hunters pursued escaped slaves, they occasionally kidnapped and sent southward African Americans who had never been enslaved or who had legally acquired their freedom. State-sanctioned force, arrest warrants, and posses could not answer all the questions of deployment of power and legal jurisdiction, however, and northern juries often failed to convict those charged with obstruction. This predictably caused southern slaveholders to cry betrayal of the letter and spirit of the agreement. Because local law enforcement, haphazard and sometimes very lax, offered little protection to free citizens of color when bounty hunters appeared, some concerned citizens, whites and blacks, formed "vigilance committees" to protect free blacks from unscrupulous abductors. Sometimes these same committees formed to protect fugitive slaves. In 1851, on another historic September 11, a group of fugitive slaves and free blacks forcibly resisted recapture in Christiana, Pennsylvania, killing the master and severely wounding several others. When they and some white bystanders were charged with resisting the Fugitive Slave Law, the government was unable to sustain a charge of treason against an unapologetic local community, only increasing southern anger at a perceived northern failure to enforce the law.

In the controversy over the Fugitive Slave Law, Congressman Abraham Lincoln kept a middle ground. He believed in obeying the law but asked for a modification to make the law more just, so that it would not "in its stringency, be more likely to carry a free man into slavery, than our ordinary criminal laws are to hang an innocent one." Antislavery northerners felt this an insufficient response when the law put them in the position of enforcers and made them directly culpable in slavery's sin.

As abolitionists grew more strident over the Fugitive Slave Law, and as southerners grew more obsessed over growing abolitionism, Stephen Douglas still believed in a democratic vision. Maintaining the status quo on slavery and enlarging the opportunities of capitalism, he believed, would both guide the nation toward social and economic prosperity and heal the sectional split. Economic prosperity would cure capitalism's vices, democratic virtue would join hands with material prosperity, and the slavery issue—one way or another—would wither away. Such a plan would also surely vault its architect into the White House.

The power of the Democrat Douglas and politicians like him was redoubled in 1854 with the collapse of the Whig Party, which for several years had been unable to draw supporters across the sectional divide. The Compromise of 1850 saved the Union, but it was a bitter draft to swallow. In the South, proslavery Whig politicians and voters threw up their hands in disgust. Northern Whigs had trickled away from the party steadily thereafter, especially abolitionists who had hoped to use Whiggery's canopy to promote the cause of antislavery. In 1855 Abraham Lincoln wrote to his friend Joshua Speed: "I think I am a whig; but others say there are no whigs, and that I am an abolitionist." Both northern and southern Whigs were drawn into the orbits of more extreme political parties. For southerners, the Democratic Party's support for free trade and limited government looked increasingly attractive. With the strength of solid southern support, Democrat Franklin Pierce of New Hampshire defeated the Whig candidate, General Winfield Scott, to win the White House in 1852. Bolstered by a flourishing economy in both sections, Pierce planted southerners in important roles in his cabinet and promoted policies that would be attractive to the South. With slavery no longer allowed in California, Pierce and his southern shadows looked elsewhere—and found Cuba, which had a thriving plantation economy and a slave system of labor (which continued until 1886).

Southerners, who coveted Cuba as a place to expand their own slavery-driven agricultural economy, had a history of supporting plans to invade the island. Lucy Holcombe of Texas was a southern belle active in encouraging Narciso López's filibustering expedition to Cuba in 1851. Holcombe, representative of "Young America," a movement of intellectuals, journalists, and businessmen within the Democratic Party who, both idealistically and ideologically, supported U.S. imperialism, wrote a novel, *The Free Flag of Cuba*, advocating liberty for Cubans; her cause, however, was not meant for Cuba's 436,000 enslaved. Many New York financiers also opposed freedom for the enslaved Cubans. Although Congress had made the slave trade a capital crime since 1820, New York City was the epicenter of this trade between Africa and Cuba. Financed by Wall Street investors, supported by sharp attorneys in admiralty law, slave ships were outfitted in New York and sailed out of New York harbor. Filibusters had ardent champions throughout the North: patriotism blended with self-interest and prevalent racism, leading newspapers throughout the country endorsed their exploits, and communities nationwide held supporting rallies and raised money for them, even though such efforts never yielded an actual result.

In 1854 Pierce instructed his minister to Spain, Pierre Soulé of Louisiana, to purchase Cuba, but the overbearing southerner had little patience for the slow ways of the Spanish court. With James Buchanan, Pierce's ambassador to England, and John Mason, the minister to France, Soulé drafted the Ostend Manifesto, a document justifying an American takeover of Cuba. The published document caused an uproar, both in the United States and in Europe, and Pierce was forced to repudiate it. But the damage had been done. Douglas Democrats in support of Pierce had tipped their hand: appeasing southern slaveholders had clearly become central to their quest for political power, which they saw, self-servingly, as central to preserving the Union.

Infuriated northern Democrats concerned with the territorial issue needed a place to turn. Some hoped to bring together the squabbling North and South under the banner of a new nationalist American Party. Initially a secret society—when members were asked about its existence, they claimed to know nothing of any such party—it was inimical to Catholicism, alcohol, and foreign immigration. For the most part, these predominantly urban northern "Know-Nothings" thought that the central problems facing the nation did not come from the plantations of the South but from the burgeoning cities of the North, where New York, Philadelphia, and a host of other urban centers were becoming havens for poverty, vice, overcrowding, and criminality. While Free-Soil advocates embraced New York *Tribune* editor Horace Greeley's admonition to the downtrodden city dweller to "Go West, Young Man" as the logical solution to these troubles, Know-Nothings thought that urban problems could never be redressed without first stemming the tide of foreigners, who they believed were corrupting American republican virtue.

Abraham Lincoln had no respect for the Know-Nothings. In the letter to Joshua Speed, in August 1855, he wrote:

> As a nation, we began by declaring that "all men are created equal." We now practically read it "all men are created equal, except Negroes." When the Know-Nothings get control, it will read "all men are created equal, except Negroes, and foreigners, and Catholics." When it comes to this I should prefer emigrating to some country where they make no pretence of loving liberty—to Russia, for instance, where despotism can be taken pure, and without the base alloy of hypocrisy.

Ultimately a grab bag of xenophobic racists, old-line conservatives, and devious southern politicos of various stripes, Know-Nothings gained a surprisingly large following in state and local elections in 1852 to 1854. In 1856, however, most of the gains melted away, except in Maryland, where anti-Catholic feeling remained strong.

Douglas's political hopes in the 1850s depended on the Democrats' ability to shut debate over slavery out of the halls of Congress and so, he believed, out of the nation's consciousness. Extremist Garrisonians continued to rant about the moral wrongs of bondage, but they were an aging, ineffectual minority, and their rants had been heard and largely ignored for two decades and more. But Douglas's grand scheme failed disastrously. The dumpy little man from Illinois had no idea that a dumpy little woman from Connecticut was about to wreck all his plans with a boilerplate novel that would stir the nation's deepest sympathies.

The crux of the problem was Americans' millennial aspirations. Wrapped up in the hopes and fears attending righteous progress, convinced that they were people of godly sympathies, even while they were eager for evidence of that truth, Americans could not simply shrug at the mawkish story of Uncle Tom. Harriet Beecher Stowe's *Uncle Tom's Cabin* told nothing new about the evils of slavery—Theodore Weld's earlier exposé, *American Slavery As It Is* (1839), had been far more graphic and revealing. Stowe, however, placed bondage in an entirely new context. What was at stake here was the family itself, and Stowe ably showed how slavery cut through ties of love, affection, and duty, afflicting white families and black. Fathers and masters discovered their powers subverted, or their passions dreadfully unleashed. Mothers in this story found their dearest impulses threatened and defeated by bondage; weeping for the enslaved mother Eliza, who is trying, in violation of law, to escape with her son before he is taken away from her, became a rite of passage for every reader.

Stowe did not demonize southerners. They too were helpless victims of a sinful system. The villain in the story is Simon Legree, a Yankee dealer in slaves who owns a plantation in Louisiana. Because of his love for money, Legree puts aside all morality for the sake of gain. In a warning to her northern readers, Stowe portrays Legree without one iota of Christian compassion. He is the embodiment of mammon-worship.

Stowe belonged to the "gradual emancipation" school. She believed that slaves should receive a basic education and a conversion to Christianity before being freed. When these two conditions were met, Stowe advocated recolonization to Africa. Stowe, as well as her brother Henry Ward Beecher, became animated abolitionists after the passage of the

Fugitive Slave Act. Daughter, wife, and sister of ministers, Stowe used her Christianity as an ideal throughout her novel. The main character, Tom, wrongly scourged and beaten to death, is the epitome of a Christian man who never sacrifices his integrity. Stowe's greatest literary trick, which modern audiences overlook too easily, was to construct a melodramatic novel that did not provide the predicted payoff. Stowe milked that shocking device of unmerited punishment and death at several points in her text. According to *The National Era*, readers' "tenderest sympathies" were "awakened by the trembling sensibility and angelic nature of the beautiful little Evangeline." For Uncle Tom, the promise of a happy ending rewarding goodness and virtue is utterly betrayed. To an audience tuned to progressing toward Christian perfection, this was shocking indeed. The unwarranted death of the protagonist allowed white audiences both to identify sentimentally with the plight of enslaved African Americans and to spring from a sob of remorse to a cry for vengeance. Aesthetically frustrated, morally confused, and bitterly angry, northern readers howled for justice for Uncle Tom.

On June 5, 1851, the abolitionist weekly *Washington National Era* began publication, producing forty installments over the next ten months. When a Boston publisher decided to issue *Uncle Tom's Cabin* as a book in March 1852, it became an instant bestseller. According to the New York newspaper the *Independent*, "Mrs. Stowe's work seems to have created a demand quite unprecedented in this country." Three hundred thousand copies were sold the first year, and about two million were sold worldwide by 1857. The success of *Uncle Tom's Cabin* derived as much from the cultural context of its production—the material circumstances of mass production and the melodramatic literary antecedents of Charles Dickens's Sam Weller and Little Nell—as from Stowe's clever construction of plot and character.

With this powerful weapon in the propaganda war against slavery, entrepreneurs quickly capitalized on Stowe's success, dramatizing her tale in theatrical productions. As people were entertained, they were also educated. Before reading or seeing *Uncle Tom's Cabin*, most white northerners, while theoretically opposed to the idea of slavery, remained apathetic. Slavery was an issue that did not seem to affect them. Loyal to the Union, they were much more opposed to sectional agitation than they were to slavery per se. That changed with *Uncle Tom's Cabin*. Readers had supposed they were not complicit in an institution in a distant section of the country, but Stowe's humanized slaves possessed genuine feelings and Christian virtue. Their subjection to atrocities rendered them martyrs to their insulted faith and struck the heartfelt emotion of northern readers. Previously uninterested in the subject of slavery, they became tainted with its sin. Freedom for the enslaved and outrage at the Fugitive Slave Law became moral issues rather than political ones. *The Western Journal and Civilian Review*, while condemning Stowe's exaggerations, nevertheless thought that her call for a "higher law" was a good doctrine "for the novelist as well as the politician." Most readers responded precisely because of the exaggerations. The political potency of the book rested on readers' general acceptance of Christian absolutes of good and evil and the knowledge that one compromises with sin at the risk of one's soul. In Stowe's declaration, "Liberty!—electric word! . . . Is there anything in it glorious and dear for a nation, that is not also glorious and dear for a man?" was a call to all Christian soldiers.

Southern newspapers decried Stowe's book as a "threat to the Union." *The Southern Literary Messenger Review* fiercely admonished Stowe for stirring up animosities, "to sow, in this blooming garden of freedom, the seeds of strife and violence and all direful contentions." The magazine's editorial of October 1852 charged the novel with making false assertions and proclaimed the South's justice in denouncing it; and in admitting to the fear that the differing opinions stoked by the book might someday lead to "the bayonet," the *Review* likely encouraged that result. Abraham Lincoln's supposed comment that Stowe was "the little woman" who caused "this big war" went too far, but no book or speech or document had so focused the nation's attention on the wrongs and dangers implicit in that peculiar institution. In response to Stowe's argument, southerners hustled out an assortment of hackneyed and equally exaggerated proslavery novels, such as *Aunt Phillis's Cabin; or, Southern Life As It Is* by Mary Eastman (1852). None gained a cultural footing outside the South.

As much as sentimental complaints about slavery irritated Stephen Douglas and his slaveholding allies, they expected material prosperity to vanquish such qualms. The crafty lawyer and caucus chief, the unrivaled master of political affairs at the federal level, the "Little Giant" who pushed through the Compromise of 1850, now used his parliamentary powers to gain massive land concessions for the Illinois Central Railroad. Construction of a transcontinental line would funnel the riches of the Pacific West into the coffers of a budding Chicago—and into his own pockets as well. The route that Douglas promoted, so dear to his national, political, and economic ambitions, was charted through the country's broad middle. Douglas Democrats believed that their plan offered something for everyone and that, just as in 1850, all parties would join hands in spite of elements that were distasteful. Instead, the projected railroad only divided and agitated all sides. For slaveowners, who had long set their sights on driving a southern route westward from Memphis or New Orleans across Texas to the Pacific, Douglas's plan sounded the death knell to their investment and development schemes. In South Carolina and Georgia especially, planters and merchants since the 1830s had sunk prodigious amounts of capital into far-flung railroad ventures aimed to bind the region together and thereby rescue the fortunes of cotton factories in Charleston and Savannah. Against Douglas's proposed shorter line to the Pacific, crossing the Mississippi River at St. Louis, southern ventures had no hope to compete. Indeed, if Douglas's route was established and the volume of trade accelerated, cotton growers in the Mississippi Valley and farther afield might well ship their crops by rail to mid-Atlantic ports like Baltimore, transforming New Orleans into a backwater.

Douglas's proposed transatlantic route presented even more immediate spurs to southern fears. Building the railroad from the Midwest rather than from Memphis or New Orleans would require organizing territorial governments in that part of the Louisiana Purchase running from the present-day southern border of Kansas to Canada. To that effect, Douglas introduced the Kansas-Nebraska Act of 1854. As stipulated by the Missouri Compromise of 1820, no slavery was allowed in these territories, yet over the years white southerners had come to resent this exclusion as a slight to their honor and a trampling on their liberty. To garner essential southern support for his railroad bill, Douglas included into his Kansas-Nebraska Act the concept of "popular sovereignty," a phrase that did not appear in the document itself but that immediately became the shorthand slogan employed by newspapers and politicians. Capitalizing on an idea first promulgated by Michigan senator Lewis Cass, Douglas suggested that henceforth the question of slavery in territories requesting admission to the Union would be left to the democratic process, to the discretion of the people—or rather, the adult white males—residing there. At one stroke, this approach redefined slavery as a local territorial issue and, more effectively than gag rule bans ever did, promised to banish from the halls of Congress all further discussion of slavery in the territories. Drawing on both the majoritarian principles of the Constitution and the conservative caveats of Calhoun's *Disquisition*, Douglas's scheme to end debate by promoting local democracy was a masterstroke of political finesse.

Popular sovereignty sounds very much like the essence of liberty and republicanism, but Lincoln called it "a mere deceitful pretense for the benefit of slavery." In his exalted moments Douglas called popular sovereignty "the sacred right of self-government"; in his franker ones he said it was to make sure government was "made by white men, on the white basis, for the benefit of white men and their posterity forever." Douglas's bill ended the Missouri Compromise that disallowed slavery in northern territory, and Abraham Lincoln was blunt in his appraisal: "I hate it because of the monstrous injustice of slavery itself. I hate it because it deprives our republican example of its just influence in the world." But what was to be done by those of Lincoln's thinking? On its face, Douglas's approach seemed the embodiment of the rule of law and self-determining individualism. Yet so transparently did "popular sovereignty" encourage rank subversion of the law that it would set off the darkest speculations that democracy was corrupted.

Under the provisions of the Kansas-Nebraska Act, white settlers were "perfectly free" to decide the slavery question. As usual, rhetoric was one thing, details another. Were settlers allowed to bring slaves into Kansas, or did they have to wait until Kansas voted as a state to allow it? When exactly did the popular sovereignty begin? If slaveholders were not welcome to settle the new territory with their enslaved workers, they would of course have to remain a minority and would never have the power to vote in a slave system. Settlers into Kansas, for the most part, were midwestern yeomen and poor farmers looking for land and opportunity—few slaveowners were among them. None of this was news to any of the interested parties, but popular sovereignty's proponents cared little about the democratic process itself. It was all too self-evident how that process could be manipulated. According to the census, Kansas territory had 2,905 eligible voters. But in the 1855 election for the territorial legislature, 6,307 ballots were cast, many by proslavery Missourians who crossed over the border to protect their interests as they saw them. The newly elected proslavery legislators then expelled the few antislavery legislators and enacted a strict slave code that said harboring fugitive slaves was punishable by death, while questioning slavery itself was a felony. In 1857, this markedly fraudulent legislature, convening in Lecompton, Kansas, wrote a proslavery constitution for the territory and applied for admission to the Union as a slave state.

To the North, Kansas's Lecompton application for statehood seemed to prove beyond doubt that Douglas, and with him the influence of the western states, was in the grip of the Slave Power. Conspiracy theory is a thread running through much of American political life, and in the 1850s, northerners increasingly focused upon a malevolent, shadowy Slave Power, bent upon warping the nation and extending its control across the free states. Who its leaders might be, none could say for sure: Jefferson Davis, Pierre Soulé, the manipulative Robert Barnwell Rhett, or some yet more shadowy cabal; regardless, all swirled around the ghost of Calhoun in these fantasies. How far back the conspiracy stretched likewise remained unclear: the Mexican War? the gag rule? nullification? the Louisiana Purchase? Yet the signs of treacherous plotting had become increasingly clear to those who looked closely: the Fugitive Slave Law of 1850, the Ostend Manifesto of 1854, the growing infiltration of slaveholders into important governmental positions, and now the reversal of free territory agreed upon in the Missouri Compromise. Roll back abolition in Kansas and, men asked, where would it be truly safe?

Nor was the Slave Power conspiracy merely an abstract, hypothetical threat to northerners. In 1854 it had seemed to reach into Boston itself, into the heart of Garrison's stronghold, to snatch away by federal force the inoffensive person of Anthony Burns. A fugitive slave, Burns had escaped from Virginia and secured a job in Boston. On May 24, 1854, two months after coming to the city, he was arrested in violation of the federal Fugitive Slave Law, and the abolitionist community in Boston mobilized to protest his capture. Reverend Theodore Parker, who had long preached to a Congregationalist society that included

Louisa May Alcott, Julia Ward Howe, Susan B. Anthony, and Garrison himself—with a pistol close at hand, intended for slave-catchers hunting the fugitives he numbered among his flock—urged a policy of mass resistance. At the same time an assemblage of disgruntled members of the black community decided to free Burns from the authorities. Getting word of this plan, the abolitionist committee adjourned their meeting to join them. Federal marshals attempted to block the protesters' entrance to the courthouse, a deputy was stabbed and killed, and chaos ensued. The wealthy young Brahmin and abolitionist Thomas Wentworth Higginson was hospitalized with an injury, and he, Parker, and radical leader Wendell Phillips were ultimately indicted for their actions.

Although unsuccessful in liberating Burns, free blacks continued to rally, gathering at the courthouse around the clock and forcing authorities to remain alert to further violence. U.S. commissioner Edward G. Loring ruled in favor of Burns's master, which set the scene for his dramatic exit from Boston. In Burns's procession from the courthouse to the harbor, the Massachusetts Infantry blocked off every street on the route as a crowd of approximately fifty thousand spectators watched from a distance and supporters of Burns adorned the route with upside-down flags and black banners. Sentiments, politics, and direct action were all thwarted. Ultimately, the people of Boston could not prevent enforcement of the Fugitive Slave Law, and Burns was shipped back into bondage. Utopian optimism of the 1840s was crushed.

With the legal system seemingly arrayed against them, northern social radicals embraced a growing determination to master law and government and to revolutionize their world through control of the democratic process. Northern reformers, never in doubt as to their moral high ground but increasingly alarmed by the nature of the threat they perceived, decided that appeals to conscience were not effective. From the spring of 1856 onward, abolitionists recognized the positive strength and refuge that resided in the law of love and the American love of law. They also recoiled from the broader prospect of where violence, unrestrained by the Bible or the Constitution, must ultimately lead. No less an intransigent than New York senator William Seward, who had risen to prominence in New York Whig politics by his untempered advocacy of a "higher law than the Constitution," now championed the moderate line. Those who stood in opposition to slavery had no need for either mob violence or moral suasion. Neither blood nor prayers would solve this problem—the answer was to vote abolition into office at the state and federal levels and then to wipe away bondage with the ballot. That strategy had succeeded in Great Britain in 1833, and with the advantage of the ever-growing population in the northern states, it could hardly fail again. But it would take time for its incrementalist appeal to gather strength and supporters.

Among abolitionists, only an isolated few in the late 1850s believed that violence offered the best solution to the slavery question. The passionate pleadings of the Garrisonians and the political maneuverings of the Tappanites were both vain delusions, declared the African American activist Martin Delaney. While whites talked year after year, millions of blacks toiled under the lash. Preaching the impossibility of overcoming white racism, Delaney urged blacks to pick up the gun themselves and win their own freedom. But there was no market for such an idea, either within the white community—which controlled the purse strings of reform—or in the black. African Americans knew that they were hopelessly outgunned, and as for the slaves themselves, Delaney's message never reached them. Advocates of violent immediatism were driven to the margins or silenced altogether. The majority of abolitionists decided that the only way to encourage God's righteous kingdom on earth was to use the law itself to undertake a new and legal sectional crusade against slavery.

That objective went a little further politically than the new Republican Party was prepared to go. Coalescing in 1854 from the wreckage of disaffected Democrats, depressed Free-Soilers, shape-shifting Know-Nothings, and devastated Whigs, Republicans from the first were a sectional party, based on a platform dedicated to activist government, rooting out corruption, and the territorial restriction of slavery. Just as the Whigs had run one war hero after another for the presidency— William Henry Harrison in 1840, Zachary Taylor in 1848, Winfield Scott in 1852—Republicans could discover no better standard-bearer in their ranks in 1856 than John C. Frémont, the victor of the nonbattle of Santa Barbara in 1846. Their campaign slogan in that year—"Free Speech, Free Press, Free Soil, Free Men"—suggested their view of liberty: the Bill of Rights, agrarian republicanism, and no slavery.

Before Brooks's precipitous act, the Republican coalition—it was not much like a unified party—seemed bound to wither away, as its Whig and Free-Soil predecessors had already done. At best it would recede to its centers of strength like Massachusetts, taking up where Federalism had left off. On the other side of the congressional aisle, Democrats were having a difficult time rallying their troops, even though they controlled both Congress and the White House. Political parties everywhere were fragmenting, with interests swirling around leading figures, newspapers, and particular issues.

By the time Democratic president James Buchanan was inaugurated in March 1857, the physically and psychologically damaged Sumner had retreated to his Boston town house and Brooks was six weeks in the grave. Fallen to an unromantic pneumonia, the Carolinian's passing provoked a spate of weepy poetry, but many probably breathed a private sigh of relief. Brooks, after all, had never shown himself to be a particularly bright fellow, and save for the shot from Louis T. Wigfall that kept him limping most of his adult life, there had long been suspicion that he was, in fact, a coward at heart. Truth to tell, caning Sumner had been anything but honorable and manly, and what Brooks might have done next, none could predict.

Brooks's caning of Sumner had shown the answer that both sides of the national debate were increasingly driven to advocate. The imposition of their own beliefs—abolitionist or proslavery—backed by the force of federal law came to seem for northerners and southerners alike the only course of safety. To slaveholders, that meant better enforcement of existing statutes protecting their property rights—and, some demanded, new guarantees that Washington would never interfere with their peculiar institution. To slavery's opponents, it meant a policy of making no further concessions toward bondage, overturning proslavery laws, and legal resistance wherever possible.

South and North were both rewarded by the caning of Charles Sumner. At last political abolition had a martyr around whom to rally its forces, and the Republican Party had a figure to symbolize its cause. However Democrats and their opponents might quarrel, who could dispute the principle of untrammeled free speech for which Sumner had fallen? Only, northerners believed, true agents of the Slave Power. By the hundreds, men who had no use for Sumner or his ideas strode to the banner of Republicanism in defense of the free speech values he was thought to embody and the rule of law that lay behind it. In congressional elections that autumn Republicans swept to power across the North and came close to winning the presidency itself. In an instant the blows Brooks struck had revitalized the Republican Party and made it a mighty political force. For their part, too, southerners crowed over the liberating effect of the stripes Brooks laid on. Each well-aimed whack had gone a little further toward the emancipation of the master class, sick of over two decades of compromise and abuse and hanging its head. For too long, extremists declared, southerners had sought common ground with Yankees who only wished them ill. For some, the time for tragic, self-serving cycles had ended. Better now to make their stand, as men of honor in defense of Christian civilization and American values, than let the mongrels and mobocrats of the North sweep it all away.

The problem was that Americans agreed at once on too much—virtue over corruption, equality over privilege, labor over commerce, white over black—and on too little. Too little usually turned on demanding rights and opportunities for themselves while scorning the same for others. South Carolinians who "nullified" tariff laws they opposed belittled the Personal Liberty Law passed in Michigan in 1855 that aimed at nonenforcement of the Fugitive Slave Law. The antislavery rioters who fought for Anthony Burns excoriated Lecompton Kansans who demonstrated their "popular sovereignty" by torching the Free-Soil town of Lawrence. Southerners who championed mercenary "filibusterers" in invasions of Cuba and Nicaragua in support of slavery's cause railed against the Reverend Henry Ward Beecher's aid to antislavery Christians in Kansas: boxes of "Beecher's Bibles" that he sent west were in fact breech-loading rifles. The truth was that in the spring of 1856 Americans had a strong sense of failure in spite of economic prosperity. Socially, communities seemed troubled, in flux, coming apart. Culturally, all that was American seemed steadily diluted, adulterated, narrowed. Political vision seemed utterly lacking. From dark horses had come little men and, at best, Little Giants of few known principles, not quite worthy of trust. Over all hung fears of abolitionist plotting and Slave Power conspiracy. "The mass of men," Henry David Thoreau summed up, "lead lives of quiet desperation." If the people were no longer looking for a Savior, they were certainly waiting for a prophet. When the Redeemer returned, He would come with the sword.

So it was, two days after Brooks cut down Sumner on the Senate floor, in far-off Kansas, which had caused all the trouble, that a little-known landless farmer and tanner, who believed he had a direct line to God, a friend to Frederick Douglass and Gerrit Smith, hacked to death with the help of his sons five proslavery settlers on Pottawatomie Creek. The murders that John Brown and his sons committed in the name of freedom and equality in 1856 were in response to the burning of the antislavery settlement at Lawrence by southern "border ruffians." The ghastly mutilation (some decapitated) of five supporters of slavery— who had had nothing to do with the violence in Lawrence—shocked Americans both North and South.

Low-level aggression continued on the Kansas prairies during the summer of 1856, but hostilities assumed a tit-for-tat feuding, uncoordinated, leaderless, and directed toward no rational political goals. Figures for those killed in "Bleeding Kansas" are wide-ranging. A close examination shows that many of the 157 violent deaths during the time that Kansas was a territory had nothing to do with the slavery issue, or came to be involved with the issue only secondarily, after somewhat normal land disagreements grew more hateful because one side was proslavery and the other side not. The death toll attributable to the slavery issue on both sides in "Bleeding Kansas" finally numbered fifty-six. No one truly wanted a war over slavery, especially in a place where slavery was still almost entirely an abstract concept. The geography and climate of the Great Plains, all knew, barred the door to slavery and cotton culture more effectively than the most stalwart abolitionist, so political conflict in Kansas was hardly more than symbolic.

In the days after Pottawatomie, Brown fled northward, embraced an alias, and eventually crossed over into Canada to continue plotting. As with most Americans at this crucial moment, the choices he had made in Kansas were largely reactive, emotional, and unconsidered. And yet John Brown was to become a man of his times and, some believed, no less than a prophet.

Four

Washed in the Blood

IN THE SPRING OF 1862 Henry David Thoreau lay dying of tuberculosis in Concord, Massachusetts. By most measures he had not made much of his forty-five years. Without family, property, or profession, Thoreau seemed an exasperating failure even to his few friends, a brilliant but relentlessly self-absorbed scribbler of impractical philosophy and rather boring travel accounts. Yet the circle that gathered around his sickbed on that last day was full of earnestness. At the moment of death, antebellum Americans believed, the nearly departed might catch a glimpse of heaven itself and pass along to the yet-living some comforting word of description or guidance. Odd as Thoreau certainly was, surely they might hear him murmur, as he breathed his last, of the angelic splendor and celestial bliss awaiting. Alas, the Transcendentalist transcended as annoyingly as he had lived. The last words he coughed out dashed—or mocked—all their comfortably pious hopes. "Moose," he muttered. "Indians."

However far Thoreau's heavenly vision was from what his neighbors longed to hear, they ought not to have been surprised by his now-famous farewell. The great iconoclast had spent his whole life telling America it was on the wrong path and that a day of reckoning would come. That theme runs all through his masterpiece, *Walden*—little read or appreciated before the 1920s—and serves as the central claim of his essay *On the Duty* (certainly not the choice) *of Civil Disobedience*. It was the astonishing point of his most head-shaking speech that had scandalized his community, *A Plea for Captain John Brown*, delivered three years earlier while the violent prophet was on trial for his life. On October 30, 1859, Thoreau had announced a public lecture in his little town and rung the meeting bell himself. Once at the rostrum he had grown ever more agitated, finally seeming to rave with a madman's violence. A man's life was at stake, to be sure, but how bizarre then that Thoreau pleaded for his death, arguing that the murderer Brown bore comparison even to the crucified Christ. "You don't know your Testament when you see it!" he had shouted to his audience of devout Christians. Hanging Brown would surely bring down heaven's vengeance, he promised, and usher in the government of God at last. The man's imminent demise was "the best news that America ever heard."

At the end of the 1850s such notions seemed to most Americans foolish and dangerous. Indeed, the once-widespread millennial vision that undergirded Thoreau's view was fast diminishing in the North. It seemed impossible to tell angels from devils, holy innocents from malicious tricksters, as Herman Melville's strange novel *The Confidence Man* showed. All of America seemed rooted in double-talk and lies. Beyond all else was a common feeling that mammon had come to rule over the republic and that family, community, social values, and political culture all were now determined by the heedless pursuit of wealth. As the antebellum era drew to a close, growing numbers of Americans were retreating from a unifying national identity in which their forefathers had taken pride. Dissatisfied over the Compromise of 1850, dissatisfied over any compromise and even over political dialogue where slavery was concerned, northerners and southerners increasingly came to see each other as irredeemably different, unreasonable, and threatening. On both sides, men and women came to fear what Seward had called the "irrepressible conflict" existing between them. How were increasingly divergent values, cultures, and economies supposed to fit together?

The whole convulsed terrain of class, race, gender, and sexuality seemed to be shaking societal foundations. Abolitionists like Garrison, Stowe, and Douglass issued their moral arguments in a fashion calculated to enrage their audiences. But after two decades of lectures and speeches, newspapers and tracts, donations and subscriptions, Garrisonian abolitionism had become as much a self-sustaining business as a quest for moral reform. It preached the evils of slavery but offered little in the way of a practical solution. By allowing readers to gaze upon all the lurid details of unrestrained violence, sexuality, and objectification to which bondage gave rise, without ever resolving the frustration that such details engendered, bestsellers such as Theodore Weld's *American Slavery As It Is*, Linda Brent's (Harriet Jacobs) *Incidents in the Life of a Slave Girl*, and even *Uncle Tom's Cabin*, rather than buttress Christian resolve, helped nurture an American taste for pornography.

Just as Republicans warned of a growing "Slave Power" conspiracy, southern radicals denounced the signs of "Red Republicanism" that they saw gathering around them: disgruntled labor unions, gabbling foreigners, polygamous Mormons, racial "mongrelism," casual divorce, and a creeping "feminization." The same logic that led northerners away from "higher law" arguments slowly drove southerners toward them. As the number of antislavery sympathizers grew, the appeal of seeking redress through due process shifted. If the written law would not protect the southern way of life, Preston Brooks had shown that the higher law of honor must be invoked. And if opportunities for that invocation did not present themselves, they could be manufactured.

So it was that, in the spring of 1858, a sleek, fast schooner, the *Echo*, docked in Charleston harbor, under federal custody, and dozens of local citizens came down to the wharf to gawk and whisper. Most had never seen a pirate ship before, and only the oldest could remember the last time such a cargo had landed. Illegal cargo had from time to time made it into U.S. ports, but it was fully fifty years since the last African captive set foot on southern soil to be sold into slavery publicly. Now, with cotton prices skyrocketing and western lands beckoning, a growing minority believed that the time was right to roll back the prohibition against the transatlantic slave trade. They had their reasons: bondage brought prosperity to the master and "civilization" to the slave. Moreover, restricting free trade in this one highly lucrative commodity—human beings—was simple discrimination, not to say pure Yankee spitefulness. That the power of the federal government would be used to prohibit this commerce and criminalize those who engaged in it incensed southern radicals and worried more than a few moderates. After all, if the slave trade was immoral and criminal, how then could slavery itself be truly and positively good? Since Washington had stepped in to curb the importation of bondpeople, what was to stop a northern-dominated ad-ministration from one day legislating against the peculiar institution itself?

While southerners bickered endlessly about how to meet this threat, moderates insisted that slavery could be maintained through control of the Democratic Party. Over three decades that control had ensured southern dominance in the national legislature and kept antislavery voices muffled. Although abolitionists had pushed their agenda within a series of political parties since the 1840s—the Liberty Party, the Free Soil Party, even the Whigs—these efforts had repeatedly collapsed. So, it seemed reasonable to assume, would the latest bubble burst. Brooks's caning of Sumner had breathed new life into the fragile Republican Party two years before, but the legislative gains they made in the fall of 1856 were, moderates insisted, bound to erode in the next elections. Re-publicans had no leader, no unity of purpose beyond "the everlasting Negro," and no strength in the South. So long as southerners hewed to the Democratic Party, and the sectional wings of the Democratic Party stood together, they thought, reason and right would prevail.

During the first half of the 1850s, as the economy rebounded and the conciliatory effects of the Compromise of 1850 calmed tempers, the incendiary words of southern radicals, the "fire-eaters," had been gen-erally repudiated across the South. Even after the caning of Sumner launched radicalism into prominence once again, the hotheads were less a group than a political spectrum—certainly nothing like a disciplined, well-organized party. At one end were moderates like Alabama's Clem-ent Clay and Mississippi's Jefferson Davis, Democratic Party stalwarts with strong northern ties who only wanted more prominent positions for slavery's friends and a greater voice for southerners in general. Others accused these southern Democrats of wishful thinking and doubtful loy-alties. Tying their section's destiny to the career of an ambitious party man like Stephen Douglas, or relying on the smiles and promises of un-trustworthy northern "friends" like New York mayor Fernando Wood and Philadelphia's William "Pig-Iron" Kelley, seemed a recipe for disas-ter. Only a unified southern party could resist northern treachery, de-clared men like Florida's David Yulee and Alabama's William Lowndes Yancey; otherwise the Union would be lost. Hang the Union, a still more radical splinter pronounced; for men like Virginia's Edmund Ruffin and

South Carolina's Robert Barnwell Rhett, it was precisely the Union-saving efforts of the moderates and the temporizers that had caused all the trouble. Southern civilization would remain imperiled, they believed, for as long as it refused to claim its rightful independence. Moreover, they insisted, southern honor was in peril from northern insults and encroachments. They denounced moderates who urged caution, branding them as "submissionists" or cowards.

As belligerent and uncompromising as such talk was, however, slavery's apologists had a yet more militant wing. Where most southern separatists urged sectional independence to avert national crisis, a few brinksmen, such as South Carolina's James H. Adams and Georgia's Cal Lamar, sought to achieve secession by manufacturing conflict with Washington and the North. Only if the South was made to face up to the urgency of its situation and overcome the immediate emergency through disunion would slavery's interests be truly safe, they argued. Even within this manipulative clique, however, divisions existed. While a few held secession up as the good and final end, more believed that once the South marched out of the Union—as it surely would one day—a chastened North, economically dependent on southern cotton, would come to its senses and beg forgiveness. In this scenario, disunion became simply the means to create a more perfect Union while securing slavery's benefits for all.

That strategy had propelled the *Echo* to Africa and back, where it was bound to run afoul of American officials on one voyage or another. With the impounded vessel docked at Fort Sumter, South Carolina, its crew was hauled before a federal court in a test case—one of a half-dozen similar piracy trials of slave traders heard by southern judges and juries between 1856 and 1860. If they were convicted of piracy, slave trade advocates believed that a howl of southern protest would surely shake the Union. If they were acquitted, the doors would swing open to a full resumption of the transatlantic trade. That would be "popular sovereignty" with a vengeance. And while lawyers twisted and talked and wrangled to defuse the controversy, the trial would drag on, popular debate would flourish, tempers would rise, and the spark of secession would ignite. It all seemed a foolproof plan to break up the Union. Instead, a crafty Carolina judge deflected the point of danger. Judge Andrew G. Magrath ruled that although federal prohibition made the slave trade illegal, nothing in the law established it as piracy per se. Since slaves were not plunder, in his eyes, the sailors were not pirates.

Courtroom reasoning, however, could not allay the social crisis that the *Echo* caused. In the end that crisis focused not on the schooner's crew but on its human cargo. Responsibility for the captive Africans and the imprisoned crew fell on Daniel Hamilton, federal marshal at Charleston. Nothing could have prepared him for the scores of "walking skeletons" he encountered. "I acknowledge most frankly to have been an advocate for the re-opening of the slave trade," he admitted, "but a practical, fair evidence of its effects has cured me forever." Enslaving Africans had seemed to some a duty of Christian civilization, but viewed face to face the cost seemed too high. These beings were naked, sick, and terrified. "I wish that everyone in So[uth] Ca[rolina] who is in favor of reopening of the Slave-trade, could have seen what I have been compelled to witness for the three weeks of their stay at Fort Sumter," he wrote. "It seems to me that I can never forget it." Ultimately, the captives returned to Africa, short thirty-five men who died in custody and seventy-one who died on the return voyage.

Instead of mobilizing southern sentiment in aggressive support of reopening the slave trade, the *Echo* incident and others like it turned slaveholders and their communities toward a more determined defense of slavery as it existed in their fondest dreams. In the same way they reacted to *Uncle Tom's Cabin*, southerners howled that their plantation world was too just and gentle to have any ties with the abominable Middle Passage. To the planter-poet William J. Grayson, the contrast between the worlds of *The Hireling and the Slave* (1854) was clear-cut. And indeed, many southern slaveholders claimed that white factory workers were worse off than enslaved blacks. Comparing slavery and free labor, agricultural reformer Edmund Ruffin argued that wage earners in the North were "held under a much more stringent and cruel bondage, and in conditions of far greater privation, painful and inevitable coercion, and of suffering, than our negro slaves." Slaveholders pointed out that their workers were provided food, clothing, shelter, and medical care that "free workers" were denied. Eliding the horrors of whip and auction, proslavery theorists made the assertion that in the South no workers starved in the streets or sold their bodies for bread, abandoned their children or wallowed in drink, or had to go begging for the chance to work, with the knowledge that when they were old or sick or simply unwanted they would become social outcasts. Smugly, slaveholders boasted that slaves were offered a measure of security that wage workers utterly lacked.

In the South, they asserted, all was quite different. Labor there was performed by African Americans, who, Grayson's friend James Henry Hammond argued, were well suited to the task, pliant, and obedient. Their material needs attended to and their duties ordered by a benevolent and superior master class, Hammond and Grayson agreed, slaves enjoyed lives entirely "free from care." Crime and social disorder were only minor concerns in the South, Hammond insisted. Entirely deluding himself, Hammond proclaimed that African Americans were "the happiest four millions" on the face of the earth, and as they became more attuned to their good fortune, warm feelings of reciprocity between white bosses and black workers were bound to flower.

Hammond explained his ideas in the U.S. Senate in 1858. Every society required a laboring foundation or "mudsill class" if others were to attain the fruits of higher civilization. How societies accommodated this inevitability was the measure of their civility. Contrast the fate of northern workingmen with that of southern slaves, he suggested. In cities like New York and Baltimore, the laboring classes were a constant source of riot and disorder, and understandably so. So-called "free" workers toiled too long for too little, Hammond argued, and had little prospect of ever rising from their degraded state. Indeed, competition with free black and immigrant labor only tended to confirm native white wage labor in its low status and its vicious ways. What then could the North look forward to, except ever-increasing poverty and social turmoil, perhaps the specter of revolution itself?

Instead, thanks to cotton and slavery, southerners promised, the conflict between capital and labor, so worrisome to Europeans and northerners, might soon be entirely overcome. Instead of seeking to overturn slavery, Hammond and Virginia's George Fitzhugh, a lawyer and proslavery writer, suggested that men of property might better join hands to extend the benefits of bondage to benighted white workers. Instead of ignorance, want, intemperance, disease, and disorder, northern laborers and their families might gain all the security, order, and discipline that the peculiar institution had bestowed upon blacks. It was an appalling, dehumanizing vision, but for southern ideologues, sickened by the changes they saw degrading northern society and threatening to overwhelm their own, the radical extension of slavery offered the best hope of retrieving conservatism and social harmony. The alternative, they believed, was chaos.

The mudsill theory ran counter to a northern view of a slow progression toward millennial perfection. Abraham Lincoln, eschewing the extremes of Grayson, Hammond, and Fitzhugh, pointed out in September 1859 that most people were neither hirelings nor capitalists. "Men, with their families—wives, sons and daughters—work for themselves, on their farms, in their houses and in their shops, taking the whole product to themselves, and asking no favors of capital on the one hand, nor of hirelings or slaves on the other." Lincoln was correct. In 1850 the number of workers aged ten years and older employed in textile mills was 92,000, compared to 4,520,000 agricultural laborers. In 1860 the number of textile factory workers grew to 122,000 and the number of agricultural workers grew to 5,880,000. The vast majority of men and their families, both North and South, were farmers and farm laborers.

Lincoln preferred that people have an equal opportunity to benefit from their own work. People in support of free labor, according to Lincoln, find it a "just and generous, and prosperous system, which opens the way for all—gives hope to all, and energy, and progress, and improvement of condition to all." Here was an incrementalist approach that, for all its presumed practicality, rested on a faith in mankind's innate goodness that was as presumed as any Millerite's expectation of the Second Coming. "Let us hope," Lincoln proclaimed, "that by the best cultivation of the physical world, beneath and around us; and the intellectual and moral world within us, we shall secure an individual, social, and political prosperity and happiness, whose course shall be onward and upward, and which, while the earth endures, shall not pass away."

The mudsill theory of labor that Lincoln opposed and Hammond, Fitzhugh, Ruffin, and others espoused essentially postulated a system of class, not race. That formulation transfigured the territorial question entirely. While most men believed that slavery's "natural" limits were determined by geography and climate, Fitzhugh noted that that perception was shaped by a racist equation of cotton culture with African American labor. Wipe away that racial boundary, open the realm of servitude to whites, and slavery might spread over all the nation, from factories and workshops to mines and farms. Wage labor, Hammond insisted, was not remarkably different from slave labor. All work that was not self-directed was, he argued, a species of bondage. He put his indelicate finger on a possibility that Lincoln's republicanism could not accommodate: if some whites had little more hope of rising from the ranks of the working class than blacks had of gaining emancipation, was it not both kind and necessary to supply those men with a greater security and a superior discipline? In a world of inherent subordinates and their betters, equality of opportunity was a cruel sham and rule of law little better than a means of keeping each in his proper place.

Southern truculence stoked northern fears. A ruling of the Supreme Court in 1857 proved to many the power of proslavery conspirators. Utterly revolutionizing the law of the land and all but destroying abolitionism at one blow, the Supreme Court decision in *Dred Scott v. Sandford* assaulted northern concepts of liberty—and ripped apart the country. A simple point of law here laid the groundwork for precisely the sort of social transformation that conservatives like Hammond, Ruffin, and Fitzhugh longed for. Born a slave in Virginia, Dred Scott later traveled with his owner in Free-Soil Illinois and Wisconsin territory, eventually returning with him to slaveholding Missouri. When his master died in 1846, Scott and his wife, Harriet, whom he had met and wed in Wisconsin, sued for their freedom, claiming that earlier residences in free jurisdictions had established their right to it. Over the next decade Dred Scott's case ascended to the Supreme Court. The doctrine affirmed by the lower court of "once free, always free" had been overturned on appeal with the explanation that "times now are not as they were"—a point the Supreme Court proved. Voting 7–2 against the plaintiff, the court ruled that neither Scott, nor any African American, could be a citizen of the United States. Indeed, Scott was his owner's chattel, and the owner was due all the protections of federal property law. Chief Justice Roger Taney, an old Jacksonian Democrat from the border slave state of Maryland who had emancipated the slaves he inherited, interpreted the equality affirmed in the Declaration of Independence as being "too clear for dispute, that the enslaved African race were not intended to be included." Crediting the men who wrote the Declaration as "high in their sense of honor," he decided they were "incapable of asserting principles inconsistent with those on which they were acting." The Supreme Court declared that African Americans were inferior to whites and had no rights "which the white man was bound to respect." The enslaved black was intended to be "bought and sold and treated as an ordinary article of merchandise and traffic, whenever profit could be made by it." Hence, explained Taney, Scott had no more legal standing to bring suit before the court than a wagon or a house might against its owner.

In this regard, Taney went further than James Madison's explanation in the *Federalist Papers*. Madison wrote that the slave was "restrained in his liberty" and "compelled to work" and was therefore property. But laws also punished slaves for "violence committed against others," so he was "no less evidently regarded by the law as a member of society." Madison admitted that the argument was "a little strained in some points," but by that founder's reasoning, slaves were both property and persons. Taney and the Supreme Court, however, did not admit any such strain; slaves were property, period.

Although on the dark side of the historical ledger, Justice Taney was prescient in his grasp of whither certain assumptions would lead. Taney listed some of the rights that would be due African Americans if they were indeed citizens, ironically foreshadowing the postwar constitutional amendments. Taney feared that citizenship

would give to persons of the Negro race, who were recognized as citizens in any one State of the Union, the right to enter every other State whenever they pleased, singly or in companies, without pass or passport, and without obstruction, to sojourn there as long as they pleased, to go where they pleased at every hour of the day or night without molestation, unless they committed some violation of law for which a white man would be punished; and it would give them the full liberty of speech in public and in private upon all subjects upon which its own citizens might speak; to hold public meetings upon political affairs, and to keep and carry arms wherever they went.

While Taney could not, or would not, see that these specific areas of freedom were part and parcel of the promise of America, Lincoln did see and would articulate that aspiration. Moreover, in the most profound accomplishment of the Age of Lincoln, he would bring about a shift in government responsibility to include the protection of personal liberties.

Confusion about bondage and freedom had come about, Taney explained, from the half-measures and compromises of generations past. The Northwest Ordinance and the Missouri Compromise were not legally binding, he found, and Congress had been wrong in 1787 and 1820 to bar slavery in the territories because the Constitution did indeed permit slavery. Bans against slavery were simply "not warranted by the Constitution."

The *Dred Scott* ruling was pure joy for proslavery southerners, beleaguered by three decades of abolitionist harassment. The supreme law of the land, which protected private property, now protected slaveowners' right to human enslaved property, without restriction. This ruling confirmed the slaveowners' right to take their enslaved property anywhere in the United States without fear that other states would grant rights to enslaved people. Northerners broadly and abolitionists specifically were horrified. Faith in law, politics, and due process seemed undone at a single stroke.

Some legal quibbling occurred over the court's use of this case to nullify the congressional ban on slavery in territory governed by the Missouri Compromise: if Dred Scott was not a citizen able to take his case to the Supreme Court, then the case ceased to exist, and the Court's statement on slavery was an obiter dictum, not essential to the case and so not binding. Even the proponents of this approach saw it as a weak effort to evade what was clear: slavery had won a sweeping victory. Not only did the South hold a majority in Congress and the power of the executive, but now the highest court in the land had overwhelmingly interpreted the Constitution to say that the peculiar institution was not peculiar at all. Indeed, it was a national institution: tamper with slavery, Taney implied, and all property rights were jeopardized. The enslaved had no claim to the law, and the enslaver had no limits upon his just rights anywhere in the nation. There were no slave states and free states: all of America was a slaveholding republic, and so it always would remain, absent specific constitutional provisions to the contrary. The *Dred Scott* decision set an almost impossible standard for slavery's abolition and provided a focused target for all the energies of political antislavery. If the North wanted to limit slavery in even the slightest way, a contrary constitutional amendment would have to be won.

Dred Scott cut away the broad middle ground of political compromise upon which the two-party system had matured in antebellum America. At this turning point in history, when compromise would no longer rule the day, the dramatic change was summed up by Republican Senate candidate Abraham Lincoln. In 1858 in one of a series of debates with his Democratic opponent, Stephen Douglas, Lincoln laid out with bold words the full implications of *Dred Scott*. While northerners had thought that slavery was dying out, he declared, now they would be forced to accept slavery in the North. While they had believed people in neighboring Missouri were "on the verge of making their State free . . . the Supreme Court has made Illinois a slave State." Ultimately, however, the decision rested not with the Court but with the people, he asserted—a trick of logic and rhetoric that wedded Douglas's popular sovereignty claims to the abolitionist notion of "higher law." "Either the opponents of slavery will arrest the further spread of it," he explained, "or its advocates will push it forward, till it shall become alike lawful in all the States." The Court's ruling had only heightened, not ended, the conflict over slavery. "A house divided against itself," he concluded, "cannot stand."

While Lincoln dissented vigorously from the *Dred Scott* ruling, Douglas argued that Taney's decision was adjustable along lines of popular sovereignty. Moreover, articulating what became known as his "Freeport Doctrine," Douglas stated that the *Dred Scott* decision did not force slavery onto unwilling people because slavery could not survive "an hour" without "local police regulations." Douglas agreed with Taney on America's racial essence: "I am free to say to you that in my opinion this government of ours is founded on the white basis. It was made by the white man, for the benefit of the white man, to be administered by white men, in such manner as they should determine."

Lincoln and abolitionists who objected to slavery on moral grounds, as well as northerners who feared that slavery jeopardized their own chances of obtaining the rewards of the American dream, were already convinced that the slave oligarchy was changing slavery from a southern to a national institution. The *Dred Scott* decision convinced many more northerners of the same. In the White House sat a proslavery northern Democrat, James Buchanan, who indeed had twisted the arm of one northern justice to vote with the southern majority. Outraged northerners became ever more convinced of a Slave Power conspiracy.

While there was no conspiracy as such, southern moderates and extremists alike saw Taney's ruling as an opportunity to further their goals. For Democrats, it proved that secession was unnecessary—almost all the concessions the South had made since 1787 had been won back in a moment. Indeed, slave trade advocates began to ponder, perhaps even the prohibition on transatlantic commerce would not stand. The South was safe at last. But not quite yet, radicals retorted: the federal government must be forced to assert the rights to property that *Dred Scott* confirmed, and to secure those rights once and for all. Either Congress would pass a constitutional amendment guaranteeing slaveholders' rights, or the South should break away. Although very few southern leaders advocated secession even as late as 1859 and the vast portion of the population opposed secession, the fire-eaters kept up their reckless demands. In South Carolina, where 57 percent of the population was enslaved; in Mississippi, where 55 percent of the population was enslaved; and in Alabama, with 45 percent enslaved, radicals proposed the idea of a federal slave code. What had seemed outlandish when first proposed by Alabama congressmen in 1848, now after the *Dred Scott* decision looked to them like a logical next step.

While emboldening southerners, Taney's opinion created other allies. Where antislavery Democrats and abolitionist Republicans had once been antagonists, *Dred Scott* drove them together. After all, the Court had struck its blow against antislavery, and now the liberty to choose a free labor system was no longer available to opponents of slavery. Northerners across the political spectrum found their central premises shattered by the Supreme Court's ruling. Unencumbered, they began to close ranks against a common foe.

Each section was the ironic mirror of the other: precisely as northerners seemed to be coming together politically, southerners appeared more divided than ever before. For all the brave promises that slaveholders made that King Cotton would raise up whites to common prosperity and cultural progress, doubts lingered and class resentment festered. In spite of high cotton prices and booming output during the 1850s, increasing numbers of nonslaveholders slipped down into the ranks of unpropertied tenant farmers and wage workers. While Senator James Henry Hammond of South Carolina asserted quite the contrary, whites worked for wages in textile mills in the shadow of his own plantation.

Mills prospered in the Horseshoe Valley and across the Savannah River in Augusta, Georgia. Even though broad new lands had been opened to slavery in the antebellum era, young men of meager means looking for a point of entry into the master class too often found their way blocked and their labors dishonored. Sturdy yeomen were stigmatized as "no-account" when they ventured to the crossroads store, "dirt-poor" as they tilled another man's fields. While the lowest slave had come to feel in some measure entitled to at least a rough subsistence of food, clothing, and shelter from his overlord, impoverished southern whites could not cling to even that slim measure of self-respect as they begged help from their supposed betters. More often, they preferred to tighten their belts, nurse their grudges, and bide their time.

Early in 1857 one disappointed North Carolinian broke his silence. Hinton Helper had already tried his luck on the streets of New York and in the gold fields of California. Those gambles had yielded only hard lessons and deepened his fears of sliding inevitably into that "mudsill class" that Hammond recommended. Upon returning home to the Appalachians, he picked up his pen in 1855 and wrote first of the faraway frauds he had seen. Few bothered to listen. Then Helper directed his bubbling resentments on the slaveholding world outside his window. What he wrote in *The Impending Crisis: How to Meet It* was not very new— journalists like Frederick Law Olmsted and James Redpath had made their reputations for many years with just such arguments, and the bulk of Helper's claims were based on statistics drawn from the federal census, southern newspapers, and commercial journals like the secessionist *De Bow's Review*. Rather, Helper's book became a bestseller and a staple of public debate because of who had written it and how he suggested to solve the crisis he saw.

In many ways *The Impending Crisis* reads like the last gasp of enlightened Jeffersonianism. In a voice southern, rural, rationalist, and progressive, Helper carried weight because his complaints steered clear of the sentimental moralizing that northern reformers could never resist. In place of Yankee hand-wringing over the ethical ugliness of bondage, the angry southerner substituted a simple, staggering claim: slavery did not and could not pay. Cotton's monocultural reign had not conferred wealth and progress on the South. On the contrary, Helper showed, the cotton-slavery combination had wrecked southern lands, pushed down wages, driven away capital, industry, and immigration, and retarded culture and education. As to the fate of slaves, *The Impending Crisis* cared little—Helper's eclectic reading and travels had nurtured in him a "Negrophobic" ethos and a vision of apartheid that went far beyond the shallow and conflicted racism that most white southerners accepted as a matter of course.

It was whites who were victimized by chattel bondage, as Helper saw it—white masters who found themselves enslaved and driven ceaselessly by cotton's demands for more land and labor, and white nonslaveholders who found their every effort to better their lot blocked and thwarted by the plantation regime. That the conflict had flared into violence on the Kansas prairie and in the halls of Congress was completely unsurprising to Helper. The "irrepressible conflict" of North and South of which Seward spoke came naturally in the struggle of social systems contending along a common frontier. The impending crisis of which Helper wrote was more frightening by far because it was essentially internal to the South, a class struggle building not along the periphery but at its heart. Without reform, Helper warned, the South would be ruined, its people plunged into poverty and conflict. The only uncertainty was whether race war would come before or after the violent rising of the nonslaveholding class he imagined.

Cotton and slavery would generate apocalypse, *The Impending Crisis* declared. Rejecting their embrace would restore the South and the nation to the path of promise. Blot out slavery, expel benighted African Americans, encourage opportunities for self-employed farmers and artisans, and nurture family and community—and America's problems would swiftly subside. The sectional crisis itself would quickly vanish, and the South would be returned to its role of honor and leadership in the country's councils. Coolly expressed, buttressed by a strong army of statistics, the alternatives of disaster or rejuvenation that Helper posed seemed clear and convincing.

Within months, Republican politicians were quoting its arguments in congressional debate and promoting publication of a handy compendium of its claims—a zeroed-in, pocket-sized weapon that antislavery northerners hoped would win their case once and for all. For decades, slavery's defenders had argued that Garrisonian abolitionists had simply missed the point: moral suasion could never trump the rational demands of economic efficiency and material progress. However repugnant, southerners had explained, slavery paid handsomely—and even if it did not, it created a way of life superior to free labor alternatives. Now Helper argued that both those excuses were lies. Clinging to them could only doom the South, the nation, and the white race. Those who denied the economic facts he laid down were worse than shortsighted: they were a selfish, evil minority opposed to truth and progress. The southern newspapers and politicians who howled against Helper's arguments seemed to provide vivid proof of just the vicious conspiracy that he railed against. When southern Democrats opposed Ohio Republican John Sherman's candidacy for speaker of the House of Representatives in 1859, it was his support for *The Impending Crisis* they focused on. If northern matrons wanted to weep over *Uncle Tom's Cabin*, that was their own affair, but for Yankee leaders to put Helper's plans in the hands of hard-pressed southern farmers seemed unforgivable. *The Impending Crisis* was the most dangerous book in America, fire-eaters believed, a southern traitor's tract for abolitionist terror.

Fear and talk of conspiracy bred loathing on both sides of the Mason-Dixon Line. Everything, including the economic depression of 1857, became fuel for conflagration. The situation was explosive, and John Brown ignited the fuse. Like an Old Testament prophet leading the way to a new freedom in America, Brown was determined to cut through the moral temporizing and constitutional chess games into which abolitionism had fallen. An admirer of Nat Turner and slave insurrectionists, Brown believed in violent retribution. He would no longer accept a deferral of liberty for enslaved African Americans; it was time again for the sin to be washed in blood.

After the events of 1859 many Americans both North and South united in an effort to describe John Brown, a white man risking his life for black freedom, as insane. Herman Melville called him "Weird John Brown," and surviving photographs of Brown reveal a personal intensity that is easily read as fanaticism. Sympathizers and Brown's attorneys recommended he make use of an insanity plea at his trial, but Brown viewed that approach as "a miserable artifice and pretext." For many struggling to comprehend his motives, insanity was more understandable than reasoned forethought for murder and violence. Yet while unusual in his advocacy for equal rights—for blacks, whites, and Indians, and for women as well as men—Brown was no madman. In the context of his times, when many Americans daily expected the Second Coming, they regarded him rather as fervent and sincere.

Since he had been taught a fierce antislavery Calvinism by his father, bowed down by a variety of familial and financial misfortunes in early adulthood, befriended by a radical community of abolitionists, it was perhaps natural that Brown would come to focus his energies on constructing what he called the Subterranean Pass Way leading toward freedom. Just what he meant by this term is unclear: perhaps it was simply a metaphor, or as he seemed to tell Frederick Douglass at one point, perhaps it was a massive project for constructing a real tunnel under the Allegheny Mountains as a stage on the Underground Railroad. The intended terminus of this passage, too, shifted across the years with Brown's own activities, from upstate New York to Kansas to Virginia.

As early as June 1855 some black and white abolitionists, working together, felt the need to move beyond talk. Douglass, Gerrit Smith, James McCune Smith, and Brown met together at a convention of the new Radical Abolition Party in Syracuse, New York. This interracial group trusted and befriended one another. Based on an intense religious belief in equality before God, they worked together as equals, which was unusual in that time and place (but not unique; Shakers, Quakers, and Universalists also shared an egalitarian vision). Brown encountered many factions of "radical abolitionists," and most wanted nothing to do with violence. Even the abolitionists at this meeting, willing to consider extreme solutions, limited their activism to soliciting funds and writing checks. The actual business of handling the guns that their money purchased or confronting slaveholders face to face they calmly left to others.

Fantasies of violence were undeniably thrilling to certain northern radicals—this was a decade when European revolutionists were treated as freedom-fighting celebrities as they toured across the region. In the aftermath of the Pottawatomie killings, Brown developed a similar cachet. He roamed around New England, giving half-clandestine lectures. His was an exciting persona, apparently free from restraint. Although the Transcendentalists became his admirers, few abolitionists were willing to open their wallets or their pulpits to someone who might have actually killed for the antislavery cause. Nevertheless, by 1858 Brown had cultivated a wealthy circle of reformers to bankroll his activities and had hired a British mercenary, Hugh Forbes, who had fought with the Italian revolutionary hero Garibaldi, to teach his few followers rudimentary tactics. Eventually, it seems, Brown intended to return to Kansas at the head of abolitionist cadres, announce an antislavery provisional government, and rally the forces of freedom to his cause.

At best, however, Brown's plans—as he explained them to others—were sketchy, shifting, and self-contradictory. In October 1858 Forbes's salary remained unpaid, and he and Brown had a bitter falling out. While the soldier went around trying to expose Brown's plans to various Republicans and reformers and generally blacken his name, Brown scrambled into action. Racing from Canada to Kansas to Maryland, Brown pulled together a small guerrilla band, five African Americans (one of whom wanted to free his wife and child enslaved near Harpers Ferry and scheduled to be sold) and seventeen whites, three of them his sons. On October 16, 1859, Brown's small group, armed with repeating Spencer rifles, marched on the federal arsenal at Harpers Ferry, Virginia, though what Brown intended to do once he had captured it remains profoundly unclear. Broadly, the plan had been to secure arms inside and hand them out to local nonslaveholding whites, whom he believed were eager to rise in rebellion, just as Hinton Helper had argued. For slaves who rallied to his cause, Brown had brought along one thousand handmade pikes—outmoded spears reminiscent of the swords he had used at Pottawatomie.

After he had been caught, after whatever his plans were had come to naught, Brown said that he had believed, mistakenly, that a limited uprising would bring the nation to its senses. Yet newspapers soon reported the mysterious map he was captured with, marked with telltale *x*'s stretching across much of the South. Further, in anticipation of a successful slave rebellion, Brown had written a constitution without slavery, which Brown termed "the most barbarous, unprovoked, and unjustifiable war of one portion of its citizens upon another portion." Espousing ideals rooted in the Declaration of Independence, Brown claimed extralegal license as he killed and kidnapped innocents. His appeal to "higher law" put him outside the law.

From start to finish, Brown's attack on Harpers Ferry was a disaster of contradictions and mixed messages. His little band seized the U.S. arsenal and took some thirty hostages, but he insisted on providing them with breakfast and care. He sent a patrol into the countryside proclaiming freedom for the slaves, then sat down and waited for revolution to unfold. He was disappointed. No slaves rushed to follow an unknown white man who urged them to seize their freedom. Instead, when one free black, the local baggage master, rushed to warn an approaching train that the armory had been captured, Brown's men killed him. Then, inexplicably, they allowed the train to carry on to Washington. His plan collapsing by the hour, he did not know what to do next. Rather than escape into the mountains, Brown dithered. When federal troops arrived the next day, under the command of Colonel Robert E. Lee, they found the abolitionist band barricaded inside a fire engine house, surrounded by local militiamen plinking away at them. One bold rush, and the revolution was over.

As soon as news of Harpers Ferry went out over the wires, some of Brown's backers proclaimed that Brown was quite mad. Yet no less than Virginia's governor, Henry Wise, attested to the sober sanity of the man he would ultimately hang. At his trial Brown declared, "I believe that to have interfered as I have done—and I have always freely admitted I have done—in behalf of His despised poor, was not wrong, but right." He was willing, he said, that his blood should mingle "with the blood of millions in this slave country whose rights are disregarded by wicked, cruel, and unjust enactments." Indeed, "the crimes of this guilty land" could "never be purged away except with blood." His mistake, he said, had been to think it could be accomplished without "very much blood."

In the immediate aftermath of the raid, southerners conjoined outrage with panic and paranoia. For several weeks every stranger in the South was suspect, every moderate voice an encouragement to rebellion. As one Atlanta newspaper saw it, the enemy included everyone "who does not boldly declare that he believes African slavery to be a social, moral, and political blessing." Even as the Harpers Ferry raid focused southern rage on northern agitation, it also assuaged southern fears, in three ways. First, given the opportunity and the means to rebel, slaves did not rise up, either in Virginia or farther afield. Indeed, the only southern African American involved in the affair had proven loyal unto death; as for Brown's five black accomplices, southerners saw them as deluded by an excess of liberty and the clever words of their captain. Second, local nonslaveholders had also proven their fidelity. Virginians of all classes and colors had turned their backs on Brown's blow for freedom. Despite the catalog of doubts that southerners had committed to their most private letters and diaries, the South had stood united against northern aggression. And the third fact Harpers Ferry affirmed for the South was that, when slavery was threatened—as pitifully as Brown's raid may be said to have done so—the power of the federal government had been exerted in its defense. For Roger Taney to proclaim slavery's rightful equality was one thing; for the swords and bayonets of U.S. Marines to defend it was quite another. A corollary, however, was that maintaining control of the government that wielded those weapons seemed more crucial than ever before.

Upon his capture, Brown took no heed of his bleeding head wound as he calmly espoused his case. His mystique increased with his courage in facing execution. He maintained his dignity as he spoke of the slavery question: "You may dispose of me very easily—I am nearly disposed of now. But this question is still to be settled." While many admired his valor and cool demeanor, most whites in the North rejected John Brown's violence, if they did not revile Brown himself. Abraham Lincoln, while admitting that "he agreed with us in thinking slavery wrong," nevertheless severely faulted Brown for lawlessness. Motives "cannot excuse the violence, bloodshed, and treason." Extremists of every stripe threatened governance by rule of law, that principle most conducive to equal opportunity among reasoning equals. Lincoln distanced his party from the actions of Brown. In his speech at Cooper Union in February 1860 he pointed out that the congressional investigation, under southern leadership, "failed to implicate a single Republican in his Harpers Ferry enterprise." He was sure: "John Brown was no Republican."

In the weeks following Harpers Ferry, as Brown and the survivors of his raid were tried and dispatched by the machinery of the state, those who had known and encouraged him denied him. Some of his financial backers, the so-called Secret Six, fled into hiding, fearing arrest. With few exceptions, abolitionists, black and white, repudiated Brown's resorting to violence, but most of them continued to sympathize with his aims. Some who spoke on his behalf tried to transform the prophet bent on purging the land "with blood" into a milquetoast prince of peace. In Philadelphia, Theodore Tilton, editor of the *New York Independent*, declared, "Today the nation puts to death its noblest citizen!" His crime, it turned out, was "loving his fellow men too well." The Virginia-born abolitionist Reverend Moncure Daniel Conway, of the Cincinnati First Congregational Church, proclaimed that Brown was "dying for a religious principle." He urged his congregants to be "baptized afresh to the cause of liberty, humanity, and God!" However well meaning, if pleasantly vague, such sentiments were, they fell far short of the example Brown had provided. Most churchmen, abolitionists, and Republican politicians—not to mention Democrats and the common run of money-minded men—assailed John Brown's attempt to overturn slavery as "a misguided wild, and apparently insane effort."

For Thoreau, this disavowal was loathsome. He derided the worthies assembled in Concord. "Ye needn't take so much pains to wash your skirts of him," he sneered. "No intelligent man will ever be convinced that he was any creature of yours." Moreover, Thoreau tacitly admitted, Brown's bold action had confounded Thoreau's own brave words. It was one thing to write and speak for freedom, as Thoreau had done, to advocate "civil disobedience" of the mildest and most unthreatening sort. But John Brown had acted—violently—on his principles, at the risk of his life, in defiance of law, hazarding his soul itself. "No, he was not our representative in any sense," Thoreau mourned. "He was too fair a specimen of a man to represent the like of us."

Thoreau's disjuncture was troubling on every level, calling into question the most basic issues of ethics and behavior—issues many antebellum Americans, even as they contemplated the distance yet remaining to bring the nation to full Christian perfection, smugly believed the republican ideology of their Founding Fathers had resolved. "Is it not possible that an individual may be right," Thoreau asked, "and a government wrong?" Was there a social obligation—a human responsibility—to fight injustice, even by violence, even in opposition to law itself? What should the penalty be for those who recognized evil for what it was, then offered only words and sentiments by way of resistance, or at most threw a handful of coins in its face? Were men finally required to be their brothers' keepers? What was the meaning of a good life? "No man in America has ever stood up so persistently and effectively for the dignity of human nature," Thoreau declared of Brown, "knowing himself for a man, and the equal of any and all governments. In that sense he was the most American of us all."

Thoreau's words dripped with bitter anger and sadness and sarcasm. Here was a hard truth of social ethics: it was not the few monsters and villains in the world who caused evil to thrive, but the mass of half-decent souls who saw it for what it was, considered their own comfort, and did nothing to stop it. Next to Brown, Thoreau believed, even the most well-meaning men and women pursued hypocritically little lives, betraying every principle that they preached. Indeed, the philosopher understood, "we become criminal in comparison."

Thoreau's *A Plea for Captain John Brown* carried on the theme its author had championed since the mid-1840s, the notion that people of conscience must live authentically, embrace individual freedom, and rise above the mundane and sinful existence of the unenlightened. But John Brown's action challenged all that Thoreau had written, and he admitted it. Could a person attain freedom for himself without striving for the salvation of all? Could a man save his life except by losing it? Could the slavery of sin—or the sin of slavery—be abolished except through blood? Thoreau confronted the problem, even as he trembled at the answer: "It seems as if no man in America had ever died before; for in order to die you must first have lived. I don't believe in the hearses, and palls, and funerals that they have had. There was no death in the case, because there had been no life; they merely rotted or sloughed off, pretty much as they had rotted or sloughed along."

John Brown was "an angel of light" whose death would swing at least "a million" souls to freedom's cause, Thoreau believed, launching the nation into action. Soon, he thought, Brown's example would impel America to take a small step toward the millennium for which many still claimed to long, "when at least the present form of slavery shall be no more here." The time for tears was not yet, Thoreau warned his listeners: before that catharsis the hearts and minds of men and women of good faith must focus on securing "our revenge." Thoreau's audience in Concord was stunned—embarrassed, annoyed, and unmoved.

A crowd of thousands cheered to see John Brown hang on a cold morning the second of December 1859. Thoreau went back to his books and his journal, not very certain at all what the first step on the path of action might be. The world went on as before, as it generally does after killing those not suited to its ways and its purposes. Yet there was a profound sense in the land that the boundless aspirations of an earlier generation had been somehow betrayed and defeated. Dreams of social perfection had been carelessly pushed aside in the quest to gain minor tangible reforms—or just to live a better, more comfortable life. In Canada, rural New England, the Ohio Valley, and upstate New York, antislavery activists like Martin Delaney, Frederick Douglass, Gerrit Smith, and Thomas Wentworth Higginson went off to their separate quarters to ponder what Brown had done and to consider what to do next. Certainly there had never been a greater crisis within the abolitionist movement, never more uncertainty about how to proceed. Had Brown been simply a fanatic and a killer—for these he surely was—or was he to be understood as an example, too? Was he something still more than a mere symbol, as the equally odd Henry David Thoreau had asserted? What kind of apostles were they supposed to be?

Bleak winter's onset shrouded private doubts and deliberations. By the spring of 1860, however, many began to hearken to the message of Thoreau and men such as James Redpath, who started writing his biography of Brown on the day of the execution. Redpath dedicated his book to abolitionists "who when the mob shouted, 'Madman!' said, 'Saint!'" Directly inspired by John Brown's action, thousands of Americans began making moral choices of their own. Within a short time northern support for Brown had swelled to such an extent that reactions mirrored the Brooks-Sumner affair in its images of heroes and villains. Even prissy William Garrison became a supporter, in a backhanded fashion. "I thank God when men who believe in the right and duty of wielding carnal weapons . . . will take those weapons off the scale of despotism," he asserted, "and throw them into the scale of freedom." His own high principles, of course, would not permit him to pick up the sword, yet Brown's deeds had merit still. In France, Victor Hugo praised Brown as "the champion of Christ" and faulted the United States "for crucifying him."

While the idea that by year's end the nation would be torn apart and on the brink of war would have been absurd to most, for brinksmen the opportunities to conjure crisis were palpably clear. Within the South a small circle had steadily grown, infatuated with dreams of southern sovereignty and abundantly tired of having northern notions of civilization and morality rubbed in their faces. They longed rather less for independence as such than for a chance to defend their own ways of thinking and doing, to stand up for the South against the belligerent Yankees as the honorable and brave Preston Brooks had done. John Brown furnished slaveholders not merely with a symbol but with an opportunity to turn their aggressions upon the meddling Yankee. In that moment the South warned the North succinctly what it would get if it did not leave off.

It may be that a centrist political party advocating rapprochement on some terms could have forestalled war. That had been Douglas's modus operandi through the 1850s, but for every effort he made to bind North and South together in pursuit of what contemporaries called the "loaves and fishes," the more they pulled apart. The more he tried to buy southern loyalty—and with it, he hoped, the presidency—the more the South demanded as the price for its continued backing. By the end of the decade both parties in the United States had become sectionalized. While Douglas thought he held the only chance of mending or compromising the differences between them, he could not prevent verbal attacks on the evils of slavery from pouring over into attacks on the evildoers themselves, the slaveholders. No one could tolerate such aspersions, least of all a culture so fixated on honor. Honor compromised was honor no longer.

The majority of northerners, of course, thought southern Democrats and their Douglasite friends went too far. The truth, they believed, was that the Little Giant, like other northern Democrats, was nothing but a "doughface," a politician who could be counted on to do the slaveholders' legislative bidding as required, his political features pushed into smiles and scowls to fit the whims of the slaveholders he served. Gradually, however, these supposedly pliant politicians, and their constituents, tired of southern hectoring. When President Buchanan and southern Democrats supported the 1857 proslavery Lecompton Constitution of Kansas, Democrats in the North could no longer stomach the fraud that theirs was a national party of balanced interests.

Even Douglas balked. Some eastern Republicans misread Douglas's opposition to Lecompton and support of popular sovereignty to be antislavery and spoke to him about forming a new party in opposition to southern disunionists. Republicans Horace Greeley and William Seward went so far as to suggest that Illinois Republicans in the state legislature choose Douglas as U.S. senator from Illinois. Abraham Lincoln complained to Lyman Trumbull about Greeley's New York *Tribune's* constantly "eulogizing and admiring and magnifying Douglas." Lincoln wondered if eastern Republicans had decided to sacrifice the party in Illinois: "If so, we would like to know it soon; it will save us a great deal of labor to surrender at once." Lincoln's supporters did not wait and see what the state legislature would do. Friends like William Herndon arranged for the first time a state party convention, whose delegates on June 16, 1858, raised up Lincoln as the "first and only choice" of the Republican Party for Illinois senator and "the successor of Stephen A. Douglas." Without that endorsement, Abraham Lincoln and Stephen Douglas would not have needed the famous six debates to garner political support for their differing positions.

The Republicans in the Illinois legislature did support Lincoln but were outvoted by the Democratic majority, who again chose Douglas as senator from Illinois. Douglas fully expected that in two years' time, he would be the Democratic presidential nominee. In April 1860 the Democrats gathered in Charleston, South Carolina, to nominate their candidate for president and hammer out a campaign platform. The former task was bound to be easier than the latter. Not only were all manner of "trimmers, trucklers, and temporizers" represented on the floor, each pursuing his own interest, but there was little of anything at all holding the northern and southern wings of the party together any longer—save the stocky figure of Stephen Douglas. By this time, however, the horse-trading style of politics aroused mutual antagonism. In the late 1850s Douglas had tacked back and forth between the sectional wings in pursuit of the main chance. His support of the Kansas-Nebraska Act lost him support in the North. His interpretation of the Dred Scott decision enraged southern slaveholders. His "Freeport Doctrine" had galvanized southern opposition to his leadership as never before. Although Douglas faced no serious challenger for the presidential nomination, with nearly a dozen southerners clinging to his coattails in hopes of scooping up the vice presidency, a small but powerful clique was determined to force safeguards for slavery into the party platform regardless of the consequences.

For Douglas, the convention that was supposed to be his coronation turned out to be closer to a mass suicide ritual. Packing the meeting with loyal followers, Douglas hoped that his personal patronage would rein in southern demands for a federal slave code that were buzzing around the hall. It was an impossible balancing act. To pass such a measure would doom the Democratic Party in the North; to defeat it might inspire a southern walkout that would split the party along sectional lines. At first Douglas loyalists succeeded in muting the slavery discussion altogether. Then up bounded the Alabama delegate William Lowndes Yancey. Since 1846 Yancey had spoken and written against the political horse-trading that had eventuated in the Compromise of 1850 and the Kansas-Nebraska Act. Refusal to bend his principles had kept him on the political margins for nearly a decade, and there was no doctrine he despised more than the "squatter sovereignty" ideas of Stephen Douglas. For the past two years he had urged the reopening of the slave trade, the creation of a "League of United Southerners," and the passage of a constitutional amendment protecting slavery. Now he rose to demand that the party platform include a federal slave code. Narrowly defeated, the honorable gentleman denounced the convention and walked out of the hall, to vigorous applause.

It is perhaps too much to say that when Yancey stood up, he accomplished the secession of the slaveholding South. But it is not far off the mark: for what choice did the rest of the honorable delegation from Alabama have, when Yancey left, except to rise and traipse out after him? And when Alabama had broken party ranks in defense of the South, what course was left to Mississippi, Louisiana, Florida, and Texas? One by one the southern delegations got to their feet, voiced their rebuke, and marched out the door to a crescendo of cheers from the galleries. At first the Carolinians were eager to avoid a party split and hoped the business of the convention would proceed. In the end, however, shouts and catcalls from the crowd prodded them out of their chairs. When South Carolina delegates walked out, their spokesman William Preston minced no words: "Slavery is our King; slavery is our Truth; slavery is our Divine Right." Finally even three delegates from Delaware—still a slave state—got swept up in the excitement and tagged along. In the space of an hour the Democratic Party, and Douglas's dreams of the presidency, were hopelessly shattered. Lacking the delegates necessary to pass the party's platform, and having already determined to resolve this question before nominating a presidential candidate, the convention was stymied. Douglas and his stunned supporters first stared at one another in perplexity, then tried to coax the runaways to return, then went their separate ways, thoroughly outfoxed.

The bolters agreed to reconvene independently in Richmond the following month, where they chose Buchanan's vice president, Kentuckian John C. Breckinridge, as candidate for the southern Democrats. Many had hoped that the split they had caused would be quickly papered over, as affairs of honor commonly were, but none could find a workable solution. Douglasites, still smarting from the humiliating Charleston breakup and terrified of alienating northern support, refused all proposals for compromise, nominated their hero, and hoped for the best. Douglas campaigned harder than most candidates had ever done, but he was ill and faced a divided constituency. In addition to Breckinridge and the Republicans, a jury-rigged Constitutional Union Party of the vaguest principles put forth the aging Tennessee Whig John Bell. Douglas was simply unable to bridge the gap between North and South. Gleeful southern radicals foretold—and hypocritically decried—the result months before ballots were cast.

The election of Abraham Lincoln in 1860 signaled that a minority of people from a sectional political party could decide the presidency. Lincoln garnered almost no votes in southern states. For one thing, voting was not done by secret ballot, and less-than-tolerant neighbors might have objected to a vote for a "Black Republican." In Virginia, which like Kentucky required voters to declare their votes in public, Lincoln still received nearly two thousand votes. In other places party ballots were color coded so that a voter's choice of candidate was easily recognizable. In nine states Lincoln was not on the ballot at all. In South Carolina electors were not chosen by the people but were appointed by the state legislature. These handicaps should have been enough to ensure the Republican's defeat. They were of minor consequence, however, because the opposition was split three ways. Throughout the country, 81 percent of eligible citizens voted. Campaigning only in the North, Lincoln garnered just 40 percent of the vote (versus 29.5 percent for Democrat Stephen Douglas, 18 percent for the Southern Democrat John Breckinridge, and 12.5 percent for the Constitutional Union Party's John Bell). In the Electoral College, however, that plurality translated into 180 of 303 electoral votes—a thumping victory achieved on strictly sectional lines.

Five

"Southern by Birth"

ON JANUARY 27, 1838, men and women in Springfield, Illinois, braved the winter weather and gathered at the Baptist Church to attend the Young Men's Lyceum, a public meeting where they were audience to talented speakers perfecting their eloquence on a wide assortment of topics. The speaker that evening was a member of the Illinois House of Representatives and a resident of Springfield, having recently moved from the frontier town of New Salem, Illinois. Disturbed by recent mob violence in Mississippi and the city of St. Louis as well as the killing of abolitionist editor Reverend Elijah Lovejoy in Alton, Illinois, Abraham Lincoln was to deliver a speech on "The Perpetuation of Our Political Institutions."

Displaying a loquaciousness he would prune in subsequent years, the young representative staked the nation's future on *"a reverence for the Constitution and law"* (Lincoln's emphasis), for which he recommended that "every American pledge his life, his property, and his sacred honor." He worried that nationwide "wild and furious passions" refused to concede to the "sober judgment of the courts," and the "mobocratic spirit" of the times rendered extrajudicial judgment against gamblers, abolitionists, suspected slave insurrectionists. Evoking the specter of dead men "literally hanging from the bough of trees upon any roadside," Lincoln called on Americans to renew their patriotic attachment to sober reason, to law and order, and to the political edifice of liberty and equal rights bequeathed them by their forebears. All too aware of human frailties, Lincoln readily granted the existence of bad laws, of grievances for which "no legal provision have been made." The "political religion" he espoused was necessarily a never-ending exercise, a halting process toward greater justice, not perfection. Bad laws were to be repealed, and new legal provisions applied to new grievances. "Reason, cold, calculating, unimpassioned reason" was the bedrock for America's future support and defense. Here was boundless commitment to, if not necessarily blind faith in, general intelligence, sound morality, and reverence for the rule of law. If the government rested on those pillars of strength, the twenty-eight-year-old Lincoln was prepared to assert, "The gates of hell shall not prevail against it."

HAD LINCOLN LOST the presidential election of 1860, there is reason to believe that the Republicans might have faded from prominence. Had southerners moderated their demands to a slight degree, northern "Wide-Awakes" who championed Lincoln's cause might have been less zealous, and perhaps the center might have held one more time. Instead, Republicans also made important gains in the Senate, where 29 Republicans balanced 37 non-Republicans, and in the House of Representatives, where 120 Republicans and 108 non-Republicans squared off. The Supreme Court, with Taney as chief justice, was still dominated by southern interests. Nevertheless, many slaveholders in the South considered the election of Abraham Lincoln to be the equivalent of a declaration of war. They regarded the election of any Republican as a reproach to their pride, but especially this one, whom they felt sure would centralize the government, would not enforce the Dred Scott decision, and would prevent the expansion of slavery.

Southern newspapers jeered at Lincoln as "vulgar," a "horrid-looking wretch," and an "Illinois ape." Some called him harder names still, usually linked with an affection for African Americans that Lincoln tried to soft-pedal in the campaign. Such unthinking hostility perplexed president-elect Lincoln. As he wrote in December 1860 to North Carolina congressman John Gilmer, "You think slavery is right and ought to be extended; we think it wrong and ought to be restricted. For this, neither has any just occasion to be angry with the other." But angry they were.

Lincoln seemed to polarize people; some felt intense animosity, others a fierce loyalty. Those who came to know him, however, even former enemies, came to like him.

One admirer, the poet Walt Whitman, considered him a man of "the real West, the log hut, the clearing, the woods, the prairie." Although Whitman called him a man of the West, Republican senator Benjamin Wade of Ohio referred to him as "born of 'poor white trash' and educated in a slave State." Antislavery journalist Charles H. Ray (future owner of the *Chicago Tribune*) wrote to Illinois congressman Elihu Washburne in 1854 of his concerns over Lincoln: "I must confess I am afraid of 'Abe' . . . He is Southern by birth, Southern in his associations and Southern, if I mistake not, in his sympathies . . . His wife, you know, is a Todd, of a pro-slavery family, and so are all his kin." When Lincoln campaigned for Frémont in central and southern Illinois in 1856, Republican newspapers stressed that Lincoln was a "southerner" and compared his eloquence to that of his fellow Kentuckian, Henry Clay. South Carolina fire-eater Robert Barnwell Rhett declared in 1860 that Lincoln was "a Southern renegade—spewed out of the bosom of Kentucky into Illinois." In later years black sociologist W.E.B. Du Bois declared, "Abraham Lincoln was a Southern poor white." Historian of the South, Bertram Wyatt-Brown names Lincoln as the greatest poet of the South. His hometown newspaper in Springfield, Illinois, clearly identified Lincoln as a southerner: "Our friend carries the true Kentucky rifle and when he fires he seldom fails of sending the shot home."

Abraham Lincoln did indeed have southern roots, roots that helped define him as a person and as a president. Lincoln once confided to his law partner William H. Herndon that his maternal grandfather was "a well-bred Virginia farmer or planter," and Lincoln attributed some of his ambition and intellect to this nobleman from Virginia. His father, Thomas, and his paternal grandfather, Abraham, were also from Virginia, and Abraham was born in Kentucky, not far from Jefferson Davis's birthplace. Beyond Lincoln's habit of greeting folks with a southern "Howdy!" his famous sense of humor emanated from his rural southern heritage. His father was a legendary storyteller, and young Abraham not only reveled in the stories but learned his father's talent and used it to good purpose most of his life.

But Lincoln's southern habits went beyond turns of speech, story-telling, and literary references. Driving his life's decisions and his handling of the crisis to come was his understanding of and respect for southern honor. Honor depended on one's standing in the community; it was an external quality that reflected others' view of the individual's place within the group. For the yeoman of the American South, this included exaggerated masculine traits of derring-do, courage, strength, and braggadocio. Traits of the yeoman sense of honor in young Abraham Lincoln are evident in the story, now part of legend, of his wrestling match with Jack Armstrong in 1831. The Armstrong family of the Clary's Grove settlement had migrated from Tennessee. Lincoln's own neighborhood of New Salem was similarly settled by southerners and was in fact a southern enclave in Illinois. Jack Armstrong was the leader of the Clary's Grove Boys, a group of tough young rowdies, and Armstrong was considered the toughest. Lincoln's employer, shop owner Denton Offutt, was more impressed with the strong, wiry Lincoln. He bet that his store clerk could whip Armstrong. Accounts vary, but apparently the two contestants struggled evenly for a long time until Armstrong threw Lincoln by cheating. Lincoln sprang angrily to his feet and challenged the entire gang, claiming that he would take them all on one at a time, but only in a fair fight. His strength and courage won over the Clary's Grove Boys.

Just a few months later when the community's militia unit was mobilizing for the Black Hawk War, Jack Armstrong and the Boys elected Abe Lincoln captain. According to Lincoln's short 1859 autobiography, the public esteem evidenced by this election by the men who knew him so well provided him "a success which gave me more pleasure than any I have had since." Abraham Lincoln craved communal approval, that essential part of southern honor. In 1832, in his first race for the Illinois General Assembly, he explained his ambition "of being truly esteemed of my fellow men, by tending myself worthy of their esteem." Although Lincoln lost the election, his own home district of New Salem gave him 277 of its 300 votes cast.

On one occasion, Lincoln's respect for southern honor almost brought him to a duel, an unusual event in the rural North. Lincoln told a friend that he was opposed to dueling, but if degradation was the only alternative, he would fight. Democrat James Shields challenged Lincoln in September 1842 because of witty, anonymous articles in the Whig paper *Sangamo Journal*. The wit may have been a little too vicious due to the added embellishments by one Mary Todd and her girlfriend. To protect his own honor as well as Mary's anonymity, Lincoln could not back down from the challenge. It was precisely this feistiness that Lincoln's colleagues and acquaintances so admired, thinking it manly. On the appointed day Lincoln and Shields, each with three friends, had to travel to an island in the middle of the Mississippi because dueling was illegal in Illinois. Since Lincoln was the one challenged, he was allowed to choose the weapons and the terms of the encounter. He demanded "Cavalry broad swords of the largest size," specifying markings on the ground that one could not step beyond "upon forfeit of life" or, more likely, "surrender of the contest." Lincoln chose cleverly. The length and strength of his arms lent themselves to the broadsword, and the prospect of being cleaved in two must have given his opponent unpalatable food for thought. As Lincoln later told a friend, "I did not want to kill Shields, and felt sure that I could disarm him, having had about a month to learn the broadsword exercise; and furthermore, I didn't want the d—d fellow to kill me, which I rather think he would have done if we had selected pistols."

The duel did not come off. As usual, seconds stepped in at the last moment to remove the fearsome weapons and proclaim honor and manhood affirmed on both sides, as it doubtless was. This event demonstrated Lincoln's shrewd belligerence, his unwillingness to yield the initiative to his opponent, and a grim refusal to be mastered by any man, regardless of the eventual outcome. Those qualities would stand him in good stead in political combats to come, win or lose, and serve him as commander of armies on the battlefield. For Lincoln, winning honor entailed more than earning the esteem of his fellows, whether fighting a duel, wrestling a rival, or standing for election as captain of his militia company in the Black Hawk War. Southern notions of honor prized the enduring remembrance of posterity for having shown one's deeds to be truly worthy. Reputation— the earning of a name—was forged both by noble deeds and by the trajectory of a man's life, the way he carried himself through victory and adversity. Over the decades Lincoln strove to attain enduring honor through the effort to make his choices matter in the world.

Lincoln's closest friend was Joshua Speed from Kentucky. Lincoln's biographer David Donald surmises that perhaps Speed, the son of a plantation owner of seventy slaves, was "the only intimate friend that Lincoln ever had." Lincoln's southern roots were reflected, too, in his choice of Mary Todd for a wife. Todd was also from Kentucky, a member of a slaveholding family, but like Lincoln she embraced a southern political and cultural tradition that vehemently opposed slavery. Lincoln was traveling a well-worn path from ambitious southern yeoman to southern nonslaveholding gentleman.

Even Lincoln's personal life reflected his southern-steeped understanding of honorable behavior. Differences of temperament and class between Mary Todd and Abraham Lincoln were obvious. When Lincoln's law partner and friend, William Herndon, wrote a biography of the martyred president (published in 1889), he interviewed many of Lincoln's acquaintances. With hindsight, people have a different view of things, but Joshua Speed recalled that Lincoln was ill matched with proud Mary and was ultimately trapped between "sacrificing *honor* and sacrificing *domestic peace*" in this union—much the same choice he later faced as president. "Lincoln married her for honor," Speed explained, "feeling his honor bound to her." In spite of percolating marital problems, his genteel behavior toward his wife was forbearingly southern, even when some of her Kentucky kin enlisted in the Confederacy. Distinctive too was his adulation of their children throughout his lifetime. For all his American representativeness, Lincoln lived as a southern man, a southern husband, a southern father.

As a young man, Lincoln stood out. Unlike most adult males on the rowdy, toiling frontier, he never smoked or drank and seldom swore. He did not hunt or carry a gun. Lincoln had a love of reading encouraged by his literate mother, Nancy Hanks Lincoln, and his illiterate stepmother, Sarah Bush Lincoln. The frontier farming culture, however, neither understood nor valued reading, and Lincoln argued repeatedly with his father, who thought him proud and lazy for "wasting" his time over books. Yet Lincoln's later greatness is said to have derived in part both from the manly individualism he showed in defending his studious habits and from grasping the larger lessons of the books he read. It is easy to suggest that "The Lion and the Three Bulls," among his favorites of Aesop's *Fables*, served to mold his future political philosophy. Three bulls pastured together as a lion lay in ambush, afraid to attack them while they kept together. At last, with charm and guile, the lion succeeded in separating them. Then he attacked them one by one. While the moral of the story seems pertinent to Lincoln's thinking, any yeoman who took part in a barn-raising or reveled at a harvest supper understood that "union is strength." Many of the tales told of young Lincoln, handed down by posterity, insist upon both his unalloyed goodness and his honest humanity. We may doubt the details of this effort to fashion the fallen president in the image of the risen Christ, yet it is imperative to grasp that those around him did glimpse a noble, independent, Christian quality about him, a sense of budding greatness that they set down for posterity.

Those who say Lincoln's choice of career was more northern than southern fail to note the southern tradition of using the legal profession as a step into the elite. In his career as attorney, Lincoln showed neither pro- nor anti-southern bias. He and his partners took cases as they came. In 1841 Lincoln defended a young enslaved woman, Nance, whose owner was in the process of putting her up for sale. Nance sued for her right to freedom. The case went to the Illinois Supreme Court, which agreed with Lincoln that in Illinois it was illegal to sell a person. In 1847 Lincoln defended a slaveholder, Robert Matson, against the petition of Jane Bryant and her four children, fugitive slaves suing for freedom. Lincoln lost the case, and the court granted freedom to the family.

As his business prospered, more of Lincoln's cases involved larger landowners, bankers, cattlemen, professionals—the growing middle class. By the middle of the 1850s, Lincoln's cases increasingly involved disputes with railroads, and he was good at his job, both for and against the railroads. One of his major cases was on behalf of the Illinois Central Railroad. Lincoln won the case against McLean County, which thought the state legislature was not within its rights to grant the railroad an exemption from local taxes. When the railroad then questioned Lincoln's bill of $2,000, Lincoln did further research as to the worth of the ruling to the railroad and sued the Illinois Central for a fee of $5,000, which he won, and luckily was paid before the railroad went bankrupt in the Panic of 1857. Fair payment did not always mean higher payment. In 1856 a client mailed Lincoln $25 in payment for some legal papers. Lincoln wrote him, "You must think I am a high-priced man." Lincoln returned ten dollars: "Fifteen dollars is enough for the job."

Lincoln's legal work in Springfield and touring the circuit gave him a broad following of friends and colleagues interested in supporting his political ambitions. In Illinois politics, where Andrew Jackson's Democratic Party was the crowd pleaser, Lincoln went his own way once more, admiring the Whiggery of Henry Clay, whose family, like the Lincolns, had come from Virginia to settle in Kentucky. Whigs supported government initiatives to construct roads, improve river navigation, and build railroads. Whigs supported a protective tariff as well as a national bank to provide capital for business. The party of national self-improvement—and, historians have judged, the economic and cultural elite—Whigs appealed to Lincoln, set as he was upon personal self-improvement.

Lincoln dove into politics and soon became a local stalwart, promoting Whig principles and contesting state offices. In 1834 he reran and won his first term in the Illinois General Assembly. Two years later, announcing his candidacy for reelection, Lincoln explained to the *Sangamo Journal* that his belief in "sharing the privileges of the government" focused his political conduct. With social responsibilities went political rights, he declared, a sentiment derived as surely from the common sense of frontier life as from the philosophy of classical Athens. "Consequently I go for admitting all whites to the right of suffrage, who pay taxes or bear arms (by no means excluding females)." At this time women attended and participated in Whig campaign rallies, to the horror of Democrats, and Lincoln here demonstrated himself as among the most radical exponents of a fundamentally conservative contemporary notion—that political rights derive from defending the country and from paying taxes, and that if women contributed, political citizenship ought to extend across gender lines on that basis.

Lincoln's views here also suggest the limits racial prejudice imposed. Lincoln's restricting the extension of voting rights to whites alone reflected the cultural prejudices of his day. Yet, his belief in freedom led him eventually to deny the equation of voting rights with property holding that had rooted the political philosophy of his idol, Henry Clay. That step across class lines was an enormous one, and too easily overlooked. Lincoln's Whiggery was thoroughgoing, and just as the Whig desired to rise to a station of independence and honor by his own labors, Lincoln would not—indeed, with any honesty, could not—withhold that opportunity from others. Whether races were socially equal was not the issue for Lincoln; what he came to insist upon was a new understanding of liberty: equality of opportunity in the race of life. Lincoln's belief in equal opportunity would continue to evolve until he was ready to assert the still astonishing claim that race was politically inconsequential, that African Americans were citizens and entitled to the suffrage and equal protection under law. Whatever private prejudices he may have harbored, Lincoln loathed the artificial bonds that society and government placed on an individual's ability to work hard, accumulate property, and rise upward. If it was the government's task to promote the common good through banks, railroads, and tariffs, regardless of class, religion, or even gender, why limit that assistance along racial lines?

The Lincolns were always antislavery. Seeing slavery firsthand in Virginia and Kentucky gained Lincoln's father, and his son after him, a lifelong antipathy to the institution. Decades later Lincoln recalled the sight of enslaved men chained together on a Mississippi riverboat, and he doubtless compared their grim journey to vibrant New Orleans with his own, a memory of slavery and freedom counterposed, gliding along life's river together. Lincoln's recollection of a similar encounter on the Ohio River was "a continual torment," he declared. As often as he saw such scenes, they always had "the power of making me miserable." To get away from slavery, the Lincoln family had moved first to Indiana and then to Illinois.

Lincoln's antislavery leanings were evident early in his political life. Reelected to the Illinois legislature in 1836, the second-term legislator from Sangamon County demonstrated courage on the antislavery issue. Lincoln was one of only six who opposed a set of resolutions that disapproved of abolition societies and that declared "the right of property in slaves is sacred to the slave-holding States by the Federal Constitution." Objecting, Lincoln and Dan Stone, another member of the Sangamon legislative delegation, conceded two points to the majority: they admitted, "The congress of the United States has no power, under the constitution, to interfere with the institution of slavery in the different States." Lincoln and Stone also acknowledged their own anti-abolitionism: "the promulgation of abolition doctrines tends rather to increase than to abate its evils." Nevertheless, they wanted to go on record that "the institution of slavery is founded on both injustice and bad policy." Their position lost 77 to 6, which Lincoln knew it would. In fact, Lincoln and Stone registered their objections only after a bill selecting Springfield as the state capital had passed. The wait of six weeks to lodge a controversial protest showed a combination of principle and political acumen. Lincoln's pragmatic politics worked with and not against his deep antislavery commitment.

Antislavery never meant pro-abolitionism. Lincoln never joined an abolitionist society, and he apparently had no objection to the Illinois state law that barred free African Americans from settling there, and that specified that blacks could neither hold property nor wield the franchise. When Lincoln moved to Springfield in 1837, six of 115 African Americans in town were enslaved, but he never spoke up on their behalf. Nevertheless, he struggled with the issues of race and justice, even as he acknowledged the underlying lack of fairness. In 1854, appalled over the repeal of the Missouri Compromise outlawing slavery in the northern territories, Lincoln spoke of his hatred of "the monstrous injustice of slavery itself." He admitted his own feelings of racial superiority, but had a sense of wondering whether "this feeling accords with justice and sound judgment." He could only accept that such a feeling was "not the sole question, if, indeed, it is any part of it." In disagreeing with Stephen Douglas over the Kansas-Nebraska Act, Lincoln reaffirmed his belief that the Declaration of Independence meant that all men were created equal, and that included African American men also: "If the Negro is a man, why then my ancient faith teaches me that all men are created equal and that there can be no moral right in connection with one man's making a slave of another."

Running for the U.S. Senate in 1858 as a Republican against Democrat Stephen Douglas, Lincoln continued to affirm his own racial prejudice. Debating Douglas, Lincoln defended himself against Douglas's charge that he was in favor of racial equality. In Charleston, Illinois, in 1858, he drew cheers from the white crowd with his unequivocal stand: "I will say then that I am not nor ever have been in favor of bringing about in any way the social and political equality of the white and black races." Getting very specific, he said, "I am not nor ever have been in favor of making voters or jurors of negroes, nor of qualifying them to hold office, nor to intermarry with white people." Lincoln readily admitted that "I, as well as Judge Douglas, am in favor of the race to which I belong having the superior position." Distancing himself from the extreme white supremacy of Douglas, however, Lincoln clarified his position at the sixth debate in Quincy, Illinois: "Notwithstanding all this, there is no reason in the world why the negro is not entitled to all the rights enumerated in the Declaration of Independence—the right of life, liberty, and the pursuit of happiness. I hold that he is as much entitled to these as the white man." Espousing an ethic both conservative and radical, rooted in the toil performed, Lincoln declared "in the right to eat the bread without the leave of anybody else, which his own hand earns, he is my equal, and the equal of Judge Douglas, and the equal of every other man."

Lincoln embraced the Golden Rule of labor's uplift: "As I would not be a slave, so I would not be a master." Thinking about the good Christians in the audience, Lincoln reflected in his notes, "Suppose it is true, that the negro is inferior to the white, in the gifts of nature; is it not the exact reverse justice that the white should, for that reason, take from the negro, any part of the little which has been given him?" Relating the Christian faith to the institution of slavery, Lincoln wrote, "'Give to him that is needy' is the Christian rule of charity; but 'Take from him that is needy' is the rule of slavery."

To the consternation (and perhaps the relief) of all denominations in the years since his death, Lincoln was not a member of a church. He was actually typical in this regard. In 1860, when about 70 to 80 percent of Americans attended church or synagogue, only about half that number belonged as members. Scholars have long scrutinized Lincoln's sense of religion, setting great store in his undoubtedly great faith. His Virginian forebears were Quakers. In his youth Lincoln attended church with his dour and devout Baptist father, though the Holy Spirit seems rather to have passed him by on these occasions. Lincoln did not appreciate the emotional excess of frontier evangelicals and in his youth mocked it. His father punished him for regaling other youths with mimics of the sermons he endured. Preferring a reasoned approach, rejecting his father's choices, and claiming his own independent path once again, Lincoln developed his own theology, more pragmatic and less doctrinaire.

From an early age Lincoln knew his Bible and later deployed biblical lessons in the stories he told and the speeches he gave. These lessons resonated powerfully with his audiences but were not employed solely for effect. For all the spare religiosity and biblical cadences of the Gettysburg Address, for example, it is worth noting that this statement, so rich in the language and phrasing of the Old Testament, contains but a single reference to God. Rather, as the address suggests, Lincoln infused God into all aspects of the world he encountered; He was surely not shuttered up inside four walls or peering down absently from the sky. Later in life, Lincoln advised his skeptical friend Speed about the simple efficacy of Christian ethics. "Take all of this book upon reason that you can," he said of the Bible, "and the balance on faith, and you will live and die a happier and better man." Lincoln felt his own destiny and believed it intertwined with God's larger purposes. "I have often been driven to my knees," he conceded, "by the realization that I had nowhere else to go." That faith, if less than biblical, would give him strength in the nation's looming crisis.

When Lincoln ran for Congress in 1846, the press accused him of scoffing at Christianity. "That I am not a member of any Christian Church, is true," he countered, "but I have never denied the truth of the Scriptures; and I have never spoken with intentional disrespect of religion in general, or of any denomination of Christians in particular." At a time of spirit rappings, antipopery, and the supposed visitations of angels on every hand, he might have done much worse. (Later he would be tolerant of Mary's attempts to communicate with her dead sons in séances at the White House.)

Lincoln's reasoned tolerance deepened into a profound religious feeling during his term as president, yet there is always a sense of him standing with the hopeless sinners, not the smugly saved. Weighed down by the uncertainty and depression he struggled with all his life, bearing the burden of leadership during a great civil war, Lincoln found his religious fatalism transmuted into a clear belief that God was working out a plan for human history, and that he himself was an instrument in that plan. Lincoln's faith included an awareness of corporate sin and God's judgment and forgiveness. His second inaugural was a prayer of confession for the entire nation. In terms not far from John Brown's last words, he talked about expiation of the national sin of slavery. If God willed that war continue, he allowed, "until all the wealth piled by the bondsman's two hundred and fifty years of unrequited toil shall be sunk, and until every drop of blood drawn with the lash shall be paid by another drawn with the sword, as was said three thousand years ago, so still it must be said 'the judgments of the Lord are true and righteous altogether.'" The

Civil War, Lincoln reckoned, was America's time on the cross: atonement, however grievous, for so vast a sin.

While neither northerners nor southerners showed much doubt about interpreting God's inscrutable thoughts and desires, Lincoln was willing to admit that he simply did not know the mind of Divine Providence. Although unorthodox in his religious views, although too humble to claim any foreknowledge of God's specific intentions, Lincoln apparently never doubted that God's blessings were intended for the national republican government: "Him, who has never yet forsaken this favored land." Lincoln's religious sensibility was key to his appeal then and now. One of Lincoln's strengths was his ability to translate his faith effectively into language persuasive to a large Protestant evangelical population. He moved forward, even if others disagreed, when he felt it was the right thing to do, careful to admit each could act only "as God gives us to see the right."

Lincoln's antislavery sentiments were fervent and real, and such formulations go far toward explaining why southern slaveholders—and a significant cluster of northern Democrats as well—saw Lincoln's elevation to the presidency as a dangerous revolutionary step. Yet Lincoln strove repeatedly in 1860 to allay fears that his party aimed at dismantling slavery. "I have no purpose, directly or indirectly," he promised, "to interfere with the institution of slavery in the States where it exists." The presidency conveyed no such power, he asserted, and the Taney-interpreted Constitution permitted no such meddling. "I believe I have no lawful right to do so," he allowed, adding, "and I have no inclination to do so." The rule of law constrained him no less than he expected it to constrain his fellow Americans.

What Lincoln failed to renounce—as all southerners noted—was the Republican commitment to being resolutely opposed to slavery's advance in the territories. Without such expansion, southerners believed, it was only a matter of time before their world was crowded into oblivion. The rule of law could promise a thoroughgoing if incrementalist revolution. The Republican president would appoint Republican judges, marshals, customs collectors, post office clerks, and more in every corner of the South. Around each man, they knew, a web of patronage and status would soon grow up, until antislavery evils would come to be whispered in their midst. The day would come, southern Democrats knew, when a southern Republican party would flare up among them—just as Hinton Helper had declared—pandering to the interests of white non-slaveholders and splitting communities between rich and poor. What then would prevent political conflict from passing over into class war—and eventually race war besides? If Lincoln could not be stopped at the threshold, the nation's house would have to divide once and for all. And in the November election for U.S. president, it became clear that he would not be stopped.

Prior to Lincoln's inauguration, fire-eaters throughout the South condemned a sectional president and escalated their threats of secession. Some members of Congress were not particularly worried, recalling many times that such threats had been used. In 1856 Abraham Lincoln himself had scoffed at such threats. "Humbug, nothing but folly," Lincoln had declared at that time. Senator Carl Schurz of Missouri recalled that in 1859 some members of the House seceded over the election of William Pennington (Republican from New Jersey): they "seceded from Congress, went out, took a drink, and then came back." Schurz predicted that in their anger over Lincoln's election, "they would secede again and this time would take two drinks but come back again."

Most members of Congress, however, were desperately trying to forestall any attempt at disunion. In December 1860 Congress attempted yet another compromise, under the leadership of Kentucky Democrat J. J. Crittenden, which would have extended the line of slave and nonslave states to the west. But Crittenden was no Henry Clay, and his stopgap fell pitifully short of meeting southern demands. Moreover, the proposal tipped Lincoln's hand, confirming the fire-eaters' worst fears. As he wrote to antislavery Republican senator Lyman Trumbull, a fellow Illinoisan, "Let there be no compromise on the question of extending slavery. If there be, all our labor is lost, and, ere long, must be done again. The dangerous ground—that into which some of our friends have a hankering to run—is Pop. Sov. [popular sovereignty] Have none of it. Stand firm. The tug has to come, & better now, than any time hereafter." Lincoln rejected outright the claim that slavery had equal rights with liberty. Lincoln was, however, willing to support a proposed constitutional amendment affirming the legality of slavery in the states where it now existed. Groveling desperately before the South, Congress actually passed this amendment, though it never completed the ratification process. For the South it offered none of the new guarantees they required; for the nation it was too little too late. Five years later, in 1865, Lincoln would champion a diametrically different Thirteenth Amendment, now specifically to *outlaw* slavery in the United States.

Traveling by train to accept the presidency, Lincoln gave short speeches along the route to Washington, D.C. On February 22, 1861, at Independence Hall in Philadelphia, the president-elect announced, "I have never had a feeling politically that did not spring from the Declaration of Independence . . . that which gave promise that in due time the weights should be lifted from the shoulders of all men, and that all should have an equal chance . . . Now, my friends, can this country be saved upon that basis? . . . If it can't be saved upon that principle . . . if this country cannot be saved without giving up on that principle . . . I would rather be assassinated on this spot than to surrender it."

Not even waiting to see what actions Lincoln would or would not take against slavery, the state of South Carolina started a split from the rest of the nation. On December 20, 1860, church bells rang and cannons boomed out across Charleston harbor. That day South Carolinians by the hundreds packed into the city's largest hall to watch delegates from all over the state add their names to an Ordinance of Secession, declaring the creation of the Independent Republic of South Carolina. Among those who flocked to Charleston was *Free Flag of Cuba* author Lucy Holcombe, now wife of South Carolina governor Francis W. Pickens. Although southern honor usually applied to men, she answered for many southerners when she wrote to her father in Texas that she wanted to be "where duty and honor demand me, and whatever dangers surround me, I will be with God's help true to my name and blood." In his campaign for governor, Pickens had announced, "I would be willing to appeal to the god of battles if need be, cover the state with ruin, conflagration and blood rather than submit." In Charleston that December the exuberant crowds greeted the news of secession with approval. Perhaps never has a people so celebrated the suicide of a world they loved so dearly.

At least part of the joy that swept over Charleston with the signing of the ordinance stemmed from a mingled sense of astonishment and ritual: after three decades of threatening secession, Carolinians had actually, unbelievably, accomplished it. Whatever happened next, most people performed the proud roles of happy radicals, satisfied with the manly way their state had vindicated its honor and defended its principles—as they had *known* it would. In the weeks ahead, as clerks and farmers drilled in defense of their boldly asserted sovereignty, politicians clustered behind closed doors, trying to figure out just what they had actually done and what should be done next. No one had much of an idea, except to wait for the other shoe to fall. South Carolina had gone out of the Union quite alone, founding a nation some derided as "too small for a republic, too big for an insane asylum." Unless it received backing from other southern states, the slaveholders' independence would soon die on the vine. With more than a little concern in his tone, South Carolina congressman John D. Ashmore wrote Washington to inquire whether the state's new status meant that federal mail service would no longer operate as before. Absurd as such a question was, it shows that secessionists had made no plans at all for the practicalities of developing a separate nationhood, largely because they had hardly anticipated winning it. That was, in turn, because many "cooperationists" had never aimed at breaking up the Union at all. Their true aim had been to scare the North into making concessions. As it turned out, Lincoln called South Carolina's bluff, and as honorable men ever will, they took the plunge, regardless of the consequences. Some South Carolinians still believed, even after they had hoisted the banner of the slaveholders' republic, that the North would come crawling, offering concessions to keep the nation intact.

Instead, the rest of the South came trailing after them, one by one. And after decades of trying to keep the slavery question out of the national arena, secessionists now could hardly stop shouting that they had broken up the Union, at root, to save their peculiar institution. The Ordinances of Secession they issued stated simply that the ratification of the federal Constitution that the state had passed originally was no longer in effect, that the "Constitution of the United States of America is no longer binding on any of the citizens of this State." Most announced themselves magically "Sovereign and Independent."

But they could not let it go at that. To Alabama legislators, the election of Abraham Lincoln signified the power of "a sectional party, avowedly hostile to the domestic institutions and to the peace and security of the people of the State of Alabama." The domestic institution at that culture's center was slavery. Texans claimed that the federal government had abandoned its lawful role of protecting "the property of our citizens." They declared that Washington was now intending "to strike down the interests and property of the people of Texas, and her sister slave-holding States."

In addition to secession ordinances, several states issued explicit "declarations of causes." Lincoln noted that states that adopted their own "declarations of independence" did not follow the words of Thomas Jefferson because "they omit the words 'all men are created equal.'" The Georgia State Assembly passed a resolution in January 1861 condemning the Republican Party, instituted as it was "for the avowed purpose of destroying the institution of slavery." "For twenty years past," Robert Toombs stormed, "the Abolitionists and their allies in the Northern states, have been engaged in constant efforts to subvert our institution, and to excite insurrection and servile war among us." When Georgia sent a representative to Virginia to try to persuade that state to secede, their advocate was Henry L. Benning, a lawyer, a Democrat, and a man who held ninety slaves. As to why Georgia seceded, he pronounced: "This reason may be summed up in a single proposition. It was a conviction, a deep conviction on the part of Georgia, that a separation from the North was the only thing that could prevent the abolition of her slavery."

Mississippi's official statement on secession, issued in January 1861, also explained its position as "thoroughly identified with the institution of slavery." If the state did not secede, militants calculated, the resultant abolition of slavery would mean "the loss of property worth four billions of money." Robert Barnwell Rhett drew up for South Carolina a Declaration of the Causes of Secession, a document especially frank, if melodramatic. The North, he charged, had "encouraged and assisted thousands of our slaves to leave their homes; and those who remain, have been incited by emissaries, books and pictures to servile insurrection." Even moderate Carolinians seemed to have lost all sense of proportion. One week after Lincoln's election, James L. Orr, who came frustratingly close to being Stephen Douglas's running mate, warned upcountry farmers of their peril. Why had this Unionist embraced secession's cause? Republican aggressions would never cease, he argued, until they had instituted racial "equality at the ballot box and jury box, and at the witness stand." An equality of such sweeping consequence, he believed, could never be allowed.

By the end of February 1861, Alabama, Florida, Georgia, Louisiana, Mississippi, South Carolina, and Texas had seized federal property and declared themselves out of the Union. Cotton-rich though they were, this group of states encompassed only about ten percent of the country's white population and about five percent of its manufacturing. Clearly they needed the support of other states. At this time, however, conventions held in Arkansas, Missouri, and Virginia did not pass secession ordinances. The Tennessee legislature was strong for the Union and refused to call a convention. In North Carolina voters defeated a call for a convention. When the rumor reached Knoxville that South Carolina was contemplating secession, an attorney at law, William McAdoo, condemned the unilateral course as criminally reckless. When it appeared certain that other southern states were also seceding, the question for McAdoo was "Shall we Tennesseans go with the South or with the North?" Reckless or not, the southern house of cards leaned in a certain direction. McAdoo confided to his diary, "My position is if they will go, now or at any time, I go with them." Nothing was unanimous, however; some in Tennessee wished the slaveholders who advocated for secession would have "their throats cut by their negroes." In Knoxville on April 27, 1861, Unionists and secessionists held simultaneous rallies on opposite ends of Gay Street.

As the slaveholding South divided forces, many expected Washington to effect a rapprochement with the breakaway states. But there was little political will for such an overture within James Buchanan's outgoing administration, and the internal divisions southerners had already demonstrated undercut the case for it. Incoming Republicans could hardly explain to their constituents why their first legislative act would be to cave in to slaveholders' demands, especially since the Upper South had shown itself unwilling to bolt from the Union. Secessionists would begin to squabble among themselves soon enough, Unionists believed, and then would come creeping back of their own accord.

Republicans meanwhile viewed this southern exodus with mounting frustration and anger. The main issue of slavery had been abruptly and unceremoniously solved by the slaveholders themselves. As delegates from one southern state after another filed out the door, the problem of slavery's place in the Union was curing itself without northern aid. All too soon Republicans would be left to govern a house shattered but no longer divided by slavery. The issue then became disunion. Did states have a right to withdraw from the Union? On what pretext? With what consequences? The Declaration of Independence asserted that government derives its just powers "from the consent of the governed," that when it failed to protect citizens' rights, "it is the Right of the People to alter or to abolish it." What was the meaning of this right to make and unmake government if a state was not allowed to assert it? What, on the other hand, did the American people's sovereignty amount to, if it could be nullified in a moment by the whim of a disgruntled few? These serious questions needed more time for national debate, moderates argued. Time and prudence, however, were in short supply in the volatile atmosphere of conflict and paranoia, and southern radicals, eager to extort concessions from the North, had no interest in turning down the heat.

Instead, on February 4, 1861, delegates from the seceded states met in Montgomery, Alabama, which was declared the capital city of a new nation, the Confederate States of America. Moderates quickly gained control of the proceedings, pushing aside the fire-eaters and nominating Jefferson Davis of Mississippi, a former Democratic leader of notably temperate credentials, as their first president. "Ambitious as Lucifer and cold as a lizard" was the assessment of Jefferson Davis by Sam Houston, the slaveholding, anti-abolition, and antisecession governor of Texas. Davis had been secretary of war under President Pierce, in which office he had vastly improved the national military that his armies soon would be fighting. When he addressed the Confederate congress in April, Davis acknowledged that their cause was perpetuating slavery. Davis declared that "a persistent and organized system of hostile measures against the rights of the owners of slaves in the Southern States" had culminated in a political party dedicated to "annihilating in effect property worth thousands of millions of dollars." Since "the labor of African slaves was and is indispensable" to the South's production of cotton, rice, sugar, and tobacco, Davis argued, "the people of the Southern States were driven by the conduct of the North to the adoption of some course of action to avert the danger with which they were openly menaced."

At Davis's side in Montgomery, as the new vice president of the Confederacy, stood the frail Alexander Stephens of Georgia, a lifelong

Whig who for years had led the forces opposing secession in his own state. Stephens was explicit that the reason for a Confederacy was to "put to rest forever all the agitating questions relating to our peculiar institutions—African slavery as it exists among us—the proper status of the negro in our form of civilization. This was the immediate cause of the late rupture and present revolution." By his account, government should rest "upon the great truth that the negro is not equal to the white man; that slavery, subordination to the superior race, is his natural and moral condition."

The newly "sovereign" southerners, instead of taking practical measures to secure southern independence, working out a strategy for attracting border states, or establishing a satisfactory foreign policy, set speedily about writing a new Constitution. The argument that this choice reflects the immature enthusiasms gripping the South misreads the central purposes of the moderate men who controlled the new nation. The new constitution they drafted was only secondarily intended as a viable instrument of government. Its main purpose was to articulate specific areas of difference so resolution could proceed.

The U.S. Constitution was a pure and good document, Confederates declared, but it had been betrayed and sullied by the "Black Republicans" of the North. Indeed, the Confederate Constitution is noteworthy for its attempt to mirror the American Constitution and the restraint with which it seeks to alter it. Both documents seek "to establish justice, insure domestic tranquility, and secure the blessings of liberty to ourselves and our posterity." Confederates argued that their freedom meant that property, enslaved or otherwise, would be protected and that states' rights would be paramount, provisions they understood were guaranteed by the U.S. Constitution.

The Constitution of the Confederate States of America was broadly similar to the Constitution of the United States. The Confederate president's term of office was six years instead of four, and had no allowance for reelection. Regarding the issue of secession, the U.S. Constitution says nothing about permanence. The CSA preamble, however, specified permanence, "in order to form a permanent federal government." This supposedly precluded other future secessions, but what would happen the first time Dixie's legislators disagreed among themselves? If a minority secedes, Lincoln reasoned, "they make a precedent which in turn will divide

and ruin them, for a minority of their own will secede from them whenever a majority refuses to be controlled by such minority." If secession was
legal, then "why may not any portion of a new confederacy a year or two
hence arbitrarily secede again, precisely as portions of the present Union
now claim to secede from it? All who cherish disunion sentiments are now
being educated to the exact temper of doing this." On what basis could
Confederates prevent seceders from seceding once more?

The Constitution of the United States dealt with the slavery issue
but did not specify slavery. The Confederate Constitution included a
provision in Article IV: "The institution of negro slavery, as it now exists
in the Confederate States, shall be recognized and protected by Congress and by the Territorial government; and the inhabitants of the several Confederate States and Territories shall have the right to take to
such Territory any slaves lawfully held by them in any of the States or
Territories of the Confederate States." This was essentially the language
of the constitutional amendment that Congress had so recently passed,
except for one crucial difference. It included the indispensable territorial
protection.

Overall, the differences between the two documents were minor because Confederate leaders hoped that their constitution would become
the basis for reconciliation. Differences between the two documents represent terms of a new bargain slaveholders hoped to drive with Washington. However much they hungered for more, rebels avoided known
deal-breakers. Omitted, for example, was any mention of reopening the
transatlantic slave trade for fear of upsetting the bargain they hoped
to strike.

The Confederate Constitution specified their central demands and
suggested the simplicity of reuniting the country. As Jefferson Davis so
rationally pointed out in his inaugural address on February 18, 1861,
"With a Constitution differing only from that of our fathers in so far as
it is explanatory of their well-known intent, freed from the sectional
conflicts which have interfered with the pursuit of the general warfare,
it is not unreasonable to expect that States from which we have recently
parted may seek to unite their fortunes with ours under the government
which we have instituted."

Their plan might have succeeded. Demands were minimal, and
brinksmanship had worked in the past. Many in the North, including

Republican William Seward of New York, were willing to offer the South further concessions. But the new Confederates underestimated the person with whom they were bargaining, Abraham Lincoln, the southerner.

Abraham Lincoln's inaugural address, given on March 4, 1861, two weeks after Davis was sworn in as the South's leader, was his answer to the Confederate ransom note, a refusal to bargain with rebels. In plain, even lawyerly, fashion, Lincoln addressed the issues of secession. "If the United States be not a government proper," he asked, "but an association of States in the nature of contract merely, can it, as a contract, be peaceably unmade by less than all the parties who made it?" Clearly not: "One party to a contract may violate it—break it, so to speak—but does it not require all to lawfully rescind it?" Violated, broken, the Union still remained unabolished. Lincoln pleaded with the South to reconsider its rash actions, refusing all responsibility for what might come next. In only another four years, he pointed out, those dissatisfied might elect a president more to their liking.

Lincoln asked, "Will you, while the certain ills you fly to are greater than all the real ones you fly from, will you risk the commission of so fearful a mistake?" Only "a majority held in restraint by constitutional checks and limitations," he counseled, "and always changing easily with deliberate changes of popular opinions and sentiments" could offer the "true sovereign of a free people." The property rights that southerners hugged so dear could find no safety except in the Union—and, Lincoln added, he was unwilling to fork over any further guarantees. He pleaded, "You have no oath registered in heaven to destroy the Government, while I shall have the most solemn one to 'preserve, protect, and defend it.'" Secessionists refused to back down. Moreover, they now had a legal document to prove that the Confederate States of America was a legitimate government. Many white southerners understood that when Jefferson Davis and southern leaders drew up a constitution, they had indeed made a nation.

Initially, some abolitionists, including Christian pacifist William Lloyd Garrison, advocated letting the South "go in peace." Charles Ray of the *Chicago Tribune* agreed, as did Horace Greeley, editor of the New York *Tribune*: "We hope never to live in a republic whereof one section is pinned to the residue by bayonets." These initial appeals to let the South secede mainly represent a different variant on Lincoln's determination to call the South's bluff. Greeley, Garrison, and Ray continued to support Lincoln's policy at this time. A weaker president might have let the southern states go without a fight, and there was considerable concern how European powers like England and France, worried whether southern cotton would continue flowing to their mills, might take it if Lincoln tried to coerce the Confederacy. Lame duck President James Buchanan, a Democrat from Pennsylvania, opposed secession but questioned whether the federal government had the power to compel states to remain in the Union if they wished to withdraw. "After much serious reflection," he concluded unhelpfully, "I have arrived at the conclusion that no such power has been delegated."

Many southern secessionists did believe the federal government would let them go. The Charleston *Mercury* found it absurd "that a people, like the people of the North, prone to civil pursuits and money-making, should get up and carry out the military enterprise of conquering eight millions of the only people on the continent, who from education and habits, are a military people." But should war come, let it come, secessionists allowed. More than one southern bravo offered to drink all the blood that such a conflict with the craven Yankees might ever spill.

War or no war, the vast majority of northerners recognized that the stakes of disunion were too high to allow Confederate rebels to succeed. A young immigrant in Philadelphia explained the problem to his father in England. "If the Unionists let the South secede, the West might want to separate next Presidential Election . . . [O]thers might want to follow and this country would be as bad as the German states." Lincoln above all recognized that democracy as a form of government was being tested. "We must settle this question now," he warned, or else "the incapacity of the people to govern themselves" would be proved before the world. For the incoming president this was a trial of sovereignty and national honor both.

Lincoln also understood the influence of the American democratic experiment in the wider world. Americans considered themselves the only major power in the world to embrace a democratic republican form of government—a system other lands might admire and would surely one day emulate. Secession meant the defeat of this grand experiment. European monarchies, which had put down their own worrisome liberal revolts in 1848, were imagined to be grinning at the prospect that secession and war would end the foolish American project. Conservatives doubtless did like the idea that disunion would weaken democratic impulses. More than one member of the British Parliament hoped that the arrogant little republic would break into "two or perhaps more fragments." America before disunion represented "a menace to the whole civilized world." Brought down a peg, it might prove rather more reasonable.

British working people had other ideas. During the war President Lincoln received a letter from unemployed textile workers of Manchester, England. They expressed support for Lincoln and had "hope that every stain on your freedom will shortly be removed, and that the erasure of that foul blot on civilisation and Christianity—chattel slavery— during your presidency, will cause the name of Abraham Lincoln to be honoured and revered by posterity." Lincoln replied, "I know and deeply deplore the sufferings which the working people of Manchester and in all Europe are called to endure in this crisis. It has been often and studiously represented that the attempt to overthrow this Government which was built on the foundation of human rights, and to substitute for it one which should rest exclusively on the basis of slavery, was likely to obtain the favour of Europe." He was deeply touched and inspired by their "assurance of the inherent truth and of the ultimate and universal triumph of justice, humanity and freedom."

Ultimately Lincoln acted from the stubborn determination, the abiding sense of honor, of a southern yeoman. "I hold," he declared, "that in contemplation of universal law and of the Constitution the Union of these States is perpetual." Confederates who disagreed would find themselves in a very different sort of wrestling match. Lincoln found that "no State upon its own mere notion can lawfully get out of the Union; that *resolves* and *ordinances* to that effect are legally void, and that acts of violence within any State or States against the authority of the United States are insurrectionary or revolutionary, according to circumstances." Confederates were not sectional patriots and statesmen, he scoffed; they were simply rebels.

Lincoln's sense of honor required following the rule of law, the Constitution, and Court decisions. Lincoln was careful not to define the war in terms of ending slavery but instead focused on preserving the Union.

That interpretation was intended to rally northern opinion to his cause, but it also let nonslaveholding southerners off the hook. By bracketing slavery, Lincoln allowed white southerners, when they took up arms against the Union, to tell themselves that they did so in defense of their families, households, and community, and not in defense of slavery as such.

A larger point about Lincoln as a southerner involves the dishonor of secession. Just as Lincoln was willing to fight Jack Armstrong and every one of the Clary's Grove Boys, and just as he believed he was honor-bound to fight a duel with broadswords, even traveling more than seventy miles to the Mississippi River to win his point, he knew that the Civil War involved honor. Certainly Confederates believed that it did. On December 14, 1860, nearly half the congressional representatives of southern states had announced that "we are satisfied that the honor, safety, and independence of the Southern people require the organization of a Southern Confederacy." For either Abe Lincoln or the secessionists to back down was to lose face with their communities North and South, to lose that esteem so essential to the men and culture of honor. When a committee from Baltimore demanded that he let the South go in peace, Lincoln replied, "You would have me break my oath and surrender the Government without a blow. There is no Washington in that—no Jackson in that—no manhood nor honor in that." In his first annual message to Congress, Lincoln emphasized that with regard to foreign powers America must maintain "our own rights and honor." In his second message to Congress, the president explained to the nation's legislators that they would be remembered in history in either "honor or dishonor."

Lincoln's southern roots were also reflected in his belief that, despite the fiery rhetoric of their leaders, the majority of southern yeomen would not be persuaded. In the end, after all, the master class had little to offer the South's common people. Growing up poor, with homesteading as a way of life, Lincoln respected hardworking, less wealthy, but self-reliant southern men and women. He knew that many southern whites opposed slavery even as they also opposed abolitionism. More to the point, he knew that most southern whites did not want to see the Union torn apart. He, and many like him, connected the prosperity of the country with its promise of "liberty for all." Lincoln calculated that most white southerners, yeomen like his own family, would reject extremism. "The people of the South have too much of good sense, and good temper," he reasoned, "to attempt the ruin of the government."

Most people conclude that Lincoln badly misjudged southern loyalty, but maybe his assessment of his fellow southerners was not far off the mark. Historian David Moltke-Hansen's cultural definition of a southerner includes people born or living in the Confederate states, the border states, and people of southern descent living in areas adjacent to the border, such as the southern portions of Ohio, Indiana, and Illinois. The number of white southerners in this "cultural South" totaled nine million. In counting these cultural southerners along with whites who supported the Union even while residing in one of the eleven Confederate states, Moltke-Hansen estimates that perhaps 40 percent or more of all white southerners fought for the Union. The border slave state of Missouri sent twenty-seven regiments for the Union and fifteen for the Confederacy. Every southern state except South Carolina had a regiment of volunteers in the Union army; South Carolina companies fighting for the Union had to travel to North Carolina or Tennessee to sign up.

Loyal southerners sometimes supported the Union in other ways. Union loyalists in Mississippi would not serve in the Confederacy and instigated the Free State of Jones. A loyal North Carolina émigré to Indiana reported that "hundreds of Carolinians have arrived in Indiana" and that the vast majority of them were antislavery as well as pro-Union. Sam Houston, who had won his race for governor on a platform of opposition to secession, warned his fellow Texans at the time, "I tell you that, while I believe with you in the doctrine of state rights, the North is determined to preserve this Union. They are not a fiery, impulsive people as you are, for they live in colder climates. But when they begin to move in a given direction . . . they move with the steady momentum and perseverance of a mighty avalanche; and what I fear is, they will overwhelm the South." Houston was forced to step down as governor when he refused to swear allegiance to the Confederate States of America. Another Texan, district court judge Edmund J. Davis, ran as a delegate for the secession convention but lost because he adamantly opposed secession. Also refusing to swear allegiance to the Confederacy, Davis went north and raised a cavalry of pro-Union Texans. Indeed, eight counties in Texas, heavily populated by antislavery German Americans who had voted against secession during that state's February 1861 referendum, opted to sit out the war, and some proposed seceding from the Confederacy.

Lincoln, of course, did misjudge the majority of white southerners in the Confederate states. Many southerners listened and obeyed their religious leaders when they preached about the ungodly North and the certainty of divine blessings in the cause of secession. Presbyterian minister James Henley Thornwell persuaded his congregation that the South was morally correct on slavery and also lectured on "the real question": "the relations of man to society" and "of States to the individual." Reverend R. L. Dabney preached: "Just in proportion to the integrity of men's principles, to their magnanimity, to their incorruptible love of right and truth, to their fear of God, have been their decision and zeal in the cause of the Confederate States." Other southerners were simply unable to cope with the rhetoric of fear and propaganda of the secessionists. Delegates in Spaulding County, Georgia, claimed that the northern states intended "to free our slaves, and make them incendiaries, to destroy us by fire, and monsters to immolate our wives and daughters at the shrine of their only god on earth—Abolitionism." Sentimental unionism calling for devotion to the Founding Fathers and the union of Andrew Jackson paled in comparison. In the war of words, fear tactics of the secessionists won. Southern pro-Union sentiments ran counter to twin cohesions: concrete fear of race war and glory of military pomp. Moreover, once southern blood was spilled in battle, loyalty to the South or to a particular state took precedence over loyalty to the country.

One week after Lincoln's election, on November 13, 1860, the son of John C. Calhoun articulated a central fear of many southern slaveholders. Speaking to the South Carolina Agricultural Society, Andrew Pickens Calhoun predicted that the antislavery rhetoric of Lincoln and his cronies would incite slave rebellions. He blamed the foreign radical ideals of "liberty, equality and fraternity" as helping to instigate the slave revolt in Haiti, and he warned of a similar disaster in the American South. To put down anticipated slave rebellions, slave patrols and militias were organized throughout the South, some styling themselves "Minute Men" to claim the mantle of the patriots of the American Revolution. With militias at the ready, with pride and honor at stake, the South reacted to Lincoln's election. As thousands of men fitted themselves with dashing new uniforms and posed for daguerreotypes, parading the streets and spouting bold sentiments, the parochial, conservative South appeared to have undergone a truly Romantic revolution. Instead of gearing up for war, it seemed that Confederates were embarked on a militant festival of self-celebration. Few imagined in these weeks that it would all truly end at sword's point.

Lincoln, though, had hardly any other choice. Providing territorial guarantees for slavery was out of the question. Strengthening the states would mean weakening the Union he cherished. Compromising with slavery now could only add a new stain on the nation's honor and on his own. While the Montgomery meeting was still in progress, with the Union threatened with disruption forever, Lincoln traveled to Philadelphia and spoke at Independence Hall. What Americans chose now, he declared, would stand as an example to the world. "It was not the mere matter of the separation of the colonies from the mother land, but that sentiment in the Declaration which gave liberty, not alone to the people of this country, but hope to the world for all future time."

So far the battle was fought with words. Lincoln's determination not to let the South go went hand in hand with his restraint. His understanding of southern honor cautioned him against striking the first blow. Only time's passage would permit moderates to solve the impasse, or at worst force Confederates into the aggressor's role. Across the South armed militants seized federal arsenals, shipyards, and forts, asserting their sovereignty and daring Washington to react. Lincoln refused to be goaded. Military confrontation was the last thing Lincoln wanted. Again and again Lincoln declared that the North would not attempt to coerce the South back into the Union. Indeed, had Confederates not struck the first blow, Lincoln probably could not have rallied sufficient political support for military suppression of the rebellion. At the very least such a course would have offered Britain and other European powers a superb opportunity to meddle in American affairs, for spite if not for cotton.

Most important, Lincoln was solicitous about keeping the border slave states from joining forces with the secessionists. For that reason he steered clear of slavery and focused on rebellion as the main issue before the nation. Reportedly Lincoln declared that he would like to have God on his side but had "to have Kentucky." His wisdom and forbearance paid off in Kentucky, where Union sentiments outshouted the strains of "Dixie." Kentucky remained "neutral" until invaded by the Confederacy in September 1861. Timely bayonets did the trick in Maryland. Rather than allow secessionists to hold a vote in the Maryland General Assembly in September 1861, Union troops arrested thirty-one legislators. They were released from jail after the elections in November, in which the voters put into office pro-Union men. Nor did Missouri join the Confederacy, though it was troubled with guerrilla fighting throughout the war and after. Farther west Lincoln was aware that Mormons were hesitant to support the Union because of its anti-Mormon attitudes. He consequently appointed Brigham Young as territorial governor; peace was maintained, and Utah did not support the Confederacy. Not all special interest groups were so easily mollified. While Native Americans in the West supported the North, the South, and neither, three regiments from the Five Civilized Nations in Indian Territory fought for the Confederacy. Some were slaveholders, and some hoped to gain greater autonomy with a southern nation than they had with the United States.

Like Lincoln, Congress was also desperate to secure the support of the Union slave states of Maryland, Kentucky, Delaware, and Missouri and also hopeful that some of the seceding states would reverse positions. In late July 1861 the U.S. Congress adopted the Crittenden-Johnson Resolution (John J. Crittenden, representative from Kentucky, and Andrew Johnson, senator from Tennessee), which affirmed that the aim of the war was limited: to "defend and maintain the supremacy of the Constitution and to preserve the Union." It specified that the war was not for "overthrowing or interfering with the rights or established institutions" of the seceded states. The resolution helped reassure nervous slaveholders in the border states. Ramifications elsewhere had to be dealt with later. In Europe, for instance, antislavery activists felt little compulsion to support the North when the paramount issue in the struggle was defined as one of the Union's life rather than slavery's death. Since "the North does not proclaim abolition and never pretended to fight for anti-slavery," one Englishman asked, why should they "be fairly called upon to sympathize so warmly with the Federal cause?"

Resolutions and words notwithstanding, major events have major outcomes, not all of them anticipated. Although few acknowledged it in

1860, a drawn-out civil war would mean that slavery was doomed. A slave system requires strict adherence to the order of things, and civil wars bring disorder. An enslaved population with some autonomy during war years became less tractable and less willing to pretend otherwise. Some who play the contingency game aver that if the South had been let alone to secede, or had been victorious in war, slavery would still have ended. The Confederacy, after all, would still have been part of a world that was increasing its denunciation of enslaved labor. Brazil was the only other major country that continued to have a slave system. Moreover, if the United States became two nations, the boundaries of bondage would have been more porous with the Confederacy's northern neighbor as opposed to slavery as its southern neighbor of Mexico, neither of which would have been required to obey fugitive slave laws. Some use this reasoning as an excuse to say that Lincoln was wrong to fight secession. It is likely that a future South, if it had been left alone, would have come to a decision to end slavery in a modernizing world (Brazil outlawed slavery in 1888), but it would have done so gradually. Furthermore, the nation might very well have institutionalized white supremacy into its legal system. Such an end to slavery in the United States might have forfeited the Age of Lincoln's most enduring achievement: inscription into the nation's founding document the principle of equal rights without regard to race.

Six

"The Coming of the Lord"

IN NOVEMBER 1863 Augustus Bennett, a white abolitionist of New York, ordered his men, African American soldiers of the United States Colored Troops, into formation to witness a firing squad, to teach them a brand of truth and discipline as well as the limits of freedom. Bennett had been astonished earlier to find the soldiers of Company A, Third South Carolina Volunteers, stacking their arms outside his tent in protest of discriminatory pay and unfair treatment. The southern-born former slaves had enlisted in the Union cause to fight their old masters under promises of equality. Instead, they had been used for all sorts of rough and degrading labor—work for menials, not soldiers, they believed—issued poor rations (and their families none at all), and paid barely half the wage earned by the lowest white private. Bennett himself had complained to his superiors of these inequities, without redress. But when his troops, tired of excuses and broken promises, refused to obey orders, Bennett stepped in to crush their strike. The senior noncommissioned officer to the company, Sergeant William Walker, was arrested, tried for mutiny, and condemned to be shot. The case aroused outrage across the North, but Walker was duly executed and his rebellious company reorganized.

Here notions of right and truth seemed to diverge all too harshly from freedom's rhetoric and bright visions, yet white military men and Republican leaders insisted that justice had been done. Although Americans might rally to a "battle cry of freedom," even radicals like Bennett understood that liberty could exist only within a context of order, maintained by law and violence both. Demands for workers' rights and racial justice could be urged only so far before the state would use its terrible swift sword to defend broader imperatives. There was a war to be won, after all, and the killing of William Walker demonstrates perhaps better than any other event what northerners and southerners thought winning required. As much as they were fighting for a spectacularly ill-defined freedom, Americans on both sides in the Civil War struggled in defense of particular notions of conservative order that they saw as desperately besieged. The contest between these mighty forces transformed a budding republic into a potent modern nation.

In early spring of 1861, while Congress discussed compromises and options, Confederate fever seemed to be waning across the South, just as Lincoln hoped. As the tasks of spring cultivation beckoned once more, men put down their muskets, picked up their hoes, and prepared to put politics aside for a season. In Montgomery, Confederate brinksmanship seemed to have failed. There had been no meaningful negotiations with the North, and few prospects that the North would yield. Southerners who were not looking for rapprochement were also disappointed. In vain they hoped that Lincoln could be needled into some rash act that would drive the Upper South out of the Union. Without activity, the rebel cause looked likely to fail. The answer was the same one John Brown had understood barely a year before, at the hour of his own death. According to the secessionist radical Edmund Ruffin of Virginia, who had hurried across Virginia to see John Brown swing, "The shedding of blood will serve to change many voters in the hesitating states from the submission or procrastinating ranks, to the zealous for immediate secession." As much as some disunionist leaders insisted that secession could be accomplished without war, most men believed that battle was the honorable road to southern independence.

Confederates were smarting with that ever-injured sense of honor that southerners seemingly loved to parade. Once they announced secession, allowing forts and military installations within their territory to remain garrisoned by federal soldiers felt injurious to rebel notions of proper self-regard. Confederates could not consider themselves masters of their home soil if Union troops remained upon it. Furthermore, southern political leaders in favor of secession understood in the weeks after the formation of the Confederacy that only the threat of war—to which Lincoln steadily refused to succumb—could hold southerners close to the radical cause. If the sense of crisis lessened, support for disunion would surely melt away. Power was for the taking, and now was the time.

Such notions drove the odd events that took place in Charleston harbor in mid-April 1861. In late December, Major Robert Anderson of the First U.S. Artillery had spiked the guns of Fort Moultrie and stolen away with a small detachment of troops under cover of darkness to Fort Sumter, the recently constructed, and not quite finished, federal fort that dominated the harbor's mouth. Local secessionists, who had demanded the surrender of all national property, were outraged, but most expected the crisis to end amicably. It almost did. While Union and Confederate politicians squabbled over the terms of Sumter's surrender, Anderson sat for photographic portraits and Union soldiers shopped for vegetables in Charleston market. Simply to preserve the status quo while negotiations proceeded, and thinking that the South Carolinians would not object to a shipment of food, Lincoln wrote Governor Francis Pickens that he was going to replenish Fort Sumter's food supplies only. But the South dared not wait.

And so it was that at 4:30 a.m. on April 12, Brigadier General Pierre Gustave Toutant Beauregard ordered South Carolina militia, now constituted as Confederate troops, to fire on Fort Sumter. The honor of firing a ceremonial first shot was accorded to Ruffin, who handed out admonitory gifts to fellow fire-eaters, souvenir pikes he brought from John Brown's raid. He then rallied the cause of disunion in the streets of Charleston.

From early morning on the twelfth till midafternoon the next day, shots of all calibers flew from scores of guns ranged around Charleston harbor, arced gently toward the wall of Fort Sumter—and bounced off. Federal troops responded in kind, and Confederate troops applauded their heroic foe and chased missiles sent their way, which rolled harmlessly along the beach. A few stray salvos did manage to knock down Sumter's flagpole and start a fire among the fort's interior buildings, which prompted Confederate officials to send emissaries across to their adversaries, offering the aid of the city's fire brigades, complete with engines, to help put out the blaze. Such assistance was honorably declined.

A stranger battle had never been fought. The South, it seems, had no idea how to fight the war it had now started. Since the South had drawn up no plans to follow the bombardment with a landing of troops, the cannonading would doubtless have gone on ineffectually until both sides had exhausted their ammunition, if not for the inebriated courage of Louis T. Wigfall. This notoriously besotted Carolinian, who had injured Preston Brooks in a duel and caused "Bully Brooks" to walk with a cane, had migrated to Texas in the 1840s in a fairly unsuccessful attempt to rescue his reputation. Wigfall, back in South Carolina and looking for a good fight, managed to commandeer a rowboat, and he and a slave rowed over to Fort Sumter. At that point the drunken Confederate weaved his way up to a gun embrasure, stuck his sword through the opening, and shouted, "Surrender!" at the bewildered Yankees on the other side. They did, amazingly enough. Wigfall then rowed back to the Confederate side, that the South might know he had won the battle for them. While the conquering hero was making the voyage back, however, a second, official southern delegation landed at the fort and demanded that Anderson give up the fight. Learning that Wigfall had beaten them to the punch, the amazed Confederate higher-ups insisted that Wigfall had no right to demand or accept the surrender, and that the battle must go on. So it did, momentarily. A couple of hours later, appropriate functionaries agreed upon terms of surrender. No duel was ever concluded in more ludicrous fashion.

The first clash of arms between Americans had been splendidly concluded. No one had died on either side, no one was seriously hurt, and only the fort itself was outwardly pockmarked and inwardly scorched. As predicted, war, so far, was a glorious thing. Anderson, a Kentucky slaveholder, seemed happy just to have concluded his responsibilities in soldierly fashion, regardless of the outcome. But there would have to be blood, as both Brown and Ruffin had affirmed. As Union troops marched out of the fort, yet another ceremony went awry. A cannon fired in honor of the colors being hauled down burst, killing a Union private.

The outbreak of hostilities at Fort Sumter precipitated Lincoln's call on April 15 for seventy-five thousand military volunteers for a ninety-day tour of duty, emphasizing in the call that the troops were needed for defense of the nation's capital. The initial response was overwhelming, and the War Department—which consisted at this stage only of Secretary

Simon Cameron and a handful of clerks—found itself swamped by the myriad problems involved in sextupling the size of armed forces overnight and setting them in motion.

With Lincoln's call to arms, the Confederates at last had evidence that Lincoln meant to coerce the South, stripping slavery's champions of the freedom rightfully theirs. Southern farmers turned away from their fields once more, responding to Confederate calls to defend their homes and their liberty. States that had not done so already began mustering troops, though far more flooded in than the best-prepared could handle. More critically, Lincoln's call for troops spawned a new wave of secession activity across the Upper South. On May 23, Virginia joined the Confederacy. Arkansas, North Carolina, and Tennessee soon followed suit, decrying the "unjust wanton war" caused by Abraham Lincoln. "The division must be made on the line of slavery," one man told a North Carolina newspaper. "The South must go with the South." Reflecting the centrality of slavery to the Civil War was the order in which the states seceded: from the first state of South Carolina on December 20, 1860, to the last of Tennessee on June 8, 1861, the proportion of the state's enslaved population predicted how quickly the legislatures voted for secession. The new Confederacy, now eleven states, authorized recruitment of an astounding four hundred thousand soldiers.

For the young men who donned the Blue or the Gray that first spring—or the many other colors that characterized uniforms in the first volunteer regiments—war seemed festive and glamorous, a high-minded frolic. Military service was a grand romantic adventure or a showcase for strutting masculinity as a practical duty of citizenship. In years past many young lads had taken part in annual excursions and exchange visits of volunteer militia companies, where they had demonstrated their prowess on the drill ground, paraded showy uniforms, struck manly poses, and toasted fraternity and honor far into the night. That was the sum of military service as most understood it: quite apart from saving their country or defending their principles, every recruit anticipated that a fellow in uniform would always stand in good stead with the ladies, and quite possibly with employers and customers too, once the little fighting was concluded.

Most white southern volunteers went to war to defend liberty as they understood it. From the first call to support a war for southern independence, white men and women interpreted the meaning of the conflict from the perspective of their own families, relatives, and friends. While the political struggle over power that caused the breakup of the Union focused on the issue of slavery, the men who filled the ranks went to defend their communities from what they deemed an implacable and godless northern bully. Southern soldiers came from both slaveholding and nonslaveholding households; either way they fought for rights they knew to be sanctioned by the Constitution and by custom. A mother in Tennessee, proud of her son's enlistment, gave this understanding its simplest formulation: "Our brave and true hearted soldiers . . . are fighting for liberty." Slaveholder James B. Griffin of South Carolina gladly rode off to Virginia as part of the Wade Hampton Legion, traveling on a fine-blooded horse, with two enslaved body servants to wait on him, two trunks, and his favorite hunting dog. He wrote to his wife, pregnant with their eighth child, that he was "battling for Liberty and independence." Like many southerners, he went further. Certain that it was better to fight "than be a Slave, *Yea* worse than a slave to Yankee Masters," Griffin and others waged war against tyranny.

Northern soldiers also were certain they fought for liberty, because the integrity of the United States was essential to that liberty. It would take some time for their concept of liberty to include freedom for the enslaved also, but the language was there from the beginning. A soldier from Vermont wrote in his diary, "I thank God my love of liberty is so large that it gives me courage to face the enemy without trembling." Another soldier wrote, "Let America set this example before the world and the time will soon come when freedom to all men of every race and color shall be universal." A soldier from Massachusetts wrote to his wife, "I do feel that the liberty of the world is placed in our hands to defend, and if we are overcome then farewell to freedom." Aware of the connections of Union, liberty, and slavery, most soldiers drew on a higher authority as they contemplated killing and being killed. Behind abstract principles stood a firm conviction that they stood with the righteous.

Indeed, soldiers on both sides were overwhelmingly Protestant and prayerful and often invoked millennial aspirations of helping to bring about God's kingdom on earth. As one Union soldier wrote, "We will be held responsible before God if we don't do our part in helping to transmit this boon of civil and religious liberty down to succeeding generations." Ministers told their congregations that God expected them to work and fight on behalf of righteousness. In New York City, Reverend Henry Ward Beecher preached that the North followed the teachings of Christ: opening prison doors, freeing "those that are bound." If Christ came "to carry light to them that are in darkness and deliverance to the oppressed," then Christ opposed the slave regime. For his part southern Methodist minister J. W. Tucker preached to his Confederate flock that "your cause is the cause of God, the cause of Christ, of humanity. It is a conflict of truth with error—of Bible with Northern infidelity—of pure Christianity with Northern fanaticism."

Fighting men both South and North proclaimed God's blessing: "Our cause is the sacred one of Liberty, and God is on our side." A Florida recruit wrote, "We look to God & trust in him to sustain us in this our just cause"; from Alabama, "I have always believed that God was with us." A Mississippian at Vicksburg wrote, "Surely the God of battles is on our side." A Union private from Pennsylvania wrote, "God will prosper us in the movements about to be made against this cursed rebellion." A soldier from New York was sure that "we can in righteousness claim the protection of heaven" and that God would "bestow in great abundance His blessings upon His and our cause." Echoing Abraham Lincoln's certainty that God did not want the American experiment in liberty to cease, a soldier wrote to his wife in 1864, "I cannot believe Providence intends to destroy this Nation, this great asylum for the oppressed of all other nations and build a slave Oligarchy on the ruins thereof."

Ultimately about two million men fought for the Union, about 850,000 for the Confederacy. On both sides tens of thousands were drafted against their will or drawn in by lucrative bounties. Most soldiers were between eighteen and twenty-nine years of age, though children of twelve and white-haired grandfathers in their sixties shouldered arms, too. Nine-year-old Johnny Clem (afterward John Lincoln Clem) tagged along with the troops passing through his Ohio town and later won fame as "Johnny Shiloh," the "drummer boy of Chickamauga" who put a pistol ball square between a rebel officer's eyes. Manhood came early too for General Ulysses S. Grant's twelve-year-old son, Fred, who witnessed the horrors at Vicksburg.

War included many tedious hours of inactivity. Some used time in camp wisely; as one soldier wrote his mother, "Maw I have lurned to write in Camp well a nuf to write letters my self." All missed home. A soldier from Alabama wrote, "When watermelons get ripe, send me one in a letter." To alleviate boredom, camp life involved prostitution, drinking, and gambling, and these profane aspects disturbed some of the very religious young soldiers, northern and southern. Some soldiers occasionally could leave camp for a visit to the local town. One soldier from Illinois recorded in his diary that he enjoyed a Shakespeare play, *Richard III*, on a trip to Nashville while his company was stationed nearby. He was particularly taken with the performance of a fine actor, one John Wilkes Booth.

Music also helped pass the time. According to Robert E. Lee, "I don't believe we can have an army without music." Liberty was featured in many of the songs of war. The proposed Confederate national anthem, penned by St. George Tucker early in the conflict and sung to the tune of "The Star-Spangled Banner," suggested that northern tyranny was crushing Liberty. The "Battle Cry of Freedom" stirred both northern and southern soldiers. Composed by northerner George Root in 1862, the song included the words "not a man shall be a slave." Southern lyricists changed the wording but not the catchy tune. Yankee Daniel Decatur Emmett's "Dixie" called on southerners to feel nostalgia as they "look away" to their homeland. In striking contrast was the Union call on God to wreak vengeance for injustice. The New England social activist Julia Ward Howe mixed the tune of "John Brown's Body" with new words more grand and terrible, urging Americans to "die to make men free," after the example of John Brown and Christ both. Howe's immensely self-satisfied "Battle Hymn of the Republic" offered warming prophecy to a grieving, bewildered people. Confederate defeat meant "the coming of the Lord" itself, she promised, the advent of "His Truth" unto a sinful nation redeemed by faith, grace, and blood.

In truth, most volunteers knew absolutely nothing of the horrors of modern war that lay ahead. Both men and women thrilled to the poetry of Tennyson and his heroic presentation of the recent Crimean War. American newspapers in the late 1850s crowded their columns with reports about the Sepoy mutiny in India and the Taiping rebellion in China—a ten-year civil war that utterly dwarfed the conflict about to break out in the United States—yet there was something wonderfully exotic and thrilling about the vague, distant dangers they depicted, hearkening back to *la gloire* of the Napoleonic era itself. Who would want to miss the chance to take part in such a magnificent undertaking, exhibiting patriotism, courage, and determination, the chief values of honor itself?

The armies of both sides presented a militarized cross-section of the publics from which they were drawn. As in peacetime, most women and children remained within the home, though scores of laundresses, prostitutes, and cooks clustered near any encampment. Just as they were beginning to filter into civilian skilled trades like printing and teaching, some women even slipped into the ranks. An estimated four hundred women impersonated men and fought. Most went undetected, but six were discovered when they gave birth; Albert D. J. Cashire, who fought at Vicksburg, was not discovered until 1911, when she had to see a doctor.* Most soldiers were farmers, mechanics, clerks, laborers, and craftsmen, the same sorts of working people and small property holders who constituted the bulk of the adult white male populations of the two contenders. Men of property and standing, unsurprisingly, filled the officer corps of both sides, though volunteer regiments were allowed to elect their leaders in the early going. A veritable flood of southern working people, black and white, nearly half a million in all, put down their hoes and went north to support the Union. Half that number joined Union forces, multiplying the host of Mr. Lincoln's Army. Within the Confederate forces, thousands of enslaved African Americans, some of them decked out in rebel gray, performed the arduous and routine labor that kept southern armies functioning. In Louisiana, one regiment of free black "Native Guards" even raised their own banner in defense of the Confederacy. A few African Americans joined northern units surreptitiously or informally before 1863.

Of all the soldiers who passed through Union ranks before April 1865, about one-fourth were immigrants, many of them enlisting and not a few going straight into the army not long after their ships had docked. These immigrants largely took up the slack for the tens of thousands of northern volunteers who decided not to reenlist after their initial terms of ninety days had expired, and still more who simply walked away from military service, particularly in the dark days of 1862 and

---

* Some at that time wanted to take her name off the Illinois monument at Vicksburg, but the men she fought with insisted the name remain.

1863. Comparatively few immigrants were drawn to the South even in conditions of peace, and even if they had hoped to lend the Confederacy a hand, almost none made it through the naval blockade that Union forces set up along the coast. This was bad news for slaveholders, who saw disease and desertion melt their armies away with each passing season after 1863. In the early part of 1861, however, no one knew the armies would need to replenish their troops.

Confidence overflowed on both sides of the conflict, and comparative strengths were tallied and debated. In 1860 northerners outnumbered southerners in the Confederate states by more than two to one, and that ratio was steadily growing. In 1860 America was rural, but one-tenth of southerners lived in urban areas versus one-fourth of northerners. In 1860 only thirteen southern towns had a population of 10,000 or more. With its population of 169,000, New Orleans was the only large southern urban center. Charleston, Savannah, Richmond, and Memphis each had between 20,000 and 50,000 inhabitants. (New York City had 805,600 residents.) Nearly half the southern population was enslaved—considered unavailable for military service and an actual fifth column in the South.

The North could move goods and manpower far more easily and quickly than the South: its roads and canals were better and more plentiful, its shipping facilities and available tonnage were much greater, and it possessed 70 percent of the nation's railroad tracks. Southerners, by contrast, could boast only a hodgepodge of railroad lines of varying gauges split by the rugged Appalachians. Another Confederate vulnerability was the lack of any sort of navy in the spring of 1861. A thinly populated coastline, stretching hundreds of miles, presented Union commanders with a host of tempting targets. Fast, new steam-powered ships armed with powerful rifled cannons could load Union troops at New York or Baltimore, sail south to any of a dozen points, pound coastal fortifications into rubble, and put soldiers ashore before southern defenses could be mobilized. For the Confederacy it was impossible to cover all its vast shores, impossible to anticipate where Federals might land, and nearly impossible to move its own soldiers rapidly from point to point to counter such threats.

In terms of the matériel needed to wage war, the Confederacy also faced deficiencies. The Union states outproduced the seven original

Confederate states by a factor of ten to one before the war, and once the crisis came, that disparity widened further still. Clothes, shoes, iron, firearms, and the raw materials that made them poured out of the North. Although Virginia was home to the arsenal at Harpers Ferry, the naval base at Norfolk, and the Tredegar Iron Works in Richmond, which could make heavy guns, northern industrial capitalists wielded considerably more economic power by far.

The South, of course, possessed cotton, and southerners believed that without adequate supplies of the staple going northward and overseas to England, hard-pressed millworkers would soon riot in the streets, bringing Yankee aggression to a halt. The problem with this theory was that worldwide cotton production had increased in the late 1850s—as some worried planters had already noted—and the bumper crop that came to market in the spring of 1860 had created vast reserves packed away in storehouses across England and New England. Furthermore, British investors, leery of the unrest in America through the 1850s, had already moved their money into Indian, Egyptian, and even Australian cotton fields. When England's factories closed, like those in Manchester, it was because markets in Asia were already glutted with finished cotton products. England's leading importer, China, was being ravaged by a bloody civil war of its own. Moreover, and more important, opium was beginning to rival cotton as England's chief export to China after British victory in the Opium Wars (1839–43, 1856–60) opened up the extremely lucrative market for that drug.

Just as King Cotton did precious little on the world stage to rescue Confederate dreams, so too the wealth created in the cotton South was not much help in financing the war effort itself. While northern capitalists channeled the profits they earned back into industrial growth or lent them out at interest to banks and corporations, southern planters sank the money they made mostly into acquiring more lands and slaves. In the Mississippi Delta or the new hummock lands of Florida, such strategies yielded stunning personal returns on the eve of the Civil War, but they made the task of finding hard money problematical from the start. The difficulty became all the more grim as the war went on.

The Confederacy, however, was not doomed to fail. Mobilization for war took time, and those states with the largest enslaved populations, those that had seceded by February 1861, had the largest militias at the ready to put down slave insurrection. Moreover, southern military tradition trained men for martial leadership. The Confederacy also had the easier job of defending its territory, whereas the Union had the formidable task of subduing a rebellion.

Southern determination, Confederate leaders predicted, would prove decisive. After all, the Bible was rife with examples of a small force of the righteous subduing a larger force of the wicked; David and Goliath was only one example southerners called upon for encouragement. American history itself showed a time when a country, weaker materially and economically, defeated a stronger one. In 1775 a smaller group with less might had taken on the greatest empire in the world, and won. Confederates so identified with the American Revolution that they pronounced secession the second American Revolution. They learned from that first American Revolution that greater will and commitment to a cause could defeat a superior power. Daring commanders who demanded the impossible and soldiers who delivered on those demands, the readiness to sustain artillery shells exploding in the midst of formations, the willingness to charge straight into enemy lines with bayonets against superior gunfire, the eagerness to die for a cause—that, Confederate leaders proclaimed, would win this war. When victory depended on which side was willing to stand its ground in spite of the punishment meted out, all the material and population advantages the North could muster would not count. Honor, however, would. Northern superiority in matériel and population would not be a factor in a very short war, and that is what southerners expected when their leaders insisted upon seeking one.

Military theorists—such as they were at the time—also expected any confrontation between North and South to be bloody and brief. This was a romantic age that believed that the fate of a nation could hang on a single battle. Europe itself, these theorists claimed, had hung in the balance at Waterloo, a single long-shot battle. That mistaken judgment grew logically enough out of a belief in the decisive role of battle that military strategists had developed gradually over the previous two centuries. The financial and logistical problems attending fielding mass armies, the argument went, propelled rivals to seek a quick solution to the pressures they faced on the battlefield. War, then, was still seen as an eighteenth-century duel, likely to be over in an afternoon or two, rather than as a long-term process of winning territory and suffering body counts.

On both sides, public men proclaimed that the conflict would be short, sharp, and decisive. One or two big battles, and the shout for "On to Richmond!" or "On to Washington!" would be realized. Neither government's treasury had enough money to wage war beyond those narrow limits, and the notion of running the conflict on credit occurred to only a few in the early stages. Neither could most men afford to devote to their country for very long the labor and time they needed to keep families, farms, and commercial concerns afloat. Even unmarried young men played an important role in maintaining family economies; only by shouldering a greater burden of work themselves could parents and siblings spare them for a season. By Christmas, nearly all felt sure, the soldiery of both sides would be back home recounting tales of military glory and preparing for spring planting or for another season of work.

Like the Confederates, Lincoln hoped for a short war, one that would beat the rebel forces decisively and return the seceding states to the Union. But the enormous size of the rebel army—and the size of the Confederacy itself—made the possibility of quick victory doubtful. The ancient veteran General Winfield Scott (who had served every president from Jefferson to Lincoln) had pressed upon the government a more patient and conservative "Anaconda" plan, encircling Dixie by land and sea, then using American material superiority to squeeze slowly inward. But this strategy seemed slow, unimaginably expensive, and too indirect to please political or army leaders. Politicians on both sides pressed their generals to resolve the crisis decisively, without delay.

What could be expected, then, of the contending armies that drew up along the small creek called Bull Run in northern Virginia on July 21, 1861? Although the assault that Union Major General Irvin McDowell planned was supposedly a secret, dozens of Washington notables had followed federal forces southward, planning to enjoy a picnic lunch as they watched the battle unfold. In truth, almost everyone must have known that a fight was in the making: northern newspapers were filled with demands for prompt action, Congress urged the president almost daily to do something, and McDowell himself was faced with the dilemma that his soldiers, still inadequately trained, were about to return to civilian life altogether as their ninety-day contracts expired.

In anticipation of a Union advance, Confederates split their smaller forces, with troops under Generals P.G.T. Beauregard, the victor at Fort

Sumter, and Joseph E. Johnston covering the approaches to Richmond, while Brigadier General Thomas J. Jackson barred entry to the rich Valley of Virginia farther west. The leadership of both sides knew each other well from previous service together stretching back to the Mexican War, and the classic rules of battlefield command that they had learned and taught together—most officers in both armies had been rather less soldiers than military instructors—made it abundantly clear what was about to unfold. In the ensuing battle the idiosyncratic Jackson, a bloody-minded, devout Presbyterian who trusted in "the vigorous use of the bayonet and the blessings of Providence," would acquire the nickname "Stonewall" for the courage of his Virginians in holding their ground—though it may also have been applied as a term of abuse for his failure to *advance* these soldiers in aid of hard-pressed comrades at a crucial moment. In either case, the notion of an unmoving Jackson lends a misleading stoicism to the battle and distorts the meaning of Confederate victory itself. To the rebels who would later call themselves his "foot cavalry," Jackson was "Tom Fool," a leader who marched his men to the point of mutiny and was almost assassinated for his efforts. What these soldiers could not know as they moved swiftly by road and rail to link up with Beauregard's and Johnston's outnumbered forces in time to stop the Yankees was that Jackson's hard charging had probably saved the day. The speed of his movement had given the slip to Union forces covering his front, and by effecting a juncture that McDowell rather rightly thought impossible, they had averted the fall of Richmond, and with it the possible end of the Confederate rebellion.

McDowell's report of the battle amply demonstrated how confused and amateurish the struggle had been. For farmers and shop clerks in uniform who faced fire for the first time here, the Battle of Manassas* was horrifyingly unlike the gallant martial pageant they had imagined war to be. Soldiers on both sides had trouble moving and firing in unison. Confederate flags looked like the American flag, and soldiers could not distinguish friend from foe. Too many failed to understand and obey the commands they received. In the heat of battle, many young men lost all sense of where they were or what to do next. Throughout the long summer day the conflict devolved into a series of reckless charges and

---

* Generally, the Union named battles after rivers; the Confederacy after towns.

desperate retreats. "We drove them for several hours," McDowell told his superiors, "and finally routed them. They rallied and repulsed us, but only to give us again the victory which seemed complete. But our men, exhausted with fatigue and thirst and confused by firing into each other, were attacked by the enemy's reserves, and driven from the position we had gained." By evening his soldiers had become "a confused mob, entirely demoralized," fleeing the field in complete disorder, throwing away their arms, and making tracks for Washington and points north, Confederate troops at their heels.

Future secretary of war Edwin M. Stanton did not expect the Confederates to stop: "The capture of Washington seems now to be inevitable; during the whole of Monday and Tuesday (July 22d and 23d) it might have been taken without resistance." That Confederates did not sweep on to crush McDowell's broken army and capture the northern capital itself owed partly to the spectacular thunderstorm that closed the day's hostilities but considerably more to the shock of battle that southern raw recruits had sustained that day. Combat was a deeply traumatic experience that few had anticipated, and having escaped with their lives, most felt little desire to undergo its terrors again on the morrow. General Johnston stressed how the exuberance of triumph actually undermined the victory they had won. "Exaggerated ideas of the victory, prevailing among our troops," he claimed, "cost us more men than the Federal army lost by defeat." Thinking they had done their duty and won the war, some Confederate volunteers simply left the ranks and went home. These cases reflected the woeful discipline that prevailed on both sides. In many more instances, soldiers reckoned that seeing battle once was quite enough and decamped to avoid facing it again. For these men the shock was overwhelming. In the space of a few hours virtually everything their culture and their leaders had taught them about war had been shown to be horrendously false. Volunteers realized that a war that killed more than a thousand Americans at one stroke without moving any closer to resolution was nothing like what politicians had promised. It would certainly not be nearly over by harvesttime that year and perhaps not the next either.

That sudden awareness was bad news especially for Abraham Lincoln. Beset on one side by jealous Republicans who angled to win power and fame by promoting their own plans for military victory, hounded on the other by Democrats who shouted for a speedy peace, Lincoln dared not admit how long and how costly suppressing the rebellion now appeared to be. And indeed, he seems in the late summer of 1861 to have been rather stubbornly unwilling to face the fact that hopes for a quick victory had been desperately misleading. Five days after Bull Run he fired McDowell, installing in his place Major General George B. McClellan as commander of the Army of the Potomac. Dashing, glib, and splendidly martial, McClellan assured the newspapers and the president that a more masterful drive on Richmond properly prepared was sure to bring the rebels to their knees. Ridiculing the tedious strategy of encirclement that Winfield Scott promoted, McClellan coaxed Lincoln into replacing him as Supreme Commander of the Union Armies on November 1. For a nation whose confidence had been badly shaken by defeat at Bull Run, this "Young Napoleon" seemed gloriously reassuring. Yet for all his promise of bold things to come when his soldiers moved south from Washington, McClellan refused to attack. While Lincoln wrote crossly that his new general had a case of the "slows," McClellan was hard at work organizing the Army of the Potomac into a disciplined fighting force. He restored morale, imposed order, and established a bureaucracy of training and logistics suited to waging modern warfare. While he played up the rhetoric of romantic victory, McClellan was steadily constructing a complex military machine.

The landing of Union forces in South Carolina demonstrated to both sides the unfolding of Scott's "Anaconda" strategy in remarkable ways that neither had anticipated. Caught in its coils were not only land and resources but people, too, and thousands rejoiced at its sudden embrace. While slaveholders fled at the sound of the first guns echoing over Port Royal Sound, and the few local nonslaveholding whites hunkered down sullenly, enslaved African Americans performed spontaneous acts of self-liberation on plantations all across the Sea Islands. They broke open storehouses and crossed the master's threshold. They donned his fine clothes, appropriated his plush furniture, drank his expensive liquor, slept in his soft beds, and called it all their own. They danced and feasted. Many of them stopped work for a season, while others went out to the fields and began to mark off the boundaries of an acreage they claimed for themselves, a long-held, impossible dream come true. A few performed minor acts of vandalism but nothing more. Everywhere

African Americans who found themselves suddenly unmastered committed deliberate acts of unambiguous self-government. By the most extraordinary decisions of everyday life—when to eat and sleep and work, how to speak, when to sing and pray and love and hate, all ordinary elements of life—African Americans made themselves free.

No sooner did Yankee soldiers step ashore, however, than they began to annul the astonishing revolution that freedpeople were creating. All the property of rebel masters was now declared "contraband," to be taken under the care of Uncle Sam. Most confounding of all to thousands of black people who had never heard the name of Dred Scott, the government of the blue-coated men with guns considered them chattels still, devoid of rights and unblessed by anything in the way of conscience or volition denoting freedom. Like all other sorts of property, the thousands of African Americans who had scarcely finished celebrating the hasty departure of Old Massa suddenly found that they had fallen under the Union government's control and might yet be delivered up to their old oppressors. The soldiers who landed near Beaufort on that November morning began the day as defenders of the Union and its laws. By sundown they had become, in spite of themselves, a slaveholders' army.

And yet though they were classified as contrabands themselves, African Americans understood that this uncertain status, as impoverished and regimented as it was, represented a pivotal break with slavery proper and voted with their feet. First at Port Royal and in northern Virginia, and then early in 1862 when Nashville and then New Orleans fell to Union forces, thousands of poor, illiterate, extraordinary black people, by ones and twos, decided to labor no more in bondage, turned their backs on slavery, and walked toward where they believed freedom lay. It was that simple and that remarkable. In the beginning it was mostly young African American men, unencumbered by children or the elderly, who dared lead the way. Black women young and old knew to fear danger from white men, regardless of the flag they followed, without going in search of it. Soon enough, however, undertaking journeys abundantly mixed with joy and sorrow, longing and trepidation, many of these former slaves too would follow along, bringing young and old after them.

As war progressed, many African Americans moved toward Union lines because the material conditions of plantation life had broken down utterly, or because their attempts to reach some sort of accommodation with their masters, balancing a measure of freedom with the security and order that working people—indeed, all people—instinctively crave, had capsized. It is clear, however, that Union soldiers and government officials were completely unprepared for this exodus and little comprehended its political import. Although treatment varied widely from one area to another, and from one regiment to another within any one place, African Americans who finally reached federal lines often found themselves turned back or abused, pressed into harsh military labor without compensation, or treated with contemptuous neglect. A few actually went back to their old masters, or set up for themselves as best they could, somewhere in the no-man's-land between the two sides. As significant as the northern "Anaconda" pressing in on the slaveholders' republic was the movement of the slaves themselves pressing out. In the ultimate destruction of the Confederacy, escape from slavery represented a powerful political act and a vital military force. By 1865 the refugees' numbers had grown to perhaps eight hundred thousand— about 20 percent of the total slave force. No population had greater right to view the war as providential. They fully intended to make liberty the measure of America's promise. More truly perhaps than any other segment of American society in the Civil War, these sojourners were freedom's footsoldiers.

Some sojourns took place by sea. On May 13, 1862, in the wee hours of the morning, federal ships off the coast of Charleston, South Carolina, noticed a Confederate transport steamer heading their way. Preparing to shoot, they held their fire when they saw the white flag of surrender. As the vessel came alongside, the pilot on board, African American Robert Smalls, shouted, "Good morning, sir! I have brought you some of the old United States' guns, sir!" Smalls, a slave who had rented himself out as a deckhand to the captain of the *Planter*, stole the boat and organized the escape with his wife, children, and others seeking freedom. In the dark of night Smalls stood boldly on the prow in the white captain's own stance, sailing the vessel past Confederate lookouts and giving the correct signals for passage. Smalls delivered to the federal fleet the boat, cannon, and guns, as well as a rebel naval code book and information on the location of rebel troops. According to the *Charleston*

Daily Courier, "Our community was intensely agitated Tuesday morning by the intelligence that the steamer *Planter,* for the last twelve months or more employed both in the State and Confederate service, had been taken possession of by her colored crew, steamed up and boldly run out to the blockades." Information that Smalls supplied to the U.S. fleet led to the Union seizure of Stono Inlet and River, an important base for future operations. In a report to the 37th Congress, President Lincoln quoted the secretary of the navy crediting the success of the operation on "information derived chiefly from the contraband pilot, Robert Smalls, who had escaped from Charleston."

By spring 1862 Union forces were determined to restrict and thwart the Confederacy's ability to utilize the little sustenance it could obtain, to starve it of economic resources. For the South, a successful defense turned on its ability to deny enemy battalions control of roads, rivers, and coastline along its borders. If rebels were still able to import the supplies they needed to make war and could disrupt the movement of matériel in the enemy's rear, it seemed likely they could prolong the war and bring the Yankees to the peace table. In the Far West, Confederates hoped to gain access to the Santa Fe Trail and gold in California. In March 1862 northern and southern forces met at Glorieta Pass, near Santa Fe, New Mexico, fighting a decisive but ultimately meaningless battle. Though Henry Sibley's army drove off Union forces at the end of three days' fighting, Confederate wagon trains had been destroyed and their expedition stymied. Even without this loss, however, it is hard to see what Sibley's thrust might have accomplished in strategic terms or how it aimed to benefit the South. Absent a railroad connection, the movement of men and supplies to and from California was an arduous task even in peacetime. Under conditions of war, the goldfields of the West and the fine harbor at San Francisco could offer little aid to the Confederate cause, even if seized.

In these months, too, southerners set to work establishing a fleet of raiding privateers and blockade runners, aimed at disrupting northern shipping and bringing needed supplies past patrolling federal vessels. Beginning in July 1861 Congress approved extensive efforts to increase Union naval forces, but how could they be expected to effectively shut off the ten ports, 160 inlets, and 3,500 miles of coastline that the Confederacy claimed? Estimates are that northern warships stopped only about one in every ten Confederate vessels in 1861, but about half of them by 1865. Moreover, southern export trade did fall to about one-third of prewar levels. Although federal seizures were relatively low, the fear of losing ships and cargo curtailed merchant activity on both sides of the Atlantic. More significant than the blockade, however, were economic disruptions within the Confederacy. Southern leaders and bureaucrats tangled up rebel shipping as effectively as northern blockaders could have hoped, and such vessels as did cross enemy lines commonly carried as many salable luxury items as vital military supplies. Without effective control, administration, and international cooperation, Confederate war needs remained at the mercy of apolitical market forces. As Union assaults took southern ports one by one between 1861 and 1864, rebels were cut off from vital outside support.

Confederate measures to threaten northern foreign trade proved just as poorly thought out as efforts to thwart the Union blockade. Confederate merchant raiders like the *Alabama*, deemed pirate marauders by Union regulations, annoyed shipping on both sides of the Atlantic, but their economic impact was negligible. There were not enough privateers to matter, and their efforts could never be effectively coordinated. Because crews frequently jumped ship as soon as they made port—as blue-water sailors were traditionally wont to do—only hopes for plunder could keep them in check, and that proved a poor basis for waging war. Politically, raiding tactics only confirmed sentiment in England and France that Confederates were backward renegades to be shunned, however tempting an alliance might have seemed in Europe's conservative corners.

More important for southern hopes was the emergence of partisans and guerrilla bands along the Confederacy's contested margins. Throughout the conflict farmers and merchants on both sides kept commodities and profits flowing across the porous borders, though some citizens more properly placed the duties of citizenship above personal gain. The trouble was, within the crucial border states, no firm consensus existed as to whether North or South upheld the right in the national quarrel. Lincoln recognized this danger in the war's first days, as rioting mobs in Baltimore pelted Union regiments moving through its streets and disrupted railroad travel toward the battlefront. His efforts to curb such resistance— overzealously abandoning civil liberties and dismissing habeas corpus—

only encouraged those who feared Republican "tyranny." In Tennessee, Kentucky, and Missouri, and even into northern states like Indiana, Confederate sympathizers worked to disrupt federal efforts and intimidate potential Union recruits. "Dark lantern" societies rallied Confederate loyalists in the North and comforted antiwar politicians like Ohio's Clement Vallandigham.

Shocked by the bloody losses at Bull Run, uncertain of the willingness of their amateur soldiers to stand and fight, and worried about the political fallout of more directly coercive measures, Lincoln and the Union leadership hoped that the strategy of encirclement and blockade would bring the South to its knees. In the West, Union troops under General Henry W. Halleck were also slow-moving until Ulysses S. Grant got permission from Halleck to attack. In February 1862, Grant's men captured the important rebel strongholds of Fort Henry and Fort Donelson, and in April, General John Pope's men scooped up seven thousand Rebels at Island No. 10, effectively seizing the Mississippi for Union control above Memphis and driving southern forces out of western and central Tennessee. When Confederates responded to these threats by shifting troops up from Louisiana, Union flag officer David Farragut (southern born and reared) waltzed in to occupy New Orleans and penetrated upriver as far as the rebel citadel at Vicksburg. The most splendid aspect of these victories, from a political standpoint, was how cheaply they had been won. During his first assignment as colonel of the Twenty-first Illinois, Grant had discovered that his Confederate adversaries in Missouri were "as frightened of me as I was of them," and he continued to use this knowledge to tactical advantage.

Lincoln, while gratified with these western victories, was deeply frustrated over his generals' lack of coordination. The president continued to press McClellan to use the enormous Army of the Potomac that he had spent so many months organizing and training. The whole point of Scott's encirclement strategy had been to strike the enemy simultaneously at many points. That tactic had won important territorial gains in the West, worn out rebel forces as they marched fruitlessly back and forth, and demoralized Confederate commanders. Strategic success was won in the West because Grant and Farragut acted. Back east, McClellan maddeningly stood still.

The problem was, as Lincoln's generals had already discovered, that southern leaders conducted battle in a far more direct, confident, and bloody-minded manner. Generals such as Stonewall Jackson thought the South erred grievously in standing patiently on the defensive. "War means fightin'," Nathan Bedford Forrest explained, "and fightin' means killin'." The more rebels took the war to the Yankees, such leaders believed, the sooner peace would be won. Southern generals at this time perhaps better understood the stunning new lethality of the troops they commanded and the shock value of that force meted out mercilessly against the foe. In some measure this explains the horrifying tactics of 1862 and early 1863, when Confederate forces so often took the offensive (or conducted an "active defense") and Union desertion rates soared. On a score of battlefields in Virginia and Tennessee, the same awful scenario played itself out: the devastating cannonade, the bloodcurdling rebel yell, the bayonet, and a field, won or lost, strewn with thousands of shattered bodies. This southern tactic could not endure because those bodies did not wear only blue. Too many wore the gray, "butternut" brown, or simple homespun of the Confederacy. Nevertheless, the revulsion that enormous casualty lists prompted in the North put Abraham Lincoln's back against the wall.

Those lessons, already hinted at in the confusion of Bull Run, came home with full force in the slaughter at Shiloh. Smarting from the string of defeats that Halleck and Grant had inflicted and from the steady withdrawal of his own soldiers from western Tennessee, Confederate General Albert Sidney Johnston turned about. "What the people want is a battle and a victory," he decided.

Early in April 1862, at a serene Methodist church amid the rolling hills of southwestern Tennessee, about twenty miles from an important railroad junction at Corinth, Mississippi, William Tecumseh Sherman and his men were enjoying a quiet rest. Over the next two days, however, the church became a hospital, and its very floorboards were torn up to build coffins. At dawn on April 6, the Confederate Army of the Mississippi, 42,000 strong, commanded by Johnston, poured out of the dense woods behind the church in a surprise attack on Union forces. Confederates hoped to beat the Union army before General Don Carlos Buell and his 35,000-strong Army of the Ohio reinforced Sherman and Grant. Unprepared, overconfident, largely untried in battle, and separated from the main body of their advancing army, northern divisional commanders at first refused to believe that they were under attack at all. By nightfall, their forces had been pushed back to the very banks of the Tennessee; thousands of their raw recruits were dead, hopelessly disorganized, or simply too stunned to defend themselves; and a violent rainstorm was pouring down. Quite possibly that tempest alone—and the death of Johnston at the head of his troops—was all that saved the North from complete disaster. With the morning came fresh Union troops under Buell, moving downriver by gunboat and steamboat. They marched into battle singing "Dixie" and rolled back the rebel gains of the day before. Northern forces would eventually pitch the Confederates back to their important base at Corinth. For the moment, however, both sides stood back from the awful scene at Shiloh and wondered what lay ahead.

"The scene on the field," remarked Sherman, who commanded one of the worst-mauled Union divisions, "would have cured anybody of war." Grant's decision, against the advice of underlings, "to attack" the enemy "at daylight and whip them" had turned the tide but at fearful cost. In one and a half days, more than twenty thousand Union and Confederate soldiers, most of them young men in their teens or early twenties, had been killed or wounded. This outcome nearly doubled the total casualties inflicted on both sides in all the battles and skirmishes waged in 1861. Gone forever were romantic dreams of what warfare meant—and hopes of quick victory as well. "I had no idea of war until then," one soldier wrote typically, "and would have given anything in the world if I could have been away."

Back east Confederate General Joseph Johnston was poised behind the Rappahannock, waiting for McClellan to make his move. Waiting just as anxiously was a meddlesome and increasingly distrustful Lincoln. What McClellan proposed was a grand seaborne invasion, taking one hundred thousand troops by water up the James River to the very gates of Richmond. While a token force froze the Confederate army along the Rappahannock, McClellan would walk in the back door. Should the Confederates turn and fight him southeast of Richmond, McClellan's vastly superior numbers would surely prevail and the road to the rebel capital would be open, one way or the other. Lincoln did not like the plan. Lincoln insisted that McClellan had two missions. One was to act decisively with the immense army he had gathered and trained to defeat the Confederate army. The other was to protect the capital, which required the Army of the Potomac to remain interposed between Washington and the Army of Northern Virginia. With those objectives in mind, Lincoln preferred an overland advance. Moreover, Lincoln believed correctly that this Peninsula campaign was predicated in part on McClellan's unwillingness to fight a major battle. At this time, however, he accepted McClellan's strategy, especially once the Peninsula campaign was under way.

It all went horribly wrong for McClellan. On April 4, 1862, the Army of the Potomac, 121,500 strong, began its march up the Virginia Peninsula. Plagued by poor roads and drenched by heavy rains, intimidated by impressive-looking fortifications manned by a handful of rebels who moved cannons around to appear more numerous, the Yankees made slow progress. A month later, as bad water and fever ravaged his regiments, McClellan had advanced only as far as Williamsburg. There, Confederate General James Longstreet delayed Union forces long enough for the Confederates to gather artillery and wagons for withdrawal. Finally, with Union forces almost within sight of Richmond, and southerners digging trenches furiously, General Joe Johnston counterattacked at the Battle of Seven Pines (May 31–June 1, 1862). James B. Griffin, part of Johnston's troops, wrote to his wife, Leila, "We marched two days and bivouacked both nights in the worst weather I almost ever saw. The men had no tents and but one blanket each." Fighting in torrential rains, the rebels (who had concentrated forces from all over the eastern theater to even the odds) halted McClellan's advance. The Union lost five thousand men, the Confederacy six thousand. And yet McClellan began telegraphing Washington about the "vastly" superior number of Confederates he believed were facing him—he estimated the almost ninety thousand troops to be two hundred thousand!—and his perplexity about how to handle the rebel host.

At Seven Pines the Confederate General Joe Johnston was badly wounded, and on June 1 Davis replaced him with Robert E. Lee. At first the men derisively called their new leader "the King of Spades" because of Lee's insistence on building trenches. Much earlier Lee had declined the Union's request for his leadership, and he joined the secessionists only reluctantly, after his beloved state of Virginia joined the Confederacy. Davis's appointment of Lee ultimately lengthened the war. A less brilliant commander would not have been able to hold out as long as Lee's army did. There is a double-edged irony here: because the early aims of the war were not construed as including the emancipation of the slaves, a quicker conclusion would have reconciled the states without eliminating slavery. Thus it happened that Lee, who would remark after the war that he had always opposed slavery, actually helped bring about the institution's demise.

McClellan responded to the appointment of Lee with a certain assurance that Lee would cause him little trouble. According to McClellan at the time, Lee was "cautious and weak. Personally brave and energetic to a fault, he yet is wanting in moral firmness when pressed by heavy responsibility, and is likely to be timid and irresolute in action." In later life his autobiography recorded a different reaction. Having fought and lost to Lee, McClellan wrote in retrospect: "Gen. Lee and I knew each other well in the days before the war . . . I had the highest respect for his ability as a commander, and knew he was not a general to be trifled with or carelessly afforded an opportunity of striking a fatal blow." McClellan excused himself for being cautious: "It was perfectly natural under these circumstances that both of us should exercise a certain amount of caution." The caution, however, was one-sided.

Apart from the near-disaster of Seven Pines, McClellan's anxiety intensified because of Stonewall Jackson, whose demonstrations far away in the Shenandoah Valley during the spring of 1862 were making fools of his opponents. Marching and countermarching a force of seventeen thousand Confederates, he led more than thirty thousand Union troops on a merry chase over the months of May and June, five times turning, concentrating his forces, and dealing out punishing blows against a superior but divided enemy. What the wily Jackson and the wilier Lee intended to do next worried and mystified their opposite numbers. When Lee sent cavalry commander J.E.B. Stuart on a scouting mission, Stuart rode clear around Union commander George McClellan's forces in the celebrated "Stuart's Ride." With these tactics, Lee, Jackson, and Stuart gained an incredible psychological advantage over Union troops, who repeatedly retreated under their assaults.

When Lee lashed out in the Seven Days battles (June 25 to July 1, 1862), McClellan simply went to pieces. Lee lost most of these tactically crude, excessively bloody engagements, but he put the Yankees on the run. From Mechanicsville to Gaines' Mill, from Savage Station to Glendale, including the suicidal rebel assault at Malvern Hill ("not war, but murder," one Confederate remembered), southerners repelled the enemy steadily down the peninsula. Yankee prisoners and deserters flooded into rebel camps, and McClellan fretted that he would have to abandon his supply train and spike his guns if he was ever to get away. "If you do not know now," he wired Stanton, "the game is lost." Union forces had suffered about ten percent casualties, but many more men were incapacitated by illness, wandering in search of their units, or simply gone to ground. They had been "overpowered," McClellan howled, and the fault lay clearly in Washington. "If I can save this army," he declared with typically self-serving scorn, "I tell you I owe no thanks to you or any persons in Washington."

Likewise fuming, and wretched at the news of soaring casualties, Lincoln considered firing him even as he went looking for more men to replenish the ranks. Recruitment was intense and emotional, with waving flags, persuasive oratory, and patriotic music. The Quaker abolitionist James S. Gibbons penned the popular poem "We are Coming, Father Abraham, Three Hundred Thousand More," which was quickly set to music by Stephen Foster. One such new recruit in the summer of 1862 was a religious college student, George F. Cram, a twenty-one-year-old from Wheaton, Illinois, who joined the 105th Illinois Infantry. Cram and his comrades in the 105th received faulty weapons. According to the *Chicago Tribune*, the unit was "extremely mortified and chagrined at the miserable apology for arms turned out to them from the Springfield armory. We had the most positive assurances that Enfield rifles should be ours, but instead we have Austrian rifled muskets of the most bungling and defective character." Typically, the 105th spent much time drilling.

Even with recruiting committees, parades, and patriotic fervor, states had problems meeting their quotas. After Shiloh and the battles on the peninsula, northerners knew that this war was brutal. The U.S. government and northern state governments added incentives for enlistment. Volunteers received an immediate $25 of the $100 bounty they would be due after their honorable discharge. Furthermore, some states, counties, and cities offered additional bounties. In order to encourage volunteers, the federal government on July 17, 1862, passed a militia law that allowed the president to call a state militia into service for nine months. The militia was to be composed of all fit men from eighteen to forty-five years of age. Only one month after the call for the 300,000 three-year volunteers, on August 4 the U.S. government used this militia act to call for an additional 300,000 militia for nine months' service. If a state did not meet its three-year volunteer quota, it would be required to make up the difference in the nine-month militia call that was essentially a draft. If a state failed to make its quota, the U.S. government would step in and handle it for the state—a blatant abrogation of state sovereignty. If a state exceeded its quota of volunteers, however, every soldier over the quota counted for four men in the militia draft. In spite of resistance, often violent, and the need to extend deadlines, many believed it was a matter of local and state pride to fulfill the quota. By 1863 the Union had 421,000 new three-year volunteers and 88,000 nine-month militiamen.

Lee understood that over the long term southerners were bound to lose a war of attrition. The Confederacy's only hope was to watch carefully for the chance to strike the North a truly crushing blow. Lee believed southern generals were compelled to meet the enemy in advantageous encounters wherever possible. Turning back from McClellan's wrecked expedition, Lee drove northward to Manassas a second time, mauling superior federal forces under General John Pope in late August. While Confederate forces west of the Appalachians sidestepped Union pressure and advanced into Kentucky, Lee now undertook a complementary offensive in Maryland. If either of those states could be rallied to the southern cause, Lee and Davis believed, or if another rebel victory could draw England or France out on their side, Lincoln would have to come to the peace table.

For the North, the stakes were equally high. Although the South's Kentucky gambit was little more than a giant raid, bound to collapse at the first touch, Lincoln was more worried by the damage Confederates might cause in the East. Federal desertion rates far outstripped those of the rebels at this point of the war, and the enormous battlefield casualties—almost sixteen thousand Union soldiers killed or wounded at Manassas (almost ten thousand Confederates)—and thousands more incapacitated by dysentery, measles, whooping cough, and fevers undercut the sturdiest efforts to raise volunteers.

Lincoln also apprehended European intervention at this time. British recognition of the Confederate States of America would probably mean a negotiated peace on Confederate terms. In England, future Prime Minister William Gladstone was contemplating such a move: "We may have our own opinions about slavery; we may be for or against the South; but there is no doubt that Jefferson Davis and other leaders of the South have made an army; they are making, it appears, a navy; and they have made what is more than either; they have made a nation."

By the autumn of 1862, desperate for men, Lincoln moved from hesitation to boldness on a decision he had been contemplating. He decided to combine two essential aspects of making war. His military problem was to find more soldiers for the ranks. His ideological problem was to articulate a stronger rationale for war—a higher purpose. A war for freedom would stiffen backbones. However moral, complex, and far-reaching this decision, Lincoln understood very well that the Emancipation Proclamation was a weapon of war. He also understood that emancipation dovetailed with a larger, millennial understanding of what was at stake in the war.

Tens of thousands of African Americans had been walking away from slavery as soon as Union forces came close enough, and their journey toward freedom caused enormous headaches for military administration at all levels. Soldier-bureaucrats created a crazy patchwork of conflicting, shifting policies as they attempted to deal with local situations that were becoming more complicated and often more dire with each passing week. Should fleeing slaves be returned to rebel masters, potentially to strengthen Confederate resistance? Six weeks after the fall of Fort Sumter, Union General Benjamin F. Butler had said no. With delicious irony, since *Dred Scott* had declared slaves property, he asserted that fugitive slaves at Virginia's Fortress Monroe were actually "contraband of war," rebel property to be confiscated and put to work against the southern cause. At the beginning of August, Congress backed him up with the Confiscation Act of 1861, denying owners' claims to fugitive slaves who had been employed in Confederate war efforts.

As early as August 30, 1861, General John C. Frémont, born in Georgia and reared in South Carolina and now commander of the Department of the West, ordered that all slaves held by rebels in Missouri were henceforth liberated. African Americans honored Butler and Frémont as pioneers for freedom, but the president was not yet ready to move beyond the war aim of preserving the Union. Lincoln first requested and then demanded that Frémont amend his order to apply only to slaves who carried out work for the rebel cause. Regardless, enslaved people were continuing to free themselves by escaping to Union lines. Even southern newspapers realized that "whenever a Yankee army has appeared practical emancipation has followed." Throughout 1862 runaway slaves, local military commanders, radicals in Congress, and Confederate victories all conspired to push emancipation upon Lincoln. In mid-March, Congress moved ahead of Lincoln and forbade military leaders to return fugitive slaves to their owners. In the District of Columbia, Lincoln had been meeting with loyal slaveholders for months, pleading, cajoling, begging, bribing them to emancipate their slaves voluntarily. Finally, on April 16, 1862, he went beyond their wishes and signed the act abolishing slavery in D.C., with compensation to slaveholders. Tellingly, Lincoln was here following the letter of the law, as the Constitution gave Congress the lawful authority to administer policy in the District of Columbia.

On May 19, 1862, Lincoln revoked another freedom order, General David Hunter's declaration that all slaves in South Carolina, Georgia, and Florida were free. In June, however, he supported another antislavery bill when Congress dealt with the issue that had touched off the whole blazing inferno: without southerners in attendance to block it, Congress passed a law excluding slavery from the territories. And on July 17, 1862, Congress passed the Second Confiscation Act, which declared that enslaved property was a military asset and that all slaves confiscated from disloyal masters "shall be forever free."

With the border states secure by mid-1862, Lincoln began investigating emancipation as a military option. Many whites who opposed slavery preferred a gradual emancipation. General George McClellan, for instance, advocated that "the negroes should be fitted for it by certain preparatory steps in the way of education, recognition of the rights of family and marriage, prohibition against selling them without their consent, the freedom of those born after a certain date, etc." Lincoln, however, listened to men like Frederick Douglass and was slowly reversing his own opinion on the ability of blacks to be equal citizens. He also was familiar with the free black communities throughout the country, especially those in Washington and Baltimore, and he could see for himself that hardworking people were being held back by discrimination. Lincoln, though still advocating colonization for those African Americans willing to move, wrote, "And yet I wish to say there is an objection urged against free colored persons remaining in the country, which is largely imaginary, if not sometimes malicious." Lincoln's views were evolving.

Lincoln was rightfully concerned about the reaction of Union soldiers, most of whom had not signed up to risk their lives to free slaves. Ultimately, however, Lincoln and the Union soldiers knew how much slave labor helped the rebellion. Freedom for that very large minority of southern Americans would hinder the Confederate war effort on the front lines and on the southern homefront. In addition, Lincoln wanted to preclude involvement of European countries on the southern side. The aristocratic elements in England and France would have preferred a southern victory, less out of any real sympathy for the Confederacy than out of a desire that America's upstart democracy should fail. A majority of people in Europe, however, even including despotic Russians, were opposed to slavery. Finally, northern consensus was building for emancipation, as Americans were growing in their own conviction that freedom could no longer include slavery. Religious groups, especially African American and white abolitionists, besieged the president to free the slaves as a moral cause. Lincoln agreed, but he was slow. He slowly accepted the need to extend to African Americans those principles of individualism that he had espoused on the stump against Douglas. He slowly came to appreciate that if his grasp of America's millennial hopes and dreams was sincere, honor required him to extend freedom to African Americans. Moreover, emancipation would free Lincoln from the confines of contradictory war goals—fighting a war for democratic liberty but not against slavery.

Once he made the decision, he was no longer slow. In July 1862 Lincoln told his cabinet that he planned to issue an emancipation proclamation. Secretary of State William Seward persuaded him to wait for a Union victory so as not to look desperate. The next month, after Lincoln had decided on emancipation but before he made the decision public, Lincoln responded to a critical editorial by Horace Greeley, editor of the *New York Tribune* and a founding member of the Republican Party. In answer to Greeley's call for abolition, "The Prayer of Twenty Millions," Lincoln wrote that, although he intended "no modification of my oft-expressed *personal* wish that all men everywhere could be free," for him saving the Union was paramount. In a brilliant political stance, he calmed conservative fears while paving a way forward. "If I could save the Union without freeing *any* slave I would do it, and if I could save it by freeing *all* the slaves I would do it; and if I could save it by freeing some and leaving others alone I would also do that." And that is what he ultimately would do. In order to save the Union, Lincoln freed some and left others alone.

While Lincoln waited for a Union victory, Lee knew that a Confederate victory on Union territory might shatter Lincoln's political support, affect him adversely in the congressional elections scheduled for November, and even encourage European powers to intervene on behalf of the Confederacy. A Federal defeat in Maryland might very well bring the war to a halt. And so in September 1862, as Union generals squabbled and Confederate cavalry menaced northern lines near Washington, Lee's rebel host marched forth to the strains of "Maryland! My Maryland!"

In Maryland the fortunes of war went against the South. McClellan, utterly perplexed as to where Lee might strike next or when, found himself presented, astoundingly enough, with a complete set of Confederate battle plans wrapped around a bundle of cigars that some careless rebel staff officer had dropped. Armed with full details of southern intent, and mustering a force more than double the size of the tired, threadbare invaders, McClellan glowed with confidence that he would "whip 'Bobbie Lee.'" With the Potomac to Lee's back, McClellan thought strategic victory was finally within his grasp. Goaded on by Lincoln, McClellan determined to fight.

On September 17, Union forces launched a series of three piecemeal attacks against the rebel line. Properly coordinated, they might have cracked southern resolve and perhaps put in motion Confederate collapse itself. Lee, however, catching wind of McClellan's drive to intercept his divided forces, regrouped and built defensive positions along Antietam Creek. McClellan waffled once more, and the battle proved a standoff, disastrous to both sides. Antietam was basically a draw. Union efforts to pursue the retreating Lee were feeble at best. But because Lee then retreated from Maryland, the battle created an enormous political victory for Union forces.

Though he winced at the awful cost—twenty-three thousand more northern and southern boys killed or wounded in the single bloodiest

day in American military history—Lincoln used this victory to announce his emancipation plan, which was to take effect on New Year's
Day 1863. Lincoln gave the South an ultimatum. He allowed them three
and a half months to come back into the Union with slavery intact. His
proclamation announced that thereafter, "all persons held as slaves
within any State or designated part of a State, the people whereof shall
then be in rebellion against the United States, shall be then, thencefor-
ward, and forever free." The Emancipation Proclamation did not grant
freedom to each and every slave. It was not effective in Confederate
states because the U.S. Army was not in a position to enforce it, and it
did not cover enslaved workers held by loyal slaveholders in the Union
border states. As one British newspaper wrote, "The principle asserted
is not that a human being cannot justly own another, but that he cannot
own him unless he is loyal to the United States." Lincoln's audience, however, well knew the ramifications. For African Americans, the meaning of
freedom from captivity ran as clearly through their spirituals as it did
through the Book of Exodus: "When Israel was in Egypt's Land, let my
people go, oppressed so hard they could not stand, O let my people go."

Like Pharaoh, Confederates were not about to let their people go
just because of a proclamation from Lincoln. A newspaper editor expressed his opinion that "Lincoln's Proclamation should be met in the
South, by Proclamations from the Southern Governors announcing
their intention to enforce strictly the existing State laws against negro
thieves and insurrectionists." The editor observed that as long as Jefferson Davis's government in Richmond was secure, such proclamations
were "as ridiculous as the Pope's bull against the comet." And yet, although it would take victory and the Thirteenth Amendment to the
Constitution to make it official nationwide, the end of slavery was now
U.S. policy.

To southerners, the most threatening part of the proclamation was
Union-sanctioned slave rebellion; governmental authority "will do no
act or acts to repress such person, or any of them, in any efforts they
may make for their actual freedom." The document recommended that
the people continue peacefully to work for wages and that they "abstain
from all violence," but—previously unheard of in race relations—that
admonition against violence did not include "necessary self-defence."

The proclamation had a major effect on the course of the war. Im-

mediately southerners had to put an even greater emphasis on controlling their slaves, leaving less time and money available for the war effort.
Moreover, it ended any question of European intervention. With northern articulation that the war was now about the moral issue of slavery,
the English and French decided that it was not in their interest to recognize the Confederacy's independence. The measure also clarified war
aims: the war for the Union was now undeniably a war for freedom.

Though it was a war measure, Lincoln clearly presented it as a
justice measure as well. When he addressed Congress, he spoke about
how, "in giving freedom to the slave, we assure freedom to the free—
honorable alike in what we give, and what we preserve." Countries
around the world supported the proclamation as a strike against slavery.
In Italy, Garibaldi named Lincoln "Pilot of Liberty." In France, one newspaper was not concerned that it was merely a first step because "time
and the contagion of liberty will do the rest."

That contagion spread throughout the enslaved population. Slaves
who could read shared the information with others. Some whites in the
loyal state of Kentucky felt compelled to ask a leader in the African
American enslaved community to explain that they were not covered by
the proclamation. Fugitive slave Harriet Jacobs reacted to the Emancipation Proclamation, as did many others, with joy: "I have lived to hear
the Proclamation of Freedom for my suffering people. All my wrongs
are forgiven. I am more than repaid for all I have endured." Frederick
Douglass wrote, "We shout for joy that we live to record this righteous
decree." The Emancipation Proclamation captured public imagination
with the idea of burgeoning freedom.

Emancipation also called for allowing African Americans to serve in
the Union armed services at a time when manpower needs were critical.
Earlier Lincoln had supported the Militia Act, which authorized him to
recruit black troops for any military service "for which they may be
found competent," and within weeks, regiments of U.S. Colored Troops
began mustering in across the North, in South Carolina's Sea Islands,
and in Louisiana. Slave volunteers were granted freedom, and this
award extended to other family members in cases where their owner
was disloyal. The Emancipation Proclamation broadened this mandate
further still. Almost two hundred thousand African American men mustered into federal service over the next two years. Although only a few

black regiments saw combat before Appomattox, they demonstrated courage and discipline in each instance, teaching the North what white southerners had always dreaded most: given the opportunity, African Americans would not hesitate to shed their own blood—and that of their oppressors—in a war to overthrow slavery.

News of emancipation both galvanized and demoralized the South; their worst fears had been realized. Controversy also roiled the ranks of the federal armies and spilled back into northern society. Was Lincoln's plan too radical or too conservative, a perversion of American ideals or their realization? Far off in London a shabby German émigré exulted. "As the American War for Independence initiated a new era of ascendancy for the middle class," Karl Marx explained, "so the American anti-slavery war will do for the working classes." For all of Lincoln's moderation, he had struck an epoch-making blow for human liberty, one he would render tangible in the effort he would soon lead to codify freedom in the Thirteenth Amendment to the Constitution.

The first of January 1863 inaugurated what the old slave song called "the Year of Jubilo." No chains fell off that morning, and the heavens did not open, but America's central meaning was transformed. If Americans had not yet realized the millennium, surely their Lord had come a decisive step closer.

Seven

"A Giant Holocaust of Death"

TALL, SAD, AND SHROUDED with a tawny mane of beard and hair, Kentucky-born Texan John Bell "Sam" Hood was too much the lion, Robert E. Lee thought, and too little the fox to make an effective commander. No one doubted Hood's courage, but by war's end, bravery had turned to irrational bloodlust. He already bore one wound from a Comanche arrow in his left hand, when he had led the Texas Brigade into battle at Gaines' Mill in 1862. His soldiers shattered the Union line that day and broke George McClellan's spirit, but by nightfall every officer under his command had been killed or wounded. Gettysburg ruined his left arm, and Chickamauga took off his right leg, but on both occasions he grasped his sword, urged his men forward, and rose ever higher in rank. On the afternoon of November 30, 1864, he was raging over the remnants of the Army of Tennessee he now led, stalled on the road outside Franklin, fifteen miles below Nashville. The fight had gone out of his men, he believed, so he set them a simple, impossible task: charge straight down the road toward the Yankee guns that blocked their way, break through their entrenchments, and carry on toward Nashville itself. It would be a fair fight, Hood figured, about twenty-two thousand men on each side. One gallant rush, and the Confederacy would drive the invader out of the heart of Tennessee.

A generation later, Sam Watkins, a private in the First Tennessee Regiment, recorded his memory of that charge:

A sheet of fire was poured into our very faces, and for a moment we halted as if in despair, as the terrible avalanche of shot and shell laid low those brave and gallant heroes, whose bleeding wounds attested that the struggle would be desperate. Forward, men! The air loaded with death-dealing missiles . . . Forward, men! And the blood spurts in a perfect jet from the dead and wounded. The earth is red with blood. It flows in streams, making little rivulets as it flows . . . The death-angel shrieks and laughs and old Father Time is busy with his sickle, as he gathers in the last harvest of death, crying, More, more, more! while his rapacious maw is glutted with the slain.

For five hours, into the darkness, Yank and Reb fought hand to hand in a slaughter of no strategic importance whatsoever. The Union forces at Franklin, Tennessee, were a minor rear guard, expertly dug in. Amassing sixty thousand bluecoats behind them for the coup de grâce was the Virginia-born and -bred General George Thomas—the "Rock of Chickamauga" and Hood's old teacher from West Point. More disastrous still, Hood's advance had been achieved only by abandoning Georgia and the Carolinas, actually easing Sherman's plan to "make Georgia howl" by marching his own sixty thousand Union troops through the countryside, "smashing things" all the way from Atlanta to the sea. Even the grandest victory at Franklin would be a crushing defeat for the Confederacy.

How much worse then was the spectacle Sam Watkins saw when the sun rose that next morning. "O, my God! what did we see!" he remembered. "It was a giant holocaust of death." The Union lines had held firm, and now that their work was done, the Federals were pulling back down the pike, yielding up quietly the ground for which so many had perished, aiming to draw southerners farther into Thomas's trap. More than one-third of the Confederates who had gone forward at Franklin the previous evening now lay dead or wounded on that battlefield, a carnage equal to any in this grim, increasingly pointless conflict. All told, six Confederate generals had been killed in this battle. Whole regiments and brigades were slaughtered. "Death had held high carnival there that night," Watkins summed up. "The dead were piled the one on the other all over the ground. I never was so horrified and appalled in my life." Two weeks later Hood's forces were crushed outside Nashville, reeling back aimlessly toward Mississippi, now less an army than a mob of hungry, filthy refugees.

BY THE END OF 1862 the Civil War was by no means over, but it was fundamentally transformed. Lincoln's Emancipation Proclamation offered only the clearest sign of that change. In the East the failures of McClellan and his lieutenants had exaggerated Confederate battlefield achievements. In the West, apart from the scare at Shiloh, northern forces had advanced from victory unto victory. Lincoln had paid dearly in blood and treasure for such successes as had been achieved, but he never doubted that he could pay. His only consistent complaint throughout the war was that his generals did not fight often enough, boldly enough, directly enough. When McClellan had proposed to swing around behind Lee's forces in the Peninsular campaign, the president was at first displeased. Nevertheless, Lincoln remained supportive of McClellan's various demands. The failures of 1862 confirmed his belief in a simple method of slaughter: if the South could not be outwitted on the battlefield, it could be outbludgeoned. After McClellan's dismissal that fall, Lincoln chose a series of generals whom he called "fighters," but those closer to the front labeled them "butchers."

In the end, more than thirty months passed after Antietam before the last rebel surrendered, Yankeedom growing steadily stronger. In his annual message to Congress in 1864 Lincoln stated that, for all the carnage, his generals had more men, more guns, and more money to fight the war than ever before. After all the "science" of warfare that leaders like Halleck preached, all the discipline and cohesion that had been drilled into recruits, and all the technical advances of weaponry that recent decades had yielded, was modern warfare to resolve itself simply into slaughter on a vaster, more efficient scale? "What is all this struggling and fighting for?" one Union general's wife asked. "This ruin and death to thousands of families? . . . What advancement of mankind [was] to compensate for the present horrible calamities?" Any assessment of Lincoln and Davis, of the Confederacy and America itself after Antietam, must include the question, Could even a goal as noble as liberty, Union, or independence possibly justify such slaughter?

From the fall of 1862 onward the pace of killing accelerated, and the conflict itself was transmuted from a war of armies into a war of peoples. Commanders and soldiers on both sides increasingly came to regard the enemy, soldier and civilian alike, as alien other. Lee himself consistently called northern soldiers "those people." Soldiers of the New Orleans Guard waiting in reserve at Shiloh in April 1862 described the Union men as covered with blood and scarcely recognizable, with "faces disfigured with hideous wounds." But when ordered to charge, they fixed their bayonets and let out "a collective 'hurrah.'" More disturbing still, military leaders on both sides hardened themselves to the human sufferings of their own troops as they lashed out against the foe. Warned that Mobile Bay was infested with mines that might decimate his fleet, Admiral David Farragut answered with a callousness that succeeding generations have chosen to interpret as a hero's shout: "Damn the torpedoes! Full speed ahead!" That cruel logic writ large unleashed a bloodbath in the last years of the war.

Lashing out against soldiers and civilian populations alike were numerous bands of Confederate irregulars that operated behind Union lines as the North pushed south. Guerrilla harassment often forced Union leaders to establish sizable garrisons along every route to protect supply lines. In northern Virginia, John Singleton Mosby's partisans disrupted Union supply routes, though ultimately the "Gray Ghost's" efforts could do little to stem the staggering abundance of equipment and munitions that Union forces put into play. In Kentucky and east Tennessee, Confederate guerrilla fighter Champ Ferguson killed captives after they surrendered, sometimes allegedly decapitating them. In Missouri and Kansas, William Quantrill's raiders devolved into a fearsome band, staging hit-and-run attacks on Union forces and exacting bloody vengeance on local civilians. Reacting to the killings of members of his men's families in Union custody (when the floor of their prison collapsed), Quantrill struck back at Lawrence, Kansas, on August 21, 1863, ordering his men to "kill every man and burn every house" in the Free-Soil town and precipitating a massacre that horrified the nation. In the hills of Tennessee, North Carolina, Georgia, and farther afield, divided loyalties sparked a host of atrocities and reprisals that left communities smoldering and still hungry for retribution at war's end. For the grim and angry men who committed these horrors during wartime in the name of cause and country, the next stop was outright criminality after the war, as in the case of Frank and Jesse James, who rode with Bloody Bill Anderson, or membership in terrorist groups like the Ku Klux Klan. In the war itself paramilitary violence counted for little because it was so poorly organized and ad hoc. Yet ex-Confederates fully understood that much more might have been accomplished by partisan tactics, and many determined to apply what they had learned in order to resist political and social change after Appomattox.

War was not the romantic adventure that the proud young gallants who today stare back from faded photographs must have imagined. Nineteenth-century battle had become remarkably bigger, in terms of both time and space, than ever before, and technological advances made it a far more grim and deadly ritual. From the conflict's first official "battle casualty"—Private Luther Ladd, felled in the streets of Baltimore by a rock hurled by prosouthern rioters as his regiment marched toward Washington in answer to Lincoln's call for troops—through the next four years, more than six hundred thousand young men would die gloriously and absurdly and horribly in defense of profoundly different visions of America: fifty-six thousand rotted in enemy prisons, another five thousand drowned, almost nine hundred were killed following quarrels with their fellows or by their own hands, three hundred thirteen expired by sunstroke. More than two-thirds of the dead perished from disease, mostly unheroic, ghastly bouts of dysentery, measles, or fevers of one sort or another as poor sanitation, bad water, and rough, crowded conditions spread viruses among populations with low immunity. Combat deaths totaled by 1865 about 95,000 for the Confederacy and 110,000 for the Union. For every soldier killed in battle, approximately 2.5 others survived wounds; about 240,000 rebels and 275,000 Yankees.

For all their organizational rigor and material resources, northern armies do not seem to have served their soldiers much better in recovering from gunshot wounds than southern forces did. Nineteenth-century armies were primarily killing forces, focused less on maneuver or self-protection than on striking the enemy a traumatic blow. For the common soldier of the ranks who found himself lying dazed and bloody in an open-air field hospital, the prospects were dire. Most of these men had been struck in the limbs, the loins, or the face by musket or artillery fire. Doctors rarely saw sword or bayonet wounds. Seldom did rival forces close in for hand-to-hand fighting with edged weapons or rifle butts, and when they did, the outcome was usually lethal. Likewise, the place on his body where a soldier had been struck by musket fire or a shell fragment offered a fairly reliable guide to his chances of survival. A wound in the lower abdomen was generally inoperable. Even if a bullet missed the liver, the hazards of infection were overwhelming. A man shot in the upper trunk had a better chance of survival, provided no vital organs had been struck and blood loss could be curtailed. Still, any Civil War soldier hit in the chest by a bullet suffered a wound rather more ghastly than one endured by his counterpart in later wars. The soft lead of a minié ball expanded and flattened out as it traveled through the air, and it struck its victim at a much lower velocity than twentieth-century projectiles, causing relatively greater trauma. Most commonly soldiers were wounded in the arm or leg, and the common remedy was amputation. Army doctors performed surgery very near the battle lines and sometimes, at Spotsylvania for example, actually under fire. Occasionally, men had to do without anaesthetic, but most operations had ether, administered on a cloth and held over the face for a matter of seconds. Veterans have left countless gruesome tales from Fredericksburg, Atlanta, and Spotsylvania of limbs stacked like cordwood outside hospital tents.

The rude conditions of general medical care dictated that soldiers who suffered major trauma would not survive, but tens of thousands went home blinded or facially disfigured, emasculated, or missing an arm or a leg. Thousands more suffered a debilitating emotional or psychological collapse. Nor was sickness evenly distributed among ranks and regiments. Officers on both sides tended to escape the worst effects of epidemic diseases, thanks no doubt to the superior living conditions they enjoyed. Conversely, their insignia of rank and placement at the front of any battle line ensured that leaders in combat were among the first to fall. For many ordinary fellows in the Union ranks, the war was a dreary and eminently safe pursuit; most of those on garrison duty in the forts ringing Washington never smelled the smoke of battle. For the soldiers of the First Minnesota, by contrast, military service was a far deadlier calling: in fifteen minutes of fighting on the afternoon of July 2, 1863, fully 82 percent of their number would be killed or wounded.

Victory would require sacrifice, all knew, and the letters that soldiers sent home are filled with sentimental and heroic professions of their willingness to die. "Oh my country," wrote one Pennsylvania corporal, "how my heart bleeds for your welfare. If this poor life of mine could save you, how willingly would I make the sacrifice." Before the grim days of 1864, however, most soldiers took comfort in the expectation that it would be some other soul who yielded up his life. Indeed, far into the war, soldiers persisted in describing combat as a grand spectacle, a form of theater in which they were less actors than spectators. Though many longed for the chance to "see the elephant," a euphemism for combat, raw recruits usually found their curiosity more than satisfied after their first experience of battle. When one company from an Iowa regiment proposed "Victory or death!" as its motto, one clear-sighted fellow objected. "Victory or pretty damned badly wounded" was his suggestion.

Approximately 200,000 Union soldiers and 215,000 Confederates spent time as prisoners of war. As no one had expected so many soldiers to throw up their hands in a short war, almost no preparations had been made to accommodate POWs. In the early years prisoners were exchanged or paroled on condition that they would return home, but when the Confederacy refused to exchange African American prisoners of war, Lincoln halted all exchanges until the South was willing to change its policy. Mismanagement and war shortages made southern prisons like the ones at Richmond, Virginia, and Andersonville, Georgia, hell on earth. The mortality rate at Andersonville was 30 percent. Northern camps like Elmira, New York, and Point Lookout, Maryland, were grim and deadly places too. The Confederate POW camp at Rock Island, Illinois, immortalized in *Gone with the Wind* as the prison camp that held Ashley Wilkes, had a 16 percent mortality rate. To avoid such a fate, some of the captured Confederates went over to the Union side and were sent west to fight Native Americans. In postwar years a small number of families who thought their loved ones had died in Union prison camps found them out west.

In recent years Civil War historians have devoted enormous attention to understanding why millions of Americans fought this war, but greater sophistication is yet needed. Clearly, the reasons why clerks and farm boys first enlisted differed from those that motivated them to keep marching along. Once drilling and training had begun, or the young gallant had stood a few turns of picket duty in a chilly downpour, the fine sentiments and political ideals that had first inspired him tended to wash away. Similarly, the motivation that sustained soldiers in camp and on campaign was far different from the reason they did not run for their lives when the bullets started to fly. Many soldiers did run, and it was not unusual for veteran regiments of both sides to overwhelm vastly greater bodies of green troops. But even soldiers who fled at the first volley or cowered behind the largest tree or rock they could reach often mustered the courage needed to rejoin the fray. Although some men showed themselves amazingly brave and others demonstrated the most craven cowardice, most soldiers tended to shift between these two poles from action to action and moment to moment. To keep their armies in the field, leaders on both sides employed strict systems of order and discipline, at which many young men balked initially. Both Yankees and rebels who trumpeted their defense of liberty when they first signed up discovered abruptly that personal freedom went out the window as soon as the drill sergeant called. Other values motivated men in battle: a desire to save one's comrades and to protect one's name, to find release in killing and to wreak revenge for friends killed. Many men, no doubt, fought because they dared not face the consequences of flight.

Historians have generally concluded that Johnny Reb and Billy Yank soldiered on against distressingly long odds "for cause and comrades," pointing to the many professions of group loyalty and personal belief contained in veterans' letters and diaries. The surprising resoluteness of amateurs under fire results from the primary group discipline, the community basis of companies. Companies were frequently recruited and organized within a single community and replenished from that same source as casualties mounted. Americans North and South generally had the extraordinary experience of standing on the firing line in company with people they had known intimately since childhood. For fathers and sons, brothers and cousins, to serve alongside one another was not strange at all, especially in Confederate and midwestern regiments. Group cohesion helped to overcome the ill-discipline of the common soldier and the fear and bewilderment in the noise, smoke, and death of battle.

The central problem was how to move soldiers forward through a zone of fire where a high percentage could expect to be killed or wounded. When men in the front rank facing the concentrated fire of the enemy knew that they were almost certain to be shot before they could close quarters with the foe—and that the odds of being hit increased as they moved forward—what made them take that first step?

Facing a lethal storm of shot and shell, the unthinking response of most soldiers was to take cover and, once they had found a place of safety, to refuse all demands that they reenter the danger zone. In such situations soldiers often simply ceased firing at the enemy and paid little heed to directions given by their officers. They froze, hunkered down, and waited for the appalling nightmare they faced to resolve itself. Battles disintegrated into ghastly, confused standoffs with a fraction of troops on each side firing away at each other for an hour or more at a reasonable remove. Ultimately such situations of terror and indecision would morph into the stalemate of trench warfare.

Civil War generals never came close to solving this problem. After 1863 the introduction of seven-shot repeating Spencer carbines transformed northern cavalry into a deadly, fast-moving force, but military thinkers little understood the possibilities of technological change. Union leaders used this firepower primarily as a defensive weapon, requiring outnumbered cavalry to dismount and stem the tide until slow-moving infantry units could be brought into play. No one on either side seems to have much believed that bullets could cause a defensive line to break and run. Their only answer was the bayonet.

So long as a defensive line kept firing, generals understood, attackers were bound to fall. Generals considered such deaths, however numerous, as unavoidable. That meant that an offensive line had to move through the zone of fire as rapidly as possible, regardless of casualties, stopping for nothing, striking the enemy with maximum force. While offensive troops would prefer the safety of dispersal and concealment, victory needed them to rally round the flag and face the foe. Then, as the defensive troops reloaded after each volley and their volume of fire became more ragged and irregular, they would strike relatively fewer targets, and the offensive would move upon them. Once the soldiers on the defensive caught a first glimpse of the long line of enemy bayonets breaking through the smoke toward them and heard the shouts of their foes above the sound of gunfire, generals believed, they would become disorganized, command itself would break down, and the men would break and run. The Union assault at Antietam had failed, Lincoln believed, because it had gone in piecemeal, with insufficient speed and determination.

After Antietam, Lincoln urged McClellan forward, demanding that he pursue and destroy Lee's crippled army. Meeting only resistance, the president dismissed McClellan in early November 1862 and appointed in his stead the very reluctant Ambrose Burnside, a divisional commander who had distinguished himself in the Maryland campaign primarily by his willingness to push his troops forward regardless of losses. Burnside was determined to prove himself at Fredericksburg, fought just before Christmas 1862, when soldiers on both sides were anxious to head into winter quarters and give up the business of war until spring returned. Lee lured the Union commander to try his fortunes, yielding up the town itself and drawing his forces back around Marye's Heights. Near the base of this steep slope he arrayed a strong force of veteran infantry behind a stone wall. Above and behind this line he positioned artillery and dug in a formidable reserve. A wiser general facing such a concentration of firepower might have opted to outflank it, but Lincoln had steadfastly rebuked any hint of indirection. For Burnside, his course was clear: to conquer by élan and the weight of numbers, launching his troops up the hill in a single, coordinated, concentric assault. The Union fist would close around the heights, Lee would break, and Richmond would fall. The war would be won before Christmas.

The best theory that day yielded the worst slaughter. Instead of inflicting a mighty, crushing squeeze, the fingers of Burnside's hand went into the rebel fire one by one, more than a dozen times in all, and came out bloody and ruined. All afternoon wave after wave of Union soldiers trudged up the hill toward the stone wall. None reached it. By nightfall more than twelve thousand bluecoats had been killed or wounded at a cost to the Confederates of less than two-fifths that number. Union regiments remained pinned down, using the bodies of fallen comrades as cover against rebel fire. "It is well that war is so terrible," Lee remarked, "or we should grow too fond of it."

The tragedy of Fredericksburg was that Lincoln and Lee both drew precisely the wrong lessons from it. President Lincoln concluded that a more capable commander could gain victory through more determined, better coordinated attacks. The southern general deduced that a riskier, more aggressive Confederate strategy could make the North call it quits. For each, there seemed to be few other choices. Lee's Maryland gamble had cost him one-third of his already grievously small army and began the steady erosion of Confederate morale. Fredericksburg did little to stop that. Had Lincoln not ratcheted up the stakes of southern defeat by playing the emancipation card, rebel forces might have dwindled more rapidly still. Instead, rebels headed into winter quarters hoping that one great triumph might yet bring about a negotiated peace. Spring raised those dreams to the zenith before summer sent them crashing down.

Come May, the Army of the Potomac, reorganized once more, marched toward Richmond again, this time commanded by Burnside's handsome rival, Joseph Hooker. Lee divided his outnumbered forces, pounced on an unprotected flank, and sent the Yankees reeling back in confusion. The Battle of Chancellorsville was Lee's masterpiece, toppling "Fighting Joe" Hooker from leadership and casting the North into mourning for another seventeen thousand sons. His words clearly showing concern over the political effects of defeat, the president lamented, "My God, my God! What will the country say?" Yet though Chancellorsville was a splendid tactical victory for the South, Hooker's army had escaped relatively intact. Lee's victory meant the loss of fully thirteen thousand rebels, nearly a quarter of his forces engaged—among them Stonewall Jackson, accidentally wounded by his own men while on reconnaissance. (The actual cause of death was pneumonia.) The death of Jackson was devastating to Lee, who had seemed invincible with Jackson's help; things would be different now.

With Ulysses S. Grant's forces in the west menacing the Confederate fortress at Vicksburg and other Union armies poised to strike Charleston and Chattanooga, Lee knew that his own decimated reserves would be shipped off to other fronts unless he took the initiative. Lee wanted a major battle with the Army of the Potomac on northern soil, and in June the Army of Northern Virginia advanced into Federal territory once more. Lee hoped either to force Lincoln to make peace by menacing Washington, D.C., or to shatter the Yankee foe in a final climactic battle. It was a desperate gamble, but some of the men were eager to keep on killing. As he marched toward Pennsylvania in June 1863, Sergeant Christopher Kendrick of the Eighth Georgia Regiment wrote how he planned to "slay them like wheat before the scythe in harvest time. I certainly love to live to kill the base usurping vandals. [I]f it is a sin to hate them; then I am guilty of an unpardonable sin."

By the end of June southern forces found themselves strung out in the rich farmlands of southeastern Pennsylvania, marching along blindly.

Lee's cavalry commander, J.E.B. Stuart, had disappeared with his squadrons in search of booty and glory, leaving the Confederates with little accurate idea of where Union forces were located. On the morning of July 1 advance elements of Lee's army bumped into dismounted northern cavalry at a minor crossroads town called Gettysburg. Though Confederates chased northern troops out of Gettysburg by nightfall, two corps of the Army of the Potomac had arranged themselves on the high ground south of town, a place warningly called Cemetery Hill. Lee left the decision on whether to press an attack on Cemetery Hill up to Lieutenant General Richard Ewell, who decided against it. Through the night, thousands of reinforcements joined the Union army and extended its line southward along Cemetery Ridge. This left the Union army in command of important high ground south of town and good interior lines of communication. The new Union leader, dour George Meade, was rallying every regiment in his command to confront Lee's army, and with each passing hour the bluecoats grew stronger. Even after Stuart returned that evening, Lee did not fully grasp how desperate his situation had become.

On the morning of July 2 Confederate General James Longstreet surveyed the Union line and urged Lee to seek battle on ground of his own choosing, or at least to outflank Meade's strong position. Sending southern soldiers uphill across the open fields fronting Cemetery Ridge was to reenact the slaughter of Fredericksburg with flags reversed. But Lee would not consider withdrawing. Ewell was to demonstrate against the Union right at Cemetery Hill while Longstreet was to attack the Union left flank. In the meantime, in a decision that has remained controversial ever since, Union Major General Daniel Sickles decided to move his troops forward into a peach orchard out of the main Union line of defense. Sickles's move opened up a gap in the Union lines. Confederate troops rushed through the gap and smashed the Third Corps. The most advanced of the Confederate brigades that charged toward Cemetery Ridge nearly captured that important defensive position, but were checked by the First Minnesota Infantry Regiment. The 262 Minnesotans, outnumbered five to one, charged forward and stopped the Confederate brigade's advance, though at a terrible cost of 215 men. With Union reinforcements arriving to back up the Minnesotans, the Confederate thrust was stopped.

The situation was just as dire for the far-left flank of the Union position. In that sector, the Confederate attack threatened to seize Little Round Top, a hill that dominated the main Union line on Cemetery Ridge. Union and Confederate forces wrestled furiously for the position, most famously the Twentieth Maine commanded by Joshua Lawrence Chamberlain and the Fifteenth Alabama commanded by William C. Oates. After throwing back several Confederate attacks, the Twentieth Maine found themselves low on ammunition. Ordering his men to fix bayonets, Chamberlain decided to charge toward the Alabamans. Shocked by the audacity of Chamberlain's decision, the exhausted Fifteenth Alabama scattered as the Maine men rushed down the hill. Union troops to the right of the Twentieth Maine blunted other attacks on Little Round Top, and the position remained in Union hands.

By day's end the Union line had held firm everywhere, and northern regiments were pouring in to shore up the defense. Longstreet urged Lee once more to disengage, but the rebel chieftain still believed he could prevail. Confederate attacks that day had come close to success, and Lee expected triumph on July 3. Although one subordinate cautioned that victory would be "at a very bloody cost," Lee was undaunted. He planned for Stuart to hit from the rear at the same time that General George Pickett and 14,000 Virginians attacked what Lee viewed as the weakest part of the Union line, the center. The rebel yell and the bayonet would finish off what massed artillery barrage had begun. The Confederates would snap the Union line in two and roll it up in both directions. The Fourth of July would see the Southern Cause saved at last.

It was not to be. As Confederate artillery rained down on Union position prior to the Confederate charge, Union General Henry J. Hunt stopped firing back, both saving ammunition for the coming attack and lulling the Confederates into thinking the Union was low on ordnance. When the South finally stepped across the broad open fields sloping up to the Union lines in the assault history remembers as Pickett's Charge, the federal center had been reinforced and every man knew what was coming. Many of the same northern regiments that had been decimated at Fredericksburg and Chancellorsville now trained their guns in anticipation of revenge. It was nothing like a battle. Fully half the rebel force was mowed down. Two-thirds of Pickett's division fell, including every

ABOVE: The only known photograph of Abraham Lincoln at Gettysburg, Pennsylvania, November 19, 1862. Lincoln is circled. Unknown photographer. *(Library of Congress)*

LEFT: "Freedom to the Slaves." *(Currier & Ives, Library of Congress)*

RIGHT: Carte de visite of a lost ambrotype of Lincoln made by Samuel G. Alschuler in Urbana, Illinois, taken on or about April 25, 1858. Attached to the photograph is a note that Lincoln borrowed the jacket of a shorter man, explaining the twinkle in his eyes as he attempted to restrain his laughter. *(University of Illinois Library at Urbana-Champaign)*

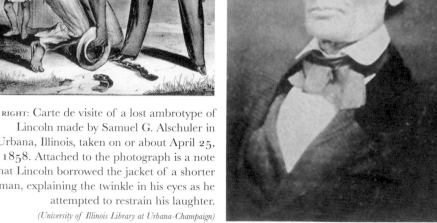

Harriet Beecher Stowe, Lyman Beecher, and Henry Ward Beecher.
(Brady-Handy Photograph Collection, Library of Congress)

Abolitionist broadside, "Am I not a man and a brother?" From 1837 publication of John Greenleaf Whittier's poem "Our Countrymen in Chains." *(Library of Congress)*

"The Assault in the Senate Chamber," from D. A. Harsha's *The Life of Charles Sumner*. Note that the Senate chamber is presented as a larger-than-life temple of democracy.

"Shakers near Lebanon state of N. York, their mode of worship" (c. 1830). Shakers performing a step dance in meeting hall. *(Library of Congress)*

William Miller (1782–1849).

Frontispiece, Timothy Shay Arthur, *Ten Nights in a Bar-Room and What I Saw There* (New York, 1854).

Edmund Ruffin.
(Brady-Handy Photograph Collection, Library of Congress)

John C. Calhoun. *(Library of Congress)*

Henry David Thoreau. *(Library of Congress)*

John Brown. *(Library of Congress)*

Gore shooting Denby.   Lloyd whipping Barney.   The last time Fred saw his mother.

Frederick Douglass at a New York abolitionist meeting, c. 1850.

(Madison County Historical Society, Oneida, New York)

"Cotton plantation on the Mississippi." Northerners and southerners portrayed the slave South as orderly compared to the disorder of the industrializing North. This image presents a vision of slavery shaped by the same sort of managerial control that would come to characterize factory life, yet the pictures below of the African American soldier Gordon belie this comforting image.

(Currier & Ives, Library of Congress)

[A TYPICAL NEGRO.]

We publish herewith three portraits, from photographs by M'Pherson and Oliver, of the negro GORDON, who escaped from his master in Mississippi, and came into our lines at Baton Rouge in March last. One of these portraits represents the man as he entered our lines, with clothes torn and covered with mud and dirt from his long race through the swamps and bayous, chased as he had been for days and nights by his master with several neighbors and a pack of blood-hounds; another shows him as he underwent the surgical examination previous to being mustered into the service —his back furrowed and scarred with the traces of a whipping administered on Christmas-day last; and the third represents him in United States uniform, bearing the musket and prepared for duty.

This negro displayed unusual intelligence and energy. In order to foil the scent of the blood-hounds who were chasing him he took from his plantation onions, which he carried in his pockets. After crossing each creek or swamp he rubbed his body freely with these onions, and thus, no doubt, frequently threw the dogs off the scent.

At one time in Louisiana he served our troops as guide, and on one expedition was unfortunately taken prisoner by the rebels, who, infuriated beyond measure, tied him up and beat him, leaving him for dead. He came to life, however, and once more made his escape to our lines.

By way of illustrating the degree of brutality which slavery has developed among the whites in the section of country from which this negro came, we append the following extract from a letter in the New York *Times*, recounting what was told by the refugees from Mrs. GILLESPIE's estate on the Black River:

The treatment of the slaves, they say, has been growing worse and worse for the last six or seven years.

Flogging with a leather strap on the naked body is common; also, paddling the body with a hand-saw until the skin is a mass of blisters, and then breaking the blisters with the teeth of the saw. They have "very often" seen slaves stretched out upon the ground with hands and feet held down by fellow-slaves, or lashed to stakes driven into the ground for "burning." Handfuls of dry corn-husks are then lighted, and the burning embers are whipped off with a stick so as to fall in showers of live sparks upon the naked back. This is continued until the victim is covered with blisters. If in his writhings of torture the slave gets his hands free to brush off the fire, the burning brand is applied to them.

Another method of punishment, which is inflicted for the higher order of crimes, such as running away, or other refractory conduct, is to dig a hole in the ground large enough for the slave to squat or lie down in. The victim is then stripped naked and placed in the hole, and a covering or grating of green sticks is laid over the opening. Upon this a quick fire is built, and the live embers sifted through upon the naked flesh of the slave, until his body is blistered and swollen almost to bursting. With just enough of life to enable him to crawl, the slave is then allowed to recover from his wounds if he can, or to end his sufferings by death.

"Charley Slav" and "Overton," two hands, were both murdered by these cruel tortures. "Slav" was whipped to death, dying under the sufferings, or soon after punishment. "Overton" was laid naked upon his face and burned as above described, so that the cords of his legs and the

GORDON AS HE ENTERED OUR LINES.

GORDON UNDER MEDICAL INSPECTION.

GORDON IN HIS UNIFORM AS U. S. SOLDIER.

"A Typical Negro." *(McPherson & Oliver, Harper's Weekly, July 4, 1863, p. 429)*

General Winfield Scott.

General George Thomas.

Admiral David Glasgow Farragut.

Lincoln at Antietam, Maryland, October 3, 1862. *(Alexander Gardner)*

General Edmund J. Davis.

General John C. Frémont.

"Incidents of the War. A Harvest of Death." Gettysburg, July 1863.

(Philip and Solomons, c. 1865, Library of Congress)

Two of the twenty-one illustrations drawn by Thomas Nast for "The Chicago Platform."

(Harper's Weekly, October 15, 1864, pp. 664–65)

"'Marching on!'—The Fifty-fifth Massachusetts Colored Regiment singing John Brown's
March in the streets of Charleston, February 21, 1865."

(Harper's Weekly, March 18, 1865, p. 165)

Hanging of Mary Surratt, Lewis Powell, David Herold, and George Atzerodt,
Washington, D.C., July 7, 1865.

(Alexander Gardner, Library of Congress)

CONFEDERATE COMMANDERS WHO SUPPORTED
BLACK RIGHTS DURING RECONSTRUCTION
(All portraits from Library of Congress)

Colonel John Singleton Mosby.

General William Mahone.

General James Longstreet.

General Pierre Gustave Toutant Beauregard.

"The first colored senator and representatives—in the 41st and 42nd Congress of the United States." Robert C. De Large, Jefferson H. Long, Hiram R. Revels, Benjamin S. Turner, Josiah T. Walls, Joseph H. Rainey, and Robert Brown Elliott.

(Currier & Ives, 1872, Library of Congress)

"Robert Smalls, S[outh] C[arolina]. M[ember of].C[ongress]. Born in Beaufort, SC, April 1839."

(Library of Congress)

Tunis Campbell.

(Moorland-Spingarn Research Center, Howard University, Washington, D.C.)

"The Centennial—The Corliss
Bevel–Gear–Cutting Machine."
(Centennial Photographic Company, Harper's Weekly,
July 29, 1876, p. 612)

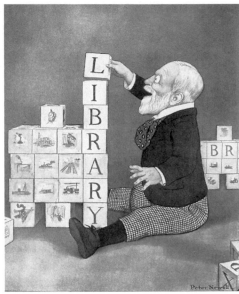

"We men are only lusty boys, / Though snowy
be our locks; / So Skibo's master still enjoys /
To sit and play with blocks."
Andrew Carnegie, by Peter Newell.
(Capitalist Benevolence, Harper's Weekly, *April 11, 1903, p. 587)*

"The Royal Feast of Belshazzar: Blaine and the Money Kings."
(The New York World, vol. 25, October 30, 1884, p.1)

Pullman car: "Interior of a palace hotel car used on the Pacific Railroad."
(A. R. Waud, Harper's Weekly, *May 29, 1869, p. 348)*

"Two unemployed railway workers seated by shack during the Pullman strike of 1893,
Chicago Ill. or vicinity." *(Ray Stannard Baker, Library of Congress)*

"The Granger Awakening the Sleepers," 1873. *(John Donaghy, Library of Congress)*

"Coxey at the Capitol. The Commonweal Army leaving Brightwood Camp."
(Frank Leslie's Illustrated Newspaper, May 10, 1894, p. 308)

Booker T. Washington. The easy-to-underestimate Washington
electrifies a large crowd in Lakeland, Florida. *(Library of Congress)*

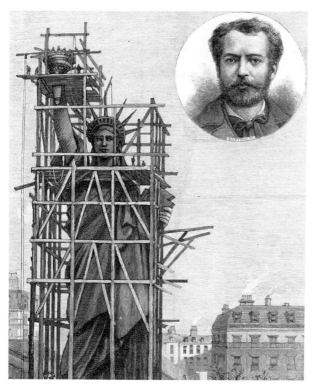

ABOVE: Dr. William Edward
Burghardt Du Bois. *(George Grantham Bain
Collection, Library of Congress)*

LEFT: "The Bartholdi Statue of
Liberty. —Drawn by John Durkin."
Portrait of sculptor Frederic
Bartholdi. *(Harper's Weekly,
January 19, 1884, p. 41)*

The TWO RAILROADS to ETERNITY

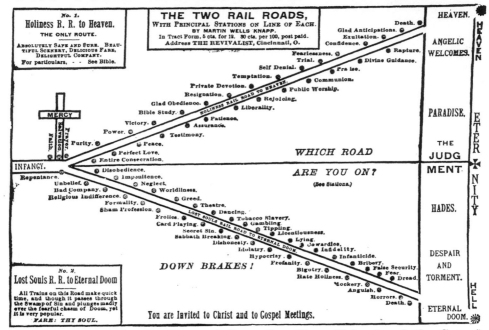

Have you your ticket for Heaven? Soon the office will be closed, the Gospel Train gone, and it will be TOO LATE. You are invited to

THE ✢ REVIVAL ✢ MEETINGS. ✢

"The Two Railroads to Eternity" (1905). The millennial theme remained strong in African American culture. *(From Martin Wells Knapp)*

senior officer. Three hundred rebels reached the Union lines, only to be bayoneted or shot at close range. Stuart, stopped by Union troops under George Armstrong Custer, never attacked from the rear.

By sunset on July 3 Lee was riding aimlessly among the bloody remains of his best regiments, begging forgiveness. "It's all my fault," he told his men. The flank attacks had been peremptory and uncoordinated, turned back with ease. The artillery bombardment had numbered fully 140 guns, but many of these were inaccurate and worn-out, and there was not nearly enough ammunition to prepare the way.

Had Meade advanced his troops against Lee's broken regiments, the war might have ended then and there. Perhaps stunned by the carnage on both sides, he gave no order. Only a minor, ill-fated cavalry assault was ordered against well-entrenched rebel infantry on the right flank. Brigadier General Elon Farnsworth knew the assault was suicidal; moments before charging to his death he protested that his men were "too good to kill." General Judson Kilpatrick, who ordered the attack, was hereafter christened "Kill-cavalry." He was hardly the only butcher on the field that day. In all, twenty-three thousand northern soldiers fell in three days of fighting, one-fourth of Meade's force. Lee lost fully one-third of his army, a shattering twenty-eight thousand men (including four thousand during the retreat from July 4 to July 13). Years later men remembered Lee moaning "Too bad! Oh, too bad!" as darkness gathered over the field. Sophronia Bucklin was one of the first Union nurses to reach Gettysburg. She reported, "It seemed impossible to tread the streets without walking over maimed men . . . they lay on the bloody ground, sick with the poisons of wounds, grim with the dust of long marches and the smoke and powder of battle, looking up with wild haggard faces imploringly for succor."

It took three days for news of another victory to reach Washington: not only had Lee's forces been sent reeling back toward Virginia, but Grant had captured Vicksburg on the same day, bagging thirty-two thousand prisoners. West of the river, Texas, Arkansas, and portions of Missouri would fight on for nearly another two years, but essentially they had been knocked out of the war. More important, with the subsequent Union victory at Port Hudson, the heart of cotton's kingdom and the Mississippi River were now firmly under federal control. Lincoln declared, "The Father of waters again runs unvexed to the sea." A week later an unescorted Union ship sailed from St. Louis to New Orleans without incident.

As gallantly as newspaper reports soon came to depict the Union victory at Gettysburg—celebrating heroes such as Bowdoin College professor Joshua Chamberlain—they painted a darker picture of triumph at Vicksburg. Not only had Grant launched a series of frontal assaults that seemed ill-considered at best, but he had waged war in a style that was anything but gallant. The whole time from late May to early July, Grant's forces successfully denied food and supplies to the men, women, and children in the city. His shelling of civilians' homes forced the populace underground. This was in stark contrast to the behavior of the noble Lee, whose soldiers had supposedly passed through Pennsylvania without molesting property or person. More shocking still to the South—and to some portions of the North, too—was word that African Americans had actually gone into combat at Port Hudson, Louisiana, on July 9. Word of their involvement outraged and stiffened rebel sentiment.

That African Americans were determined to fight and die for freedom was proven abundantly on the evening of July 18, 1863, when the African American Fifty-fourth Massachusetts Regiment took part in an ill-starred frontal assault on a rebel fort near Charleston. The attack on Battery Wagner was a bungled, pointless affair that cost hundreds of casualties and ended in defeat. Forced to advance along a narrow front due to the fort's proximity to the ocean, the Fifty-fourth Massachusetts suffered heavy casualties before even reaching the fort. Lengthy hand-to-hand fighting was fierce. As the regiment approached the fort's ramparts, its commanding officer, Robert Gould Shaw, son of noted abolitionist parents, was mortally wounded. Undaunted, the regiment continued fighting and actually captured part of the fort, where it planted its colors at the parapet. Against superior Confederate firepower, however, the Federals were forced to withdraw. Although unsuccessful in its assault, the Fifty-fourth Massachusetts fought bravely and earned laurels and commendations for its actions. The regiment included Charles and Lewis Douglass, sons of Frederick Douglass. Charles was sick and did not fight. Lewis later wrote a personal narrative of the combat, describing the death of Shaw and the valor of Sergeant William Harvey Carney. The battle occurred just days after serious draft riots in New York City, in which white rioters viciously attacked the African American community. The heroic assault by African American troops at Fort Wagner and at Port Hudson showed skeptics that black troops would make an important contribution to the Union war effort.

After the battle, Confederate troops buried the Fifty-fourth Massachusetts' casualties in one long ditch and disposed of Shaw in the same mass grave, reputedly saying, "We have buried him with his niggers!" They assumed that such a burial with black soldiers would bring shame, but Shaw's father disagreed. Reflecting an idealism that was growing among white northern abolitionists, he clarified, "I can imagine no holier place than that in which he is, among his brave and devoted followers, nor wish him better company."

After the Emancipation Proclamation, the Confederate South regarded Lincoln's armies, African American and white, as bent on more than vanquishing southern soldiers. Increasingly, it seemed, they were determined to wreak vengeance on southern civilization itself. Bitter rebels perpetrated atrocities of their own, murdering Union sympathizers in a host of hamlets in North Carolina and eastern Tennessee, killing black prisoners of war at Ocala, Florida, burning Paducah, Kentucky, and offering no quarter to surrendering black and white soldiers at Fort Pillow in Tennessee, where a Confederate soldier recorded: "Human blood stood about in pools and brains could have been gathered up in any quantity." In such crimes Confederates displayed the pure evil of racism at the heart of their regime. Vengeance wreaked more of the same. When eighteen-year-old Confederate soldier Albert Padgett died from his wounds at Antietam, his fellow soldiers, friends from home, explained that his death "can have no other effect than to alienate our affections towards the invaders and sow deep in our bosoms an undying hatred." His death invited others "to the banquet of blood prepared by Lincoln and his fiendish Cabinet" and called for "revenge in this our struggle for National Liberty." Union soldiers reciprocated the bloodthirsty hatred. Private Robert H. Strong, of the 105th Illinois, wrote in May 1864 about a captured rebel soldier begging for his life: "He had his shirt off, and on one arm was tattooed in big letters, 'Fort Pillow.' As soon as the boys saw the letters on his arm, they yelled, 'No quarter for you!' and a dozen bayonets went into him and a dozen bullets were shot into him. I shall never forget his look of fear."

After Gettysburg and Vicksburg, many rebels recognized that the slaveholders' republic was doomed. Although Longstreet and General Braxton Bragg inflicted a tactical defeat on Federal forces at Chickamauga, Georgia, in September and briefly besieged Chattanooga, they could not halt the northern drive. With victories at Missionary Ridge and Lookout Mountain, Tennessee, Grant pushed Bragg out of the Appalachians. And yet, they would not capitulate. According to historian James McPherson, religion kept both armies, and especially the Confederates, going in the face of these crushing deaths. "It may not be an exaggeration to say that the revivals of 1863–64 enabled Confederate armies to prolong the war in 1865."

In the spring of 1864 Lincoln brought the relentlessly hard-hitting Grant from the Tennessee front and appointed him the new American lieutenant general to oversee all Union forces, the first such appointment since George Washington. Against Robert E. Lee, George Meade still technically controlled the Army of the Potomac, but he functioned primarily as a chief of staff for Grant, who made all the major decisions. In the early going, those consisted first of prodding the cautious Meade forward and keeping his troops battering on the door to Richmond. But it was Lee who struck Grant first, his army crossing the Rapidan at the beginning of May 1864. Outnumbered more than two to one, Confederate forces caught the Federals in the tangled woods near Chancellorsville in the confused and terrifying two-day Battle of the Wilderness, inflicting more than seventeen thousand casualties. To Lincoln and Lee's equal surprise, however, Grant did not shy away from the slaughter, instead "sidling" to the left and crashing into fresh Confederate entrenchments at Spotsylvania Courthouse on May 10. For the next eight days Grant launched assaults that came close to shattering the Army of Northern Virginia, at a further cost of eighteen thousand men. Undaunted by such massive losses, he promised Lincoln that he would "fight it out on this line if it takes all summer." Such pugnacity in the face of staggering casualty lists with no end in sight was a mixed blessing for the president. It was worse still for Lee, whose sixty thousand soldiers suffered more than 30 percent casualties in three terrible weeks. "Lee's army is really whipped," Grant declared, "our success . . . is already assured." If the South could not be beaten, it would be bled to death.

In the days that followed, however, Grant overreached himself as disastrously as any of Lincoln's most bungling generals ever had. While Lee augmented and entrenched his troops on a strong line near Cold Harbor, Grant replenished his losses with fresh troops stripped from the defenses of Washington. The men had been training for two years in heavy artillery regiments, but they had not seen combat. Yet they knew enough to anticipate the coming carnage, some of them pinning to their uniforms slips of paper with their names to ease identification. Grant sent them forward in a single wave—and saw them met by a concentrated rebel fire that one man described as "simply murder." In a matter of minutes more than seven thousand Union troops fell, at a cost to Lee numbering in the hundreds. By the time Union forces disengaged on June 12, Grant's losses had nearly doubled. Newspapers across the North branded Grant "the fumbling butcher" and called for his dismissal. Lincoln held his breath.

Grant's strategy had been to lure Lee into open battle away from the safety of prepared defenses. But Lee did not dare risk so much. Confederates by this stage had no ready supply of men or matériel to draw upon. After Cold Harbor Grant abandoned his hopes of quick victory, shifting his troops deftly across the James River and laying siege to Petersburg on June 15, 1864. Despite the formidable earthworks that protected it, he decided, that town held the key to Union victory. If Lee failed to maintain its defense, northern troops could march quickly through to seize Richmond. If he manned its trenches, Grant would bleed him white.

Around Petersburg nearly two hundred thousand men fought over the complex system of forts and earthworks. As soldiers on both sides dug ever longer trenches—extending more than thirty miles in all—in a fruitless effort to outflank each other, the world glimpsed the grim face of modern war. On July 30, 1864, Union forces exploded a mine totaling eight thousand pounds of gunpowder under a portion of the Confederate works. In the ensuing Battle of the Crater northern forces tried to storm through the gap blasted open, only to find themselves trapped by the steep walls that the detonation had created. Almost four thousand black and white bluecoats were shot down or captured to no purpose. In the months that followed, Grant stuck more closely to his strategy of attrition, biding his time. Snipers plied their deadly art across no-man's-land, siege mortars rained down death, and small-scale raiding parties made trench life miserable for both sides. From June 1864 through the next ten months, Grant's siege continued.

When Grant had gone to Washington, D.C., in the spring of 1864, he turned over command in the western theater to his divisional subordinate, William Tecumseh Sherman. The pitiless, plain-spoken Sherman had relatively free rein to destroy what remained of the Army of Tennessee as it fell back across Georgia. In May and June 1864 Confederate General Joe Johnston, recovered from the wounds he received at Seven Pines, gave ground to Sherman in a masterful series of skirmishing withdrawals, digging in on terrain of his own choosing again and again and daring the Yankees to come at him. Sherman took the bait only once, at Kennesaw Mountain on June 27, 1864, losing three thousand men in a single charge. Thereafter he stuck to flank attacks, driving the southerners back steadily and whittling away at their numbers. To Illinois private George Cram, battle now seemed more ghastly than ever. "Now a poor boy has his leg shot away," he recorded, "another has his face blown off by a shell, and one by one they fall." A month later he wrote, "Bullets are continually whistling and monster shells flying from line to line . . . the very air seems full of death and destruction." By mid-1864 such scenes suggested nothing of gallantry. To staunch such massive bloodshed, Sherman pursued a feinting, jabbing style of warfare in the late spring. If the Confederates could be pushed toward defeat by light skirmishing, so much the better for all concerned. Sherman would "never go to hell," one Yankee declared proudly, "for he'll flank the devil and make heaven in spite of all the guards."

In mid-July, however, such regimental waltzing came to a sudden, bloody halt. Alarmed by Sherman's steady advance and Johnston's shrewd but obvious reluctance to attack him, Jefferson Davis replaced the cautious Johnston with Lee's most celebrated warrior, the much-maimed Hood. It was a disastrous choice, as even the author of Pickett's Charge could see. "Hood is a bold fighter," Lee demurred. "I am doubtful as to the other qualities necessary." Within eleven days of taking the reins, Hood had thrown away nearly fifteen thousand irreplaceable troops who had been hammering against Sherman's lines around Atlanta. Total Union casualties barely topped six thousand men. Instead of falling back upon Savannah or Augusta, Hood responded to strategic defeat in the only way he knew how: by attacking. In this case, he turned his back on Sherman and marched his battered, bewildered soldiers back up toward Tennessee on a mad scheme to liberate Kentucky itself. Sherman simply detached a subordinate to keep an eye on Hood's ruined Confederates, who wound up shortly enough on that awful road into Franklin. With Hood's departure, Sherman entered Atlanta on September 2, 1864.

A continued defense of Atlanta might have been the last hope for Confederate survival because it might have ensured the political defeat of Abraham Lincoln in November 1864. Lincoln fully expected to lose that election, writing in August of that year, "It seems exceedingly probable that this Administration will not be reelected." Hood's loss of Atlanta changed that political dimension, and Lincoln won overwhelmingly. The end of the Confederacy was ensured, and yet the butchery by Lincoln and Davis continued.

Hood's bizarre departure gave Sherman's troops a clear path to the Atlantic, yet military wisdom argued against any further advance. With supply lines menaced by rebel raiders stretching all the way back to the Ohio, Sherman had been hard-pressed to keep his troops armed and fed during the Atlanta campaign. If guerrillas disrupted the flow of supplies in his rear once he moved forward again, they might wreak much more havoc than Hood's wild thrusts had accomplished. Clearly the path of safety was to build up his supplies in Atlanta, reequip his troops, and set out slowly and gingerly toward the next goal.

Instead, Sherman announced on October 19 a stunningly different plan: "I propose to abandon Atlanta, and the railroad back to Chattanooga, to sally forth to ruin Georgia and bring up on the sea-shore." Instead of allowing southern insurgents to make war on him, he would make war on the South itself. "War is cruelty," he told a delegation of Atlanta civic leaders, "and you cannot refine it." First he would burn their city and abandon his supply lines. Marching his forces in three parallel columns toward Savannah, he proposed to live off the land like the plundering armies of old. On November 15 he set the city ablaze and marched down the Decatur road. As they marched, Sherman remembered years later, "some band, by accident, struck up the anthem of 'John Brown's soul goes marching on'; the men caught up the strain, and never before or since have I heard the chorus of 'Glory, glory, hallelu-

jah!' done with more spirit, or in better harmony of time and place."
Over the next month Sherman's "march to the sea" cut a path across
the state sixty miles wide and two hundred miles long; troops pillaged
according to their needs and desires, and burned and destroyed whatever they could not carry. Before secession Sherman had warned a
southern acquaintance of disunion's folly: "You people speak so lightly
of war, you don't know what you're talking about. War is a terrible
thing." Now he set out to prove the accuracy of his judgment. By the
time he rendered Savannah to Lincoln as "a Christmas present," Sherman and his men had caused more than $100 million damage to the
state's infrastructure and demoralized Confederates everywhere.

Sherman turned to the Carolinas in February 1865, his troops pursuing even crueler retribution. Columbia fell to Federal troops on February 17 and went up in flames that night. Retreating Confederates started
some fires to keep supplies out of Union hands. Confederate troops
evacuated Charleston the next day. Riot, arson, and plunder accompanied northern regiments everywhere as they moved across the state that
had given birth to secession four years before. "The truth is the whole
army is burning with an insatiable desire to wreak vengeance upon
South Carolina," Sherman had warned Henry Halleck. They did their
work well. Union soldier Charles Wills wrote on March 5, 1865, about
a dispatch the Union soldiers had found. At least one Confederate general from South Carolina, Wade Hampton, had not wanted Sherman
to dally in the state. He wrote his fellow South Carolinian, General
Matthew Butler, "Do not attempt to delay Sherman's march by destroying bridges, or any other means. For God's sake let him get out of the
country as quickly as possible." The soldier from Illinois added, "Were I
one of the S.C. chivalry I'd be in favor of turning out en masse and
building up roads for him."

As Grant sieged in Virginia and Sherman marched in Georgia and
the Carolinas, desertion in the Confederate ranks spiraled out of control, stretching Lee's forces paper-thin. Given the awful odds that they
would suffer death, disease, or injury—or that they would shed the blood
of others, wrecking families and communities just like their own—
desertion on each side ran into the hundreds of thousands. An estimated
one in eight Confederate soldiers deserted (on the Union side, one in
ten). Soldiers frequently fought for a term, slipped back home to man-

age their affairs, then returned to the ranks as conditions allowed. Thousands of others on both sides went home reckoning that fighting would be of no benefit to their private interests or ethical concerns. In addition to those thousands who simply walked away from the war, perhaps an equal number surrendered to the other side. After emancipation, white northern soldiers sometimes refused to fight "for the Negro." Southerners frequently rooted their decision to desert in class terms, decrying "a rich man's war and a poor man's fight." A leading cause of military desertions was the privation suffered by families back home. State and district taxes were inadequate for relief. Soldiers were caught between patriotism and the need to care for their families.

Deserters were arrested, court-martialed, sentenced, and sometimes shot. With only one month left in the war, a court found seventeen-year-old Antone Ricker guilty of "willful desertion." It ordered his execution "without delay as a just punishment for your crime and a fitting example for your comrades." A. Baron Holmes, whose prominent Charleston family had used its influence to get him a furlough, observed another group of four deserters so sentenced. He wrote, "Thank God I was not in the shooting squad. Those men were 'regulars' who had not been home in three years, their families were starving, and they could not get furloughs, but went anyway and were convicted of desertion, and were murdered." The situation of young aristocrat Holmes contrasted sharply. First, he had been assigned to "duty in the Charleston Post Office." Then he was "detailed by the Confederate Secretary of War as Assistant Superintendent of the Nitre and Mining Bureau." Transferred in 1863 to the Palmetto Guard Artillery, he often obtained passes home.

As Confederate armies retreated from state to state toward the end of the war, desertion rates rose dramatically. One extended family from South Carolina, the proud Gunter clan, had been fighting together for four long years, first in Virginia, then in Tennessee and Georgia. Now the company in which they served sat on the last car of a troop train as it wound its way close by their home, moving slowly northward out of the state to continue the fight in North Carolina. One of the Gunters noted that if the linchpin was pulled, the car would be left behind. Mysteriously, the linchpin did come out, and as the rest of the train pulled away, the entire company got off and walked home. When the state agent came to take one of the Gunters back to the army, this seasoned fighter, rifle held across his lap, informed the agent he'd just as soon die on his own land. The agent left him alone. Other areas of the South broke out in local warfare as deserters battled Confederate and state militia. One Confederate judge confided his joy when the Union army of occupation arrived, thereby ending the local "civil war."

The large number of deserters, however, was good news for Grant, whose lengthy siege of Petersburg finally succeeded in March 1865. When Grant ordered an assault all along the line, Confederate resistance crumbled. Richmond fell on April 3, 1865. Lincoln visited Richmond shortly after the Union victory there. He signaled a new meaning of freedom, a meaning of mutual respect, when he, the president of the United States and a white man, returned in equal manner the bow of a black man and former slave. Another former slave fell to his knees before the president, to which Lincoln responded, "Don't kneel to me. That is not right. You must kneel to God only, and thank Him for the liberty you will enjoy hereafter." To African Americans, the man they called "Father Abraham" was all too easily conflated with a new Moses, rendering the still-unfolding Confederate collapse part of a divine destiny.

Upon leaving the city, Lincoln asked the band accompanying his entourage to play "The Marsellaise" to honor his guest from France, the Marquis de Chambrun. Then, asking the band to play "Dixie," he said it was "good to show the rebels that, with us in power, they will be free to hear it again." Lincoln's bow to the former slave and the former Confederates meant more than mutual respect. The near providential right of self-mastery now extended to former slaves as well as to former rebels. To disallow this self-mastery would be to undercut the very principles, even articles of faith, that had driven Lincoln's evolution over the course of the war.

Days later, Lee told his troops that he was "compelled to yield to overwhelming numbers and resources." He commended their steadfastness and valor but "determined to avoid the useless sacrifice of those whose past services have endeared them to their countrymen." The remains of Lee's proud Army of Northern Virginia, fatigued but still a fighting force, surrendered on April 9, 1865, at Appomattox Courthouse. In mid-April General Joe Johnston likewise conceded. "Our people are tired of the war," he summed up, "feel themselves whipped, and will not fight." He was out of options: "My small force is melting away like snow before the sun." General Johnston surrendered his forces on April 26 near Durham, North Carolina. On May 26 General Kirby Smith surrendered his army. On June 23 in Indian Territory (now Oklahoma), Brigadier General Stand Watie and the last Confederate soldiers formally surrendered. These troops of Cherokee, Choctaw, Creek, Seminole, and Osage, however, continued guerrilla actions in the West.

When Jefferson Davis and the Confederate government escaped from Richmond, they urged the struggle to continue and planned to form a government in exile. Davis and the remnant of his cabinet and generals met on May 2, 1865, in Abbeville, South Carolina, for their last council of war. They stayed in the home of Leila Griffin's kinsman, former U.S. congressman Armistead Burt, where Davis reunited with his family. Four years earlier Burt had believed so strongly that the North would not fight against the South that he declared he would drink all of the blood shed as a result of secession. At this meeting, however, Burt was not the gracious southern host. He offered Davis and his cabinet no refreshments, and he certainly drank no blood. Two weeks later the President of the Confederate States of America was captured at Irwinville, Georgia. Though the story wasn't true, taunting northern newspapers reported that he had been disguised as a woman. So ended the Great Rebellion of the most powerful slaveholding class the world has ever seen.

At the conclusion of the war Sergeant Cram and the 105th Illinois Infantry returned home. The unit had suffered 494 casualties, either killed or disabled. Only 460, fewer than half of the men who marched away to win the war for the Union in 1862, returned home. The survivors arrived in Chicago with no celebration, no notice. No one even gave them food or water. As the *Chicago Tribune* reported, "These things ought not so to be."

After four years of butchery, what had the conflict finally meant? Had anything truly changed? As the conflict wound down, three veterans among many millions summed up best the cause and consequence of the war. Two African American soldiers from Massachusetts, in the hospital recuperating from wounds, discussed their motivation in the fight. One had lost an arm and said, "Oh I should like to have it, but I don't begrudge it." The other, who lost a leg, answered, "Well, 'twas in a glorious cause, and if I'd lost my life I should have been satisfied. I knew what I was fighting for." So too did Virginian Edmund Ruffin,

slaveholder and agricultural reformer, spectator at John Brown's hanging, secessionist who fired the first shot against Fort Sumter. For four
years he had served the Confederacy. At last from his ruined plantation
outside Richmond, he penned one last note of defiance on June 17, 1865.
For Ruffin, as for his class, there could be no true surrender. "May such
sentiments be held universally in the outraged and downtrodden
South," he declared, "though in stillness and silence, until the now far-
distant day shall arrive for just retribution for Yankee usurpation, oppression, and atrocious outrages, and for deliverance and vengeance for
the now ruined, subjugated and enslaved Southern States!" One last
time Ruffin proclaimed "my unmitigated hatred to yankee rule—to all
political, social, and business connections with Yankees, and with the
perfidious, malignant and vile Yankee race." Then he blew out his
brains.

Eight

"I Want You to Come Home"

> The Federals proceeded to Gallatin, but found no Confederates upon
> whom to be revenged. But their insatiable cruelty must be gratified,
> and with that fiendishness characteristic of the Yankee soldier, they
> sought out the aged and peaceful citizens, and dragged them from
> their homes, to incarcerate them in their wretched dungeons.

THUS DID SALLY ROCHESTER FORD'S 1863 NOVEL, *Raids and Romances; or, Morgan and his Men*, depict her idea of Yankee behavior on the southern home front. Yankees insulted ladies, abused the elderly, and even desecrated the Bible. Ford and other southern novelists announced clearly that the Confederacy, and not Yankeedom, deserved the loyalty of its citizens.

By contrasting the North and South in terms of evil versus good, southern authors, as well as Confederate political leaders, tried to convince southerners to stay the course. If battles were lost, if times were hard, God was testing their faith, and they must persevere. But however dramatically media portrayed the evil North, however valiantly slavery's defenders fought at Antietam or Spotsylvania, their benighted regime ultimately failed on the home front. Southerners were willing to sacrifice but were divided on what this war for southern liberty meant. Their opposing ideologies created internal conflict, and that instability contributed to their downfall. Confederate victory, predicated on a dream of internal unity that crossed lines of class, gender, and race, was never realized. For all the stirring successes and desperate defeats of the Rebel host at Antietam, Shiloh, Chancellorsville, and beyond, the real heart of the military struggle lay far from what most would have understood as the lines of battle. In the end, as the African American historian W.E.B. Du Bois argued, it was not the clash of Blue and Gray that ultimately brought down the slaveholders' rebellion, but "a general strike" of black workers defecting from southern fields and factories to join Union forces "as a new labor force." Even as they struggled to fend off the armies of Grant and Sherman, Confederates proved unable to check the steadily swelling movement of southern blacks to liberate themselves from bondage, and of nonslaveholding southern whites to reject participation in a military conflict for which they increasingly felt no commitment. By 1865 those twin rebellions had merged unwittingly into a powerful democratic revolt that shattered the solons' regime. Few should have been surprised. "If we are defeated," the *Augusta Chronicle* had predicted in February 1861, "it will be by the people at home." And indeed, what occurred on the many-fronted home front almost guaranteed the Confederacy's collapse.

Three groups of southerners varied in their views of what the war meant. One group, constituting about 40 percent of southerners, thought it meant freedom: God was finally ending their captivity. This enslaved population, the majority in South Carolina and Mississippi, wanted the Confederacy to lose. In 1831 the French aristocrat Alexis de Tocqueville had visited the United States to study a functioning democracy. At that time he predicted, "If freedom is denied negroes in the South, they will seize it themselves." And they did.

The other 60 percent of southerners in the Confederacy, the whites, were also divided. Of white southerners, 66 percent held no slaves. This group of nonslaveholding yeomen included Unionists, whom Lincoln had erroneously thought would prevent secession. Most of these nonslaveholders, however, supported the Confederacy because it represented their hearth and home. This group, which included a large minority of landless and poor whites, wanted freedom from government interference. In this regard they encountered three major problems: conscription, poverty, and the unevenness of wartime sacrifice.

The Confederacy's slaveholding master class also faced internal contradictions. As people who were opposed to a strong national government they also opposed a strong national military, and Jefferson Davis found himself continually in the position of having to convince southerners to defend "their birthright of freedom and equality."

The question of Confederate victory or defeat depended on the ability of its labor force, black and white, to sustain southern armies in the field. The masters' rebellion would survive only as long as their slaves continued to toil on their behalf. The slaves were the ones, after all, who raised the food and cared for the animals, who grew the cotton and made the clothes, who worked in factories including munitions plants, who built fortifications. While responses to the war varied widely among African Americans, many purposely worked against the Confederacy, both subtly and blatantly. Freedom did not await official proclamations; it began at the outset of war. While southern whites often ignored the presence of the slaves who filled their plates and poured their tea, those enslaved people listened and learned and spread the news. In early September 1860 whites had to chase African Americans away from political meetings. A local editor complained that "every political speech . . . delivered in Macon [Georgia] had attracted a number of negroes, who, without entering the Hall, have managed to linger around and hear what the orators say." One woman remembered how whites foretold southern victory against the horrible Yankees. She had a different viewpoint: "From dat minute I started praying for freedom. All de res' o' de women done de same." Whites also acknowledged the precariousness of slavery during wartime, even as they noted that a change had come over their enslaved property. In September 1861 Mary Chesnut wrote that her enslaved butler "scents freedom in the air." Although Chesnut had always thought African Americans were an excitable group, now she found, "They go about in their black masks, not a ripple or an emotion showing."

Southern whites' greatest fear was slave rebellion. Remembering the aftermath of Haiti's revolution, southerners feared "anarchy, horrible carnage, and crimes too revolting to mention." The need to fight Union soldiers on one front and to guard against insurrection on another set the stage for conflicting mindsets. Confederate measures to avoid a general insurrection meant that fewer resources were available for the war. Weapons and manpower needed for the Confederate army were also needed for state militias that had to handle all slave patrols. Many on the home front felt defenseless. "There is not sufficient men left in the county for patrol duty," worried one. To forestall insurrection, whites clamped down. Eavesdropping, spying on black worship services and gatherings, interrogating enslaved children, and rewarding informants all helped to preclude a general uprising. In 1862 authorities in Mississippi hanged "some forty for plotting an insurrection, and there has been about that many put in irons." Slaves caught with guns were hanged. Some were hanged simply for stating that "Lincoln would set us free." Ties to kin and community, however, restricted plotting; most enslaved people kept their heads down, kept the southern economy running, albeit more slowly, and watched carefully.

Slavery required such extensive supervision that anything apart from the status quo jeopardized the system. As the war progressed and more and more white men left rural southern communities, enslaved African Americans who remained on farms and plantations enjoyed greater autonomy. With the war's disruption of routine, institutional control and personal supervision of slaves slackened, and enslaved families took advantage of the situation. They expanded their garden plots and traditional spaces around their cabins. Black women spent more time with their own children, and black men affirmed parental authority. Enslaved workers gained some leverage in bargaining when white women, in charge of the farm or plantation in the absence of husbands, had to rely on enslaved men for details on management. In many instances slaves were running the plantations. At the same time other slaves stopped or slowed their work efforts. An Alabama slaveholder worried, "In the negro population in some places there is manifested a disposition to mis-rule and insubordination." The very threat of violence upon which employers of enslaved labor had always relied for motivation was undermined. "Some of them are getting so high on anticipation of their glorious freedom by the Yankees," whites complained, "that they resist a whipping."

One form of rebellion was escape, and the front lines beckoned. The diary of Rufus Kinsley of Vermont contained many entries about fugitives arriving at his Union military encampment. One wrenching story told how he had to release a fugitive "from his iron yoke, and ball and chain, with which he had traveled 18 miles. His ear had been cut off, to mark him, and he had been well branded with the hot iron. His flesh was badly lacerated with the whip, and torn by dogs; but he escaped."

Slaves working on the Confederate front lines often found their way to the northern army—sometimes to the complete bewilderment of the slaveholders. Slaves who escaped surprised slaveholder Edmund Ruffin, whose proslavery views had not anticipated that "happy" slaves would leave of their own accord. James B. Griffin was confounded when his enslaved body servant escaped near Yorktown in 1862. "It is very singular and I cant account for it," a perplexed Griffin wrote. Imagining that Abram would return in penitence, Griffin continued, "I am sorry he was such a fool—I'll bet he will always be sorry for it." Other officers would not take that bet. Writing home to request an enslaved attendant, one southerner specified that they should not send Bob: "He would be in Lincoln's army before you could say Jack Robinson." As war and Union troops presented opportunities for freedom, more family and kin groups—sometimes even entire plantation communities—fled slavery. A Texan warned that the state's vast borders with Mexico and the Gulf Coast needed guards because of the opportunities they afforded to escapees. One white woman recorded in her diary, "The runaways are numerous and bold." Many escaped to the woods to await Union approach. With Yankees not far off, James McCutcheon, a Louisiana sugar plantation owner, reported in 1863 that 233 of his 250 slaves had run away. Near Natchez a plantation owner who had 118 slaves in January 1862 had 33 in December of that year. One Mississippian complained to the governor, "There is a general disposition among the negroes to be insubordinate, and to run away, and go off to the federals."

The enslaved population on the home front supported the Union in many ways. In addition to organizing work stoppages and slowdowns, in addition to escaping to Union lines to help fight or work for the Federals, slaves also provided an intelligence infrastructure for invading Union armies. In a common occurrence, a Union spy in Tennessee reported, "I found that my best source of information was the colored men, who were employed in various capacities of a military nature." And Grant's success at Vicksburg relied on information and help from the countryside's enslaved population. They showed him little-known roads and locations of food stashes; they warned him about Confederate forces. African American Albert Johnson, for example, served as a scout and pointed out the location of Confederate gun batteries. In a thousand ways, both spectacular and virtually unnoticeable, African

Americans, backed by Union armies, tore away at the foundations of bondage during the war years.

The situation was very different for yeomen and poor whites who supported the Confederacy. Most whites were landowning yeoman farmers who wished for a degree of personal independence and self-sufficiency that was beyond their reach. Already precariously perched within the idealized civilization that proslavery advocates claimed the antebellum South had achieved, the war for southern independence intensified the hopelessness of that aspiration. Most in this group, like most white Americans in the North, preferred a racialized society where white people were treated equally and African Americans were kept subordinate. Prior to the war, class conflict in the South was largely hidden, diffused through categories of slave and free. Whites tended to share the assumptions of a society oriented primarily around small rural communities led by a slaveowning elite. Pride, revolutionary heritage, and race-defined notions of liberty gave them a basic consensus for fighting. And yet this consensus, and indeed that postulated civilization, presupposed that planters would take care of the poor and intercede on behalf of the yeomen when necessary.

Some yeomen, often from upcountry areas, dissented from the start. In North Carolina, when slaveholder William Pettigrew was encouraging volunteers, a local farmer objected. Ellsberry Ambrose, who owned no slaves and worked the family farm with his wife and two sons, flatly declared, "The rich people are only going to make the poor people do all the fighting; the rich only pretend to go." Pettigrew, who was the county justice, arrested Ambrose, who spent two months in the local jail. Another member of the Ambrose clan also went to jail, this time for shouting, "I am a Lincoln man, and I'll be damned if anyone who voted for Jeff Davis ought not to be hanged." The advent of war—whose purpose was to maintain the slaveholders' way of life—demanded consensus among white social classes as to the benefits of that way of life for all. But when nonslaveholders began to go hungry, they increasingly resented the planter class that represented no more than five percent of the white population. For yeomen and poor families, evading the sacrifices of war was not an option. It meant doing without necessities and suffering poverty, and they were galled by the disparity. Even prior to war the yeoman church-based culture had looked askance at aristocratic extravagance. During wartime, from the yeoman perspective, revelry, banquets, or the purchase of a fashionable Parisian gown to lift upper-class spirits bordered on treason.

Over time many yeomen came to feel betrayed. As the war forced an expansion of southern industry in textiles and steel, some southern investors earned huge profits. A very few wealthy planters even made fortunes during the Civil War by investing in railroads and other northern enterprises. Poorer southerners did not fail to notice that some of their wealthy neighbors seized opportunities to buy the inexpensive lands and homes of deceased or financially distressed yeomen, some of whom were fighting on the front lines. This seemed the very antithesis of the harmonious Anglo-Saxon civilization promised by the war's advocates. George Alfred Trenholm, Confederate secretary of the treasury, was a wealthy Charleston shipowner, businessman, and politician who bought up such property. For most elites the war's early austerity meant giving up luxury items. When the Confederacy required each household to contribute a horse, yeomen may have given their one and only horse, needed for plowing and transportation; the wealthy gave one out of many. As early as 1861 discontent was evident. A Georgia citizen asked his local newspaper, "Is it right that the poor man should be taxed for the support of the war, when the war was brought about on the slave question, and the slave at home accumulating for the benefit of this master, and the poor man's farm left uncultivated, and a chance for his wife to be a widow, and his children orphans?"

Southern slaveholders, a large majority in the new Congress of the Confederate States of America, held to their faith in their perfected way of life and the narrow and crabbed freedom on which it primarily rested. That no one could be truly free without protection of his property was a proposition to which most in the leading ranks of the North would have assented. That every other freedom depended on the safeguarding of one particular form of property, however, was not. Ironically, while the protection of this "property" was a major cause of the war, the Confederate government empowered itself to appropriate it in the name of that war. Impressed enslaved laborers were the war workers of the Confederacy; their labor relieved white soldiers so they could fight. But using enslaved labor so close to the Union lines meant that soldiers had to guard the hands at all times. Many times a planter refused the army's emergency request for slaves; many a planter agreed with James Allen, who wrote in his plantation notebook, "Declined sending any." When armed forces came to collect enslaved workers, some plantation owners hid them in the woods or paid bribes to the soldiers.

Dissension from the slaveholders beleaguered Jefferson Davis throughout his tenure. The constitution that Davis had to work with, written as it was for negotiation rather than for governing during war, left him floundering. Governors Zebulon Vance of North Carolina, Joseph Brown of Georgia, and Pendleton Murrah of Texas refused to accept Confederate national authority over their "sovereign states." Davis also had rebellious pockets of pro-Unionists. In Virginia, Stonewall Jackson had to put down a local "Blue Ridge Rebellion" of several hundred. Davis downplayed his autocratic response in relation to that of Lincoln, who clearly considered the Constitution a document of national power and did not hesitate to use the war powers granted to him as commander in chief. Yet the reactions of both leaders were similar. The same time that Davis was giving an address to the Confederate Congress on February 22, 1862, contrasting the Confederacy's refusal to restrict "personal liberty or the freedom of speech, of thought, or of the press" with Lincoln's abuse of these same rights, William G. "Parson" Brownlow was in prison in Knoxville, Tennessee, for his pro-Union newspaper. Five days later, that Congress gave Davis the authority to declare martial law, and he was quick to suspend habeas corpus and order the arrest of dissenters in areas seething with pro-Union sentiments. Davis declared martial law in Norfolk, Portsmouth, Richmond, and Petersburg, Virginia. He suspended civil liberties in eastern Tennessee, which was in open rebellion against the Confederacy. The Confederate vice president, Alexander Stephens, condemned Davis's suspension of habeas corpus as military despotism. Better to lose the war, he declared earnestly, than to lose "Constitutional Liberty at home." It was that sort of democratic nicety that helped fashion Confederate defeat.

Most southerners had little thought of habeas corpus or liberties abridged—that is, until the need for soldiers brought the government to their front doors. The hope of those who planned to sit out the war was dashed in the spring of 1862, when the Confederate Congress enacted a draft. Men aged eighteen to thirty-five had to report for a period of three years. Soldiers who had voluntarily enlisted in 1861 and whose terms were up were required to remain in service another two years. Certain occupations, such as teachers and government officials, were exempt, and the Confederacy allowed religious exemptions for pacifists. Most contentiously, anyone wealthy enough could hire a substitute to take his place.

Dissatisfaction over the draft was immediate and brought class conflict into focus. Caleb Herbert of Texas warned that it might provoke Texans into "raising . . . the Lone Star Flag." Although the vast majority of yeomen accepted conscription in 1862 as a sacrifice they were willing to make, their level of willingness decreased when they saw that some of their wealthy neighbors were not so willing to sacrifice. Yeomen observed the ease with which the wealthy received exemptions from fighting or got "safe" army jobs behind the lines or in the state militias. Some complained that doctors who gave medical excuses to friends were "quite partial toward the rich." An Arkansas judge wrote in his diary, "Most of those who were so willing to shed the last drop of blood in the contest for a separate Government, are entirely unwilling to shed the first." For some, universal conscription changed antiwar feelings from a passive resistance to an active strategy of forming antiwar leagues, arming themselves, and devising plans for resistance, though nothing occurred that approached the antidraft riots in the North.

One of the most controversial laws passed by the Confederate Congress was the Twenty Negro Law of October 1862. This act, which exempted one white man from military service for twenty or more slaves under his control, prompted huge class resentment. Issued in response to Lincoln's announcement that he was preparing to issue an Emancipation Proclamation, planters made the most of the new exemption. Slaveholders with eighteen or nineteen slaves immediately tried to purchase one or two more in order to qualify. The *Savannah Republican* reported that certain plantation owners divided their slaves into gangs of twenty or more, put them on separate tracts of land, "and made their sons and other relatives overseers to protect them from conscription." Planters justified themselves in patriotic terms, citing their importance in keeping the enslaved workers from insurrection and in aiding the southern economy with food production. When yeomen and poor whites saw them growing more cotton than food, planters responded that cotton production, with its longer cultivation cycle, helped keep idle slaves busy. As food shortages mounted, the claim struck many fighting men as hollow.

Reaction to the Twenty Negro Law tore the fabric of the home front. Even before the new law took effect, yeomen had believed conscription was unfair to them because their departure left women alone to look after farm and home, while elite women had enslaved workers to help them. The new draft exemption became a powerful symbol to common white southerners that the war benefited the rich at the expense of the poor. Again, common soldiers and their families raised the issue that "we poor soldiers . . . are fighting for the 'rich mans negro.'" Farmers in Virginia swore that "they will be shot before they will fight for a country where the rich men's property is to be taken care of and those who have no overseers are to go and fight first." An anonymous letter to a South Carolina editor asked why members of the legislature were exempt from Confederate service: "Justice demands that they should be in service, for all of them were acknowledged Secessionists, and many of them members of the Convention that voted South Carolina out of the Union." When it appeared that the elite had abrogated their responsibilities, the ideals girding the southern way of life frayed as the needy pondered their traditional deference.

Too late to keep these conflicts submerged, the Confederate government did amend conscription in an emergency session in December 1863. They repealed substitutions as well as most exemptions, and they expanded the power to impress enslaved workers. In February 1864, even more desperate for manpower, they expanded the draft to include all white men seventeen to fifty years old and also free blacks, but they did not repeal the Twenty Negro Law. Finally, they even suggested recruiting slaves as soldiers, though their promise of freedom to those who would serve was limited to a second-class citizenship without equal rights. Debate over the issue was hot. When Major General Howell Cobb wrote to Confederate secretary of war James Seddon, he stated what abolitionists had been saying all along: "If slaves will make good soldiers our whole theory of slavery is wrong." Some soldiers said that if it helped the South win independence, they should do it. Most said that they would refuse to fight alongside blacks. Because Lee needed troops, he supported the measure, and in late March 1865 the Confederacy authorized the enlistment of African Americans under orders specifying only recruits already freed by their masters. One company of black Confederate soldiers drilled in Richmond and served with Confederate forces in Virginia in the last days of the war, but the Confederacy's decision to sacrifice slavery for independence came too late to have any effect on the battlefront.

Just as yeomen noticed that they bore the brunt of enlistment, they also saw the discrepancy of hardship on the home front. With fewer men at home to plant and till crops, poverty and want were gnawing realities for many. Almost from the onset of the war the South suffered from shortages in every category of goods due to the cessation of northern trade, their own rudimentary transportation system, the desertion of enslaved labor, the deterioration of irreplaceable tools, military impressments, and a growing reluctance near battle areas to plant at all lest the crop be confiscated by the Confederacy or destroyed by the Union.

Shortages also weighed heavily on the poor. Although blockade runners were able to bring in some military items, these private entrepreneurs also used precious cargo space for luxury items rather than necessities. Coffee and sugar all but disappeared from the Confederacy within a year of the war's outbreak. The lack of salt was a particular problem because it was needed to cure meat. In May 1861 a sack of salt cost sixty-five cents. By October it cost seven dollars. As early as spring 1862 food prices for wheat, flour, cornmeal, and bacon were four to six times greater than they had been in 1860. Other essential articles—fabric, iron, tin, copper, and utensils—underwent similar radical increases in price. The price index for commodities that equaled 100 in 1861 reached 763 by early 1863. Inflation on food was worse. The average family food bill was about $6.65 per month in the spring of 1861; in early 1863 it was $68. Inflation became even more acute after the Union victories at Gettysburg and Vicksburg in the summer of 1863. In 1864, $46 purchased what $1 did in 1861. Regional differences existed, but the general pattern of spiraling, uncontrolled price increases made the purchase of many goods impossible for a poor family or those dependent on a private's pay of $11 per month (if they got that).

As much as shortages, Confederate monetary policy caused rampant inflation. States required to fulfill their financial quota for the Confederacy did so simply by printing their own money. Many state banknotes showed very clearly the origin of southern wealth—pictures of slaves working in cotton fields or driving cotton-loaded wagons. Without that labor the currency was a symbol of nothing. Worst of all, the Confederacy pumped out a steady stream of shaky currency to supplement shaky state banknotes. Although Confederate treasury secretary Christopher Memminger had incomparably better banking credentials than did his northern counterpart Salmon Chase, the conditions on which his actions would rest were chaotic at best. The Confederate congress, counting on future generations to redeem the notes, never passed legislation authorizing this new money as legal tender. Soldiers paid in these banknotes were unable to pay bills with them. Paper money was increasingly regarded as useless.

The rhetoric of King Cotton, insiders knew, was desperately hollow, and even in peacetime the Confederacy lacked the resources needed to nurture a growing internal market. Southerners had learned to depend on northern goods, and no new flag was likely to change that fact in the short run. Whereas the North had a tariff to raise revenue, the federal blockade limited southern means of raising money. As in the North, Davis imposed a host of consumption taxes. He also allowed Confederate agents to impress southern crops, draft animals, and slaves to further the war effort. Not surprisingly, such efforts drove resources underground, killed off the desire to grow larger crops, and inspired open revolt in some localities. Agricultural and industrial production dwindled, while inflation skyrocketed. By Appomattox consumer prices in the South had risen 9,000 percent over Fort Sumter levels. Grant's and Sherman's armies were in some sense irrelevant by war's end; given time, inflation itself seems to have been enough to uproot the slaveholders' republic.

Populating the southern home front were those white men unable or unwilling to serve in the army—mainly the disabled, the elderly, the too young—and women. With sometimes as many as 70 percent of white men eighteen to forty-five years of age absent from a community, white women had to fend for themselves, obtaining food and supplies and making family decisions. Women responded to the challenge by doing whatever needed to be done, running farms and businesses with increasing confidence as the war progressed.

At first exigencies of war required and enabled elite and yeoman women to make more substantial contributions to family and community than had been previously possible. With the enthusiasm that comes from doing God's work, they transformed their everyday church groups and sewing circles and benevolent societies into organizations to support the war effort. Typical was a fund-raising event organized and run by the Southern Sisters' Aid Society in South Carolina in November 1862. The "Fair and Tableaux" in the Masonic hall sold "fancy articles and refreshments, including *real store-bought Coffee*." Women had more power to make decisions, but as the war continued, hunger and want limited their range of choices.

Whether to keep food on the table or to contribute to the war effort (and probably for both reasons), women availed themselves of job opportunities. The Confederacy set up factories to produce tents and uniforms for its army, and in addition "clothing bureaus" contracted with women in their homes. In cities like Augusta, Georgia, fifteen hundred seamstresses worked for the Confederacy. Jobs in southern textile mills expanded for all whites during and after the Civil War. Prior to the war most mills hired men but also employed some children and some young, unmarried women. During the war adult married women also began to work in textile mills. The war opened vocational opportunities in government agencies as women took over traditional male jobs as scribes and clerks. In the Confederate capital of Richmond, "large numbers of females" were "employed to cut money." One South Carolinian noted in his diary in August 1864 that "govt. work has been the means of giving a living to many persons who have lost their all during the war. Widows of Officers & soldiers, refugees without a home, & other destitute persons thus have been enabled to live." He commented that "the necessities of war have given rise to many kinds of business & employment before unknown." In 1862 Lila Chunn wrote to her husband about local happenings in Georgia. She was somewhat dismayed that "ladies keep the stores here now . . . It looks funny in Dixie to see a lady behind the counter, but it would be natural if we were in Yankeedom as it has always been the custom there, a custom however I do not like." Nonetheless, she was in the process of changing her mind that clerking was suitable only for the "brazen faces" of northern women. "But I say if it is necessary, our ladies ought to shop keep and do everything else they can to aid in the great struggle for Liberty."

Elite women entered teaching. *De Bow's Review* advised southerners in 1861 that they must overcome the predisposition to "rank teaching among the menial employments" or to regard it as "socially degrading" or "fit for Yankees only." Yeoman women took on a larger role in industry, working in munitions factories, suffering an equal fate with male workers when a plant blew up or caught fire. Both elite and yeoman women entered nursing as volunteers or paid staff, and early in the war women opened their homes to the sick and injured. Mary Rutledge Fogg, descended from Edmund Rutledge and Arthur Middleton, both signers of the Declaration of Independence, recruited "a corps" of women from the Ladies Hospital and Clothing Association to open a hospital in Tennessee. She wrote her friend Jefferson Davis to request assistance, reporting to him that brave soldiers were dying "for the want of proper nurses." In 1862 the Confederate Congress passed the Hospital Act, allowing women to serve. Women who volunteered in hospitals read to soldiers and wrote letters for them. Some became matrons in charge of hospital wards. Nurses sometimes angered their male superiors by objecting strenuously to unnecessary amputations; especially problematical for some men were the women who refused the male doctors and staff their nips of "medicinal" liquor. Despite objections, male doctors and nurses needed the women's help, and in hospitals run by southern women the mortality rate (five percent) was half that of hospitals run by men.

Class disaffection shaped women just as it did men. The few job openings tended to go to elite women who could read and write. All employers were less likely to hire the poor. Yeoman women who were willing but unable to find jobs were often too proud to accept charity. While all had to contend with shortages and inflation, elite women had the resources to do so; yeoman women more quickly moved from subsistence to deprivation. Early in the war elite southern women shared food with their neighbors and helped raise money for relief efforts. As deprivation grew, however, elite women were less able and less willing to help, and some tired of the beggars streaming to their homes. As their resources ended, they resented queuing up in food lines alongside poor women. The famed noblesse oblige of the planter class failed.

When individuals in the community did not "come forward with open hands to the relief of the destitute," poor women begged for government relief. Some got angry and wrote letters to the Confederate government complaining of hunger, high prices, and severe shortages. In the official "Letters Received by the Confederate Secretary of War" from 1861 to 1865, the most poignant and poetic were often from poor women. One from Virginia wrote, "I have tried to do without calling for any help but I cannot hardly get bread for my children." One woman wrote to Governor Vance of North Carolina, "I am a pore woman with a pasel of children and I will have to starve or go naked." Across class and gender lines the implicit and explicit promises of the antebellum-touted southern way of life broke down.

In 1863 a group of starving women marched to Governor John Letcher's office in Richmond to complain about the price of bread. When the governor asked them to come back later, the women decided that was not good enough. Joined by men, the hungry women became a mob. Shouting "Bread," they stole flour, groceries, and other provisions. Looting expanded into taking anything and everything. Confederate president Davis tried to reason with the crowd. In later years Davis's wife, Varina Davis, recalled that he emptied his pockets and hurled all his money at a crowd of beseeching women. Nothing calmed them. Only when he ordered the public guard to shoot into the crowd did they slowly disperse. Other "bread riots" occurred in Alabama, Georgia, North Carolina, South Carolina, and Texas as well as in other areas of Virginia. Richmond newspapers did not cover the stories because the authorities decided that it would be demoralizing to the population. Increasingly, southerners who wanted the real story and could still afford a newspaper had to wait for the rare copy of the London *Times*.

In 1863 twenty-eight highwaywomen, brandishing guns and knives, ambushed a load of cloth in transport. This action prompted South Carolina textile mill owner William Gregg to purchase "150 fine rifles for the defense of our property against insurrection and raid," rifles the army needed desperately. When Gregg was attacked in the papers for making too much profit, he feigned surprise that people who made heroes of the blockade runners harassed him for similarly following the simple economics of supply and demand.

One southern newspaper warned of the consequences of not providing for soldiers' families: "If you do not do it, can you be surprised to see the poor soldier desert the army . . . Sickness, death, famine, and cries of entreaty for help, in the poor family of the soldier, however brave and loyal in our cause he may be, are far more terrible to him than all the bayonets, powder, steel and bullets of the enemy." In the autumn of 1863 Confederate General Kirby Smith reported to President Davis that "the common folk were tired of fighting; they simply wanted the boys to come home." One wife's letter pleaded, "John come if you can."

Their son was "lying at death's door" and calling out for his pa. A woman in North Carolina sent this message to her husband: "The people is all turning Union here since the Yankees has got Vicksburg. I want you to come home as soon as you can. The conscripts is all at home yet."

Letters had a powerful effect on the soldiers and contributed to desertion rates. Having gone to war to defend their community, many soldiers came to the conclusion that they could best fulfill that obligation by returning home. Once the men got there, however, civil authorities, military tribunals, and bloodthirsty home guards had to make an example of deserters and showed no mercy. In one incident where three men from North Carolina were shot for desertion, an onlooker said, "I heard that they were caused to desert by letters from home." When Edward Cooper was put on trial for desertion, he used for his defense a letter from his wife, which read in part, "Before God, Edward, unless you come home we must die." The court condemned Cooper to death, but Robert E. Lee granted him a pardon. Lee, desperate for men, hoped he and others would reenlist after a time at home with family. And besides, would the Confederacy kill every one of its hundred thousand deserters?

To come home to plant a crop and care for family was not the only reason for desertion. Black and white women and children needed protection as lawlessness became an issue as important on the home front as hunger. White women became scared of unsupervised enslaved workers. One woman wrote, "I am surrounded on all sides by plantations of negroes—many of them have not a white person on them. I am now begging you in kindness to a poor unprotected woman and her child give me the power of having my overseer recalled." In the Confederate senate, James Phelan of Mississippi shared a fear of African Americans but blamed the slaveholder for the predicament: "Why not let the poor man stay at home to protect his own family against the slaves of the rich man?" Southern civilians were also afraid of army deserters and stragglers, pillaging with "insults and depredation." Towns especially were in disarray with refugees and fights and thefts. Many blamed liquor. A woman told a friend it was no use quoting the price of corn because it increased weekly "on account of so many stills being put up in the country." Farmers could actually make some money by turning corn into liquor.

In areas close to the action, foraging Union troops, in addition to bushwhackers, plagued families, stealing, harassing, and destroying. Looters took more than food and tools. They scavenged through bedrooms as well. Sarah Morgan in Baton Rouge was outraged at the treatment and disrespect for private belongings: "As I looked for each well-known article, I could hardly believe that Abraham Lincoln's officers had really come so low down." Confederate looters also roamed the countryside. In late December 1864 a group of about one hundred deserters passed through Edgefield, South Carolina. Pretending to be on their way to join Nathan Bedford Forrest in Tennessee, they used a forged petition to collect forty bushels of corn, fifty pounds of bacon, and ten bushels of potatoes, precious goods all.

The old days were gone when women could expect—in return for wifely devotion and subservience—to receive men's protection. James Griffin, who was serving in the state militia on the coast, wrote his wife, Leila, in February 1865, "My Darling you are now thrown upon your own resources and you must do the best you can." Frankly confessing his inability to help them, he continued, "I will try to [take] care of myself, and you take care of yourself and the Children. God bless you and them." Both armies severely punished rapists, and soldiers charged with the crime faced either the gallows or the firing squad. In June 1864 three Union men were shot by firing squad for a rape committed near Memphis. In August of the same year two members of a New York regiment were hanged for rape. Confederate court-martial records did not survive the burning of Richmond, but conjecture is that southern soldiers acted in a similar fashion. Most women confronting any strangers in their homes were terrified, but some were amazingly brave. One Confederate woman announced to a marauding Yankee soldier who held her at gunpoint, "If you kill me I shall go straight to heaven. I am a Christian." Civilization having broken down, hearth, home and home front violated, such Christianity was what remained.

Most of the battles in the Civil War took place on southern soil. With the sounds of Union and Confederate shelling, women and children cowered in their homes until they were able to flee. The refugee situation affected battle and home front alike. When Confederate civilians who supported the war effort fled the area, the army had fewer resources to turn to. On the home front a massive flow of people, predominantly wealthy refugees and their enslaved servants, brought a new mix of people to isolated southern communities and shook attitudes toward outsiders. In 1865 a young girl wrote about her visit with an upper-class refugee family, "cultivated and refined." She wrote about how the local residents would embarrass the refugee daughter because of her love of reading. "The people in the neighborhood, who are plain working people, think it a waste of time to read, so when any of them chanced in she put out of sight the stray volumes that she might not merit their contempt!" Many refugees were not treated well.

War rarely facilitates kindness, though some remained kind. Shortages do not facilitate generosity, though some remained generous. Resources became more and more scarce over the course of the war, but in many cases southerners adjusted by becoming more accepting of travail. Although class conflict fragmented community spirit and thievery broke trust, communities did not totally disintegrate. Instead, realism replaced sentimentalism. Religious faith helped women in all sections and in all social classes cope as about one-third of families suffered the loss of a loved one. As Sarah Espy wrote when her twenty-four-year-old son died in camp, "What a change from the sick, weary, harassing camp life to the joys of Heaven! I feel we should not grieve for him; for it is a happy release from these distressing times."

Most of the southern home front was never invaded, but in the summer of 1864 parts of the South lay in utter ruin. Farms near battlefields were annihilated; those only slightly distanced were completely depleted of animals and produce. Confiscation of crops meant that farmers simply stopped producing above the subsistence level or hoarded what surplus they had. Armies on both sides foraged crops from the fields and stole whatever livestock they could lay their hands on. Early in the war army officers who confiscated food wrote out promissory notes for what they took. By the end of the war these outstanding and worthless receipts were estimated to have covered half a billion dollars' worth of food and equipment. Without workmen or tools to maintain them, houses fell into disrepair. On January 24, 1864, Union soldier George Cram wrote home about the devastation he witnessed: "You cannot realize the terrible destruction which attends those countries where active war exists, but I have seen it. All traffic ceases except a little in the largest towns. The work of a lifetime is destroyed in a few minutes, fences are burned down; education ceases; whole towns are in ruins and in others beautiful buildings, once used for thriving business, are now filled with dirty soldiers for a large percent of soldiers will be dirty—but were I to undertake to tell of one half the awful ruin and devaluation exhibited even in Tenn. I should want four such sheets of paper as this."

The desolation of farmland, shortages, inflation, and an unofficial work stoppage of enslaved workers meant that a hungry population filled the landscape. A planter from Mississippi bemoaned, "The whole country here is a perfect waste, not a ear of corn scarcely to be found." A man from North Carolina wrote to his brother in the Confederate army, "I would advise you to go to the other side whear you can get plentey and not stay in this one horse barefooted naked and famine stricken Southern Confederacy."

The Confederate home front could not hold together. Antebellum society and its "God-ordained" hierarchy and harmony split wide open. Only half the population supported the war in the first place, and class conflict grew as resources dwindled. The rationale for war disintegrated when people on the home front faced all the false assumptions that once defined a supposedly perfected way of life. While African Americans worked for their own freedom, slaveholders thought their freedom depended upon making sure the enslaved got none or little. The majority of white southerners, nonslaveholding yeomen and poor, expected that the burden of fighting would be shared equally among whites. They found instead that they bore an inordinate amount of the suffering. Southern yeomen and poor increasingly understood southern civilization as a zero-sum game: more freedom for the slaveholder meant less for themselves. There was not enough manpower to fight Yankees, maintain slavery, and grow the necessary food. There were not enough supplies for both armies and civilians. There was not enough shared ideology to overcome class conflict. Contradictions within and among southerners doomed the Confederacy to collapse, and Divine Providence did not intervene on the Confederate behalf.

Nine

"To Square Accounts"

TWELVE DAYS AFTER they had turned back Lee's forces at Gettysburg, the soldiers of the 69th New York Regiment formed against a different enemy. Under a fierce July sun they, and four other regiments of mostly Irish soldiers from New York, had moved swiftly by road and rail southeast, nearly two hundred fifty miles home to Manhattan. Although reluctant to relinquish soldiers pursuing Lee's army in retreat after Gettysburg, Secretary of War Stanton had a telegram sent to New York governor Horatio Seymour: "If absolutely necessary, troops will be sent from the field in Maryland." It was necessary. Gunfire crackled and fires raged across the city from the mansions of midtown down to Battery Park. In the vast new "central" park near the city's northern edge, hundreds of African Americans had escaped the fray, climbed into the trees, and watched as New York burned. The tired, sunburned bluecoats could hardly restrain themselves from lashing out in anger against the howling white mob rioting in protest of the draft. The soldiers leveled their muskets against one group of sixty—some said eighty—thousand, fired a volley, and charged with bayonets into the horrified crowd of men, women, and children. By nightfall, scores of protesters were dead, hundreds were wounded, and millions of dollars in property had gone up in smoke. Although the streets ran red in what yet remains the greatest urban riot in American history, the back of this rebellion had been broken.

For the mob in the streets, all talk of Union and liberty rang false. They looked at the stupefying casualty lists from Fredericksburg, Chancellorsville, and now Gettysburg, and questioned if it was not the poor—especially the immigrant Irish poor—who were paying for this war with their lives. New York's Democratic politicians, hoping to make gains in the next elections, ruthlessly stoked discontent against the draft, against expanding powers of the national government, and against a war increasingly understood by the poor whites in the city as a war for black people. When government officials in New York began drawing fifteen hundred names for the draft on Saturday, July 11, 1863, working people in the city held their breath. The next day they prayed and talked and drank and organized. On the third day the Catholic Irish—perhaps a quarter-million strong—rose up, torching draft offices and fighting police. They attacked the mayor's residence and Republican Horace Greeley's *Tribune* newspaper building. They looted stores and shouted "Down with the Protestants" as they burned the Methodist Episcopal mission in the brawling Five Points neighborhood. Republicans were also targets; in the eyes of the Democratic Party regulars, they were the apparent recipients of Lincoln's bounty. They plundered German druggists, low dramshops, and fine tailors like Brooks Brothers, because "the boys wanted the clothes," even though it was "a shame to stale them." After stoning fine houses, some turned their anger on a scapegoat, burning down black churches, hanging African Americans from lampposts. The rampaging mob destroyed the Colored Orphan Asylum; while his fellows cried "Murder the damned monkeys!" Paddy McCaffrey rescued twenty children from the flames. Over on Clarkson Street, however, no Irish voice spoke up for the black man beaten and lynched by the mob: he was a cartman, perhaps the most economically precarious of occupations in the whole city in 1863. In addition to being an expression of racial hatred, his murder was a scream of working-class despair.

Not so their torture and murder of Colonel Henry O'Brien, commander of the Eleventh New York Volunteers, just come from Pennsylvania. Grievous wrongs had been inflicted upon local working people, and the soldiers, themselves mostly Irish, had killed women and children, also mostly Irish, that very day. "Bedad, I suppose it was to square accounts," one rioter explained, and regardless of religion or ethnicity "a sojer had to suffer." In all likelihood, the bluecoats who formed up to inhibit this violence saw things the same way: black or Irish or German or some other variation, it did not matter in the end. The state would maintain order and assert governance. Those who challenged that order would suffer, be they named Patrick Dougherty, Catharine Waters, or Robert Edward Lee. After four days the fires from the riot burned out, the corpses were pushed into mass graves, and life returned to something rather like normal. President Lincoln called in New York Democrats to handle New York's problems and continued to prod General Meade to take up the chase after the retreating Army of Northern Virginia. The draft went on unabated, and several thousand more New Yorkers were drawn into the net against their will, but a crucial tipping point, all knew, had been reached.

Questions of Union and slavery that had focused national attention for decades had been for a moment roughly thrust aside. The real problem, men of property now told one another, was how to control the burgeoning, volatile "working classes." Properly harnessed and disciplined, their labor power promised to create a new regimen of unrivaled prosperity in America. Unchecked, however, this reeking, gabbling mob could only wreck the national dream. Such arguments, of course, were exactly what southern ideologues had been preaching throughout the 1850s. Perhaps the greatest irony of the Civil War era was that even as their troops destroyed the southern slaveholding class, northern elites and federal officials came to imbibe central elements of that class's worldview.

The home front got a visceral image of battlefield carnage from gruesome photographs of death. Mathew Brady decided early in the war to make a photographic history. He and his twenty teams of photographers captured images of bloody, bloated dead after many battles. Pictures exposed every man's vulnerability, even as the sheer numbers bred callousness. War snuffed out sentimentalism. By 1863 each day's newspapers brought fresh news of federal success, and yet the Union remained sundered. Although religious revivals swept through both armies periodically, most soldiers prayed simply to be spared in the next fight and sent home soon. Social perfection, harmony, and the millennium seemed further away than ever. Perhaps God was simply mocking the arrogance of a people he had never chosen. Many pondered: Were Christ to come again, what would He find? His people awash in the blood and dirt of Civil War, their hearts set on self-righteous murder and personal gain, their spirits set on victories temporary, finite, material, and squalid.

Certainly northern society by the fall of 1863 looked very little as it had just two years earlier. Before Manassas many southerners had predicted that Lincoln's regime would be quickly toppled once hostilities disrupted the cotton trade, once southern bales could no longer reach northern factories. Yankee capitalists would have to lay off workers by the thousands. Unemployed hands would go hungry, consumer spending would collapse, and the nation would spiral into a depression far worse than the setbacks of 1837 and 1857. Riot and class war would divert Union troops into the streets of northern cities, and Lincoln would have to make peace with the Confederacy to avert social collapse. Other rebels argued that a more prosaic circumstance would stop the North: without money, they reasoned, there could be no war, and Washington in 1861 had nothing like the gold reserves needed to purchase the means to put down secession. One or two battles would exhaust the northern treasury, and then the South would be left alone.

How confounding, then, to watch the war drag on, season after season, through dozens of catastrophic battles, long after the capital reserves of both sides had been consumed. How demoralizing for Confederates to see the Yankee economy actually thrive on war, to see the social turmoil they had forecast for the North, when it finally came, quickly crushed. How shocking for many northerners, too, to witness how their own government in pursuit of victory had twisted the principles and institutions they so adored. While Lincoln proclaimed a new birth of freedom in the land, some feared that the war had spawned its own tyranny of wealth and big government. By 1863 almost no one believed any longer that it would be possible to restore American government or society to the terms of 1860. The abolition of slavery was the root but not nearly the sum of the mighty changes sweeping over the land. In squaring accounts with the flawed vision of the Founding Fathers over the questions of states' rights and slavery, America itself underwent a tremendous, troubling social revolution. The modern nation was decisively shaped in the crucible of civil war.

The key to this explosive transformation was simple enough: credit. Although North and South alike lacked the deep pockets necessary to purchase arms, uniforms, food, shelter, and the thousand other sundries

required to keep millions of men fighting, international financiers—
specifically the Bank of England—never doubted that, in time, they
would make good on the billions that Americans borrowed. Moreover,
by the winter of 1861, treasury secretary Salmon Chase had underwritten the cost of the war, thanks to the crafty Philadelphia financier Jay
Cooke, through a system of short-term loans and privately held bonds.
Jefferson Davis told the Confederate congress that "Our foes must sink
under the immense load of debt," but long before Shiloh and the Seven
Days, the war had been transformed into a source of speculation and
private profit, returning a pleasant six and seven percent interest to investors. With bonds marketed to the public in denominations as low as
fifty dollars per share, many northern families anted up the funds to pay
the price of waging a war that would see their own sons killed or dis-
membered. Men and women did not consider it that way at the time, to
be sure. They spoke of their patriotic duty and whispered of golden opportunities as they plunked down savings. Capital flooded in.

All told, Lincoln's government raised more than $1.2 billion through
contracted bond sales, fully two-thirds of the total cost of the northern
war effort. Since many of these notes fell due after three years—just after the 1864 presidential election—offering them represented a tremendous political, military, and economic gamble. But there was simply no
other way to finance war on the Confederacy except by driving the nation into deep and perilous debt. The Republican-controlled Congress
had run mounting budget deficits since the depression of 1857, calculating, as the old-line Whigs most truly were, that higher tariffs would both
stimulate domestic industry and yield revenue sufficient to balance the
books. The onset of war seemed to ruin those plans, but Republicans
only plunged deeper into debt.

Before 1861 the federal government was a remarkably small, simple
organization. The Department of State was housed in a couple of offices;
the Department of War, warriors apart, numbered a corporal's guard of
clerks and secretaries. For most Americans, government reached into
their daily lives primarily through the coins it minted, the mail it delivered, and the flag that fluttered overhead. Elections, which came around
less often than traveling circuses, were distant and stranger forms of en-
tertainment, and the tariffs that nudged prices and production were only
an indirect form of pickpocketry. The local institutions of state and

community—the family, the workplace, the church, and the store—played a far more prominent role and assumed much greater importance in estimating social relations and personal identities than anything emanating from Washington. Most people considered themselves first as citizens of Maine, Maryland, or Michigan; Bostonians, Brooklynites, or folks from Liberty Hill; they were wives or fathers, backstairs girls or prodigal sons; Episcopalians, Catholics, or Jews; printers, iron puddlers, or shoemakers, Odd Fellows or Masons, Ulstermen or Saxons or Cherokees or Creoles, Democrats, Republicans or Whigs, teetotalers, Swedenborgians, Shakers, Transcendentalists, phrenologists, vegetarians, Grahamites, anti-Sabbatarians, Mormons, Millerites, and much more. Each of these constructed identities trumped broader notions of nationality.

The war changed all that. It turned a squabbling set of profoundly disunited states into what Abraham Lincoln called—five times in the 266 words of the Gettysburg Address—a nation. The truest measure of the alchemy that conjured American nationality may be, however, that it was achieved not through blood—though this played a mystical part, to be sure—but through silver and gold. The great symbol of America, which commerce and battleships soon carried to every corner of the globe, the great arbiter before which ancient cultures and high moral traditions all bow down even today, was made manifest in 1862. The Revelation of John had foretold how Armageddon would usher in at last the millennium, but in the heady years of the Gilded Age not a few Americans thought that the preachers of perfection before the Great Rebellion had missed the most sacred sign when it finally appeared. What was the sign of freedom, then or now? What, after all, had won the war, freed the slaves, and healed the nation except the new commercial order and the almighty dollar?

In the spring of 1862, when southern soldiers pawed through the pockets of fallen Union recruits at Shiloh searching for something to eat, they were astonished by the wads of new paper money they found. Indeed, in both armies the irregular arrival of the paymaster was rightly taken as a sign that battle was at hand. Soldiers were thought to fight harder with a little cash in hand, and having mustered to receive their pay, they were harder-pressed to claim they were too ill to go into battle a day or two hence, or to slip off to a corner of safety. Such immediate considerations no doubt flashed through rebels' minds, but more astounding was the tangible evidence that the Civil War was in fact the first conflict waged by paper-money armies.

Back in the closing days of 1861 all across the North depositors had staged a frightening run on urban banks, compelling almost all to suspend payments of gold and silver specie. There was, in a word, no real money in the vaults. As the war carried into a new year, Americans who had sweated, saved, and banked their funds began to panic. Great revolutions are fashioned out of such fears, and Lincoln's administration chose fiscal transformation over raging mobs. Already in August 1861 Republicans had hiked tariffs and passed America's first—and it was assured, temporary—income tax law to pay the interest on its war bonds. Fearful of antagonizing the workingmen who constituted the bulk of the nation's potential soldiery, Congress exempted those with annual incomes under $800 from the new three percent levy, but the regressive features of Republican taxation, viewed as a whole, were plain to see. In 1862 higher tariffs touched the luxury goods that elites purchased, to be sure, but they also raised prices on a range of imported items upon which ordinary Americans had come to depend. Moreover, Congress taxed almost "everything but the air." For the minority of farmers who still practiced a "safety first" method of cultivation (raising the crops and animals they needed to survive and selling the surplus on the market) and for the urban journeyman who "gave her jiminy" (worked extra hard when wages were high, then took his leisure), the steady drain that taxation imposed on nearly every act of consumption acted as a stern goad to steadier labor.

The "food of the poor" was not taxed, Republicans promised, and perhaps it was possible for the skint to escape the worst of Washington's demands. But anytime a workingman drank a beer, or rode an omnibus, or went to the music hall, or took a smoke, the government filched from him. However bearable the economic loss inflicted by the Internal Revenue Act of 1862 might have been, an unspoken diminution of manhood, a subtle demand for obeisance, went along with each payment. Taxation played a crucial role in creating American identity—and in cutting it down to size.

Even as the mass bowed down, a chosen few were lifted up. In early 1863 the National Bank Act provided for a supervised system of national banks—unthinkable in the years of Democratic ascendancy. The National Bank notes were bonds that paid interest and, backed by gold, they did not inflate. Almost all these gold-backed bank notes were invested in Northeastern banks, giving that region tremendous financial power in the years to come. In addition to the bank notes, Congress authorized more than $300 million in new treasury bills—greenback dollars—to be pumped into the broader economy. As with the whole package of Republican fiscal measures, legislators and private citizens gravely doubted the constitutionality of funneling paper money—backed by promises alone—through the mechanism that an earlier era had labeled "the Monster Bank." Everything was "a war measure," advocates assured the community, a desperate course to be sure, but "necessary and proper" under the circumstances and destined to end once the rebellion was vanquished. In fact, federally issued paper currency served only to augment and replace the ragged and oft-refused notes of hundreds of state banks. As greenbacks, declared good for settling all debts public and private, flooded the market, their ubiquity instilled money markets with a new sense of confidence and stability. Instead of sending the North into a deadly inflationary spiral, as some had predicted, federal paper currency drove state bank currency out of circulation. The North had discovered a powerful new mechanism of economic stimulus and restraint.

Inflation on the northern home front rose 80 percent over four years. That means, as dollars chased scarce goods, that prices for the average northerner shot up at about the same rate as in the two world wars. The culprit here again was government itself, intruding on every market, offering top dollar for food and cloth, steel, paper, draft animals, lumber, and more. The *New York Tribune* estimated in 1864 that it cost $18.50 a week for a family of six to live in the city, not counting clothing, medicine, or transportation. Average wages were $16 a week. As prices shot up, real wages, amazingly, fell on average by one-fifth: as if other economic advantages were not slanted enough to gain victory, Lincoln made war on the South at a 20 percent discount!

To keep up with inflation, workers sometimes went on strike for higher wages. The independence and human dignity of labor had long been a cornerstone of Republican ideology, central to Lincoln's political philosophy. Comparing labor and capital, he said, "Labor is the superior of capital, and deserves much the higher consideration." To Lincoln, freedom meant free labor and the opportunity for upward mobility as opposed to enslaved labor without hope of a better life. The promise of Lincoln's republican worldview was simply this: a hired laborer was not "fixed to that condition for life." Lincoln, like virtually all Americans at that time, thought that a self-reliant person, like himself, who may have started life as a "prudent penniless beginner in the world," could labor for wages, save and continue to better himself, and acquire property. Like most Americans, Lincoln expected the wearying term of wage labor to end with the acquisition of property. "Property is the fruit of labor," he explained; "property is desirable; is a positive good in the world. That some should be rich shows that others may become rich and hence is just encouragement to industry and enterprise." Lincoln did not want government to obstruct the worker's way; he wanted government to ensure that opportunities were open to all hardworking people. "We do wish to allow the humblest man an equal chance to get rich with everybody else."

As much as Republicans held wage labor to be a transitory step on the ladder of life for most Americans, they deployed this labor form into the national experience as no other political administration ever had. From 1861 to 1865, in hiring millions of greenback-earning soldiers, the federal government became the largest single wage-paying employer in the nation's history—a title it would never relinquish in the years to come. These new government war workers were schooled sternly in the ways of discipline. Foot-draggers were flogged, fined, or imprisoned. Strikers, commonly called deserters, the army often shot.

In 1860 Lincoln made several favorable remarks about a shoemaker strike in New England. Comparing the right to strike with the absence of such a right for enslaved labor, he appreciated that "we have a system of labor where there can be a strike. Whatever the pressure, there is a point where the workingman may stop." Before the Civil War, however, few strikes were more than a one-man affair. Unsatisfied with the terms of his labor, or finding his dignity affronted by the boss who hired his time, the workingman simply packed up his tools and marched out. Laborers uniting in organized groups to defend their interests implied that the owners were less than virtuous, fair, and hardworking men themselves— more like overlords. They showed a failure of republicanism.

Neither did Lincoln malign capital. Certainly capital "has its rights," he understood, "which are worthy of protection as any other rights." He saw the two working in harmony to produce "mutual benefits." Relations were increasingly unharmonious, however. When miners in the coalfields of LaSalle, Illinois, went on strike in 1863, the state legislature sided with the mine owners, making it a criminal offense for labor to organize or for anyone to interfere with another person's work. Certainly by late 1863, with a war to win, the federal government intervened to put down strikes. In the New York longshoremen strike of 1863, the federal government sent in soldiers and civilians to replace striking workers at New York piers so that military supplies could be distributed. This was the first time a federal administration interfered against the wishes of both employers and striking workers. The replacement of striking longshoremen, however, was limited exclusively to the unloading and loading of governmental vessels, not of private ships. As a result, this strike was somewhat successful in that workers got a wage increase. Many strikes at this time were less about wages than about broader notions of employer-employee working relations, but those issues were harder to address.

When coal miners in Pennsylvania struck in 1863, the owners called for cavalry troops to guard the mines and "scabbing" replacement workers. This government coercion on behalf of the mine owners broke the strike and attempts at unionization. More alarming, Republicans used Federal soldiers to break strikes and hold workers to their tasks against their will. In 1864 General William S. Rosecrans gave orders prohibiting disgruntled shipbuilders, tailors, and printers in St. Louis from going on strike. The strikers, however, petitioned Lincoln personally, after which the military withdrew. A month later in Louisville, General Stephen G. Burbridge took similar action against striking machinists, but no orders withdrew the army. During a strike at the Philadelphia & Reading Railroad in July 1864, the federal government went further still. At the behest of Charles E. Smith, president of the railroad, they seized control of the entire operation. More than half of the striking workers were discharged, and union agitation ceased. Here as elsewhere Lincoln showed himself willing to bend deeply held principles in the service of wartime necessity.

Low wages continued to be a problem. Even as about two million men (a significant portion of whom had not heretofore entered the workforce as wage laborers) joined the Union army, they were replaced by other hands in the civilian workforce. The premium wages such employment might have commanded, however, were undercut by the influx of female workers. Without women willing to take up the slack in eastern factories and on western farms, the northern war economy might have failed altogether. Yet gender differences were perceived to merit lower wages. Even if she could cut and bind wheat at the same pace as her male counterpart, or was as nimble in sewing lasts to soles in some Massachusetts shoe factory, the Yankee working girl was thought to be laboring for "pin money." On some not-distant day she would marry and quit work altogether, and till then the real costs of feeding and housing herself seemed rather lower than those for some strapping family man. Employers gave no consideration to arguments of "equal pay for equal work"— no one except a cadre of foreign fanatics did. The great desideratum, as of old, was one of "competency," whether the worker could provide for a family's need. All understood that competency was the concern of married men alone; single women or single men were considered failures and misfits as they drifted through middle age and were written out of the social narrative as merely "queer" or "odd."

For tens of thousands of single young women in the years of war and immediately after, what the Great Rebellion meant was the opportunity to go to Washington or another regional urban center, sit at a desk in respectable clothes for a number of years, surrounded by other girls of similar background, hopes, and concerns, and scratch out in duplicate longhand every word and phrase of every order issued by soldiers at the front. The Civil War began to allow women into the nation's secretarial class, just as it opened the ranks of teachers and nurses to "career girls" and made vast—but temporary—inroads for women in a host of skilled trades. How stunningly improbable, how completely insurrectionary it must have seemed to the citizens of Lynn, Massachusetts, to see scores of young, single women marching in the streets of their city in the fall of 1861, holding banners aloft and chanting the slogans of labor united. They were not daughters and sisters merely; they were skilled shoemakers, independent-minded income-earners, producers, consumers, and citizens, to boot. This was a revolutionary moment akin to emancipation.

Just as women found themselves laboring "like men" as never before, many men came to believe that the demands of war had robbed them of the privileges and status of masculinity itself. It was not just that journeymen and craftsmen labored alongside women, or that farm wives, left to fend for their families while their husbands sought to kill other husbands, turned out crops as large as their menfolk ever had. Even without the incursion of female labor, farmers and workers found themselves driven to increase productivity—to work harder and longer, for lower wages— than ever before. Especially in rural areas in 1862 and thereafter, northern boys were evidently driven to the army as a means of making more money from less effort. The introduction of labor-saving machinery on a mass scale in important war industries altered both the quantitative output and the qualitative meaning of the labor experience.

"This is essentially a people's contest," Lincoln told Congress in 1862, sweeping up the "whole family of man" in its prosecution. The Union fought "for maintaining in the world, that form and substance of government," he explained, "whose leading object is to elevate the condition of men." Victory would mean "an unfettered start, and a fair chance" for all "in the race of life." Winning the day, however, required Americans to enter into a devil's bargain. "Shoddy" became a much-used word for the times. To feed and clothe, shelter, and move its massive armies, the government needed to abridge notions of fair competition, awarding contracts for all manner of goods not to the lowest bidder but to the fellow who could supply the largest quantity of a minimum average quality with greatest certainty. For meatpackers like the Armour family of Chicago, producers of iron furnaces like Bethlehem Iron Works in Pennsylvania, E. S. Sanford and Andrew Carnegie of American Telegraph Company, and oil merchants like John D. Rockefeller, colossal government contracts promised windfall profits. The consequence for such well-placed men, or for those who supplied crucial technology at a secondary level (like Cyrus McCormick's "Virginia Reaper") was wealth on a spectacular scale protected by government monopoly.

Moreover, northern legislators in pursuit of military victory dramatically enlarged and transformed the legal status and economic rights of American business. Before the Civil War most Americans who went into business for themselves assumed unlimited liability for debts incurred and other attendant risks. If sued by suppliers or customers, a vendor or manufacturer stood to lose everything he was worth, and those who invested in his firm, signed his notes, or backed him in some more marginal way might also be drawn into the general wreck. As a consequence, most people invested capital or risked their names and fortunes only where risks were small and returns were steady and certain. Business was usually associated with a single individual or a small circle of partners. As with a person's life-course, a business was assumed to have a predictable and finite trajectory, from the humble beginnings of youth through the vibrancy of middle age down to that final day when the books were balanced one last time and the concern dissolved. Economic life paralleled human existence, complemented it, and enriched it.

The Civil War, however, affirmed what northern businessmen and politicians had begun to grasp as early as the 1840s, that canals, railroads, factories, and banking houses had needs and responsibilities different from those of the local dry-goods shop. Unless a greater measure of security and continuity was extended to such ventures, each time an elderly entrepreneur wound up or passed along his life's work, enormous economic uncertainty and dislocation were bound to result.

While historians have rightly focused upon the revolutionary character of emancipation in winning the war and changing the lives of ordinary Americans, just as important is another singularity: the growth of corporations and of big government under Lincoln's administration. For the first time, Congress, instead of the states, chartered corporations. In the war years the extraordinary use of incorporation as a tool for business expanded across the North and extended to businesses an enduring character independent of the men who built and invested in them. Indeed, incorporation extended to a business such protections as no individual citizen or freedperson could hope to enjoy. Just as Lincoln affirmed that African Americans were persons, not property, and that they enjoyed a particular—if yet still vague—set of civil rights, northern Republicans during the war years armed corporations with a distinct social identity and a set of legal and social rights. Moreover, by granting to capitalists and proprietors "limited liability" for debts and suits incurred by the corporations with which they were involved, legislators opened the door to an enormous volume of venture capital.

In 1863, of course, no one could have imagined that the pragmatic legal changes in incorporation and limited liability that Congress enacted to help vanquish rebellious slaveholders would ultimately go far toward subverting revered political values. Making such amendments seemed an easy choice: incorporation brought predictability, order, and social stability. It kept prices on an even keel, regulated demand, and conferred security of employment. Production boomed. Profits rallied. War plus incorporation brought dynamic economic growth to the northern states. Newspapers and public speakers hailed newly minted millionaires as "captains of industry," as essential to and responsible for Union military victory as Grant or Sherman.

Overturning slavery, Abraham Lincoln steadfastly insisted, had been part and parcel of the struggle to restore the Union. But once emancipation had been accomplished—first proclaimed by the president, then ratified by the votes of state and federal representatives—the broader question arose: What could America *not* do? Were there *any* real limits to the powers of the president and the Congress? Despite the American love affair with "checks and balances," did such self-satisfying formulas provide any real safety from governmental tyranny? Such questions were not entirely new to the Civil War years, but under Lincoln's administration they assumed an urgency and a difficulty that earlier observers had hardly imagined.

Efforts to trace the roots of an "imperial presidency" back to Lincoln usually point to the cavalier way in which the former Illinois lawyer sometimes dealt with questions of civil liberties. To mute support for secession in the border states, Republicans had no qualms about using methods of intimidation, threatening Maryland and Kentucky politicians with summary arrest and confinement should they lend their voices in favor of disunion, and stationing impressive military garrisons in crucial centers of doubtful loyalty. Later Lincoln undeniably gave short shrift to rights of free speech and habeas corpus in deporting Ohio congressman Clement Vallandigham, an irascibly antiwar Democrat. In May 1863, with Union military fortunes at their lowest ebb, General Ambrose Burnside, commander of the Military District of Ohio, ordered Vallandigham, without Lincoln's knowledge, to be brought before an army tribunal. He was convicted of "uttering disloyal sentiments" and sentenced to two years' imprisonment. Anxious to avoid turning the loudmouthed Vallandigham into a political martyr, Lincoln arranged for him to be expelled across Confederate lines. Vallandigham refused to be silenced, traveling from Tennessee to Bermuda, then to Canada, insisting all along that he acted in defense of the Constitution and free speech against those who would "enslave" America's citizens. He ran for the governorship of Ohio on the Democratic ticket in 1863, campaigning in absentia, and lost by a landslide.

In February 1864 a federal appeals court affirmed that the president had not exceeded the "war powers" allowed him under the Constitution. That the nation might be properly divided up into "military districts" and administered by soldiers under a distinct body of law went entirely unchallenged; that civilian courts had no right to compel military officials to obey the doctrine of habeas corpus was affirmed. This was a sweeping legal victory for Lincoln. Wartime Americans seemed to care much more about order, security, and military victory than about infringements of the rights and liberties of marginal political activists. That choice, however popular, carried with it devastating consequences for advocates of social change in generations to come. At that time, of course, if disgruntled plaintiffs had won habeas corpus lawsuits against the draft, the U.S. Army would have crumbled.

As a true believer confronted by intransigent opponents, Lincoln magnified the danger he faced from "a most efficient corps of spies, informers, suppliers, and aiders and abettors of their cause"—even as he crushed it. Although Lincolnites labeled antiwar Democrats "copperheads," after deadly poisonous snakes, their actions and arguments ranged across the spectrum of political action from opportunistic anti-Republicanism to pro-Confederate racism to principled defiance of what seemed to them like presidential tyranny. In predominantly Democratic urban centers like Chicago and New York, antiwar sentiment focused on feelings that the conflict was a "poor man's fight," victimizing Catholic Irish immigrants most of all. In rural sections of Indiana, Ohio, and Illinois farmers rebelled against fears that the war for the Union had turned into a war for the African American, and that Lincoln had subverted the cause of republican government itself. In newspaper editorials, public rallies, and secret societies like the Knights of the Golden Circle, conservative northerners vented their anxieties and made plans for opposition.

In some cases, big talk overflowed into subversive plotting. In 1864 five Indiana members of the "Sons of Liberty" were arrested for scheming to launch a Harpers Ferry–style raid on a northern prisoner-of-war camp. In another incident, attorney Lambdin P. Milligan and his follow-ers hoped to seize control of the state government and carry Indiana out of the war. Instead, a military court-martial sentenced the harebrained conspirators to hang, and they doubtless would have hanged had not the Supreme Court intervened in December 1866. *Ex parte Milligan* re-mained silent on whether the president might suspend habeas corpus in-dependent of congressional support, but it ruled that citizens could not be tried by military authority where civilian courts were functioning. In dozens of cases where army provost marshals had held prisoners for long periods without charge, then, the detentions were deemed legal, though military prosecutions such as Vallandigham had faced were ruled invalid.

As disturbing as that ruling seemed to some, it fit well with the broad, warlordlike powers that Lincoln wielded in his struggle against the Con-federacy. Republicans used federal marshals, Pinkerton detectives, and agents of the newly formed U.S. Secret Service to silence political op-ponents as well as Confederate spies. While Lincoln took an unprece-dented hands-on approach to war-making, goading and advising his generals on tactical points, he demonstrated little desire to intervene when his commanders abridged civil liberties or political rights in pur-suit of military success. The "hard war" policies of Generals William Sherman and Philip Sheridan, waged more against the southern citi-zenry than against its government, aroused no complaint on his part. Neither did he intervene in 1864 when Maryland rewrote its state con-stitution to disfranchise disloyal slaveholders. Although Lincoln tried to follow the Constitution and precedent, tried to limit action to specific places and distinct periods of time, his wartime administration spon-sored a contraction of civil rights and an expansion of executive power.

Antiwar Democrats and draft rioters were more than just assorted crackpots, traitors, and racists. Certainly their ranks were swelled by such types, but their arguments held truths also. The president, the Con-gress, and the courts sometimes *did* ride roughshod over civil rights. The army *did* include a large proportion of poor, uneducated immigrants. Al-though the Conscription Act that Congress passed in March 1863 was levied impartially in terms of geography, social class, and age (twenty to forty-five), it protected a large class of elite men in "bombproof" occupa-tions—from aldermen and ministers to railroad engineers and ships' pilots—and it allowed anyone unlucky enough to be drafted to escape through payment of a $300 "commutation fee." Theodore Roosevelt's father, to honor the request of his southern wife, served with the U.S. Sanitary Commission and was one of about 118,000 northerners who hired a substitute to take his place in the ranks. Many of these soldiers-for-hire soon learned to duck their contracts after pocketing their various fees and bonuses. Some lit out for Canada or the West; others turned up in another county or state, trying the same lucrative trick a dozen times or more. One New England soldier called such "bounty-jumpers" the "grandest scoundrels that ever went unhung." Ultimately about 116,000 substitutes and about 46,000 conscripts actually served in the federal army.

To help finance the war, the United States had a great resource: federal lands in the West. Some of the land was sold, some was given away. Since the mid-1840s Free-Soilers like Horace Greeley had advocated using western territories as a safety valve for urban poverty and discontent in the East, but southern Democrats had steadily blocked such programs. In 1862 Republicans passed a far-reaching Homestead Act, providing a quarter-section (160 acres) of farmland to any household head, male or female, for a land office fee. After five years, and making improvements such as buildings, fences, and plowed fields, title would be given to the homesteader. As a social engineering measure, the Homestead Act's virtues were mixed. There is little evidence that the measure did much to turn slum dwellers into prairie farmers, or that the Jeffersonian vision that framed the legislation withstood market pressures. The more successful farmers soon gobbled up the acreage of their less fortunate neighbors, and in areas where cattle ranching or extensive cultivation predominated, a quarter-section was never sufficient to achieve stability or success. Without access to water or good grazing acreage, many agriculturists (especially in the Southwest and the mountain states) quickly sold out for the best price they could get and looked for greener pastures. Nevertheless, it did provide opportunity for some and hope for even more. During the 1870s and 1880s homesteaders settled much of the frontier.

Western land, more than ninety thousand acres, was also given to states to establish colleges for "agriculture and mechanic arts." Lincoln signed the Morrill Act in 1862 (Buchanan had vetoed the legislation in 1857). Lincoln firmly supported education, and land-grant colleges promised to enlarge the educational opportunities for those eager to learn progressive farming, engineering, or military science. Actually, few sons and daughters of farming families enrolled, and those who did attend rarely went back to a career in farming. African Americans, almost all of whom were still enslaved at the time, did not benefit from the act, and it was thirty years before Congress prohibited racial discrimination at land-grant colleges. Some opponents questioned these grants by the federal government to support education.

One of the giveaways few complained about at the time was the land to help establish a railroad to the West Coast. Congress wanted access to California, to the enormous wealth in western mines, and also a closer link to Asia for markets. For capitalists, however, interested in building railroads only where there were cities and plenty of people, the West was a risky venture. In an effort to encourage entrepreneurs, Congress passed the Pacific Railway Act of 1862, giving railroads the right of way as well as half the sections of land along the route. Between 1862 and 1871 Congress gave railroads almost 110 million acres of land. The railroads could sell the land to pay for the cost of construction, and because farmers wanted access to the railroad, the railroad could charge more for their acreage.

Companies like the Union Pacific and Southern Pacific Railroads also used these lands for speculation and profit, accumulating enormous wealth and building the rails that traversed the nation at no cost whatsoever. The vast railroad land grants and the farm concessions of the Homestead Act did much to populate the prairie and mountain states and to set the wheels of commerce spinning, but they also sounded the death knell for the Indian and métis cultures of the Great Plains. Even as Lincoln's Republicans were proclaiming freedom to the slaves, they were denying it to tens of thousands of Native Americans.

In the fall of 1862 American troops under Colonel Kit Carson burned Navaho farms in the Rio Grande Valley in an effort to seize their valuable lands. In Minnesota the Native people, systematically cheated and neglected by Washington and literally starving, rose up in bloody rebellion. For more than a month Sioux warriors raged across the state, killing about 350 whites. (Some estimate as many as 800.) General John Pope, sent by Lincoln to put down the Sioux rebellion, frankly declared, "It is my purpose utterly to exterminate the Sioux if I have the power to do so." No tally of Native American losses is known, but about 1,500 men, women, and children were arrested. Preferring to study each case as an individual, Lincoln ordered Pope to execute no one, then personally examined each of the 303 recommendations for execution. Among these warriors Lincoln found that 38—men he considered guilty of more heinous crimes of rape and murder of women and children—were deserving of death. When Republican leaders in Minnesota, angered at Lincoln's clemency for the 265, announced that it would cost him votes, Lincoln replied, "I could not afford to hang men for votes."

As these events suggest, the social, cultural, and economic forces that Republicans unleashed in their effort to win the war had far-reaching and unforeseen consequences. In nearly all cases, however, Lincoln's men acted to overturn the rebellion and to strengthen the power of the nation. However much their respective situations varied and clashed, working-class Irish rioters in New York, outraged Native Americans in Minnesota, and Confederate rebels in Tennessee all saw their worlds vitally threatened by outside forces and were determined to defend themselves through violence. In each case the new birth of freedom that Lincoln had promised was tenuous at best and suggested nothing but conflict, defeat, and destruction to the ways of life they cherished.

Every four years the Constitution allows voters in the United States a plebiscite on presidential policies. The Democratic National Convention in Chicago that summer of 1864 nominated General George McClellan for president and George H. Pendleton for vice president. The Democratic desire for an immediate armistice was opposed by the Republican platform, which called for victory on the battlefield as the way to reunify the country.

Generals on the battlefield knew very well the close relationship between home and battle fronts. This late in the war, Lee and Longstreet knew that the main chance for Confederate success was Lincoln's defeat at the polls, and he might indeed be defeated if the Confederacy could prevent a Union victory in battle. As Longstreet explained, "If we can break up the enemy's arrangements early, and throw him back, he will not be able to recover his position or his morale until the Presidential election is over, and then we shall have a new President to treat with." That was a distinct possibility. No president had won a second term since Andrew Jackson more than thirty years earlier.

Lincoln also understood the tenuousness of the situation. For four years he had worked unceasingly to shore up support for the war. His door was always open to friendly reporters, to the Sanitary Commission, to volunteer associations with their bits of advice, scorned by Sherman as "the grannies." More important, Lincoln met regularly with evangelical church leaders, whose continued loyalty was absolutely essential for supplying troops and for maintaining the country's morale. Nevertheless, the problem of political support was real. Lincoln knew many blamed him for Union losses. And he had to worry about the Radical Republicans until it was clear they were not going to split the party.

Racism played a huge role in campaign literature in 1864. Ohio Congressman Samuel S. Cox introduced a pamphlet in Congress in a vicious attack on Lincoln and the Republicans. Titled *Miscegenation: The Theory of the Blending of the Races, Applied to the American White Man and Negro*, it was supposedly a secret Republican document promising African American men that they would have white women when the Union won the war. But congressional leaders soon discovered the pamphlet was a deliberate falsehood to scare whites. It was written and published by David Goodman Croly and George Wakeman, the managing editor and a reporter of the Democratic paper, *The New York World*. A more upfront election poster for the Democrats in 1864 warned the electorate that a vote for Lincoln meant "You will bring on NEGRO EQUALITY, more DEBT, HARDER TIMES, another DRAFT! Universal Anarchy, and ultimate RUIN!" A vote for McClellan meant, "You will defeat NEGRO EQUALITY, Restore prosperity, re-establish the UNION! In an Honorable, Permanent and Happy PEACE."

Republicans did not flinch but appealed to antiracist elements in the population, which had been growing with the enlistment and fighting of African American troops. They reprinted a powerful political cartoon by Thomas Nast and distributed it as their campaign poster. Nast, born in Germany, was a full-time cartoonist with *Harper's Magazine*, and during this political campaign he determined to show the racist underpinnings of the Democratic rhetoric. Lincoln appreciated Nast's steadfast opposition to slavery and is reported to have said, "Thomas Nast has been our best recruiting sergeant. His emblematic cartoons have never failed to arouse enthusiasm and patriotism." On October 15, 1864, Nast presented to the 1.25 million readers of *Harper's* two pages of twenty ironic vignettes illustrating the white supremacy that was endemic in "The Chicago Platform." He used phrases from the Democratic platform, as well as statements by McClellan and Pendleton, to show the difference between rhetoric and reality.

Democrats said, "Security, and Happiness as a People and as a Framework of Government Equally conducive to the welfare and prosperity of all the states, both northern and southern." Next to this Democratic platform phrase, Nast drew two fleeing slaves under vicious attack by dogs.

With the Democratic Party's claim that "the constitution itself has been disregarded," Nast drew Lincoln presenting the Emancipation Proclamation to a cheering and dignified group of African Americans. With the "rights of the states unimpaired," he showed a master overseeing two whites whipping a slave. Near the center of the two-page illustration, over "preserve the Federal Union," two white men smirk lustily at an attractive enslaved woman being sold away from her brokenhearted child and husband. Nash illustrated "PUBLIC LIBERTY and PRIVATE RIGHT" with the 1863 New York draft riot: background fires burning, a crowd beating and kicking defenseless African Americans, and a caricatured Irishman lifting a black child by one foot, a club raised in his other hand ready to bash the child's head. *Harper's* did not comment on the cartoons, except to say, "We do not undertake to describe or explain the picture, but we commend it to the thoughtful study of every patriot in the land."

An issue on the Republican platform illustrates that party's support for the industrialists who needed low-paid workers: "Foreign immigration which in the past has added so much to the wealth and development of resources and the increase of power to this nation . . . should be fostered and encouraged by a liberal and just policy." That "liberal and just policy" led that year to the Bureau of Immigration, which was given authority to import workers bound by labor contract. (The act was repealed in 1868, but the practice continued until contract labor was declared illegal in 1894.)

In the election of 1864, Lincoln garnered 2.2 million votes or 55 percent; McClellan 1.8 million or 45 percent. Confederates, of course, did not vote in this election, and for the most part neither did most northern African Americans. Some of the northern states authorized a new system of absentee voting so that soldiers, widely anticipated to be pro-Lincoln, could cast ballots. Among absentee votes tabulated separately, Lincoln received 119,754 to McClellan's 34,291. Democratic-controlled legislatures, such as those in Illinois, Indiana, and New Jersey, did not allow for absentee voting. Lincoln wrote to Sherman about the importance of the soldiers' vote: "The loss of [Indiana] to the friends of the Government would go far towards losing the whole Union cause." Lincoln requested that Sherman grant furloughs to as many Indiana soldiers as possible, and Sherman did furlough several thousand. All told, however, it was the close relationship between the battlefront and the home front that ultimately proved determining. Lincoln's reelection owed just as much to Sherman's taking of Atlanta as to any politicking.

The Republican Party's success in 1864 meant the continuation of its wartime program of railroad construction, homestead laws, land-grant colleges, income tax, and national banks—a new commercial order. Republicans, for all the military miscues of the generals they sponsored, demonstrated great consistency in developing and marketing this particular vision of freedom and order. It was a political triumph the Confederates were never able to match.

Ten

The Promised Land

ON FEBRUARY 18, 1865, blue-coated soldiers of the Twenty-first U.S. Colored Troops Regiment marched into Charleston, South Carolina, capturing the rebel citadel with surprising ease after four long years of war. White southerners had long dreaded the coming of the Yankees, but how much more dreadful to discover, when they finally did arrive, that the invaders were black. U.S. Colored Troops, free African Americans and former slaves, commanded by white abolitionist Augustus Bennett of New York, who had earlier overseen the execution of his black sergeant for insubordination, marched through the fallen city's streets, securing government offices and establishing strongpoints—and wreaking a revenge of looting and burning as well. Grim and gleeful soldiers sang words that had come to haunt the slaveocracy from battle to bloody battle: "John Brown's body lies a-mould'ring in the grave, but his soul goes marching on!"

The strains of "John Brown's Body" had offered fair warning of the social cataclysm that engulfed the master class between 1861 and 1865. But it suggested something more fearsome still: the prospect of sweeping social change, which overturning slavery only began. Thereafter it threatened to erupt into egalitarian demands for property, freedom, and justice, promising as it did so to cut down traditional barriers of gender, race, and class altogether. America in 1865 looked remarkably different than it had in 1861. Virtually no one could have imagined the bewildering new nation that emerged from the fires of fratricidal war.

Four million African Americans were free from bondage. Yet in this revolutionary by-product of the struggle for the Union, white and black Americans lacked anything like consensus about the possible place of freedpeople in a reconstructed United States. Commentators as diverse as Martin Delaney, Hinton Helper, William T. Sherman, and Lincoln himself had wondered doubtfully whether different races could ever be brought to peaceful coexistence, much less to the common purpose of joint citizenship. Equally uncertain was the question of what to do with the defeated southerners, all the men and women who had aided and encouraged the slaveholders' rebellion. Were these traitors, at the hour of their defeat, to be handed back the privileges they had scorned and with them the reins of local power? Should ex-rebels be permanently disfranchised? Should they be penalized for their treason, after the example of other republican governments, by execution, confiscation of their property, or loss of their political rights? How the victorious nation dealt with southern masters and former slaves at war's end would foretell the providential meaning that Americans would impose on the blood and sacrifice of the past four years.

The Civil War cost more than $6.5 billion, not including the pensions to wounded and elderly soldiers and widows and orphans of the conflict (by 1890, over 40 percent of the federal budget). That money was more than enough to cover the cost of purchasing from all the slaveholders all the four million slaves, which, after all, is what Lincoln had advocated all along. In addition, there would have been enough money left over to give each African American family forty acres, a mule, and some cash.

Worse than the financial cost, the war had seen more dying than any could have imagined—fully six hundred thousand soldiers as well as many civilians. Tens of thousands of dinner tables included a vacant chair, once filled by a father or a son, now forever empty. More than half a million more were filled by men suffering wounds, many mangled or crippled, with one sleeve empty, an eye gone, their minds distracted or their nerves shattered. The war's cost, too, was borne by women and children who had endured dark fears and long nights, and too often found those fears of loss dreadfully realized. Even men who did not go into battle, due to advanced age or infirmity, special position, self-interest, or simple cowardice were compelled ever after to concede in private that at the hour of crisis they had failed to act the part of a man. The diminution of spirit such admissions entailed, however tiny and personal, were magnified by their social pervasiveness. True heroes there were, all knew, but they were fewer than anyone had thought, and now they were mostly dead or gruesomely maimed. Even the best of men, though they had given full measure in the struggle, now knew that their bodies, their families and communities could never be restored to what they had been before. Many wondered why God had put them—and their country—through the horrifying ordeal.

Historians have noted that the Civil War created a "theological crisis." Antebellum Protestants, both North and South, had been certain they were wedded to notions of national destiny, but they were less certain now. Religion had not solved the nation's political problems. Religion had not prevented war. More than that, political extremists had used religion to justify war. Many decided that they should no longer base public policy on interpretations of the Scriptures. The Civil War took the moral energy out of Protestantism.

Southern white theologians had a dilemma in how to explain defeat. They did so by preaching that God was testing their reliance on His providence. As had happened in Biblical times when God allowed the enemy to smite His chosen people, southerners needed to keep the faith. Theological underpinnings for slavery would become underpinnings for racism, discrimination, and segregation. As southern Presbyterian minister John Bailey Adger wrote in 1868, "God has so constituted the two races as to make their equality *forever* impossible."

Northern white theologians also had a dilemma. Although the Civil War determined that the northern interpretation of Biblical scripture on slavery was the political winner, many northern clergy did not want to preach racial equality. Moreover, many thought the larger problem was young white men. The young men they had sent to fight for noble ideals were supposed to return home more purified and less self-centered. Some of the soldiers sent "to die to make men free" had instead become killers, or at least drunkards and blasphemers. Northern newspapers editorialized that the war did not redeem the Union. The war had not brought sanctification or godliness as hoped. Northern American Protestantism would never be the same. The failure of white American Protestantism to come to terms with the Civil War meant that it would have only a marginal voice when it came to issues of accelerated industrialization and the Civil War's unleashing of unfettered capitalism.

African Americans faced no such dilemmas. Unlike white evangelicals, their theology held no ambitions for cultural power and prestige and thus was not overturned. Rather than a theological crisis, the Civil War was proof of God's plan for His children. In April 1867, African American minister Simeon Beard interpreted the meaning of the war for fellow former slaves: "God intended, through this war, that, like the Red Sea, while the nation rendered itself asunder, you should pass through free. This war was God's work." AME minister Andrew Brown drew upon a millennial imagery of Revelations: "God's horse was tied to the iron stake. The day the first fire was made at Sumter, I saw the Gospel Horse begin to paw. He continued to paw until he finally broke loose and came tearing through Georgia. The colored man mounted him and intends to ride him."

Lincoln's war had been fought to prevent the disorder of secession from ending the American experiment of democratic freedom. When the war uprooted the twisted tree of chattel slavery once and for all, it also unleashed a broad new debate across the land about just what freedom actually signified, what it meant to be American, and what sort of a new nation had been ushered in at such horrific cost.

For North and South alike, April was the cruelest month. Amid ruined cities, ruined fields, and ruined lives arose a profound uncertainty. Once-valiant Confederates were now vanquished traitors awaiting the justice of victorious Yankees. No one knew how far that justice would be meted out. On April 4, as Jefferson Davis abandoned Richmond and fled south hoping to reach Texas, he defiantly urged Confederate troops to fight on, suggesting even guerrilla warfare, "with our army free to move from point to point," and with "the foe . . . far removed from his own base . . . nothing is now needed to render our triumph certain but . . . our own unquenchable resolve." Lee contravened that last order of his president, refusing to turn his remaining 27,805 seasoned soldiers into guerrillas.

On April 9, with marked graciousness and leniency, General Grant accepted General Lee's surrender. Reactions to the surrender were varied. Some Union officers hooted and jeered Lee as he rode away in defeat, and federal soldiers stared curiously at the rebel soldiers who stacked arms three days later. The famed "mutual salutation and farewell" at the formal surrender ceremony disbanding Lee's army was only one gesture among thousands. Another was made by General Martin Witherspoon Gary of South Carolina, whose brigade earlier in the war had massacred a brigade of African American soldiers so that "only a corporal's guard survived the slaughter." Ignoring Lee, Gary rode away from Appomattox with his men in an attempt to join the fleeing Davis and fight on.

Just like war, war's aftermath involved matters of moral integrity and sheer power. Lincoln began considering the issue of Reconstruction almost as soon as war broke out, and in 1864 he had written to a Quaker constituent: "Surely He intends some great good to follow this mighty convulsion." Lincoln also considered the place of African Americans in a nation undergoing a new birth of freedom. His views had evolved and expanded throughout his presidency. As he pondered racial issues, he became acquainted with people such as Frederick Douglass, whom he called "my friend," and Martin Delaney, about whom he wrote to Edwin M. Stanton in February 1865, "Do not fail to have an interview with this most extraordinary and intelligent black man." Asking about Douglass's reaction to the Second Inaugural, Lincoln said, "there is no man in the country whose opinion I value more than yours."

The *New York World* criticized Lincoln for not having a plan for Reconstruction, comparing him to "a traveler in an unknown country without a map." Not true. Lincoln knew where he was headed and had already taken several important steps in the right direction. Of critical importance was the appointment of a new Chief Justice to replace Roger Taney on the Supreme Court. Taney, whom Andrew Jackson had appointed in 1836, had written the majority opinion in the *Dred Scott* case. For twenty-eight years, until his death in October 1864, he had presided over a conservative court. Many of Lincoln's supporters, good and qualified people, wanted the position, but Lincoln knew that Reconstruction would need an unfaltering advocate of black rights: Salmon P. Chase. When questioned why he appointed a rival, a critic, a thorn in his side, Lincoln admitted that he "would rather have swallowed his buckhorn chair than to have nominated Chase." But more important to

Lincoln: "To have done otherwise I should have been recreant to my convictions of my duty to the Republican Party and to the country." Just a little over a month after Chase was confirmed, Charles Sumner introduced the first black attorney, John Rock, to practice before the highest court, and *Harper's Weekly* commented that future historians would interpret this "as a remarkable indication of the revolution which is going on in the sentiment of a great people."

An early step in his Reconstruction plan was his decision on amnesty for the rebels. He determined that a general amnesty should be granted to all who would take an oath of loyalty to the United States and pledge to obey federal laws pertaining to slavery. Unworthy of amnesty were officials and military leaders of the so-called confederate government, who were to be at least temporarily excluded. Again, Lincoln was putting his trust in southern yeomen and not their leaders.

On April 11 from the White House balcony, after Lee's surrender but before Johnston's, Lincoln made some remarks to the gathering crowd, reminding them to remember Him "from whom all blessings flow." He then addressed "the re-inauguration of the national authority—reconstruction." Lincoln the southerner knew that he did not confront a single, unified South. "We must simply begin with, and mould from, disorganized and discordant elements." Nevertheless, he hoped and expected that a majority of white southerners would support efforts to reunify the country. Lincoln's plans for Reconstruction required cooperation between the executive and legislative branches of the government. The executive branch had the right to determine when the rebellious states were back in "proper practical relation" with the government, and the legislative branch had the right to determine who were admissible as members of Congress.

Lincoln pointed to Louisiana as an example of what Reconstruction might look like. That state had already passed the Thirteenth Amendment granting total emancipation with no middle step of apprenticeship for freed slaves. Louisiana's "free-state constitution" gave "the benefit of public schools equally to black and white." Lincoln noted that some criticized Louisiana's constitution for not granting African American suffrage, but it did empower the state legislature "to confer the elective franchise upon the colored man." In part Lincoln agreed with the critics: "I would myself prefer that it were now conferred on the very intelligent, and on those who serve our cause as soldiers."

One year earlier, on March 13, 1864, Lincoln had shared those sentiments in a confidential letter to Michael Hahn, "the first-free-state Governor of Louisiana." He suggested that Hahn advocate black suffrage in Louisiana. "I barely suggest for your private consideration, whether some of the colored people may not be let in—as, for instance, the very intelligent, and especially those who have fought gallantly in our ranks." And yet, while he knew that "important principles may, and must, be inflexible," he emphasized the need for flexibility in the management of principles.

From his balcony, Lincoln ended on an anticipatory note: "In the present '*situation*,' as the phrase goes, it may be my duty to make some new announcement to the people of the South. I am considering, and shall not fail to act, when satisfied that action will be proper." One listener at this speech, John Wilkes Booth, read his darkest fears into Abraham Lincoln's vision and told his companion, "That means nigger citizenship. Now, by God, I'll put him through. That is the last speech he will ever make." What the near future held was anyone's guess, and while some held their breath, the majority, in ways large and small, planned their next moves.

In mid-April the flag of the United States was raised once again over Fort Sumter, where it had been replaced four years earlier by a Confederate flag very similar in design. Speech-making was the order of the day, and America's most famous and beloved preacher, Henry Ward Beecher, was invited to do the honors. Abraham Lincoln had greatly appreciated the minister's support for the war and particularly his role in lobbying England to remain neutral. His series of speeches in England were so important that Lincoln believed "without Beecher, there might have been no flag to raise." At Fort Sumter, Beecher asked why the country had "shed this ocean of blood." Lincoln, one month earlier in his Second Inaugural, assigned the South blame for resorting to war: "Both parties deprecated war, but one of them would *make* war rather than let the nation survive." But Lincoln was not charging guilt to the South alone. He acknowledged that "American slavery" was a national sin, and that God gave the punishment of war "to both North and South." At Fort Sumter on April 14, however, Beecher answered with a total and unambiguous consignment of blame: "I charge the whole guilt of this war upon the ambitious, educated, plotting, political leaders of the South." America's preacher would later change his view, but in the war's immediate aftermath he declared that reunion ought to go hand in hand with the vengeance and retribution of a patriotic God. Only after the rebel chiefs had been smitten could the nation be healed. "God shall say, 'Thus shall it be to all who betray their country.'"

Tragically, that very evening America suffered a blow from which it has never recovered: the stunning assassination of President Abraham Lincoln. The little circle of resentful southerners and immigrants who clustered around Mary Surratt's H Street boardinghouse where John Wilkes Booth resided almost succeeded in beheading the national executive branch at one stroke. Lewis Powell tried to kill Secretary of State William Seward and almost accomplished the task. George Atzerodt, assigned to kill Vice President Andrew Johnson, got drunk and backed down. Booth's shot to the back of Lincoln's head cost the nation its statesman and commander in chief. The North lost its hero. African Americans lost an ally for fair and equal opportunity. The South lost a leader, southern-born, who called for "charity toward all" and "malice toward none."

In a letter home dated April 19, 1865, Union soldier George Cram wrote, "Yesterday our camps were filled with intense sorrow over the death of Mr. Lincoln . . . the feeling in the entire army is deep mourning." Cram appears sympathetic even to the North Carolina "secesh" whom he had despised at the time of his enlistment: "The citizens of this place held a meeting yesterday and made some resolutions expressing their sorrow at the occurrence and even the old rebels seem to feel a kind of horror at such a dastardly deed."

By some accounts, when Jefferson Davis learned on April 19 of Lincoln's death he expressed regret. "There are a great many men of whose end I would rather hear than his," he was recalled as saying. Superintendent of the Southern Express Company for the State of North Carolina Lewis F. Bates, at whose home Davis was staying in Charlotte at the time he learned of the murder, however, remembered Davis expressing a different sentiment, one more in keeping with the fleeing Confederate president's April 4 proclamation issued in Danville, Virginia, that southerners "meet the foe with fresh defiance." In late May, Bates testified, "Jefferson Davis and John C. Breckinridge [Confederate secretary of war] were present at my house, when the assassination of the President was the subject of conversation. In speaking of it, John C. Breckinridge remarked to

Davis, that he regretted it very much; that it was very unfortunate for the people of the South at that time. Davis replied, 'Well General, I don't know, if it were to be done at all, it were better that it were well done; and if the same had been done to Andy Johnson, the beast, and to Secretary Stanton, the job would then be complete.'" Bates's veracity was affirmed by five individuals at the trial of the Lincoln murder conspirators.

In the North grieving crowds lined the streets as Lincoln's funeral procession made its way home to Springfield, Illinois. Americans, white and black, clearly treasuring Lincoln's message, held up placards with phrases from his Second Inaugural Address as the coffin passed. In his remarkable eulogy to the fallen sixteenth president, poet Walt Whitman captured some of the grief felt nationwide:

> When lilacs last in the dooryard bloom'd,
> And the great star early droop'd in the western sky in the night,
> I mourn'd, and yet shall mourn with ever-returning spring.
>
> Ever-returning spring, trinity sure to me you bring,
> Lilac blooming perennial and drooping star in the west,
> And thought of him I love.
>
> O powerful western fallen star!
> O shades of night—O moody, tearful night!
> O great star disappear'd—O the black murk that hides the star!
> O crucial hands that hold me powerless—O helpless soul of me!
> O harsh surrounding cloud that will not free my soul.

By assassinating the president, on Good Friday no less, Booth had ensured Father Abraham's place in history as a beloved martyr for freedom. Even though soldiers tracked down and shot Booth soon after he fled Washington, aggrieved Federals would not be deprived a public ritual of blood atonement. On July 7 four of Booth's accomplices, including Mary Surratt, were publicly hanged. Days later, the trial of Confederate Captain Henry Wirz began in the Capitol a short walk from the gallows. Accused of causing the deaths of more than thirteen thousand northern prisoners of war at Georgia's notorious Andersonville camp, Wirz seemed the military equivalent of the Booth cabal: unheroic, treacherous, and vile.

When he was hanged in November, some called for Robert E. Lee to join him on the scaffold. Some advocated hanging Jefferson Davis with the lot. Davis had been captured and clamped in irons in May and was then languishing in a federal prison. Three weeks earlier the rebel guerrilla chieftain Champ Ferguson had been executed at Nashville for assorted war atrocities, including the murder of African American prisoners of war. By Christmas it was still uncertain whether the meting out of these sentences would serve to appease northern fury or would merely whet its appetite for southern blood.

There was more to Reconstruction than revenge. It was a period of unity and disunity, of racial coalitions and racial hostilities. During Reconstruction a majority of southerners, fractured by class and by race, nevertheless moved uncertainly, incrementally, grudgingly, and enthusiastically along a path of equality. They encountered an intransigent white minority, increasingly bound together through paramilitary organizations, insistent upon inequality. The essential character of Reconstruction was based on traditional American values, with parties on all sides concerned with establishing local systems of workable order in their own communities, according to their own notions of justice and fair play. Like antebellum conflicts between enslaved and master, abolitionist and planter, and Free-Soiler and slaveholder, the conservative drive to resolve practical problems at the local level in Reconstruction generated tremendous unforeseen conflicts that propelled events along a startlingly revolutionary course. This interplay of conservatism and revolution, this interweaving of concerns with order and with freedom define Reconstruction in its achievements and failures both. At Reconstruction's start only one certainty prevailed: thousands had reason to anticipate its advent and thousands had reason to dread it.

Most optimistic of all was the political course that hundreds of thousands of African Americans took in the years after slavery ended. Lincoln's republicanism was taken up anew by freedpeople at the local level across the South. It is fitting that in the years after 1865 those most newly arrived on freedom's doorstep held the clearest sense of its precepts. The freedoms they fought for grounded citizenship in self-mastery and independent property. From Plato to Thomas Jefferson, from James Harrington to Abraham Lincoln, republican theorists had emphasized that the political duties and opportunities of citizenship were founded on the ideal of property ownership. Emancipation not only marked the birth of African American freedom, it sparked an African American rebirth of republicanism, argued and defended more cogently and fervently than at any time in American history. Reconstruction is the story of that promise.

Viewed from Capitol Hill, the history of slavery's sequel seems straightforward, progressive, and ultimately tragic. In courts and legislatures on both the state and national levels, politicians wrangled over and ultimately reached important decisions about the nature of the Union, the characteristics of citizenship, and the proper relation between the races in social and political terms. The political and legal history of these changes is important, exceedingly complex, and heartbreaking. But in the end, to tell the story of Reconstruction in the shadow of the Capitol dome, or even in state legislative bodies in capital cities throughout the nation, is to miss how uncertain, how revolutionary, how conservative, and how profoundly democratic this era of change truly was. No one knew what the end of bondage might bring in its wake. Slavery's death did not automatically confer any positive rights upon African Americans. It only liberated them from the control of the master, eliminating at the same time the latter's motive for self-interested benevolence, which under bondage enslaved blacks had tried to use to their benefit. Between the captivity they had known and the freedom they dreamed of, African Americans found themselves suspended in a limbo of social and political uncertainty. While on the federal level the president and Congress worked to reconcile states within the Union, on the local level former slaves and rebels could do little except feel their way forward tentatively, staking claims to new ways or old habits in their own communities, defending their choices on a daily basis to those they ran up against in the course of labor and community life. In this way ordinary Americans reconstructed their nation according to their own uncertain, conflicted ideas. The passage of new laws played a central role in shaping the contours of that struggle, but Reconstruction was a far more diverse, all-pervasive process than legislation alone. The effects of the tensions it created crept into all aspects of everyday life, and they persist in common behaviors and social values down to the present day.

The tasks that confronted the nation after the war were enormous and multifaceted. Reconstruction was political: rebellious states required loyal governments and representatives who were deemed fit to serve in Congress. Congressmen thought the problem of postbellum southern race relations was how to integrate former slaves into freedom and citizenship, but the effort became how to integrate former Confederates into a nation undergoing a new birth of freedom and justice under the law for all. Reconstruction was economic: with the destruction of chattel bondage, former masters and former slaves alike would have to take recourse in wage labor, and farms laid waste by four years of war would somehow have to be made profitable again. Reconstruction was religious: reformers like Lewis Tappan and other white and black abolitionists saw the opportunity to do God's work in structuring a new order on moral principles. The American Missionary Association sent teachers into the South to bring "the glorious liberty of the gospel." Granted the freedom to worship as they wished for the first time, African Americans would have to decide whether to kneel before God in prayer alongside their former enslavers or to establish their own churches. Whites and blacks alike would have to ponder whether to turn the other cheek or to smite their oppressors when the chance presented itself. Reconstruction was legal: as thousands of African Americans troubled themselves to record marriages long since consummated, or paid taxes, or set their mark on a labor contract, or simply called the sheriff in time of trouble, they asserted their right to live in peace among their fellows under the shade of the Constitution and all subsequent acts of legislation. They were neither chattels nor dependents, interlopers nor charity-seekers; they claimed rights, endured responsibilities, and enjoyed freedoms guaranteed by the power "of the people." If the Civil War was the period in which American freedom was expanded for African Americans, the Reconstruction era established institutions and bureaucracies that determined or undermined this freedom.

Most of all, Reconstruction was indeterminate, a blank slate to be drawn on by federal resolve, African American self-determination, and the toxic stew of emasculated masters and embittered yeomen. The world had been turned upside down and would continue topsy-turvy for at least twice the number of years the Union and Confederacy had fought and killed each other during the official Civil War. That killing had inspired Beecher's April 14 call for Confederate reckoning as well as the assassin's response.

The call for vengeance infected both victors and defeated. In the retribution of war, simmering hatreds boiled over: northerners and southerners against each other, rich and poor, whites and blacks, political parties, all against all. One southern white woman wrote about the nation that Lincoln touted, "While I have no personal feeling towards any one of them I hate the nation from the bottom of my soul, Even as I hate Satan, and all things low, mean and hateful." Such bitter intransigence was widespread, bloody-minded, and openly declared. Some postwar poetry spoke in exaltation of hatred. One such postwar poem, attributed to former Confederate Major James Innes Randolph, Jr., of Virginia, used the vernacular of poor whites to express his feelings, thereby both appealing to that group and putting the blame for such passionate hatred onto them rather than his own aristocratic self:

> I hates the Constitution, this "Great Republic," too,
> I hates the Freedman's Bureau and uniforms of blue!
> I hates the nasty eagle with all its brags and fuss,
> And the lying, thieving Yankees, I hates 'em wuss and wuss!
>
> I hates the Yankee nation and everything they do,
> I hates the Declaration of Independence too!
> I hates the "Glorious Union"—tis dripping with our blood,
> And I hates their striped banner, and I fit it all I could.
>
> . . . I do not want no pardon for what I was and am,
> And I won't be reconstructed, and I do not care a damn!

A desperate and humiliated rage smolders in many of the letters and diaries that have come down from this hour. Yet the uncomprehending expressions of shock, loss, trepidation, and aimlessness that fill the letters of the South's planter class in the months after surrender suggest that most rebels did not respond to the utter collapse of their way of life with quite the anger expressed in these lines. But anytime former Confederates passed around the jug, or considered changed times in front of a crossroads store, or steeled their eyes as a former slave passed them on the street without doffing his hat, a bitter militancy came to the fore among a minority.

Most southerners, though, greeted the news of Confederate defeat with some relief, and many nonslaveholders, even as they pondered what the future would bring, were quietly pleased to see the gentry taken down a notch and the Union that many of them had always revered restored once more. Taking a loyalty oath to the U.S. government that they had been iron-clad Unionists throughout the war were 22,000 citizens seeking reimbursement for war damages. The Southern Claims Commission validated 41 percent of the claims. Rich and poor alike came before the commission. The widows from Mississippi requesting compensation for stock and corn included a former slaveholder and an illiterate tenant. The former, Debbey E. Clark, testified, "My Grand father was killed in the Revolutionary war. My brother was with Jackson at New Orleans and I had nephews in the Mexican War and nephews in the late war in the Union Army. I believed in Genl Jackson and did not think it was right to destroy what he saved." The poorer neighbor proclaimed, "I never believed in the war of Jeff Davis I always believed in the United States Government I did not believe in secession . . . had I the chance I would have shot Jeff Davis." A neighbor corroborated her report mentioning that she came from the Piney Woods in Copiah County "where there is a great many Union people."

For the four million African Americans suddenly loosed from bondage, no single stereotype can comprehend their reaction: some were overjoyed, others fearful of events to come; some were disbelieving, others just as confused and cast adrift as their former masters. Countless thousands set out immediately on the roads—searching for kin and loved ones lost or sold away, seeking out a better chance of employment, abandoning plantation labor for the perceived joys of yeomanry or city life. Just as many defined emancipation for themselves by the quest to bring together families divided on the auction block, some lost no time in breaking up vexing unions held together by the threat of the lash. Everywhere freedpeople congregated across the South in the weeks after Appomattox witnessed the same remarkable transformation: African American families vaulted outward, as if by centrifugal force, setting up independent households. Here and there a few former slaves embarked upon freedom by settling scores with hated drivers and overseers or with the master. At most, however, such declarations of independence were usually verbal, even if vociferous and salty. Nothing like the nightmares of rape and pillage that planters predicted were acted out. Perhaps this speaks to the deep roots that Christian virtue had already struck within the African American community; perhaps it suggests that former slaves saw the redemption of former masters as only a little further off.

In the most practical, confounding, head-scratching sense, Reconstruction was a social process, a daily working out, by white and black, male and female, rich and poor, of how they ought to treat each other in these changed times. In some cases these social dramas played themselves out over old ties sundered or renewed—or reversed, as when freedpeople brought food to "old massa," now steeped in poverty. In others they were enacted through new behaviors: a white man hauled before a black judge, African Americans defending their homes with rifles, a black militia instead of a white slave patrol, interracial crowds of Union League supporters whooping it up on Independence Day. Other changes were smaller: freedmen driving newly bought buggies, poor black or white children learning to scratch out ABCs on a dearly bought slate. Of such seemingly insignificant things mighty revolutions are made; against such dread changes the forces of reaction launch their strongest battalions. So it was in the Reconstruction South.

Black and white, rich and poor, male and female, southerners shared no common definition of what freedom for former slaves should mean in practical terms. African Americans' desire for personal and family autonomy conflicted with the social interests of some whites, who still needed workers even if they could not have slaves. Most white people of the South were of the mind that African Americans must not receive the abundant freedom that whites enjoyed. Many agreed with the South Carolina newspaper editor who argued that "freedom from being sold on the block and separated from his wife and children is all the freedom he ought to have." Using the example of antebellum free blacks as a model, whites offered to go as far as they could toward establishing a labor system just short of slavery. Few, however, argued for a return to chattel bondage in public declarations or private correspondence. Emancipation, as it turned out, loaded all the responsibilities of freedom—finding food, clothing, and shelter, and the money to gain these good things— onto the shoulders of former slaves who had absolutely no resources. Newly relieved ex-masters sighed deeply and plotted how to keep as much of that money in their own pockets as possible. African Americans strode toward a providential liberty defined by property ownership and legal rights, but whites contested every step.

As former slaves grappled with a new world beyond slavery, responding hopefully, quizzically, doubtfully to the changes they encountered, the same adjustments viewed from the perspective of the southern white community seemed positively cataclysmic. Wealthy whites who had invested heavily in Confederate bonds lost fortunes, as did those few Confederate patriots who accepted payment in worthless Confederate currency. Slaves had been the defining symbol of status and wealth, an assurance of loans and advances on future crops, a sign of personal identity itself. Emancipation eliminated this collateral for purchases and negotiations, struck down solid systems of social definition, and cast the meaning of masculinity, honor, and selfhood in doubt. With a profound sense of insulted pride, some men became psychologically as well as physically scarred. "To our father it was a distress, and something of a mortification that he could no longer be the main stay of his family," wrote the daughter of Charleston planter Frank Frost, a grandee who had often stated that the Bible declared, "A man was no good who could not support his family." His girls saved the family financially by going out to work for wages, turning "over our earnings to him . . . that he might still feel the dignity as head of the family." Whether such labors retrieved paternal pride in this case and countless others, or wounded it still further, is a problem beyond solving, blended as it is with a thousand similar individual negotiations within vastly changed circumstances and expectations.

Elite women were confused and fearful, too. One was distressed to see carts of her possessions commandeered by departing Yankees heading north, stolen and stuffed into boxes marked "Family relics, from Rebeldom." She pointed out to her daughter that at least they would probably get their homes back because "houses, fortunately, not being like chairs, tables etc [were not] removable to Northern states." Older white women remained in traditional roles at home and tried to help financially by renting out carriage houses or empty rooms to those few with greenbacks or gold. Others asserted themselves in church and civic activities. Some became small-scale entrepreneurs, selling homemade jellies or using their flower gardens to make and sell corsages and bouquets. In April 1867 white men in upcountry South Carolina complained about the entrepreneurial spirit among two supposedly dependent groups. It seems a group of white women "and negroes" was operating stills "where spirits were retailed."

Lucy Pickens, comparatively untouched by the war in material terms, wrote a friend about "a gloom dark & bitter indeed to all who love our desolate & helpless land . . . the dreary clanking of our chains comes shudderingly on every breeze." The reason, to Emilie McKinley of Mississippi, was plain: the world they had known was gone forever, and "Negroes rule the land." How far that social revolution might ultimately extend, none could say for sure. "Political reconstruction might be unavoidable now," another plantation mistress wrote in late 1865, "but social reconstruction we hold in our hands & might prevent." Certainly it was not at all clear to ex-Confederates in the months after surrender just what would be required of them in order to reestablish civilian control of state and local governments, much less how they could restore what seemed to them a shattered world of honor, balance, propriety, and purpose.

Thousands of white southerners left the South. Many Confederate leaders fled in fear to Europe. Eight to ten thousand emigrated to South America in hopes of re-creating the South's slave-based society (many later returned). Neighbors who had disappointed their communities through a lack of zeal for the Cause during wartime now contrived reasons or discovered inducements to pull up stakes. Others simply wanted to turn their faces away from a scene of catastrophe. One rice planter's son moved to California to practice law and delve into land speculation. He urged his parents to join him. "Is there any hope in the future?" he asked. "Has there been any day, since the closing of the war, when property was not lower and hope fainter than the day before?" Each new disaster seemed to "double all [the] evils" of existence, he believed, "and lessen all its good." Many abandoned their homeland in a different fashion, giving up agriculture in favor of new ventures in industry, banking, insurance, and other Yankeefied pursuits. Countless southerners scrawled the letters "GTT"—Gone To Texas—on their homes and in a great postwar folk movement headed for the country of long-horned cattle and tall cotton. Texas was as far west as one could go without leaving the South altogether. Most whites, however, like most blacks, stayed put.

African Americans realized immediately that political rights were essential for their economic and social health. In the summer and fall of 1865 African Americans called conventions to discuss how to make ideals of liberty their own. African American minister Garrison Frazier spoke for his Baptist congregation in Savannah, Georgia, about what freedom meant: "taking us from under the yoke of bondage, and placing us where we could reap the fruits of our own labor, take care of ourselves and assist the government in maintaining our freedom." Federal military commander Nathaniel P. Banks reported the results of his inquiries in the Louisiana plantation belt "to ascertain what the negroes wanted." They wanted sanctity of family, education for their children, the end of corporal punishment, and the payment of reasonable wages. R. H. Cain, an African American minister and newspaper publisher in South Carolina, wrote that he wanted to "be dealt with as others are—in equity and justice." According to Reverend James Keelan of New Orleans, "All we want now is our rights and religious privileges—to live as Christians in a Christian country. We like our rebel friends, and we don't want to hurt them. We want them to give us our rights and to receive us as distant brothers . . . We have raised your children, cleaned up your grounds and enriched you. Now let us go." Most wanted to be left alone.

Others went further. African Americans in Louisiana called a meeting near the conclusion of the war and resolved "that the right of the employee to freely agree and contract . . . is the unquestionable attribute of every freeman." They protested, "as friends of freedom, equal rights, and liberty," against any form of segregation. They denounced any attempt "of the former slaveowners to transform, the book of Liberty . . . into a disguised bondage." In April 1865 freedmen from North Carolina wrote about their willingness to fight for their country. Having performed their duty, they now expected more: "We want the privilege of voting." The African American leader in Vicksburg, Mississippi, Peter Crosby, declared, "We do not intend to be satisfied until we have all the privileges belonging to all citizens. We do not intend to be satisfied in part." Reverend James W. Hood of North Carolina listed demands: "First, the right to testify in courts of justice; Secondly, representation in the jury box; Third and finally, the black man should have the right to carry his ballot to the ballot box." The African Methodist Episcopal minister Henry M. Turner insisted on the most fundamental of political freedoms, "our rights in common with other men."

Sometimes freedom meant withdrawal from white society, a withdrawal into one's own family, farm, and church, away from surveillance by whites, to be self-sufficient. Sometimes freedom meant accommodation, as blacks worked with and for whites in employment. Sometimes it meant assertion and confrontation. In politics, freedom meant involvement in the governance of the community—directly, through the supervision of one's household; and indirectly, through the mechanisms of petition, party, voting, and legislation. Whether or not they were able to read the Constitution's guarantee of the right to assemble, African Americans knew they wanted to exercise that right. On Charleston's Battery, in New Orleans's Congo Square, and in ten thousand crossroads stores, churchyards, and muster grounds, blacks came together to speak their minds, swap stories and opinions, complain and boast, plan and organize. Relative homogeneity, strong kinship ties, and developing economic and occupational possibilities fostered a group identity among African Americans. Many had come from cohesive plantation and interplantation communities, a source of strength and unity for them in captivity. Almost immediately African American communities in the rural and urban South developed thriving voluntary groups such as burial and mutual benevolence societies, fraternal orders, Union Leagues, Grant Clubs, and other grassroots political organizations to advocate for voting and holding office. Overwhelming historical documentation shows that in every southern state former slaves grabbed hold of freedom and asserted themselves in the postwar era by securing their families, learning and teaching, and seeking and wielding political power. And that political power was accompanied by economic strength and personal independence. Each element was necessary for the others, both in republican theory and in daily life. African Americans gained in means and social prestige as long as they held political power.

From the moment of liberation, then, most former slaves saw freedom in traditional terms: they focused, with careful self-regard, on building strong families, obtaining property, and accumulating wealth. They expressed the republican virtues of the Founding Fathers themselves as they set out to balance self-interest with the well-being of local communities. Central to the African American definition of liberty was religious freedom, and many whites complained that former slaves were "religious fanatics." As a rule, white people did not request that former slaves sever connections with the white church; state religious associations instructed churches to continue to minister to African Americans. Nevertheless, except in rare cases, establishing its own churches, away from white control, was one of the first things the African American community chose to do. African American religion frustrated pious whites with its emphasis on joy and hope and forgiveness rather than on personal guilt, punishment, and self-denial. With very few exceptions, integrated Baptist and Methodist churches from antebellum times, which whites firmly controlled, split into black and white, for reasons of theology and for reasons of governance.

As under slavery, whites continued to fear African American meetings and religious ceremonies that took place without whites present, and they sometimes monitored services. Throughout the southern states whites heard a different version of the creation story. In His own image, African American preachers declared, God created Adam and Eve black. They turned white, and their hair straightened, from sin and guilt, from encountering God after eating the forbidden fruit. Such revisionist theology did not go ignored or unanswered. In South Carolina, where Franklin Moses was a native white Republican leader during Reconstruction, white Democrats objected to the text of a sermon delivered by Reverend Thomas Sease, "The Lord has delivered his sheep out of the hands of the enemy and placed them in the care of Moses"; it was too political, they said, and was meant "to stir up race hostilities." White neighbors entered the black minister's home and killed him. The local paper did not condone this murder but explained that the reverend had been "in the habit of talking in a somewhat turbulent and threatening manner." One sugar planter in Louisiana complained about a former slave who "preached that he was the servant of Christ &, as such, was not required to work" except for the Lord. The same rule "applied to them that joined his church." The planter considered this interpretation of religious liberty to be "very bad doctrine."

The African American church advocated civil society and community activism. It provided a meeting place, solidified community spirit, and often focused activism toward social and political ends. A source of strength for black leaders, the church inspired the application of ethics to the political problems of the postwar period. Through Christian doctrine black culture preached reconciliation rather than revenge as a reaction to past bondage. Black leaders thought it best to move past animosity and "exhibit a christian universality of spirit." Typical was a discussion among African Americans in Vicksburg about whether whites, those "lately in rebellion," should have the right to vote. The majority believed in democracy so much that they thought whites should be able to participate in a fair system where each man had a meaningful vote. Only a minority of the African Americans present at this particular meeting thought it was unwise to give former rebels "this substantial weapon." Churches and religious faith helped black leaders see that their freedom was not dependent upon whites but derived directly from God, the African American religious community, and the autonomy of their own families.

Churches fostered education. All across the South in the months after Appomattox, African American communities opened up whatever building was available to create a space for volunteers to gather, teach, and learn together. Often proceeding under church leadership, freedpeople contributed their labor and their very limited funds to build new schools, hire teachers, and organize supervisory committees. White minister Reverend William Richardson of the American Missionary Association went to Savannah in early 1865 to check the feasibility of starting a school. He found that the Savannah freedmen had already collected $730 and launched a school with several local teachers. Throughout the South white and black teachers taught, often through songs, civic responsibility and patriotism, hard work and patience. In Georgia a group of seven hundred students upset local whites by singing "The Battle Cry of Freedom." Black students in Florida gave their own version of the law in songs for visiting Supreme Court chief justice Salmon Chase—"We'll Hang Jeff Davis to a Sour Apple Tree" and "John Brown's Body."

In Beaufort County, South Carolina, Robert Smalls, who had hired a tutor during the Civil War to teach him to read, described himself as "deeply interested in the common school system." He bought and donated the land for a school to which freedmen came "at all hours . . . expecting to catch a lesson." The vast majority of freed African Americans saw educational opportunity as integral to freedom, part and parcel of their determination "never to be made slaves again." Freedman Charles Whiteside of North Carolina said that education was "the next best thing to liberty." Northern schoolmarms, such as African American Edmonia Highgate from New York, came south to help. A member of the American Missionary Association teaching in Louisiana, she wrote,

"The majority of my pupils come from plantations, three, four and even eight miles distant. So anxious are they to learn that they walk these distances so early in the morning as never to be tardy." She also wrote about local opposition to the school and how she and some of her students had been shot at. "The nearest military protection is 200 miles distant at New Orleans." Opponents of black education in New Orleans showed their disapproval of one northern schoolteacher: they stabbed him and left a note in his pocket, "The damned Yankee won't teach any more niggers."

Even such threats and dangers, however, could not halt the deep thirst for knowledge in African American communities. Each gain proved cumulative: from basic literacy and rude arithmetic, freedpeople mounted upward. Among the hundreds of secondary schools and colleges founded during Reconstruction were Fisk in Nashville, Tennessee (1866), and the Augusta Institute in Georgia (1867), the latter moving to Atlanta onto land donated by fellow Baptist John D. Rockefeller; the college was subsequently renamed Morehouse College. These religious institutions grew to be prestigious academies that opened and clarified a vision of higher education beyond the achievement of agricultural and vocational skills.

Despite acts of violence and arson committed against churches and schoolhouses, African Americans persisted and made progress in educating their children and reducing illiteracy. In 1860 only about 10 percent of the adult African American population could read; by 1870 that figure had increased to 30 percent. (In 1900 it was 55.5 percent.) Poor whites even complained that freedmen would surpass them in literacy, though that never happened; white rates remained at about 80 percent. (Louisiana saw a decrease in white literacy when it quit funding education at the end of Reconstruction.)

One of the dearest aspects of newly acquired freedom was to have a family that could no longer be sold. The first exercise in personal independence for many African Americans was to bring together missing family members who had been torn apart during slavery, an endeavor that proved very difficult. Ads in newspapers looking for family members who had been sold by "a trader then in human beings" were numerous and, sadly, usually futile. Typical was an ad placed by Samuel Dove of Utica, New York, in the *Colored Tennessean* in 1865. He wanted to know "the whereabouts of his mother, Areno, his sisters Maria, Neziah, and Peggy, and his brother Edmond, who were owned by Geo. Dove, of Rockingham country, Shenandoah Valley, Va." They had been sold in Richmond "after which Saml and Edmond were taken to Nashville, Tenn. by Joe Mick; Areno was left at the Eagle Tavern, Richmond."

Some whites saw the reorganization of family units as a direct challenge to a master's authority. At the end of 1865, when Annie Burton's mother, who had escaped during the war, came for her three children, the white ex-slaveholder in Alabama refused to let the children go. Annie Burton's mother sneaked back later to spirit them away, but the onetime master's two sons came after them and demanded that the children be returned. According to Burton's memoirs, "My mother refused to give us up. Upon her offering to go with them to the Yankee headquarters to find out if it were really true that all negroes had been made free, the young men left, and troubled us no more."

Troubling to many white observers was the exercise by African Americans of a much-appreciated freedom to move at their own free will without "passes" and without having to answer to slave patrollers. They moved to find or join families, to seek economic opportunity, to satisfy curiosity or a yen for adventure, or simply to get away. As one freedman stated, "I must go, if I stay here I'll never know I am free." When Private John Smith Watson of Georgia, father of future Populist leader Tom Watson, came home from Confederate service, he held a meeting to tell his recently enslaved workers that they were free. He reported that by the next day "not a negro remained on the place" and "every house in the 'quarter' was empty." While the majority of African Americans, for financial limitations or by choice, stayed in the same area, the theme of travel, journey, and sojourn acquired a special significance in black culture. In art and music, trains especially offered a powerful metaphor for a physical and a spiritual journey to the Promised Land of freedom. At the same time rootless wandering suggested a lonely experience, cut off from family and community, an antecedent of the blues.

Under slavery no one could leave the plantation without permission. That supposedly was over. But in 1866, after former slave Elbert MacAdams visited his wife, "who lived on Basil Callaham's plantation," a group of whites took MacAdams from his house, shot him three times, cut his throat, and dragged him into the woods. Callaham and two other men were arrested for the murder, but the white law enforcement system, which did not yet include blacks in the judicial process, did not convict them. Although such stories were not unusual, the majority of free men and women were able to enjoy the newfound liberty to care for their own home and children instead of, or in addition to, someone else's. Emancipation resulted in the withdrawal of a significant number, though not the majority, of black married women from paid employment, a source of exasperation to planters (who lost women's labor in the fields) and to white women (who lost their "beloved servants"). When Cretia, a long-time servant of Mary Pringle in Charleston, South Carolina, informed her that she was going to live with her son, a carpenter, Mary wrote, "It was a great shock to me." Cretia offered to continue to work for Mary during the day, but Mary wanted a live-in servant who did her bidding no matter the inconvenience: "None of these demoralized negroes would make up my chamber fire at daylight in the morning."

Freedom did not guarantee a former slave the right to decent housing. Whether they had lived on large plantations in concentrated slave quarters, on smaller farms in houses close to that of the white owner, or even within the white household, many freedpeople preferred to move away from white control. But options were limited; very few former slaves had the fortunate housing situation of the extraordinary Robert Smalls. After the war Smalls used the prize money he received for capturing the Confederate *Planter* to purchase the home he grew up in, the Beaufort, South Carolina, residence of his former master (who was also quite likely his father), John K. McKee. Often freedpeople stayed in their same houses, but a good many whites evicted former slaves who did not "act slavish" any longer. One planter who had taken in five orphaned children of former slaves wrote, "Their parents were among my best and most faithful servants." But recognition of past free service was not good enough, and he complained about the burden: "I am unwilling to bear it longer unless there can be some assurance of reward at some future day." Catherine Hammond, widow to proslavery ideologue James Henry Hammond, complained in the aftermath of the Civil War, "We have not lost many negroes . . . [but] I wish we could get clear of many of the useless ones." Paternalistic impulses thinned out precipitously in the postwar period as economic motivations shifted.

Coming out of slavery with only "freedom," most freedmen's families across the South struggled in conditions of desperate poverty. There was "not much house room," one former slave remembered, and the quality of most quarters was inadequate at best. Few adults and fewer children acquired more than one change of clothing, often of the roughest and cheapest sort. Freedom did not put food on the table either, African Americans quickly learned; emancipation left southern blacks now fully free to starve. According to southern theologian and apologist Robert Lewis Dabney, previous to the war no "Africans" had resided in "the poorhouse." Now that the North had taken upon itself "conquest of the South," he said, it must not expect white southerners to bear the burden of providing food, shelter, clothing, and medical needs for African Americans. One former slave asserted their capability: "We used to support ourselves and our masters too when we were slaves and I reckon we can take care of ourselves now." Carl Schurz, Republican senator from Missouri who studied conditions in the South in the summer of 1865, found that, although many former slaveholders accused former slaves of laziness and unwillingness to work without coercion and the threat of whipping, those accusations for the most part were unfounded: "Certain it is, that the larger portion of the work done in the south is done by freedmen." On the contrary, Schurz found that many whites were not reliable paymasters.

Few former slaves confused wage labor with freedom. Real freedom, as republican ideology understood it and religious expectation framed it, required autonomy. In an agricultural economy, that meant living off one's own land, or at least working with the expectation of acquiring property. For centuries African Americans had been told they did not belong; owning land proved they did. Surely the "Day of Jubilo" that Mr. Lincoln's armies had brought on must entail an act of retribution toward the master class, at least the minimal transfer of "forty acres and a mule" as token of redress. Everywhere across the South (except in the sugar lands of Louisiana and eastern Texas, where tillage required larger acreages and gang labor) African Americans raised the cry for land. "Gib us our own land and we take care ourselves," one freedman pleaded, "but widout land, de ole massas can hire us or starve us." For almost 250 years enslaved people had tilled the soil of their masters and had watched them become rich and powerful thereby. "Our wives, our children, our husbands," declared one Virginia freedman, "has been sold over and over again to purchase the lands we now locates on." Carl Schurz pointed out in his report to Congress that the abolition of serfdom in Russia resulted in little or no vagrancy because "the emancipated serfs were speedily endowed with the ownership of land, which gave them a permanent moral and material interest in the soil upon which they lived." African Americans were wise enough to understand the meaning of Lincoln's republicanism: without land of their own, they remained rootless, dependent beings, possessing nothing like independence.

Early in the war abolitionist William Goodell called for the confiscation of Confederate land and its redistribution to freed slaves. Charles Sumner also advocated redistribution "so that at least every head of a family may have a piece of land." Charles K. Whipple wrote in *The Liberator* in June 1862 that "rebels against a government forfeit their property, as well as their other rights and privileges." At first President Lincoln, unsure of its constitutionality, objected to the Confiscation Act of 1862. Two years later, however, in July 1864 he told congressman George Julian of Indiana that he had changed his mind: the confiscation of rebel property was constitutionally within presidential authority. One of the first places where freedman took hold of the land was on the Sea Islands and coastal areas of Georgia and South Carolina, after whites abandoned their rice plantations when Union troops arrived in November 1861. In 1863 Secretary of War Edwin M. Stanton appointed Tunis Campbell, upon recommendation of a mutual friend, to help with the resettlement of freedmen on the Sea Islands. A resident of New York, Campbell had tried to volunteer for the army in 1861 before the government was ready to accept African American soldiers. Two years later he had sent to President Lincoln a plan to educate the freedpeople of the South, a proposal that Lincoln ignored. In January 1865 Campbell was working to establish an independent freedmen's government on the islands. He wrote a constitution, organized an eight-man senate and a twenty-man house, a judicial system, and a militia of approximately 275 citizen-soldiers.

On January 16, 1865, with the approval of Abraham Lincoln, General William Tecumseh Sherman's Special Field Order no. 15 subdivided hundreds of thousands of acres of farmland along the South Carolina and Georgia coast "so that each family shall have a plot of not more than forty acres of tillable ground." The experiment was successful. Within six months, more than forty thousand freedmen were farming land they thought was theirs for keeps. The success was short-lived, however; President Andrew Johnson rescinded the plan in August of 1865. Conservatives in Congress also opposed distribution of confiscated Confederate land to the freedmen as a threat to private property writ large.

In September 1865 Thaddeus Stevens called once more for substantial land redistribution. He wanted to appropriate land owned by the top ten percent of southern landowners and sell it in forty-acre plots to the freed slaves who had worked it. Republican ideology equated liberty with independent property holding, and Stevens agreed with former slaves, true republicans in that sense, that landownership would be one of the bedrocks of black freedom. African American independent landholders would be "the support and guardians of republican liberty," Stevens argued, a bulwark against traitorous southern whites. His plan garnered little support.

The Southern Homestead Act of 1866 provided that all remaining public land in five southern states (and the best land was already taken) be made available to freedmen. Former slaves supposedly had the right to enter these public lands without competition from "disloyal" whites until January 1, 1867, but many freedmen were already locked into subsistence-level wage work or lacked the cash needed for purchase. Congress failed to extend the time for the exclusive entry by freedmen. South Carolina was the only state to form a land commission, and it met with some limited success. When the commission began to purchase land in 1869 and to sell tracts to small farmers at low prices, white Democrats cranked up their propaganda in opposition, tarring the program as "confiscation." Over the next seven years about two thousand farmers in South Carolina, most of them African American, were able to purchase land from the commission.

In nearly every state in the Deep South, some African Americans instituted communal self-help programs. Farming communities that pooled resources to purchase land, implements, and supplies included Davis Bend, Mound Bayou, and Renova in Mississippi; Burroughs, Harrisburg, and Gullinsville in Georgia; Kowaliga and Klondike in Alabama; Thomasville, Arkansas; and Promiseland in South Carolina.

In 1860 only twenty-six antebellum free blacks owned land in Mississippi and twenty-two in Arkansas and Texas combined. By 1870 in Mississippi 2,875 blacks owned land, and in Texas and Arkansas combined it was 3,056. Emerging from slavery essentially landless, within five years 4.8 percent of black household heads in the South owned real property averaging $746. Opportunities were greater in the Upper South of Delaware, Kentucky, Maryland, Missouri, North Carolina, Tennessee, and Virginia, where one in sixteen household heads (6.25 percent) owned land compared to one out of every twenty-six (3.8 percent) in the lower southern states of Alabama, Arkansas, Georgia, Louisiana, Mississippi, South Carolina, and Texas. While the large majority of African Americans lived in rural areas throughout the South, in the Upper South 15 percent lived in urban areas (7 percent in the lower South), where they had more opportunities to earn wages. The success of these efforts relied mainly on personal initiative of individual African Americans, some of whom had prewar freedom, education, and savings.

Economic disparity in land distribution was a major flaw and lost opportunity of federal Reconstruction strategy. Early in 1865 a special commission went to the South for inspection and observation. One of the participants, Whitelaw Reid, a wartime journalist for the *Cincinnati Gazette*, recorded his observations and published a book in 1866, *After the War: A Southern Tour. May 1, 1865, to May 1, 1866.* His assessment of the chaotic southern situation in the early months of peace was that the southern states "expected nothing; were prepared for the worst." It was his opinion that the southern people would have accepted any terms. "They were stung by the disgrace of being guarded by negro soldiers; but they made no complaints, for they felt that they had forfeited their right of complaint. They were shocked at the suggestion of negro suffrage; but if the Government required it, they were ready to submit." He compared the southern policy to wax: "It needed but a firm hand to apply the seal. Whatever device were chosen the community would at once be molded to its impress." In the immediate postwar confusion as to how the South would be punished for rebellion, whites might well have given up land in exchange for amnesty, particularly if the alternative was swinging at the end of a rope on a charge of treason. Reid ended his observations prophetically: "But if the plastic moment were suffered to pass—!" It was not long before that moment passed.

With or without land redistribution, Republicans in Congress held a transformative notion of what Reconstruction would entail. Former masters and former slaves alike would have to be educated in the ways of the capitalist marketplace before they could become truly American, Congressman Thaddeus Stevens argued. They would have to learn to replace the antagonism of chattel bondage with the reciprocal voluntarism and mutuality of the marketplace. At the heart of this process was a new accent on contractualism, and driving it forward was an ambitious government agency familiarly called the Freedmen's Bureau. Established in March 1865, the Bureau of Refugees, Freedmen, and Abandoned Lands was authorized to rent abandoned and confiscated property to the freedmen in forty-acre plots, which tenants might purchase if legalities could be arranged. As it turned out, such lands were few and hotly contested in the months after Appomattox. Mostly the bureau spent its time mediating between white landholders and former slaves, trying to revive some measure of agricultural stability. To the indigent, both white and black, bureau agents handed out food, clothing, and medicine—the first federally administered social relief program. Those former slaves able to work, however, gained no handouts. To earn cash to purchase tools, draft animals, and eventually land, agents urged freedpeople to sign on as laborers for their old masters. The wages they gained could be held in the newly created Freedmen's Savings Bank, drawing interest and serving as collateral. Real potential did exist for fair dealings and upward mobility, northerners insisted, if former antagonists learned to toil together for mutual profit.

In having to arrange a contract, and one that was satisfactory to the Freedmen's Bureau, whites felt a demeaning loss of freedom. From the vexing task of finding and persuading laborers to come to work, bargaining and signing contracts with them, and paying attention to their complaints and suggestions, down to the final moment of rendering accounts, bosses chafed under all the regulations and petty humiliations of wage labor management. But some made money. Stephen Duncan, Jr., hired and directed scores of workers on his five Mississippi cotton plantations. Men were paid $9 per month, women $7, and children $3.50. "The plantations under my control have done pretty well notwithstanding the disadvantages attending the new system of labor," he allowed. "It requires a good deal of Macchiavellean [*sic*] diplomacy to get along with them, and were it not remunerative it would be unbearable."

White Freedmen's Bureau agents were well disposed to white complaints. When landowners explained that former slaves were mere novices to the harsh ways of freedom, requiring the guidance and tender mercies of paternalistic whites, not a few agents nodded their heads knowingly. Even the estimable John Eaton, who had commanded a USCT regiment in the Mississippi Valley and ultimately took charge of all "contraband" affairs in that region, insisted that emancipated blacks (and Native Americans, too) had to be "educated" in the ways of capitalism. In books like *John Freeman and His Family*, *The Freedman's Book*, and *The Freedmen's Catechism*, abolitionist do-gooders like Clinton Fisk and Lydia Maria Child sought to instruct former slaves in the benefits of steady labor, moral purity, and quiet perseverance.

Former slaves were far from being innocents and novices when it came to bargaining, however, as bureau officials quickly discovered; they were keen to work out the best deal. While landowners sought to lock in workers to contracts for the length of the growing season at the lowest rates possible, freedmen in turn demanded short contracts, ready wages, and a host of social benefits. Some required that contracts include a garden patch for their personal tillage, or payment with a share of the crop. Others insisted on better housing or education for their children. Labor's power was limited, however, especially once the contract was signed. As one Freedmen's Bureau agent pointed out, "Your former masters and owners own all the lands and homes and houses and you are dependent on them." Another sent out a notice on August 8, 1865, informing the freedmen and -women on a certain plantation that although they were no longer captives, "the lands, buildings, furniture, and animals, including the swine, still belong to the planter," and that they had no right or title to any of them, except by purchase or gift, or by some other way of obtaining a right of ownership.

Contracts could not specify every detail—or to put it another way, former slaves and masters demonstrated a remarkable ability to discover points of contention. Complaints and petitions to the bureau were numerous. Most workers complained about nonpayment of wages; bosses lamented the nonperformance of duties. On the Louisiana plantation where freedman Henry Adams worked, two former slaves protested to the plantation owner that they had been working for three months without pay. In answer to their complaint, the owner "took his gun and shot at them, and did not pay them a cent." Adams and other witnesses reported that landowners in Louisiana continued to whip black workers as they had done under slavery, and that many freedpeople who attempted to leave plantations in 1865 had been killed. Planters brought questions to the Freedmen's Bureau also. One man asked if one of his workers could bring her sick child to work. The magistrate told him that she had that right, to which he complained that it was "d——d strange if a man could not control his own property &c."

Planters and freedmen both commonly complained that the under-staffed Freedmen's Bureau made a bad situation worse, but usually agents balanced where they did not ameliorate circumstances. When one planter stipulated in a contract that he would have "control of the children on the plantation and make them behave either by constraining them themselves or by requiring the parents to do so," the bureau agent rejected his demand, requiring parents to correct their children. Agents often eliminated clauses allowing whites to whip workers. Masters had been accustomed to using corporal punishment against black workers for hundreds of years, and landed whites bewailed the loss of this privilege. Freedmen's Bureau agents justified themselves as working to improve white "antipathy to the colored race," but actually an agent's efforts to do so depended on his own integrity and fair-mindedness. The few African American agents in the bureau did advocate for the freedmen. Agent Jonathan Jasper Wright, future justice on the South Carolina supreme court, cooperated with attorney William Whipper in the first recorded case tried by an African American attorney in South Carolina. They successfully prosecuted a white man for attacking an African American worker. Other agents, who believed that former slaves had to be forced to work, dealt very harshly with African American workers. Where African Americans dared to withdraw their services or go on strike, they quickly came face to face with the legal power of the Freedmen's Bureau, backed by the military in its determination to enforce contracts.

Ultimately the bureau coaxed and bullied most former slaves into signing pitiful wage labor contracts. These contracts, sanctioned by law, assured the landowners that workers would be in the fields. The Freedmen's Bureau was short-lived, but it set the precedent of contract wage labor that became the social order of the rural New South.

With or without contracts, landowners had to rely on their same labor force, though now free, to plant and hoe and harvest the labor-intensive cotton crop. One former master, Colonel P. H. Anderson of Tennessee, wrote to Jourdan Anderson, a former slave living in Ohio, with a request that he return and work for him. In an unsentimental reply dated August 7, 1865, the unusually articulate Jourdan responded to his former "master" in a lengthy letter. He was happy that his children had the opportunity to attend school and that his daughters were free from sexual exploitation. Testing the former owner's sincerity, Jourdan asked for past-due wages. "I served you faithfully for thirty-two years and Mandy twenty years. At $25 a month for me, and $2 a week for Mandy, our earnings would amount to $11,680. Add to this the interest for the time our wages has been kept back and deduct what you paid for our clothing and three doctor's visits to me, and pulling a tooth for Mandy, and the balance will show what we are in justice entitled to." As a parting shot, which very clearly showed he had no intention of trusting his former enslaver, he wrote, "Say howdy to George Carter, and thank him for taking the pistol from you when you were shooting at me."

Whites expected labor practices to continue as before—that is, black laborers working in gangs under a white supervisor or overseer; the new wrinkle, wages, would be paid only after the crop was sold. African Americans had a vastly different idea about how to use their new freedom. Eager to throw off the close supervision of gang labor and the slave quarters both, former slaves decided freedom meant not being coerced to work from sunup to sundown under the labor system preferred by white landowners. For African Americans unable to purchase land, the opportunity to till a patch of land on the basis of family rental seemed like a step toward actual ownership. For workers who abhorred the gang labor reminiscent of slavery, tenancy provided a mechanism for self-directed labor. For cash-strapped white landholders with little ability to pay daily wages, renting provided an opportunity to get fallow acreage back into production on a shoestring basis. While not an easy or smooth transition, large sections of land were consequently parceled and rented in small holdings to white and black farmers, fragmenting the antebellum plantation system though not the ownership of the land.

Prior to the Civil War tenancy had been widespread among whites, and some free blacks were tenant farmers. (Some of them even sublet land to other tenants, including white farmers.) Under postwar tenant arrangements, perhaps two-thirds of tillers were freedpeople, though whites predominated among cash renters. People who rented for a set fee owned the crop and had the power to decide what to plant. These tenants, usually sufficiently well off to own a mule, were economically better off than sharecroppers, whose payment for their work was the proceeds of a share of the crop owned by the landowner. Most whites paid an inadequate share of between one-tenth and one-fifth of the crop. Sharecroppers gave up financial control and legal ownership of the product. The landowner decided what to grow, when to harvest, and where and when to sell the crop. White agricultural clubs across the lower South dissuaded landowners from renting to African Americans for a set rental fee. These groups specified that laborers should be hired "either for wages, or for a share of the crop," and they retaliated against whites who did not join the club or follow the rules. In Mississippi from 1865 to 1867, African Americans were legally proscribed from renting farmland.

Cultural mores dictated gender divisions in agricultural labor; since plowing was considered a man's job, landlords rarely rented out land to a woman (unless a widow had older sons). For the most part, men dealt with men on business matters, reinforcing the patriarchal culture of the South. African American tenant and sharecropping families lived in households traditional at that time; a pattern of two-parent families and long-term marriage among black families was predominant. But African American women were used to self-reliance, and after the war, freedom within family relations, so different from liberty in a political system, had to be negotiated on a personal level.

While sharecropping did not fulfill the African American desire for autonomy, the end of the coercive authority of planters did represent a shift in the balance of power and allowed blacks a greater degree of control over their time, labor, and family arrangements. Too often, though, greater freedom over their day-to-day labor routine translated into grievous overwork. Freedmen established a degree of control over their own households that slavery had long denied them, but this new individualism rooted in the labor of nuclear families left them vulnerable to economic exploitation and paramilitary violence. Dispersal on sharecropping or tenant fields meant that the African American citizenry was more isolated. Remoteness made organizing politically and militarily difficult. Nevertheless, African Americans clearly embraced sharecropping as a means to attain some social and economic independence. For African Americans coming out of slavery, those who made it into the tenancy system, either as renters or sharecroppers, climbed an economic step above the majority of African Americans, who had to find work as day laborers.

For most of the men who signed on as tenants and sharecroppers, the chances of their earning returns that would allow them to rise up into the ranks of landed property holders were unlikely. As the worldwide production of cotton drifted upward, postwar prices tumbled by more than 80 percent. For planters and freedpeople striving to revive a shattered economy already desperately short of tools, fertilizer, and draft animals—not to mention provisions, cash, and credit—the cotton crash all but doomed successful cultivation. Worse, old seed, flood, drought, and the dreaded "army worm" combined to ruin crops across most of the South in 1865—and then again in 1866 and 1867. By the beginning of 1868 the hardest work and best will could not assure economic independence—or even enough to eat. By 1880, when the U.S. census enumerated farm operations for the entire South, farm owners operated 64 percent of the farms, share tenants and sharecroppers operated 24 percent, and fixed-rate rental tenants operated 12 percent. Of all "white farm operators," 26.5 percent were sharecroppers, share tenants, or livestock sharers. For nonwhites, that figure was 54.4 percent.

Although few were able to reconcile ideas of freedom with the reality of subservient wage labor for white landowners, the truth was that families not able to buy land or to secure a tenant situation, even as sharecroppers, had to find other employment. White landowners needed workers; newly freed African Americans needed employment. In the early aftermath of the war, this usually meant agricultural wage labor.

While African Americans were defining and living their new lives with new freedom, whites felt the need for imposing on the African American population some code of conduct. For the wealthy white conservatives who sat down together in provisional assemblies across the South in the fall of 1865, drafting new state constitutions hardly seemed to require much in the way of innovation. Once they had stomached the painful abolition of slavery and rejection of secession, the rest would be easy enough. The new codes of law defining the rights of freed blacks would structure black economic and social roles precisely, much as neighboring northern states such as Illinois, Indiana, and Ohio had done for their free black populations. In 1865 throughout southern states, legislative bodies—often the very members who had held control during secession and war—adopted new state constitutions to clarify race relations without slavery. In Texas the new state constitution prohibited "intermarriage, voting, officeholding, and jury service by freedmen." Like others, the South Carolina constitutional convention restricted voting and officeholding to white males. "This is a white man's government," explained provisional Governor Benjamin Perry, "and intended for white men only."

The white man's government of the antebellum South had never had more than a few free African Americans within its jurisdictional authority. Slavery was the law. Frederick Douglass captured the essence of slavery's legal order: "That plantation is a little nation of its own, having its own language, its own rules, regulations and customs. The laws and institutions of the state, apparently touch it nowhere. The troubles arising here are not settled by the civil power of the state. The overseer is generally accuser, judge, jury, advocate and executioner. The criminal is always dumb. The overseer attends to all sides of a case." With that legal system no longer operational in 1865, legislatures throughout the South voted to create county courts and to expand "Black Codes" as white southerners prepared for what they believed would be an avalanche of black crime. From state to state and locality to locality, laws and customs shaping freedpeople's lives differed only in their details. The central concern of every ex-Confederate state, however, was to keep former slaves under white control and laboring steadily for white landowners.

Most state codes required African Americans to sign annual contracts to perform agricultural labor, unless they could obtain a license from a local magistrate attesting that they possessed skills requisite to pursue an industrial trade, or could pony up prohibitive fees to trade and peddle goods. The hours of farmwork were commonly defined to be just as they had been under slavery, from sunup to sundown, half a day Saturday, with Sunday reserved as a day of rest. Black Codes specified how African American children could legally be taken away from their families and used as apprentices, "bound by indenture, in case of males, until they are twenty-one years old, and in case of females until they are eighteen years old." Whites sometimes stole black children, even as the children walked to school with books in hand. In South Carolina workers were to be addressed as "servants," bosses as "masters." Labor would be performed by task or by gang, as it suited the landholder, with discipline usually coming in the form of wages forfeited for poor work. Black Codes also gave white employers the power to administer "moderate corporeal chastisement." All codes employed vagrancy laws as a device to bind the newly freed people to the land. As under slavery, moving around without a pass from one's employer was forbidden. Those who fled a bad master in search of a better one surrendered all wages earned up to that point, and anyone who hired truants or provided them with food or shelter faced fines and jail. In such cases, the codes echoed the Fugitive Slave Law: "every civil officer shall, and every person may, arrest and carry back to his or her legal employer any freedman, free negro, or mulatto who shall have quit the service of his or her employer."

In most states it became nearly impossible for blacks to rent land, to market their own produce, or to seek effective legal redress against whites. Freedpeople were not allowed to possess knives or firearms, to buy or sell alcohol, or to preach the Gospel without license from white authorities. More egregious regulations were mere replicas of slave code clauses with the substitution of *freedmen* for *slaves*. Section 40 of the New Orleans code went further still. "Free people of color ought never to insult or strike white people," it declared, "nor presume to think of themselves equal to the white." The system would bind blacks to the land, impoverished, uneducated, disfranchised, and unorganized, in perpetuity. Codes defined race by statute, expressly affirmed social and political inequality, and prohibited interracial marriage. The goal was to meld labor exploitation with social subservience. Freedpeople were compelled to compete with whites in the new capitalist marketplace on a decidedly unequal footing, with none of the buffers and protections that slave status had formerly offered.

Prior to the war Abraham Lincoln had claimed, "Those who would deny freedom to others deserve it not for themselves; and, under a just God, cannot long retain it." During the war, Lincoln had worked diligently to ensure passage of the Thirteenth Amendment, for which he received congratulations from the incorruptible William Lloyd Garrison: "As an instrument in His hands, you have done a mighty work for the freedom of millions." Garrison was confident that Lincoln's efforts would continue: "I am sure you will consent to no compromise that will leave a slave in his fetters." And close to the end of the war, and of his life, Lincoln himself had commented upon the essential need "in some trying time to come, to keep the jewel of liberty within the family of freedom."

Eleven

"The Safeguard of the Republic"

ANDREW JOHNSON HAD SUCCESSFULLY RISEN from the city council of Greeneville, Tennessee, to the state assembly, the governorship, and finally the U.S. Senate. He was a true disciple of Andrew Jackson, as he saw it, a lowborn apprentice tailor from North Carolina who had lit out to make his fortune, taught himself to read and write, and doggedly scratched his way upward in the world. He fully shared Old Hickory's obstinacy and his deep hatred toward anyone who sought to master him, and rode that bootstrapping class resentment all the way to Washington. Johnson's guiding principle was his belief in limited government. He also believed in the people. In his 1853 inaugural as governor of Tennessee, he declared that the "voice of the people" was the "voice of God." Comparing democracy to the Biblical ladder of Jacob, he explained that those who merit it "may ascend." While it reaches down "to the humblest of all created beings, here on earth below," it also "reaches to God on high."

From 1860 to 1861 he had been the only congressional representative of the seceded states who refused to resign his federal seat. That unwavering determination—which looked like patriotic loyalty at the time—coupled with the rhetorical salvos Johnson unleashed at the corrupt and wealthy southern slave-drivers who had so treacherously broken up the Union, brought him to national prominence. For Lincoln and his circle, a pragmatically antislavery southern Democrat like Johnson seemed just right for the National Union coalition Republicans sought to build, and Lincoln installed him as military governor of Tennessee in 1862. Johnson was in his glory, ruling by fiat, excoriating his enemies, and promising grand changes to all who would accept his leadership. As military governor he paved the way for Tennessee to reenter the Union. He supported taxes for public education. Although he believed in "a white man's government," he spoke of the need to be fair to African Americans. In October 1864 when African Americans in Tennessee called him their "Moses," he replied that he would lead them to a "fairer future of liberty and peace."

Johnson recommended harsh penalties for former Confederates. He would strip disloyal southern leaders of property and political rights. "Treason must be made odious," he thundered. For the rich planter secessionists he vowed, "I would arrest them—I would try them—I would convict them and I would hang them." Ordinary Confederates who asked pardon, on the other hand, would receive the hand of fellowship. It was this mixture of mercy and retribution that ultimately catapulted him from local power to become Abraham Lincoln's running mate in 1864. A drunken and incoherent speech at his inauguration did nothing to encourage confidence in his leadership, but there seemed little reason for practical concern at the time. No one could have foreseen that, three months after being sworn in as vice president, an assassin's bullet would place him at the head of government itself.

As president Andrew Johnson would prove himself to be neither Moses nor Aaron; if anything, he seemed more to resemble the inflexible Pharaoh whose mulish heedlessness brought his regime to ruin. His collision course with Congress was not immediately self-evident. He actually supported limited black voting rights as president. In August 1865 he advised Mississippian William Sharkey, a staunch Union supporter throughout the Civil War and Johnson's appointee as provisional governor of Mississippi, to allow certain African Americans to vote: "all persons of color who can read the Constitution of the United States in English and write their names" and African Americans "who own real estate valued at not less than two hundred and fifty dollars, and pay taxes thereon." This was a practical idea to "disarm the adversary and set an example the other States will follow." In October, Johnson suggested that Tennessee "introduce negro suffrage gradually." He recommended suffrage for those who served in the army and those who could read and write. "It would not do to let the negroes have universal suffrage now," he advised; "it would breed a war of the races." While limited black suffrage was his personal choice, he never changed his mind that voting was a matter for each state to determine.

Many expected the Confederate-hating Andrew Johnson, upon becoming president, to seek retribution against the former slaveholders. Instead, he appeared to out-Lincoln Lincoln in his leniency. While congressional Republicans called for the final destruction of the planter class, Johnson opened up a virtual pardon mill in the president's office, restoring Confederate veterans to political standing with startling eagerness. Following his predecessor's example, he reached out to prominent Unionists in the defeated states—or the nearest thing to loyalists he could find—urging them to establish provisional governments and charging them to write new constitutions repealing secession, abolishing slavery, and working out the civil status of the newly liberated freedmen. Once these relatively straightforward steps were taken, federal troops might be removed from the state, and its representatives readmitted to Congress; all might put the unpleasantness of disunion and Civil War behind them. Reconstruction would be a swift, simple affair, patching up the nation's wounds and putting it back on the track it had pursued before sectional controversy threw it off course. That was Johnson's view of Presidential Reconstruction.

Republicans in Congress saw things in a different light. Thaddeus Stevens, an early and impassioned critic of Johnson, announced, "This is not a 'white man's government' . . . To say so is political blasphemy, for it violates the fundamental principles of our gospel of liberty. This is man's Government; the Government of all men alike." By the end of the war many U.S. congressmen, while not egalitarians like Stevens, had overcome previous racial attitudes because of reports from the frontlines that the freed slaves had proven themselves valiant soldiers and industrious workers.

At the end of 1865, when Johnson announced that the Union was restored, the 39th Congress disagreed. Stating that it alone had the power to seat delegates, Congress refused to seat officials elected from the former Confederate states, Democrats and secessionists as they were. Without these newly elected officials, the House of Representatives kept its

Republican majority of 136 versus 38 Democrats (21 from other parties). The Senate kept its Republican majority of 39 versus 11 Democrats (4 others). That spring Congress repudiated the Black Codes and passed the Civil Rights Act of 1866 defining citzenship. African Americans as U.S. citizens were guaranteed the right to own or rent property, to make and enforce contracts, to have access to the courts as parties and witnesses, and generally to enjoy the "full and equal" benefit of all laws enjoyed by white citizens. Depriving a citizen of these civil rights was a federal crime, enforceable by the federal courts and military. Congress also formed a joint committee of senators and representatives under the leadership of Stevens to examine issues of suffrage and southern representation in Congress.

Congressional determination solidified in May 1866 following a bloody rampage in Memphis against the African American population, which had swelled after the war as men came to the city seeking work. Freedmen's Bureau investigators of the riots reported: "There was an especial hatred among the city police for the Colored Soldiers." The report detailed events on the evening of April 30, 1866, when white police pushed a gathering of African Americans off the sidewalk. One of the black men fell down, and a policeman stumbled over him. Thereupon police officers pistol-whipped the group. African Americans, including Union army veterans, protested, and a group of black citizens assembled. About this time the white city recorder, John C. Creighton, gave a speech urging mayhem: "Boys, I want you to go ahead and kill every damned one of the nigger race and burn up the cradle." Whites did their best to comply. The report summarized, "Negroes were hunted down by police, firemen and other white citizens, shot, assaulted, robbed, and in many instances their houses searched under the pretense of hunting for concealed arms, plundered, and then set on fire." Men, women, and children were killed, some shot in bed. Law enforcement personnel were themselves the murderers and arsonists. Moreover, the police stole money from African American soldiers who had just received their pay. Any white person protesting these atrocities was labeled a Yankee or an abolitionist and forced to shut up. The lawless mob reigned over Memphis during the next five days, the mayor unable or unwilling to establish control. "His friends offer in extenuation of his conduct, that he was in a state of intoxication." In the end white rioters killed about thirty African Americans and wounded about seventy others. They burned four churches, twelve schoolhouses, and eighty-nine homes, all belonging to African Americans, as well as five government buildings. The bureau investigators noted that, though the perpetrators were well known, no one was charged with a crime.

This Memphis riot and other atrocities throughout the South stirred northern anger at recalcitrant ex-Confederates. In June 1866 Congress decided that America's most sacred document, the Constitution, must codify the new birth of freedom that Lincoln had called for. An end to slavery was not enough. Freedom had to be available to all citizens, and race was no longer an excluding factor. Congress proposed a Fourteenth Amendment to the Constitution to define American citizenship.

"All persons born or naturalized in the United States . . . are citizens" and as such are entitled to "due process" and "the equal protection of the laws." This amendment instituted a vast and critical change in the distribution of government power. In a transformation of a core American belief in the need to limit governmental power, the majority in Congress wanted the federal government to exhibit its "strong arm of power, outstretched from the central authority." This, along with the other postwar constitutional amendments (Thirteenth and Fifteenth), radically changed how power was and is delegated. Rather than listing the limits to government authority, or what Congress "shall make no law respecting," these Civil War amendments specify government authority: "Congress shall have the power" to enforce the provisions. The extent of a citizen's social, civil, and political rights, and whether those rights were separate or unitary, remained open to debate, but the Constitution now committed the power of the federal government to the equal extension of those rights.

Congress sent the Fourteenth Amendment to the states for ratification, and in short order the following states refused to ratify it: Texas, Georgia, North Carolina, South Carolina, Virginia, Kentucky, Louisiana, Delaware, and Maryland. Had it not been for the unrepentant course these states pursued, significant political change might have been delayed in the South or derailed altogether. As it was, Congressman James Garfield of Ohio declared that military authority was needed to "plant liberty on the ruins of slavery." Congress felt bound to a higher purpose than a simple reconciliation of the sections. In the fall elections of 1866 civil rights were the central issue. "Support Congress and You Support the Negro," said the Democrats in a campaign broadside featuring a grotesque caricature of an African American. "Sustain the President," the broadside continued, "and You Protect the White Man." Northern voters did not buy it. They returned "radical" Republicans to Congress in a thunderous repudiation of accommodation of former Confederates. Republicans won almost three-fourths of both houses, enough to override easily any veto.

Congress played its trump card, the Reconstruction Act of 1867. Congress divided the South into five military districts. State governments were abolished across the South, federal military commanders were placed in charge, rebels were broadly disfranchised, and new constitutional conventions were set in motion, based on universal manhood suffrage. New state legislative bodies would need to ratify the Fourteenth Amendment before their elected officials could again sit in the U.S. Congress.

Congress showed little patience with attempts to block their vision of sweeping social change, and when President Johnson vetoed the civil rights bill of 1866 and the bill to extend the Freedmen's Bureau (both vetoes overridden), he marked himself for vengeance at the hands of the Republicans. In the spring of 1868, when Johnson removed secretary of war Edwin M. Stanton, a Lincoln appointee who was out of step with the president's conservative views, Congress declared that he had violated the Tenure of Office Act. The House of Representatives charged Johnson with "high crimes and misdemeanors," as allowed by the Constitution, and voted to impeach him. Johnson's trial in the Senate concluded with an acquittal, one vote short of the required two-thirds that would have cast him out of office. Some feared that a proper balance of power between government branches would be lost altogether if Congress could get rid of a president for disagreement on policy issues alone. Northern capitalists also feared impeachment. The would-be successor, Senator Benjamin Wade of Ohio, was considered "unsound" on economic issues. According to one editor, securities and federal bonds "are strong reasons for preserving the Constitutional Powers of the President." Politically, however, Johnson was a dead man long before the final vote was cast.

In November of that year, 1868, the chief issue in the presidential election was Reconstruction and suffrage. Democrats and their presidential candidate, Horatio Seymour, favored declaring the Reconstruction Acts "null and void." Seymour's running mate, Francis P. Blair of Missouri, declared that African American citizens were still "a semi-barbarous race . . . who are worshipers of fetishes and polygamists." Without straying from their platform of white supremacy, Democrats began broadening their issues. After the Civil War, Democrats offered criticism of industrialization and capitalism, focusing on the evils of corporations, especially monopolies that had government support. Whereas slavery had been an "open system of undisguised force," corporate slavery, declared South Carolina Democratic leader Francis Pickens in 1866, "is a system of disguised fraud." In the corporate system of slavery, "Whites and blacks shall both be owned by the capitalists." The Democratic Party continued its economic appeal as the United States embraced a more unrestrained version of capitalism unleashed by the Civil War. Campaigning in the Midwest in 1868, Democrats proclaimed, "You freed the negro; you put down that awful curse '*negro* slavery' and fastened eternal white slavery upon yourselves and children by lowering and knuckling to . . . the monied monopolies of the country. Good bye laboring man! The bondocracy of New England have fixed your status." Republican nominee Ulysses S. Grant won by only 300,000 votes in an election in which 700,000 African Americans voted.

The year 1868 saw mighty changes throughout the states of the former confederacy. The Reconstruction Act authorized new state constitutions, and U.S. military commanders took charge of registering all male voters to elect delegates to state conventions. It is hard to imagine a more momentous occasion, at once deeply conservative and boldly revolutionary, fraught with pathos and irony. African Americans, most of them illiterate former slaves, responded overwhelmingly as citizens and as men; often marching en masse to the very spot where they had been whipped or sold, they cast ballots that would determine the political fate of their families, their fellows, and their former masters, too. Louisiana was typical: with a fair and efficient system of registration, approximately 90 percent of African American men of voting age in the state registered to vote in 1867. In November 1867 in South Carolina, 80,832 African Americans and 46,929 whites were registered to vote. Across the South whites who thought the newly freed slaves would not bother voting were proved dramatically wrong. However unlettered they may have been, freedmen here grasped the path-breaking political lesson of the Black Codes: for all their repression and wrongheadedness, those ordinances represented the establishment of a rule of law in the South that transcended and abrogated the former power of master over slave. Now, given the chance to affirm that fundamental rule of law, to substitute good laws for bad, and to demonstrate their own freedom and self-mastery in the bargain, African American men turned out in droves, preachers alongside plowhands, patriarchs leading sons and grandsons. It was a spectacle of democratic faith and independent purpose. As one white Republican from Alabama put it, "The negroes voted their entire walking strength—no one staying at home that was able to come to the polls." With that act African Americans ended an age-old history of elite privilege and popular subservience. They stood up and brought their states into the modern world.

Nineteenth-century political thought was divided on whether suffrage was a right of citizenship. Many argued that voting was a privilege and that democracy could work only when suffrage was based on education, property, and responsible citizenship. Because citizenship imposed responsibility as well as conferring rights, republicanism excluded those who were "dependent" on others: insane persons, paupers, children, women, and enslaved workers. Lincoln himself opposed equal suffrage for free blacks as late as 1858. At the outset of the Civil War only five states in the nation, all in New England, permitted African Americans to vote on the same basis as whites. All states denied women the vote, and many states from each section of the country had additional suffrage restrictions, denying Chinese, illiterates, or those too poor to pay property taxes.

But compelling voices articulated a different vision. Frederick Douglass declared that the right to vote was "the keystone to the arch of human liberty." At the Republican national convention in Baltimore in 1864, one of the delegates from the recaptured Sea Island area of South Carolina was Robert Smalls. Along with three other elected African American delegates, Smalls was denied his official seat by reason of color. At this convention several participants tried to get the Republican Party to advocate universal male suffrage but could not muster the strength to bring it to a vote. As the editor of the *Beaufort Free South* wrote, "All were ready to have the negro fight for the Union, die for it, but were hardly ready to have him vote for it." Americans still had miles to go in the march toward a democratic suffrage.

War service, blood sacrifice, however, made the privilege part of the nation's promise. In January 1865 freedmen in Tennessee, equating citizenship with military service, asked the delegates to their state constitutional convention to grant them the vote. "If we are called on to do military duty against the rebel armies in the field," they asked, "why should we be denied the privilege of voting against rebel citizens at the ballot-box?" Abolitionist Wendell Phillips was an early supporter of black suffrage as a consequence of African Americans' war service. "The nation owes the negro," he affirmed, "after such a war, in which he has nobly joined, not technical freedom, but substantial protection in all his rights." Later that year the Reverend Henry Ward Beecher went further still, defining the right to vote as "God given." It was "not a privilege or a prerogative" to be earned or bestowed, in his view, "but a right" due to all men, as men.

Republicans took up the cause of suffrage for the freedmen for two main reasons. First of all, postwar reckoning of population for representation in the House was increased by the newly freed African Americans. Now each person counted as one whereas before the war, enslaved blacks counted as three-fifths. If African Americans could not vote, southern white Democrats would reap the benefit of increased representation, but would not use it for the benefit of those constituents. The second reason was simply principle. It was the right thing to do. Advocating black suffrage entailed considerable political hazard. Campaigning to add freedmen's votes for the party in the South, Republicans risked disenchanting thousands of lukewarm supporters in the North. In midwestern states especially, Republican functionaries had always counted on an undercurrent of "Negrophobia" to help win election day. For Lincoln's party to champion black suffrage, then, looked to many at the grassroots level like straightforward political suicide. "Anybody that dares to advocate it is stigmatized as a dangerous fanatic," wrote Carl Schurz. Republicans, after all, did not need to convert southern states to their cause to hold on to national power; they simply had to keep the North solid, no easy task. And indeed, Democrats and conservative Republicans welcomed radical altruism on voting rights as an opportunity to shatter the dominance of that political coalition. Publicly, most Americans agreed with President Andrew Johnson that it was wrong to give the right to vote to "a new class, wholly unprepared" for democracy. Privately, many believed that African Americans would never be ready. Base prejudice blinded them to the remarkable evidence of their own eyes.

Any community of people enslaved and oppressed for a term of centuries should hardly be required to demonstrate its fitness for freedom and self-government to those who have held it down so long. In these years, however, African Americans kept up the fight for political rights and democratic rule through countless acts at the local level. The church, voluntary organizations, and freedpeople gathering by ones and by twos in political factions and Union Leagues knew that achieving the right to vote was essential to securing meaningful liberty. In meetings, parades, and petitions to Congress, former slaves pressed for the ballot as a prime weapon of community development and self-defense. Without the right to vote, all other rights could be too easily subverted and liberty quashed. As Carl Schurz wrote, "In the right to vote [freedpeople] would find the best permanent protection against oppressive class-legislation, as well as against individual persecution." Wendell Phillips declared that without the right to vote "freedom, so called, is a sham." By 1868, with eyes squarely focused on the shocking behavior of ex-masters toward former slaves, a majority of white Republicans finally reached the same conclusion: the ballot was necessary to enable the freedmen to protect their own rights and perhaps to protect the nation itself.

In the process of writing new state constitutions, both African American and white men were eligible to vote for delegates. Unpardoned rebels and a handful of ex-Confederate officials remained disfranchised, but thousands of other whites simply refused to take part in the balloting because it meant they would have to "vote with a nigger." Putting voter registration under the supervision of military commanders and twenty thousand troops, every southern state had a black-white Republican coalition in the majority, and this majority voted for delegates who were determined to grant suffrage to African American men. Although Arkansas elected only eight African Americans as delegates to the state constitutional convention, those delegates demanded provisions for schools, an end to segregation in transportation facilities, and equal suffrage. Virginia delegate George Teamoh worked to eliminate whipping as a legal punishment. In South Carolina the constitutional convention included black and white delegates, most longtime residents of the state. They advocated universal male suffrage, reorganization of the courts, the division and sale of unoccupied land among the poorer classes, and caution in the restoration of rights of those lately guilty of treason. Delegate William Whipper argued for women's suffrage. Delegate Robert Smalls introduced and won a provision for compulsory education for all children between the ages of seven and fourteen, "to be opened without charge to all classes of the people." Nor did African Americans mindlessly advocate a single "racial" program, as some detractors charged. In convention after convention, important divisions developed, usually over whether African Americans should devote their energies to education as a strategy of group uplift or whether they should broaden programs of land reform. Ultimately these divergent emphases, often between wealthier, urban constituencies and their rural proletarian colleagues, sometimes between lighter- and darker-skinned delegates, sometimes between geographical sections of a state such as upcountry and lowcountry, culminated in the creation of political factions that could stymie legislative progress. Nevertheless, truly impressive was the vibrancy, independence, and frankness of the political debate, and the cogency and vision of the platforms for which they argued. These were men, usually newly freed, with clear and dynamic ideas about how to reshape southern society to promote new opportunities of economic prosperity, racial harmony, and personal enlightenment.

By June 1868 seven southern states had passed new constitutions granting citizenship and the right to vote to previously enslaved men. Congress readmitted Alabama, Arkansas, Florida, Georgia, Louisiana, North Carolina, and South Carolina into the Union. The Reconstruction South and the Republican Congress alike were tested for seriousness, and the latter was found to be in earnest. After Georgia was readmitted to the Union, the Georgia assembly voted to expel all its African American legislators, having first ruled they were not allowed to vote on the issue. Governor Rufus Bullock asked Congress to investigate the situation, and African American leader Jefferson Long of Georgia wrote to Congress: "Ask those white Republicans who love their God and their country if they are satisfied with the reign of terror that now

exists in Georgia." The Congressional Reorganization Act of 1869 ordered purging the former confederates and reinstating African Americans in the Georgia Assembly.

With voting open to all men, and with election procedures supervised by the military power of the federal government for the first time,
a thriving interracial democracy took hold in the former Confederate
states. By the steady repetition of ordinary democratic acts, southern
blacks and whites created a biracial political system out of the welter of
their own pragmatic choices, shaping their own lives in their own communities. However small and conflicted, such changes promised, in
time, to liberate southern white consciousness from the chains of racism
itself. What had first seemed unthinkable had become merely outlandish; soon enough it might seem simply vexing, then curious, then
run-of-the-mill. Throughout the southern states African Americans
served on juries, and a majority coalition of African Americans and
whites elected former slaves to office, though nowhere did African
Americans hold offices in proportion to their population.

Between 1867 and 1877 about two thousand freedmen held federal,
state, and local office. They won elections and served in various appointments as cabinet officers, superintendents of education, justices of the
peace, city council members, sheriffs, judges, and numerous other posts.
Fourteen African Americans won election to the U.S. House of Representatives. Two African Americans from Mississippi won election to the
U.S. Senate. One, Blanche Bruce, was the first and only former slave
elected to the U.S. Senate. Enslaved in Virginia, Mississippi, and Missouri, he escaped to Kansas in 1861. Settling in Mississippi in 1867, he
became very active in the Republican Party. The other, Hiram Revels,
born free, had been a barber and minister. In 1854 he had been imprisoned "for preaching the gospel to Negroes." During the Civil War he
helped recruit black troops, serving in the Vicksburg campaign as army
chaplain. Provisional governor Adelbert Ames, a former Union officer
from Maine, appointed him to the Natchez City Council, and as it did
for many other whites and blacks, local political experience provided a
springboard to broader service. Revels won election to the state senate
and then the U.S. Senate, serving the remainder of his career in the seat
once held by Jefferson Davis. That was a high climb indeed. Across the
South, however, effective black sheriffs, magistrates, and juries proved

just as important in advancing democracy's goals as African Americans in Congress, maybe more so.

In Louisiana the new state legislature in 1868 was approximately half white and half African American. Black legislators never constituted a single like-minded bloc. Well-heeled Creole politicians often advocated programs far more attuned to moderate white Democrats than to landless black farmers. African Americans in Louisiana held the offices of lieutenant governor, state superintendent of education, and state treasurer. In South Carolina, African Americans controlled a majority of seats in the lower house (and from 1874 to 1876 both the senate and the house), and African Americans won elections as lieutenant governor, secretary of state, and state treasurer, as well as a significant number of local offices. Reconstruction in South Carolina lasted longer than in any other state, and South Carolina's black Republicans achieved as great a degree of political power as did African Americans anywhere. Their achievements were the consequence of clear-eyed pragmatism and considerable political horse-trading.

Newly freed African Americans understood the give-and-take of politics. When a white newspaper reporter asked an African American leader in Vicksburg, Mississippi, whether it was appropriate for black candidates to disagree on issues, the official chided the reporter's paternalistic attitude. He had no wish to prevent other candidates from expressing differing views, he explained. Had he so wished, he "could have followed the course whites had so often pursued: using cow hide, a bucket of tar, and a bag of feathers." Vigorous and honest debate promised a better way forward.

In a speech entitled "An Honest Ballot Is the Safeguard of the Republic," delivered in the U.S. House of Representatives (1877), Congressman Robert Smalls told how slavery had taught white masters "to ignore and trample the rights of those they could not control." The right to vote brought protection against that trampling. It meant political power and elected officials responsive to the needs of the new constituency. The new state constitutions, formed by various coalitions of African Americans and moderate whites, brought about important reforms in women's rights and divorce laws. They reformed orphanages and asylums and ended some of the exploitation of children in apprenticeship. A lasting legacy of Reconstruction was the vigorous advocacy of public education for all children in the South. Republican legislators also initiated important changes in the penal system, ending inhumane punishments such as disfigurement and imprisonment for debt.

The tendency of this legislation seems overwhelmingly radical, given its accent on fair play, aiding the underdog, and holding back the hand of unjust power. But once again the vision of Lincoln shines forth, meshing the drive for equal opportunity with a concern for emerging order. African American and white Republicans saw the suffrage as a means of radically altering their society, to be certain, but altering it along lines that would seem familiar and palatable even to the most socially conservative of Americans: erasing racial preference, guaranteeing the rule of law, upholding the operation of the free market, securing the strength of families and the promotion of churches and schools in the local community, and advocating personal responsibility, voluntarism, honest government, and civic service.

As Republican Party operatives and legislators tried to reestablish order and promote racial harmony, new biracial administrations flowered all over the region after 1868, and the gradual strengthening of local communities attested to their success. Although Confederates and conservatives tarred Republicans as illiterate, inept, free-spending, and corrupt, Republican achievements under increasingly difficult circumstances remain impressive. Faced with empty coffers, a wrecked cotton economy, and the sullen intransigence of the white elite that had done the wrecking, they acted swiftly. To revitalize the state and local economy and reestablish credit, they floated massive new bond issues and wrote protective lien laws. They established the rule of law on a basis stronger than had ever been obtained in the antebellum era. Vastly enlarged public education programs in particular offered a broad road for social advancement for ordinary southerners, white and black. Beyond everything else Republican legislators did in this decade, they got the southern economy up and running again, reviving banks and railroads, promoting trade and agriculture, creating jobs and wealth for ordinary citizens.

The most revolutionary of legislative initiatives, or so it seemed to propertied conservatives, were the Republican tax reforms. Emancipation and war had completely dismantled the existing tax system. Antebellum taxes that white slaveholders paid for the enslaved population had accounted for 30 to 40 percent of tax revenues in southern states (60 percent in South Carolina); wealthy whites also paid taxes on luxuries and capital. Many poorer whites, in fact, paid virtually no taxes before secession. During the war the Confederacy shifted a tremendous tax burden onto the shoulders of ordinary southerners; what it could not jingle out of their pockets by means of levies both major and minor, it seized by outright impressment. Much of the critique of the "Cause" as a "rich man's war and a poor man's fight" referred to this crushing weight of increased taxation. After the war, as freedpeople were defined as people rather than property, the potential tax base more than doubled, but former slaveholders were no longer responsible for the hefty bills they had paid annually to the state for the privilege of holding human chattel. A new taxing structure was needed.

At the same time, southern legislators were tasked with greater responsibility: reviving a decimated economy and sponsoring a raft of egalitarian reforms. For the first time taxes accrued to land itself. Although Republicans granted homestead exemptions, the burden of taxation fell on small-farm owners, most of whom were white. Still reeling from Confederate exactions, even those whites who favored the new regime were hard-pressed to pay the taxes. Higher land taxes, after all, hit the most marginal property holders hardest. In South Carolina, for example, the half-million acres confiscated in 1873 for nonpayment of taxes included many former plantation tracts, but they also included the holdings of hundreds of white hardscrabble farmers who became sworn enemies of the Republican regime the moment they lost their land. Although the drift in Republican policy, requiring patience and racial forbearance, was to increase opportunity for African American and white yeoman farmers and laborers and ultimately to enrich their lives, many poorer whites turned away from all Republican programs. Here again, as so often in southern history, racist rhetoric served to mask troubling class concerns. Resentful and mistrusting of African Americans, whites found it easier to scapegoat newly risen freedmen than postwar economic woes for their steadily falling status. Complaints against taxes also shed much-needed light on government corruption and waste. Massive bond issues to finance railroads had little oversight. In 1871 and 1874 Taxpayers' Conventions made public a host of Republican fiscal sins across the color line.

Despite difficulties and challenges, African American voters across the South joined with enough white voters to form majority coalitions and elect Republican-dominated legislatures. While some have argued that intervention from the federal government created these Reconstruction legislatures of the late 1860s, Republican power in the South was not imposed by force of arms. Few federal troops were stationed in the South, and those were usually limited to outposts in major cities. In 1869 there were only 11,237 total federal troops in the former Confederate states, 4,612 of whom were in Texas primarily to subdue Native Americans. In Mississippi, 978 soldiers were stationed in seven posts, in South Carolina only 417 troops in two posts.

While many white southerners had trouble accepting that freedom for African Americans included rights of citizenship, a sizable minority of whites, varying from 15 to 35 percent depending on the state, felt otherwise. These whites joined with African American Republicans, about 90 percent of all African American voters, and they worked together. In late 1866 Tunis Campbell moved from the Georgia Sea Islands to Darien, Georgia, where blacks outnumbered whites by a four-to-one majority. Campbell built a political machine of African American and white voters. He registered voters and helped draft the Georgia constitution. He sat in the state senate and on the state Republican central committee. Because he was justice of the peace for the county, local whites consulted him when problems arose. In 1871, presenting the opening remarks at the State Convention of Colored Men in Atlanta, Campbell said that African Americans must "move wisely, carefully, steadily, [but] without compromise. We must act in harmony with all acts in behalf of liberty." A sort of pragmatic quid pro quo became the hallmark of electoral politics from 1868 to 1874 in the South as well as the North. On the one hand, it gave rise to some power-hungry politicos; on the other, it gave voice to the aspirations of ordinary citizens, provided a mechanism for united action, and ensured their material well-being.

Southern states were developing an open and progressive political process where law applied equally, all male citizens had access to due process, and the courts were open to blacks as well as whites. African Americans who were literate and educated (many of them, like Alabama's James Rapier, enjoying—or enduring—the status of free blacks before the Civil War), skilled artisans like South Carolina's Joseph

Rainey, and military veterans like Louisiana's P.B.S. Pinchback or Florida's Josiah Walls, emerged as the initial leaders of the freedmen. Increasingly, other former slaves like Mississippi's John Roy Lynch and those who had been mere youngsters during the Civil War became leaders as well. Formerly enslaved women and children also gained opportunity, though not the vote. Freed people formed a host of political associations and social clubs, with high participation rates and a sophisticated understanding of their interests. They worked with white allies such as Mississippi's Adelbert Ames, who felt that "there should be no servile class among a free people." Few expected government to eliminate entirely problems of poverty, vice, and intolerance, but they shared a keen awareness of how much good common democratic action and hard work could accomplish.

African American political power directly and personally influenced economic opportunity at the local level. For the first time and to a significant degree, jobs in towns were offered to African Americans—government positions of postal workers and court clerks. Decent non-agricultural jobs were a boon that provided cash instead of credit until the next crop. Blacks and whites became business partners. Schools, including colleges, were open to African American students. Over time former slaves became attorneys. Black political power meant laws were responsive to community needs. Lien rights went to the worker first. Tenants' rights were guaranteed. Sheriffs and local officials, often former slaves or political allies of the black community, decided landlord-tenant disputes. Reconstruction in the South was politically and economically successful for many African Americans on the local level. In his first annual message to the Mississippi legislature in 1872, Governor Ridgely Powers reported that a relative tranquillity existed throughout the state and that a "new era of good feeling has sprung up." Mississippi should be recognized, he said, as "an example of reconstruction based upon reconciliation."

Broadening this democratic revolution meant guaranteeing new constitutional rights. While southern state constitutions allowed universal male suffrage, most nonsouthern states did not. Although Congress insisted on voting rights for freedmen in the former Confederacy, equal rights initiatives failed in Connecticut, Ohio, Wisconsin, Minnesota, and Colorado. In 1868 Iowa Republican Peter Melendy had strongly urged his state to extend to African Americans the franchise: "Vote to give other men, as President Lincoln expressed it, a fair start and an equal chance in the race of life." According to General Ulysses S. Grant, Iowa was "the bright Radical star," and he hoped the state would be willing to grant suffrage to its African American citizens. Iowans met Grant's challenge.

To secure the right to vote nationwide, congressional leadership mobilized members of Congress to propose a Fifteenth Amendment to the Constitution, providing that "the right of citizens of the United States to vote shall not be denied or abridged by the United States or by any State on account of race, color, or previous condition of servitude." This guarantee of the right to vote was ratified on February 3, 1870, approved by eight of the former Confederate states as well as states in the North and West. With citizenship secured by the Fourteenth Amendment and the right to vote secured by the Fifteenth, African Americans could protect themselves from their former owners through the rule of law, could shape those laws by standing for political office, and could choose their own leaders with free debate and an honest ballot.

The Constitution now defined the new birth of freedom—citizenship and the right to vote. A potent force for change, the rule of law was poised to preserve liberty for the freedmen and for all Americans. The goal of democratic rule seemed well within reach. And yet from early on there were limits to freedom that Republicans themselves were not prepared to see clearly.

Women saw those limits. Scornful that the new amendments did not include them, hopeful that they also would be swept up in the new birth of freedom attending the expanded rule of law, suffragists expected to be included in the Fifteenth Amendment. The ideological and organizational thrust of the women's movement, which had preceded the outbreak of war, continued to grow. African American suffragist Sojourner Truth pointed out that everyone, "whatever their sex or color," had a "common cause" in needing the right to vote. Lucy Stone, a graduate of Oberlin College in 1847, had been an outstanding orator against slavery and for women's rights. Because each of those groups jealously guarded its own interests, Stone agreed to speak against slavery on weekends and for women during the week. In 1858, when Stone refused to pay her tax bill in protest of her political disfranchisement, she recalled the freedom demanded by early patriots in the American Revolution. "Women suffer taxation and yet have no representation," she warned male tyrants, "which is not only unjust to one half of the adult population, but is contrary to our theory of government."

As the Civil War ended and Reconstruction began, women like Truth, Stone, Elizabeth Cady Stanton, and Susan B. Anthony were optimistic about the future. Anthony and Stanton published a magazine centered on women's suffrage, *The Revolution*, whose motto was "The true republic—men, their rights and nothing more; women, their rights and nothing less." These women anticipated that the democracy outlined in the proposed Fourteenth and Fifteenth amendments would also be applied to women. Their optimism badly misjudged the conservative Republican vision that propelled even the most radical social changes. Men were not willing to give women the right to vote, claiming that they were already "virtually" represented by the men within whose sovereign households they sheltered.

For suffragists who found themselves compared once more to children and imbeciles, this refusal seemed no more than a hypocritical betrayal of the women who had subordinated their cause to join with abolitionists. That African American leaders like Frederick Douglass and Martin Delaney, or newly raised freedmen like Blanche Bruce, failed to speak out in favor of votes for women only compounded the irony. To be sure, Anthony and Stanton were among a majority of middle-class suffragists who favored "educated suffrage," believing that voting was a privilege better left to the educated and well off. Precisely because of these sentiments, these women thought they were better qualified to vote than poor, "ignorant" former slaves or, for that matter, northern immigrants who might be dependent upon machine politics for jobs.

Those who opposed educated suffrage pointed out that without the vote most African Americans might well be unable to secure an education, were it left to the supervision of racist ballot-wielding whites. At an Equal Rights Association Meeting in New York in May 1869, some declared their stark opposition to limited suffrage. One man declared himself "as an enemy of educated suffrage, as an enemy of white suffrage, as an enemy of man suffrage, as an enemy of every kind of suffrage except universal suffrage." Still others insisted that practical politics imposed a hierarchy of priorities. A supporter of women's rights, Frederick Douglass explained, "I do not see how any one can pretend that there is the same urgency in giving the ballot to woman as to the negro. When women because they are women are dragged from their homes and hung upon lampposts," he pleaded, "then they will have the urgency to obtain the ballot."

Julia Ward Howe, a staunch suffragist who prioritized black suffrage over women's, thought the most pressing issue was peace. Horrified by the butchery of civil war, the author of "The Battle Hymn of the Republic" now called for the coming of the Lord of Peace. Addressing women at a meeting for international peace, Howe declared, "Our husbands shall not come to us, reeking with carnage, for caresses and applause. Our sons shall not be taken from us to unlearn all that we have taught them of charity, mercy and patience. We women of one country will be too tender of those of another to allow our sons to be trained to injure theirs." Howe and other women, motivated by the lessons of war and the fight for suffrage, remained active politically.

The unsuccessful crusade of northern suffragists to include gender equality in the Fourteenth and Fifteenth amendments split the women's movement. Some followed Anthony and Stanton, who ceased calling for racial equality. Others, following Stone and Howe in continuing to fight for African American rights as well as women's rights, concentrated their efforts on state constitutions. Wyoming and Utah territories granted women the vote in 1869 and 1870 (measures that Congress rescinded in 1884). Women continued to take collective, direct action by attempting to register and cast ballots wherever they could. In a few cases such bids succeeded; other challenges were turned away or channeled into the court system.

The most important female political association of the era, the Women's Christian Temperance Union, endorsed women's suffrage, guardianship rights for mothers, better wages and working conditions for women, and a single standard of sexual morality for both sexes. In 1879 Frances Willard, president of the organization, argued that women must venture beyond their traditional domestic realm to protect the home. Northern women also lobbied for political solutions to poverty and urban problems and state intervention on social issues of public welfare.

As communities negotiated new rules in the light of emancipation and new economic realities, race relations remained in a state of flux.

Symbolic of the best of racial equality and the worst of racial antipathy was interracial marriage. In South Carolina native white Republican judge William Ramey wed a former slave in 1872 and chose to do so in a symbolic ceremony on the prominent Edgefield courthouse steps. People seemed accepting; no one expelled him from the board of deacons at the Baptist church. They remained married all their lives, only to be separated at their deaths because of laws on segregated cemeteries that were enacted in the intervening years. On November 9, 1870, in Hines County, Mississippi, white state senator Albert T. Morgan was handily reelected after having married earlier that year Carrie Highgate, a beautiful black teacher from New York City. Another prominent interracial marriage in Mississippi, this time an African American man and a white woman, however, enraged some whites. In Mississippi in 1874 the union of the daughter of a wealthy plantation owner to one of her father's former slaves, the new state senator Haskins Smith, infuriated that white community and precipitated rioting.

No one knew what rules would prevail now that slavery was gone. Legal codes provided one system of guidance, religious principles another, the cult of honor a third, and Victorian respectability another still. With conflict over every meaning of freedom, days were filled with anxiety and tension for whites and blacks both. Yet life went relentlessly onward. People courted, wed, and bore children; gambled, drank, fussed, and bragged; attended church and prayed for the right balance of sunshine and rain; nursed the sick and mourned the dead. People of all colors continued to fish and hunt together as well as to work side by side. Human relationships in all their complex variety continued on steadily in spite of dissonant power relationships. Gazing around at the changes Reconstruction had brought in the early 1870s, Frederick Douglass wondered at how vitally America had changed. "I seem to be living in a new world," he exclaimed.

For white conservatives, too, changes made the South seem almost unrecognizable, and increasingly they determined to turn back the clock. Black achievements aroused the deepest white fears. After African Americans succeeded in establishing families, churches, and schools, after they fought for and won the right to vote, after they were elected to many offices in all southern states, some war-hardened ex-Confederates and some bitter racists could take it no longer. Hundreds if not thousands re-formed their army units and prepared to fight African American leaders, who were often former Union soldiers, and their white allies. Armed resistance sprang easily from emotions of injured pride and racial hostility. Earlier, during the war itself, Major General J. M. Schofield, commander of northern forces in Arkansas, warned that "the rebel army west of the Mississippi is rapidly breaking up into small bands for guerrilla operations in the vicinity of their homes." He reported to General Halleck, "The habit of waging guerrilla warfare, which amounts to a passion with the western people, will, I apprehend, give us more serious trouble than the organized rebel armies have done." The prediction proved true.

A heritage of slavery, violence was always a component of U.S. history, but after the Civil War it reached new heights as southern slaveholders no longer protected African Americans as their own personal chattel property. The Civil War continued in the South as counterrevolutionary paramilitary units took the law into their own hands across the former Confederacy, murdering African American and white legislators and community leaders. Immediately after the war, gangs of outlaws offered to dispatch anyone for twenty dollars, collecting body parts as trophies. Anyone known to be fair to the newly freed population was at risk.

Adelbert Ames, reflecting in 1914 on his Reconstruction experience, wrote of how too many white southerners refused to accept the tenets of Congressional Reconstruction and how northerners misjudged the depths of white southern enmity: "The condition of the freedman is simply this, so long as he is subordinate after the manner of a slave and not of a freedman . . . he is safe from violence; but when he attempts to depart from his old discipline and assert a single privilege, he meets opposition; and in localities is punished with death."

Throughout the South, as blacks and whites negotiated new political, social, and labor arrangements in the postwar period, rage and violence could flare up at any moment. Terror became more methodical in the early summer of 1867, when Nathan Bedford Forrest, infamous for his massacre in 1864 of 231 African American soldiers under a white flag at Fort Pillow, became the Grand Wizard of a new organization, the Ku Klux Klan. Contrary to the stereotypical image of "poor whites" who hated freedmen as economic rivals, Klansmen represented all classes of white society in the South and included planters, lawyers, merchants, teachers, and even ministers. Although there were a number of exceptions (in South Carolina's upcountry, for example), the Klan was strongest where the two parties or the two races were nearly equal in number, and it was least likely to flourish where the population was either overwhelmingly white or black. The Ku Klux Klan was highly decentralized. With no formal connection to the original order in Tennessee, "Klansmen" became a generic term referring to any group of masked vigilantes who targeted African Americans and their white allies, groups like the Knights of White Camellia and the Knights of the Rising Sun. Before 1867 Klan violence focused primarily on securing black acquiescence to unfavorable labor arrangements, though it also targeted teachers. The Klan's broad goal here was to tie the mass of black workers firmly to the land on terms favorable to its members, and to kill or drive away those who would not be cowed.

After the removal of the Freedmen's Bureau from the South at the end of 1868, the establishment of a relatively stable sharecropping system across much of the region, and the rise of biracial Republican governments at the state level, however, Klansmen launched a second campaign of terror, more bitter than the first. The Klan attacked the fledgling democratic institutions that African Americans had begun to create. Night-riding terrorists turned their attention to political activists and appointees, legislators, and voters. Most broadly, white vigilantes determined to assert that the rule of law grounded in constitutional reform would not be allowed to triumph in the South. Although the Confederate cause had been vanquished on the battlefield, former rebels and their civilian allies determined that they would use terror and brutalization, like that which had undergirded the slave system, to maintain their hegemony in the postwar South. In general Democratic leaders and newspaper editors supported the Klan, often by denying its existence.

They often did so despite damning contradictory evidence. In 1867 Republican judge Albion W. Tourgée, a white from New York who served as a delegate to the North Carolina constitutional convention and helped create the state's new legal code, counted twelve murders, nine rapes, fourteen cases of arson, and more than seven hundred beatings in his judicial district. While it is impossible to know the total number of murders, one estimate for 1868 in Arkansas alone claims more than

, three hundred Republicans killed, including U.S. congressman James M. Hinds. Union League activists were also targeted. Union Leagues acted closely with the Republican Party and were crucial for mobilizing African American citizens. Between 1868 and 1871 in Alabama and Mississippi, whites murdered or forced into exile at least seventy members of the Union League. Between 1866 and 1876 more than thirteen hundred African Americans were estimated to have been killed by whites in rural Louisiana; political motivations underlay the vast majority of these murders. Death and intimidation devastated the Republican organization and the community. Between 1868 and 1876 whites murdered seven state legislators in South Carolina alone.

African American legislators responded, employing the rule of law against brute force. In 1871 South Carolina African American state senator Lawrence Cain, in an effort to undercut local support of racist violence, introduced a bill to tax the five square miles surrounding any neighborhood "in which a man shall be murdered on account of politics, race, or color to support the widows and orphans of such martyrs." Governors in some southern states were aggressive in fighting the Klan and were somewhat, though temporarily, successful. Powell Clayton in Arkansas, William "Parson" Brownlow in Tennessee, and Edmund Davis in Texas—all mobilized biracial or all-white state militias to combat the Klan. Governor William Holden in North Carolina was so angry over the Klan murders of leading black Republicans in 1869 and 1870, and especially of state senator John Stephens in the courthouse itself, that he organized 670 soldiers under the command of Union veteran Colonel George Kirk with orders to suppress the KKK. They arrested more than one hundred Klansmen. The Klan attorney objected to Holden's denial of habeas corpus and appealed to the federal district court, which ruled against Holden. During the next state election the Democrats won a majority in the state legislature and in December 1870 impeached Holden. He was found guilty and removed from office.

Fighting against the Klan needed federal help, and at first Washington took action. When President Grant suspended habeas corpus in nine counties of South Carolina, mass indictments followed. The Ku Klux Klan Act of 1871 specified that anyone preventing citizens from voting, holding office, or serving on juries could be prosecuted by the federal rather than the state government. This was a major shift in government power from the state to the national level. As Benjamin Butler explained, if the federal government were to guarantee "the rights, liberty, and lives of citizens," it had to provide the muscle to protect those rights. Ultimately, however, northern Republicans proved unwilling to provide that level of protection. The Klan and its allies would prevail simply by avoiding federal forces. Few rebel paramilitary organizations ever clashed with army troops. They steered clear when soldiers arrived, preferring to bully county sheriffs and smaller state militias. Had there been an adequate military presence—Grant sent only nine hundred troops to back up his anti–Ku Klux measures—plus a few salutary hangings, reactionary violence might have been crippled and Lincoln's Republican vision saved. Instead, Washington's actions showed conservative white Democrats that Federals lacked the political will to turn back their assault.

Many Klansmen who raided African American communities must have felt as if they were merely embarked on a new military campaign in a very long and fratricidal war. Vigilantes often hollered the rebel yell as they swooped down on victims. Hostilities at street level, as one African American former slave wrote, were entirely driven by white hatred: blacks wanted reconciliation, whereas Klansmen wanted war. In 1871 South Carolina governor Robert Scott declared that Klan violence in his state "differed in its destructiveness from actual war only in this, that *the killed and wounded were all on one side.*" With ample weaponry and practical experience in guerrilla tactics, Klansmen made a formidable foe, eager to fight old battles to a more satisfying conclusion. Indeed, whites in local militias even applied to their state Civil War military pension boards for their time of service fighting in battle against duly elected Republicans during Reconstruction.

Fighting white militias without, and fighting factionalism within, Grant faced a difficult reelection in 1872. Some of his abolitionist reformer supporters faulted him for not suppressing southern whites. Charles Sumner, for example—for a number of reasons including personal antipathy, disagreement over foreign policy, and Grant's failure to halt white violence—proclaimed that Grant was "radically unfit for the Presidential office." Others faulted him for even trying. William S. Robinson disagreed with using the federal military to protect voting rights of African Americans: "The war is over: we must get back to peace fashions; martial law must give way to civil government . . . Sooner or later . . . the work of pacification must begin." Corruption was a major issue in the campaign. Many were outraged at the Credit Mobilier scandal (1872), when slick, winking congressmen were given stock that quickly doubled in value in exchange for favorable legislation. Organizers paid off government investigators. The scheme cost taxpayers more than $23 million and indirectly blackened the reputation of the too-trusting president, U.S. Grant. Blaming Grant for corruption not only in his administration but also in southern Republican governments, Theodore Tilton proclaimed that the "rottenness" of the "alien and carpet-bagging governments in the southern states" had "never been matched in our history save by the Tammany Ring."

North and South, black and white, politicians of the day were corrupt, but southern bribery was minor compared to that of the nation as a whole, and it never attained the outraged and outrageous self-justification of its northern and western cousins. Few balked at the appropriation of $1,000 by the South Carolina legislature to cover the gambling losses of the white speaker of the house. More typical is the career of William Whipper, who pushed reform while he also pocketed "gifts." The two went hand in hand. That the national spotlight focused on southern corruption reflected the ease with which the defeated South could be blamed for national sins. Moreover, it was easy to focus on black malfeasance at a time when for some the inclusion of any black person in government was corrupt by definition.

Some Republicans splintered, formed the Liberal Republican Party, and endorsed Horace Greeley. Grant continued to receive the support of the large majority of abolitionist reformers in the North and the Republican coalition of black and white voters in the South. The Democratic Party, in disarray and without a candidate of its own, also supported Greeley rather than Grant and the Republican Reconstructionists. While it billed itself as the party of small government, low tariffs, noninterventionist policies, and states' rights, the Democratic Party stood for white supremacy above all. Horace Greeley received 44 percent of the popular vote but died on November 29, 1872, prior to the electoral college vote. According to a good friend, it was the "weight of ridicule" heaped upon him by cartoonist Thomas Nast that caused Greeley's death.

Factionalism split the reform movement in the northern Republican Party. In New York City, Plymouth Church's pastor, Henry Ward Beecher, America's most beloved celebrity, now supported women's suffrage, argued for Darwinian evolution, and announced he no longer believed in hell! Beecher enjoyed hobnobbing with the rich and famous and gladly accepted money for his advertising support for insurance companies and throat lozenges, as well as for his wife's endorsement of eye products. He also changed his mind over the need for the sort of Confederate retribution he had demanded at Fort Sumter on April 14, 1865, instead calling for leniency and the return of control to the former southern elite.

Having ramifications for the old abolitionist coalition in general, an 1872 scandal peeled the veneer of virtue and integrity off the Reverend Beecher. During the election of 1872 suffragist Victoria Woodhull nominated herself on the Equal Rights Party ticket. (Frederick Douglass declined her offer to be the vice-presidential candidate.) In both North and South many were appalled and thought that her candidacy itself demonstrated that the system was corrupt to the core. When the establishment press maligned her for her heretical views on women's rights and free love, Woodhull reacted by attacking the person she thought responsible for the bad press. On November 2, 1872, her magazine, the *Woodhull and Claflin's Weekly*, claimed that America's most influential preacher was having an affair with his parishioner, the wife of fellow reformer Theodore Tilton. Arrested under the Comstock Act for sending "obscene" literature through the mail, Woodhull spent Election Day in jail but was afterward cleared of charges. In 1874 Tilton did indeed sue Beecher for "criminal conversation" with his wife, Elizabeth Tilton, who had accused Beecher, recanted, and retracted her recantation. In a highly public and sensationalized trial, the tawdry side of law, Beecher was acquitted in 1875. The salacious public gossip about Beecher shifted the sand under reformers' moral high ground. Questioning the meaning and sincerity of Beecher's moral rhetoric, some doubted his exhortations to strive toward a godly, perfect future. Although Beecher remained a popular clergyman, corruption had reached such a depth that some despaired of all honesty and propriety.

At certain times throughout U.S. history, the public gets concerned about political corruption, and at other times it appears to ignore it.

While hardly unique or even more widespread than after Reconstruction, corruption during Reconstruction received extensive press. And yet the destruction of black voting rights, the only weapon former slaves had to protect themselves from white supremacists, attracted comparatively little attention, except in one respect. As corrupt government became a symbol of Reconstruction, interracial democracy and black voting rights became implicated in the public's perception of widespread political malfeasance.

The attention given to southern corruption was deliberate. It turned focus away from the successes of Reconstruction. The late 1860s and early 1870s were nearly a decade during which whites and African Americans throughout the South forged tentative but real economic and social bonds and demonstrated the vision of Lincoln. Despite tax revolts and hard times, a biracial political coalition proved viable at addressing issues of the day. In 1860 nearly four million African Americans were held in slavery, and free blacks had little political, social, and economic liberty. In 1870 all were legally free and equal citizens. In 1860 there had never been black elected officials in the South; in the 1870s African Americans held elective office at almost every level of government. They served on juries. They were able to attend school. African American landownership was increasingly on the rise. Emancipation was a successful and lasting revolution, brought about by the actions of African Americans, the courage of black and white abolitionists, and the convictions of Abraham Lincoln. From Benjamin Butler's refusal at Fort Monroe, Virginia, to return a fugitive from slavery in May 1861, through the Confiscation Acts of 1861 and 1862, Lincoln's Emancipation Proclamation, and the Thirteenth Amendment, emancipation was a successful revolution based on limited goals. The goal of reconstructing government on racial equality, while far more wide-ranging, was never predestined for failure.

Adelbert Ames wrote that the people who served during Reconstruction were "all young, each and every one believed he was doing God's service and that the final result of his labors would be the elevation of an unhappy class of the human race." People coming south after the Civil War included African Americans who were returning home without fear of being reenslaved. Harriet Beecher Stowe moved to Florida parttime in 1867, taken with the natural beauty of the land and the "tumble-

down, wild, panicky kind of life—this general happy-go-luckiness which
Florida inculcates," and neighbors made her feel welcome. For the most
part it was northern missionaries and teachers who came south. They
barely made a living, and their lives were in daily jeopardy. These teachers, nurses, ministers, philanthropists, and honest businessmen, however,
have come to be painted with the same smear of "carpetbaggers" given
to unscrupulous speculators who arrived to exploit the South, carrying
all they owned in cheap suitcases made of carpet material.

At that time of struggle for decent race relations, some southern
whites stood up for reconciliation and racial justice even while the majority of whites refused to do so. An Alabama newspaper described any
white who joined the Republican Party as "a mangy dog, slinking
through the alleys, haunting the governor's office, defiling with tobacco
juice the steps of the capital." Such men included governor Edmund
Davis, the Texan who as brigadier general in the U.S. army accepted the
surrender of Confederate forces in Texas. Advocates of racial harmony
also included former Confederates, such as cavalry hero John Mosby (the
"Gray Ghost") and General James Longstreet, Lee's "Old Warhorse."
The man who hanged John Brown, Governor Henry Wise of Virginia,
became a Republican supporter of black rights. These men were labeled, and still are today, with the epithet "scalawag." But nothing so insults the legacy and sacrifice of these and others than the term still used
in historical writings for the time when fraud and violence prevailed:
"Redemption," a beautiful term of religious faith that would be a better
label for the promising years from the early 1860s through the early
1870s than so grossly to misconstrue the decades that followed.

Twelve

"A Dead Radical Is Very Harmless"

MORE THAN ANYTHING ELSE, it was the new black militias that ruffled southern white supremacist sensibilities. One white man, infuriated about a Fourth of July parade by a black regiment, wrote in 1874, "No orgie of the Paris Commune surpassed this in the subversion of God's law and order." A white woman wrote to a friend that her attitude toward blacks had grown into hatred at the sight of "negro soldiers marching so grand in their blue uniforms . . . with their fine swords, and their scarlet sashes, making a fine show." For another, whereas enslaved African Americans had made her "heart bound with pride, hope and respect and reverence," black soldiers with weapons produced "a loathing that I feel when looking at a venomous reptile." Although desperately searching for house servants, this woman would not hire any African American woman whose husband was a soldier.

In Edgefield County, South Carolina, the local militia was commanded by a former slave, Captain Edward Tennant. A dashing officer who bore himself with great dignity, Ned Tennant was both a symbolic and a substantive threat to southern white hegemony. In July 1874 a local white paramilitary group, the Sweetwater Sabre Club, assembled near the place where Tennant's militia drilled. Enraged by the black militia's use of large bass drums, which had been banned under slavery, the Sabre Club attacked Tennant's house that night. Immediately the

African American militia went into action, pounding the drum in a "long roll," calling neighboring townships for help in protecting Tennant. Hearing the drum echo, whites decided that the "negroes meant to kill all whites," and the white irregulars also congregated at Tennant's home. In the morning more than two hundred whites, many of them Confederate veterans, faced one hundred black militia members. Despite an explosive atmosphere, no bloodshed occurred, the leaders agreeing to dismiss their troops. Following this incident, whites asked Republican governor Daniel H. Chamberlain's permission to disband Edgefield's black militias. Chamberlain, who endorsed African American voting rights but also wanted to attract moderate whites to the Republican Party, gave assent. Led by former Confederate Cavalry General Matthew Calbraith Butler, one thousand white men searched for Tennant's militia throughout the county. Tennant and his troops, however, had no desire to turn over their weapons to Butler's group. Marching twenty-five miles through a country swarming with whites, they arrived in full force at Edgefield Court House and instead surrendered their weapons to African American state senator and regimental commander of the state militia Lawrence Cain. Potential violence was averted, but the political outcome for freedmen was disastrous.

NO UNIFIED WHITE SOUTH rose up against Reconstruction's interracial democracy. While the numbers are not known, court cases show that it was a minority of white men, perhaps hundreds in a given locality, who resorted to extralegal terrorist tactics to overthrow Reconstruction. Some whites spoke out against the violence, and the 1870s investigation of the Ku Klux Klan records are filled with the KKK attacks upon whites who opposed them. Most white men just did nothing—nothing to break the law and nothing to prevent their friends and neighbors from breaking it. Even as many southern whites accepted the legality of Reconstruction governments, others thought their liberty required white supremacy. Troublemakers sincerely believed that a polity in which African American men were truly equal citizens with the right to vote, hold office, and serve on juries was not a "legitimate" government. And that being the case, they felt no compunction to limit themselves to legitimate dissent. With a new sense of pride for their violent extremist measures, many of the new white vigilante groups no longer hid behind masks and silly white robes.

White "Restoration" of the mid-1870s and 1880s ushered in a new phase of southern white violence, an era wherein no act, no matter how heinous, went untried in the effort to eliminate African American voting power. Ultimately what brought down the republican vision in state after state was a bloody reign of terror, sponsored and carried out by the very leaders who posed as champions of conservative "order." Waning in power were groups such as the 1873 Unification Movement in New Orleans, which included blacks and whites, Republicans and Democrats, Jews and Gentiles, former Union soldiers and former Confederates such as General P.G.T. Beauregard. This group and others advocating racial equality, and freedom and justice for all, were slowly losing out to the largely unchecked flood of white supremacist rhetoric and violence.

The very success of Reconstruction drove white Democrats and their vigilante lieutenants to acts of terrorism. A Democrat from Louisiana pronounced, "This state of affairs could scarcely be tolerated by the proud former masters of slaves." Refusing to work with the interracial coalitions that had won elections during the first several years of Reconstruction, too many whites deliberately chose lawlessness precisely because they demanded a system that would adjudicate their interests only. Violence was the only way white Democrats across the South could end the record of electoral and appointed success. The Democratic Party created a paramilitary wing that shadowed the opposition and generated unrest. While party leaders promoted the peaceful electoral process, it was a facade. Whether through secretive activity or through open mob fighting, Democrats resorted again and again to political assassination and murder, although physical beatings, arson, and threats of death were more common. A constable, white or black, who tried to serve a warrant on a white man put his own life in jeopardy. While adopting a policy of winning elections peacefully if possible, Democrats did not shrink from fraud and violence in areas with large African American populations.

Corruption of the electoral process became the norm. One northern Louisiana newspaper bespoke the depth of white feeling when it editorialized that it was a "religious duty" to rob votes and "any failure to do so will be a violation of true Louisiana Democratic teaching." With a might-makes-right mentality, whites used extralegal activity because they were not legally able to break the majority control of the state and local governments. Ultimately, it was not African Americans or Republicans they opposed but the rule of law itself.

In Louisiana in 1867, former Confederate General James Longstreet, then commander of the state militia stationed in New Orleans, was surprised that the newspaper accused him of "joining the enemy" when he expressed his support for equal rights: "If I appreciate the issues of Democracy at this moment, they are the enfranchisement of the negro and the rights of Congress in the premises." Longstreet had only acted as he thought right. He had integrated the militia and appointed black as well as white officers, including Confederates and Union veterans. He ordered that each militiaman swear on oath to "accept the civil and political equality of all men, and agree not to attempt to deprive any person or persons on account of race, color, or previous condition of any political or civil right, privilege or immunity enjoyed by any other class of men." By 1871 Longstreet claimed that "one half of our force is composed of officers and soldiers who were in the military service of the Southern States during the late civil conflict," and in 1872 and 1873 this militia defended the governor and state legislature from two attempts at violent overthrow. Thereafter, the White League, the paramilitary arm of the Democratic Party, grew stronger, enforcing tighter discipline in its ranks. It replaced wanton, indiscriminate terror with carefully orchestrated violence to achieve specific political ends. In the "Colfax Massacre" of April 13, 1873, the more numerous White League defeated the Louisiana state militia as it attempted to protect black voters. White Democrats in Colfax, determined to rid the county of black voters, strode into the black section of town and killed the fleeing people. When some African Americans took refuge in the courthouse, whites set it afire and then shot those exiting the burning building.

After the massacre, the federal government was able to convict only three persons for more then 100 murders. The defendants appealed their case all the way to the Supreme Court, which ruled in October 1875 in *U.S. v. Cruikshank* that the federal government did not have the right to prosecute individuals under the Enforcement Act of 1870. The Supreme Court had already severely limited the enforcement of Reconstruction law in its rulings in the *Slaughterhouse Cases* of 1873. Justices used those cases, which were initiated by butchers, to define what could be brought to trial under the auspices of the Fourteenth Amendment. In a split decision 5 to 4 (Chase among the dissenters), the court ruled that very little could be so brought. In effect, the court gutted enforcement of civil rights legislation.

President Grant was outraged that guilty parties went unpunished. "To say that the murder of a negro or a white Republican is not considered a crime in Louisiana would probably be unjust to a great part of the people, but it is true that a great number of such murders have been committed and no one has been punished." He denounced the idea that "the spirit of hatred and violence is stronger than law."

Six months later, on September 17, 1874, the Louisiana state militia again lost to the stronger forces of the White Leaguers in the battle of Canal Street, an attempt to get rid of the Republican governor William Kellogg. Democrats also prevented elected Republicans from organizing the state legislature. After an emergency cabinet meeting President Grant authorized federal troops to preserve the peace. Three months later, on December 24, 1874, Grant sent Lt. Gen. Philip Sheridan to Louisiana to investigate reports of massive disorder. Sheridan verified the reports and recommended the arrest of the leaders. U.S. troops reinstalled the duly elected officials. Republicans in Louisiana were grateful, but White Leaguers did not approve of the military intervention. Reaction in the North was also hostile.

In the midterm election of November 1875 Georgia native white Republican Richard Whiteley was defeated in his bid for reelection to the U.S. House of Representatives. Like other southern white Republicans, Whiteley had built a coalition that depended upon getting African Americans to the polls, winning over or appeasing some whites, and minimizing the certain obstruction of Democrats. By 1875, however, white supremacy had become a major issue in Georgia. By limiting the vote of African American Republicans, Democrats won every single congressional race in Georgia. In both north and south, the Republicans felt the repercussions of the Panic of 1873. For the first time since the Civil War began, Democrats gained control of the House of Representatives. The Forty-third Congress, which served from 1873–75, included 88 Democrats and 199 Republicans (5 other). The Forty-fourth Congress, 1875–77, included 182 Democrats and 103 Republicans (8 other).

With victory in Congress, the white counterrevolution at the state level moved to limit local Republican political machines such as Tunis Campbell's. Because Campbell still wielded considerable power, state authorities changed regulations so that appointed commissioners rather than elected officials would govern counties. Even then the African American Republican coalition resisted; white Democratic state authority had to physically remove Tunis Campbell from power. He was arrested on a trumped-up charge of malfeasance, found guilty, and sentenced to the state penitentiary. Arrayed against intransigent racists, Campbell could still articulate his class-based appeal as the best means to bridge the racial divide: "No matter what might be the moral worth or respectability of a mechanic or laboring man, his interests or rights must not stand in the way of the wishes of the capitalists or property-holder . . . How long will it be before you will have no rights that the capitalists or property-holder is bound to respect?" And indeed, the interracial coalition Campbell built in Georgia continued to be an active force in local politics for years, even as he himself, at age sixty-three, served on the chain gang leased out under Georgia's new convict-lease law. But the forces unleashed by rank prejudice would otherwise overwhelm such reasoned claims to mutual self-interest.

In an extraordinary message to Congress on January 13, 1875, Grant pleaded with its members to support fair elections in the southern states, reminding them "that Congress shall have power to enforce" the Fifteenth Amendment to the Constitution, that it was a duty. Grant detailed some of the atrocities, describing "wild scenes of anarchy . . . sweeping away all restraint of law and order" and the murder of "Union men or Republicans on account of their opinions." The president proclaimed that "to the extent that Congress has conferred power upon me" he would work to prevent "Ku Klux Klans, White Leagues, nor any other association using arms and violence to execute their unlawful purposes." The president concluded with an indictment of the congressional lack of attention to the problem: "I can not but think that its inaction has produced great evil."

The forces of reaction in Mississippi saw northern hesitation as a green light. The overthrow of the legitimate government in Mississippi in 1875 was a major turning point in ending Reconstruction's interracial democracy. In that state a year of organized political violence lay the groundwork for the upcoming statewide elections in the fall. The Republican governor of Mississippi, Adelbert Ames, called for federal intervention to protect Republican voters from white vigilante "rifle clubs" and to stop the terror tactics. This time, however, Grant declined. Grant knew he had failed to muster a national consensus of support. Yankees were weary of the seemingly endless disputes in the former Confederate states. Edwards Pierrepont, attorney general for the Grant administration, echoed Grant's frustration in his response: the public was "tired out with these annual autumnal outbreaks" of violence. Moreover, Grant's earlier decisions to send troops to Louisiana hurt the Republican Party at the polls. To northern Republicans, party politics were just too important at this key moment. Like Mississippi, Ohio was in the midst of state elections. Many believed that presidential intervention in Mississippi would cause the Republican gubernatorial candidate, Rutherford B. Hayes, to lose in the Buckeye State. Grant did not help Mississippi, and Hayes became governor of Ohio. Too many northerners were in agreement with Grant's Darwinian assessment: "If a Republican State Government cannot sustain itself, then it will have to give way."

In Mississippi on Election Day 1875, armed horsemen terrorized African Americans and prevented them from going to the polls. Democrats destroyed ballot boxes and threw away ballots, substituting their own. Landslide Democratic victories brought the Mississippi legislature under the control of the white elite, who then instituted new methods to keep themselves viable against an opposing majority. White election boards abolished voting precincts in black areas, so people had to walk many miles and even cross rivers to cast a vote. They complicated registration and confused voting-box arrangements. They instituted at-large elections wherever African Americans had the ability to elect representatives from districts. They gerrymandered electoral districts to create safe havens for conservative Democrats. They changed local elective offices to appointments. They instituted all-white Democratic primaries. By these and other means, Mississippi cut the percentage of black voting-age men registered to vote from over 90 percent in 1868 to less than 6 percent in 1892.

If Grant had done more to counter white terrorists, if Congress had persevered in safeguarding the right to vote and in compelling fair elections, white southerners would likely have come to accept the law. Senator Joseph Fowler of Tennessee had warned that the work of Reconstruction would need enforcement for some time, until the "second generation" after the war. Indiana congressman George Julian suggested a twenty-year military occupation. But voters in the non-South had grown impatient. In contrast to his stirring message to Congress in 1875, Grant's message in 1876 made no mention of the South.

Some northern white civil rights activists in Congress never gave up on trying to legislate fairness. Year after year Charles Sumner had advocated for a new civil rights bill to forbid discrimination in public places. Somewhat to honor him after his death, and somewhat to address southern race relations in a last-ditch effort before their political hegemony would come to an end, Republicans in Congress passed the Civil Rights Act of 1875. Although Sumner had wanted no exceptions, Congress had to exempt churches and schools from requirements or the bill would not have passed.

Southern whites knew their main problem was on the state and local level. If they had charge of government there, they could ignore such federal mandates. Looking to how the national government treated Mississippi, other states learned the lesson: they would be safe from federal interference.

Mississippi was the model for the South Carolina plan. Although violent clashes between whites and blacks occurred throughout the South, the scale of battle in the mid-1870s was nowhere as great as in South Carolina, and in South Carolina nowhere as great as in Edgefield District. In 1876 in the black-controlled town of Hamburg, Democrats under Matthew Calbraith Butler's leadership brought in a cannon and several hundred armed horsemen to do battle with the town's African American militia, killing six (four by firing squad) and pillaging the homes and shops of the town's black population and their white allies. The Hamburg massacre was a piece of the larger Ellenton Riot, and in the wake of that violence Democrats orchestrated an overthrow of state government. The Democratic campaign of 1876 was conceived and organized by former officers of the Confederate Hampton Legion, and the Civil War hero General Wade Hampton III led the party's ticket. Only one officer of the Hampton Legion played no part in the "Edgefield Plan": Colonel James B. Griffin. Griffin and his family had gone to Texas in 1866, forsaking cotton for the world of business. Like some other whites, he preferred to move on rather than continue to fight a civil war on local streets and against neighbors belonging to a different political party.

Major General Matthew Calbraith Butler and Brigadier General Martin Witherspoon Gary mapped the campaign. Gary favored waging all-out guerrilla warfare and organized three hundred "rifle clubs" throughout the state. Armed bands of horsemen, attired in symbolically defiant red shirts like Garibaldi's men in Italy, intimidated and attacked potential black voters. Gary wrote out thirty-three points for the organizers. Point Number 16 reads: "Never threaten a man individually if he deserves to be threatened, the necessities of the times require that he should die. A dead Radical is very harmless—a threatened Radical or one driven off by threats from the scene of his operations is often very troublesome, sometimes dangerous, always vindictive."

For Democrats, killing Republican leaders was an effective way to gain and maintain control. For African Americans and other Republicans, if voting became dangerous, holding office was more so. In one incident the "Red Shirts" surrounded their state representative, African American Simon Coker. The captain of the unit, Nat Butler, informed Coker that he had only a few moments to live. Coker gave them a key to his cotton house and said, "I wish you would please send it to my wife and tell her to have our cotton ginned and pay our landlord rent just as soon as she can." Having agreed, the group then gave permission to Coker to pray. After a few moments Butler said, "You are too long," and he gave the order to shoot the legislator still kneeling in prayer. Witnessing this murder was Benjamin Ryan Tillman, a future South Carolina governor and powerful U.S. Senator. "It will appear a ruthless and cruel thing to those unacquainted with the environments," he wrote. "The struggle in which we were engaged meant more than life or death. It involved everything we held dear, Anglo-Saxon civilization included." The old justification had been reburnished, and in the election of 1876, more than seven hundred armed and mounted Democrats in red shirts seized control of the Edgefield County Courthouse, outnumbering the few federal troops, and prevented African Americans from voting. "Gary's doctrine of voting early and often changed the Republican majority of 2,300 in Edgefield to a democratic majority of 3,900," recalled Tillman proudly. Statewide, Hampton's "victory" resulted from the casting of 2,252 more votes than eligible voters. Some considered Hampton a "moderate" because he appointed African Americans who "knew their place" to some local offices. But Hampton was no moderate. Later, as a U.S. Senator, he justified fraud, intimidation, and violence to deny South Carolina African Americans the franchise, claiming that "the very civilization, the property, the life of the State itself, were involved."

The state of Virginia took longer to establish white restoration. In Virginia, General William Mahone, who had commanded rebel troops that turned back the assault on the Crater in 1864, came to perceive the advantages of doing business with Republican regimes and found himself avidly courting white and black Republican legislators to gain concessions for his railroad and coal-mining ventures. "Little Billy" grew rich and rose to high office promoting economic renewal, racial harmony, low taxes, and clean government. There is scant evidence to reveal that Mahone embraced any deep commitment to the freedman's cause when he embarked on his postwar career in business and politics. By the 1880s, however, he had shifted steadily away from the Democratic conservatism that many ex-Confederates championed. Mahone moved as he did for the sake of his state and the well-being of his neighbors and himself; embracing the politics of racial animosity and reaction just made no sense to him.

Whites and blacks in Virginia worked together between 1879 and 1883; Mahone's Readjuster Party has been called "the most successful interracial political alliance in the post-emancipation South." This black-majority party controlled the state legislature and the courts and distributed the state's many coveted federal patronage positions. The party promoted African American suffrage, officeholding, and jury duty. The Readjusters won the governorship, two seats in the U.S. Senate, and six of Virginia's ten congressional districts. But this situation did not last. By 1883 Virginia had succumbed to white power as had the other southern states—through violence, electoral intimidation, and fraud.

White restoration in Florida added a new technique in the typical pattern of election fraud in the late 1870s. After winning back control of the Florida legislature in 1877, whites in the Florida Senate enacted a statute, meant to be used exclusively against African American voters, allowing partisan poll-watchers to challenge the qualifications of "any person offering to vote." African American senator Fred Hill, in an effort to invoke the Fifteenth Amendment, unsuccessfully moved to emend the title of the bill to the more transparent "To provide for disfranchising one-third of the legal voters of the State of Florida." Another statute to diminish African American voting in Florida was the requirement that boards of county commissioners divide their counties into election districts and to designate voting places within each district. This requirement ended voting by substantial numbers in towns and replaced it with voting dispersed throughout the countryside, effectively increasing rural white landowner influence and decreasing the sway of the black and white political leaders in the towns. In addition to the package of disfranchisement measures, the Florida legislature modified jury selection. The boards of county commissioners were to choose from among registered voters jurors "who shall be such persons only as they know, or have good reason to believe, are of approved integrity, fair character, sound judgment and intelligence."

On the national scene, charges and countercharges plagued the 1876 presidential election. The Democratic nominee was Governor Samuel Jones Tilden of New York, the antislavery (also anti-black and anti-Semite), conservative reformer who had won his popularity by successfully taking down the infamous William "Boss" Tweed. The Republican nominee was Rutherford B. Hayes, governor of Ohio, a former Union officer and, like Tilden, an attorney known for his opposition to corruption. Up against another reformer, Hayes relied on the tried-and-true technique of "waving the bloody shirt," reminding voters that a Democratic victory would put the country in the control of the very people who instigated the rebellion. When the election returns came in, almost every Democrat agreed that Samuel Tilden won the presidency. He won the popular vote and secured all but one of the electoral votes he needed to be elected, and the fifteen undecided votes were mostly from states with significant Democratic majorities. To the southern white Democrats of the day, Tilden's election signaled the end of Congressional Reconstruction. Once in office, Tilden would remove the few remaining federal troops from the South, and elite white Democrats would finalize local control and patronage power without regard for minority rights. Republicans, however, found that in a fair contest Hayes would have won in Florida, Louisiana, and South Carolina. They refused to accept the Electoral College votes in these states, as well as the state of Oregon, also in dispute. Without these states, Tilden remained one vote short of election.

Congress had to decide who would count the electoral votes. Seldom have the math skills of two groups of men differed so pointedly. If the

Republican-controlled Senate counted votes, all knew, Hayes would win; if the Democratic-controlled House tallied up, it would be Tilden. Instead, Congress set up a commission of five House members, five Senators, and five Supreme Court justices. The House appointed three Democrats and two Republicans; the Senate appointed three Republicans and two Democrats. The Supreme Court appointed three Republicans and two Democrats. Voting 8–7 along party lines, the commission gave the votes in all four disputed states to Rutherford B. Hayes. Hayes was inaugurated in March 1877.

When Hayes was selected by the Electoral College and sworn in as the nineteenth president, no violent resistance erupted in the South, as had happened sixteen years earlier over the election of Abraham Lincoln. It has been argued that the South did not challenge the installation of Hayes because southern Democratic politicians had struck a secret deal with him. This argument presupposes back-room promises made by Hayes to withdraw federal troops from the South and to end federally directed Reconstruction policies in exchange for the support of southerners in Congress. In return for the White House, Hayes supposedly agreed that the federal government would not interfere with southern whites and their "race problems."

Popular imagination of "the withdrawal of federal troops from the South" might envision occupational forces departing en masse—a large undertaking. Hardly. From 1876 to 1877, barely six thousand (more than half in Texas) federal soldiers in fifty-two posts remained, and these were no match for white paramilitary leagues and rifle clubs, whose greater firepower was able to prevent open elections. Federal troops were active in protecting duly elected state legislatures only in South Carolina (683 troops in 10 posts) and Louisiana (529 troops in 9 posts). President Hayes did indeed order those troops to leave the statehouse grounds and return to barracks—in other words, federal troops would not be used to ensure voting rights—but no dark conspiracy is required to explain why. Hayes most likely wanted to leave the South alone because, unlike Grant, he did not have any interest in fostering interracial democracy. Hayes opposed the idea of "forcing" the races together, believing that the "let-alone policy" was "the true course." Hayes accepted southern leaders' rhetoric that they would maintain peace and abide by the law. He described his southern strategy as one of trust: "My policy is trust—peace, and to put aside the bayonet." Moreover, federal bayonets were needed against Native Americans in the West and railroad strikers in the North.

Whether as part of a secret "Compromise of 1877" or not, the Republican Party had that year turned away from Lincoln's vision of government of the people, by the people, and for the people. The party had lost its most idealistic leaders as well. Thaddeus Stevens had died in 1868, choosing to be buried in a cemetery without racial barriers, Salmon Chase had died in 1873, and Charles Sumner in 1874. While the brightest and most hopeful spirits who had guided and propelled the antislavery movement from the 1830s onward continued to support equal rights for African Americans, some white abolitionists understood freedom only in opposition to a slavery system. These men were unprepared to embrace newly freed Republicans' insistence on justice. Reformers who had accused the slave system of being so overwhelmingly oppressive that enslaved humans could not function on any level—family, church, or society—were not able or willing to reconcile their philosophy with the de facto citizenship of the newly freed people. Their emphasis on individual achievement and social respectability left them ill equipped to confront postbellum circumstances. White supporters of black rights came to question their own portrayals of African Americans when southern whites told them tales of lazy, recalcitrant freedpeople, too eager to dispute their imagined wrongs with employers and officials, too reluctant to put their back into their work of raising themselves upward. They all too easily believed white elite southerners that, because African Americans had been denied political experience, they lacked the skill needed to govern. Less experienced, the freedmen were therefore said to be more prone to corruption or at least less able to prevent it. They pronounced black suffrage a failure and blamed African Americans for the violence perpetrated against them. In all of American history there is perhaps no spectacle of abandoned ideals more wrongheaded or depressing.

The Republican Party was split on whether its political and economic interests would be better served by cooperating with the traditional southern elite. Enough Republicans sided with the Democrats in Congress to prevent the use of federal power to assure African American, or for that matter yeomen, meaningful liberty in the South. Imbued with widespread northern self-interest, apathy toward the problems of others, and racial prejudice, Congress gradually acceded to southern demands that it return power in the South to white elites who claimed that they were better suited to handle their own institutions of state and local government. Changed policy showed in lower numbers of federal prosecutions. In the single year of 1873 more than one thousand federal prosecutions were launched under the enforcement acts (including the Ku Klux Klan Act), and the effectiveness of the KKK shrunk accordingly. Between 1878 and 1890 the annual number of federal prosecutions averaged below one hundred, and the KKK revitalized.

The weakness of Lincoln's new meaning of freedom was that it had to be vigorously defended. Republican free labor ideology, which had provided the political support for the eradication of slavery and the passage of laws granting black male civil rights, had never condoned governmental intervention to enforce workers' rights. Too many in the North were growing callous from hearing about the atrocities. Moreover, some whites assumed that the reports were exaggerations, not willing to believe the savagery that terrorists inflicted on black activists in the South. At the same time, when northerners also felt threatened by disorder, nonsoutherners cheered on southern white elites trying to "restore order" in their region. Northern Republican support for African American rights waned when African American voters, while loyal to the party, expressed political sentiments that paralleled the class-conscious demands of the northern white working class.

By the late 1870s the northern press was equating the demands of southern African Americans for justice and freedom of opportunity with the demands of organized labor. E. L. Godkin of *The Nation* came to support southern Democrats. When Godkin became editor of *The Nation* in 1865, he had declared that the paper would support issues that were "likely to promote equal distribution of the fruits of progress and civilization." Once an avid supporter of women's suffrage and equal rights for African Americans, however, his and other influential papers came to oppose a democratic vision. They called instead for government by that "part of the community that embodies the intelligence and the capital."

In *Harper's Weekly* the onetime political cartoonist for Lincoln's Union cause, Thomas Nast, led the nation in turning away from African American rights. In his classic "The First Vote" (November 10, 1867)

Nast portrayed dignified African Americans lining up to cast their ballots. In "The National Colored Convention" (February 6, 1869) he showed an orderly assembly gathering to discuss their rights. Five years later, in a blatant racist caricature, his "Colored Rule in a Reconstructed (?) State" (March 14, 1874) shows grotesque faces of African American legislators in South Carolina as they argue and disagree and accomplish nothing.

Interracial democracy was failing and the supreme law of the land stamped its imprimatur on the failure. In the *civil rights cases* of 1883, the Supreme Court struck down the Civil Rights Act of 1875, holding that the act exceeded congressional powers. Justice John Harlan alone dissented, vigorously, charging that the majority had subverted the Reconstruction Amendments: "The substance and spirit of the recent amendments of the Constitution have been sacrificed by a subtle and ingenious verbal criticism." In 1884 in *Hurtado v. California*, the court ruled, with Harlan again dissenting, that the Fourteenth Amendment did not guarantee enforcement of the Bill of Rights.

If civil rights, as defined by the Supreme Court, were a matter for the states, certain states took that imperative and enacted state civil rights statutes. The Midwest predominated: Iowa and Ohio in 1884; Illinois, Indiana, Michigan, and Nebraska in 1885. Former Confederate states, however, took no such steps.

Aware of the horrendous assault on African American rights in the South, and with no recourse to the federal judiciary for enforcement, U.S. representative Henry Cabot Lodge offered practical steps toward enforcing the Fifteenth Amendment. The Massachusetts Republican, who scorned corruption of all kind—in business, in politicians, and in elections—sponsored the 1890 Federal Election Bill to ensure fair state elections. Democratic opposition was fierce, starting with the propaganda victory that labeled the measure the "Force Act."

Lodge tried to counter, stating, "There is no question of force in the present bill. One able editor referred to it as bristling with bayonets in every line; but as there is absolutely no allusion to anything or anybody remotely connected with bayonets . . . So anxious, indeed, are the opponents of the measure on this point that, not finding any bayonets in the bill, they themselves have put them in rather than not have them in at all." Lodge also clarified that the bill was not sectional: "Those who rave against the bill as sectional that is, as directed against the South, for Southern and sectional appear to have become synonymous terms, admit by so doing that they have a monopoly of impure elections."

Republicans in the House, supporting their African American allies in the South and wanting to protect the Republican majority (which it lost overwhelmingly in 1892), passed the bill by a narrow margin, an outcome tellingly different from the overwhelming support for fair elections displayed in 1866, when southern Democrats were not present. But by one vote the Senate failed to pass the Federal Election Bill, the last attempt of the party of Lincoln to protect black voting rights. Its defeat in Congress signaled to the southern states that the reformers could no longer muster enough votes to do so. While the majority of southerners wanted racial justice, justice required fair elections. The federal government had to be willing to ensure that African Americans procured an honest ballot. That it was unable and unwilling to do.

On December 10, 1892, a Victor Gillam cartoon in the Republican magazine *The Judge*, "The Weakness of the Republican Party," shows two men, one young, virile, and handsome, the other old and decrepit, "courting" the Republican Party, symbolized by an attractive young woman. The party looks in disgust at the stooped, balding, paunchy Republicanism of the 1870s and 1880s while the "Young Republican" explains, "A generation has been born and voted since the war; pensions have been amply provided for; new measures demand young men. We are sick of being led by old fossils on the war issues, and the time has come when young Republicans must be recognized!" A central war issue was black rights, especially the hard-earned right to an honest ballot; after 1892 the Republican Party dropped the policy from its platform. A Democratic Congress in 1893 dealt a fatal blow to black voting rights. It repealed laws allowing federal supervisors to investigate voting fraud or federal soldiers to protect the right to vote.

Without any real resistance from northern politicians, Democrats throughout southern states moved beyond the violence and political maneuvers of the 1870s and 1880s. The next stage of white restoration was legal disfranchisement. White supremacy demanded that political power belong to whites alone, and southern whites preferred a racially constructed rule of law to an informal system of terror and fraud. Throughout the Deep South white Democrats organized new constitu-

tional conventions, this time to codify African American disfranchisement. Here, however, is tantalizing evidence that Lincoln's faith in the
southern yeomen was well founded. When Mississippi's 1890 state convention passed a new constitution, delegates decided that statewide ratification was not required. Neither did South Carolina and Louisiana
require ratification. Leaders, in short, did not trust the majority of
whites in their state to do their bidding.

In 1896 only 5,500 African Americans were registered to vote in
South Carolina; African Americans constituted a majority in the state
but a mere ten percent of all registered voters; but whites demanded
a constitutional convention to eliminate more African American voters.
One delegate to that South Carolina disfranchising constitutional convention was Robert Smalls, who spoke in favor of a "Constitution that is
fair, honest and just." Whatever the disqualifying techniques, Smalls
asked that they apply to white and black equally: "We care not what the
qualifications imposed are, all that we ask is that they are fair and
honest, and honorable, and with these provisos we will stand or fall
by it." South Carolina senator Tillman, in contrast, declared defiantly:
"We have done our level best. We have scratched our heads to find out
how we could eliminate every last one of them. We stuffed ballot boxes.
We shot them. We are not ashamed of it." He announced, "The whites
have absolute control of the government, and we intend at any hazard
to retain it." In Mississippi a Democrat declared that "we have been
preserving the ascendancy of the white people by revolutionary methods." In Louisiana, Governor Murphy Foster bragged to that state's
legislature in 1898, "The White supremacy for which we have so long
struggled . . . is now crystallized into the constitution." By the end of
the 1890s African American disfranchisement in the Deep South was
nearly complete. White Democrats worked from the belief that their
freedom, their world, all that they held dear, depended on these measures. They were unable to grasp the promise of America, even as it was
sanctified in the Constitution, that individual liberties had to be open to
everyone.

Whites had stopped most African Americans from voting, but some
brave souls refused to give up. Whites forced the issue in a particularly
bloody encounter on November 8, 1898, near Ninety Six, South Carolina, home of Preston Brooks and Benjamin E. Mays, future president

of Morehouse College and civil rights activist. Mays's first childhood memory was of fear and torment during this Phoenix Riot. Local newspapers blamed the African Americans for instigating the riot, but a Charleston newspaper wrote that the white mob was "made with the lust of blood." Whites "killed the men whom they thought they could kill with the least, or no risk to themselves." White allies of African Americans were also targets of violence. These attempts to vote came three years after the disfranchising convention of 1895. In 1900 in Georgetown, South Carolina, a similar four-day white riot ended the sharing of county offices between white Democrats and African Americans (mostly Republicans).

Even amid the violence, some few African Americans continued to vote, and remnants of African American political activity persisted. Tunis Campbell's machine in Georgia and the African American Populists working with Garrett Scott's organization in Grimes County, Texas, proved that in elections where the vote was counted fairly, even racist white elected officials paid some attention to the needs of their black constituents. Although some white supremacists believed black Americans would never again be elected to office, more prophetic was the 1901 farewell address by African American Republican Congressman George White from North Carolina: "This, Mr. Chairman, is perhaps the Negro's temporary farewell to the American Congress; but let me say that, Phoenix-like, he will rise up and come again."

With next to no African American voters to consider, racist white regimes immediately worked to undermine the gains of Reconstruction. Without the fundamental right to vote and protect themselves politically, African Americans were powerless to stop the legislative onslaught. Southern legislatures resegregated universities and public schools, then failed to fund education properly at all, with black schools faring much worse than white ones. The Georgia state legislature repealed the homestead exemption that had provided substantial help to small farmers black and white.

Not just in the South but throughout the nation the Fifteenth Amendment's guarantee of the right to vote was effectively nullified as whites found legal means to eliminate or dilute the black vote by redistricting, gerrymandering, and instituting at-large elections. The 1890 Mississippi constitution reduced black voting from 88 percent in 1888 to virtually zero thereafter. Estimates of African American voter turnout for the whole South show 61 percent in 1880, 36 percent in 1892, 17 percent in 1900, and 2 percent in 1912.

African Americans throughout the South protested their disfranchisement, calling conventions and meetings, campaigning vigorously against disfranchising amendments. When they were excluded from political meetings, they presented petitions. They instigated lawsuits. Among others, *Mills v. Green* (1895) sought to overturn disfranchising election laws in South Carolina. *Williams v. Mississippi* (1898) challenged the laws in Mississippi. The Supreme Court concentrated on procedural questions and basically refused to enforce the Fourteenth and Fifteenth amendments. And yet African Americans and some white Republicans continued to resist, becoming a principal redoubt of Lincoln's legacy, a commitment to egalitarian constitutionalism.

Lack of the vote meant lack of political clout. Lack of political clout meant lack of economic opportunity as the white-only government protected white propertied interests at the expense of black citizens. Restored white Democrats repealed laws favorable to tenants and sharecroppers and instituted lien laws to favor landowners and merchants. Debt became a way of life for many poor whites and nearly all African Americans, the former, however, having avenues of escape that the latter did not. Politicians went beyond custom and wrote employment discrimination into state law. In towns where African American men held jobs as postal clerks, sheriffs, and judges, they were fired from those positions and relegated to janitorial work and the stereotypical agricultural jobs associated with slavery. Henceforth they were denied access to jobs in the trades as skilled artisans. Whites made sure that the textile industry developed as a white-only enterprise. Between 1880 and 1885 the number of cotton spindles in the southern states doubled, but this major employment opportunity for the landless and jobless in the postbellum South excluded African Americans.

At the same time that employment was limited, African Americans were unable to use their right to refuse to work as a bargaining tool in negotiations; they could be arrested as "vagrants," and the chain gang replaced the whip as the symbol of punishment for black southerners. With the development of convict lease labor, wealthy planters, mill owners, mining operators, and railroads benefited by "purchasing" forced convict labor. Joseph E. Brown of Georgia, once an antebellum governor of that state and now heavily invested in railroads and coal companies, was happy to employ convict laborers at seven cents a day. In 1880 Tom Watson, a candidate for the Georgia legislature, attacked the convict lease system for exploitation: "Men of high standing and great influence, governors and United States Senators, were making fortunes out of it."

The political onslaught complete, southern whites moved to limit freedom in other ways. Without the captivity of slavery to define race relations, southern whites took their cue from northern examples and redefined race relations in terms of segregation. In 1890, for the first time in its history, the city of New Orleans segregated trains. African Americans fought the law in court. On June 9, 1892, the *New Orleans Daily Picayune* reported that "a Negro named Plessy was arrested . . . for violating section 2 of act 111 of 1890, relative to separate coaches." Homer Plessy, an activist and a member of the New Orleans Committee of Citizens (a group of African American Republicans, former Union soldiers, and local writers and businessmen), volunteered to challenge the constitutionality of segregated transportation. The chosen individual had to be white enough to purchase a first-class ticket and black enough to be arrested for sitting in that car. Plessy, born in 1863, son of a free black mother and father, was the man for the job. He had grown up in a New Orleans where he was free to vote, to engage in politics, and to ride any train and streetcar. The Civil War, emancipation, constitutional amendments, and civil rights acts had promised a life of freedom—a promise that was now increasingly empty.

Plessy's arrest went according to plan, and *Plessy v. Ferguson* worked its way though the court system, reaching the Supreme Court in 1896. In ruling against the plaintiff, the Supreme Court, while not using the exact words, instituted the infamous dictum of "separate but equal." Justice Henry Billings Brown presented the majority opinion. The Court found that segregation was legal as long as the separate facilities for blacks were not inferior to those for whites. "The most common instance of this," he wrote, "is connected with the establishment of separate schools for white and colored children, which has been held to be a valid exercise of the legislative power even by courts of States where the political rights of the colored race have been longest and most earnestly enforced." In refuting the argument that white privilege deprived African Americans of due process, he stated that they are "not lawfully entitled to the reputation of being a white man."

Only one judge on the Supreme Court dissented from the majority opinion: Justice John Harlan, the son of a former North Carolina slave-holding family. Himself from Lincoln's birth state of Kentucky, Harlan alone articulated Lincoln's vision of freedom: "Indeed, such legislation as that here in question is inconsistent not only with that equality of rights which pertains to citizenship, national and state, but with the personal liberty enjoyed by every one within the United States." Harlan echoed Lincoln in claiming that the preservation of one's own liberty depended upon the willingness to grant others' liberty, but it was a crabbed echo because Harlan could not embrace this notion without caveat: "There is a race so different from our own that we do not permit those belonging to it to become citizens of the United States. Persons belonging to it are, with few exceptions, absolutely excluded from our country. I allude to the Chinese race." Harlan found it offensive that, while the Chinese were allowed to ride on white train cars, African Americans who "risked their lives for the preservation of the Union" and supposedly have "all the legal rights that belong to white citizens" could not.

However incomplete his understanding of Lincoln's new meaning of liberty, Harlan did not mistake its likely momentum. "The judgment this day rendered will, in time, prove to be quite as pernicious," the justice predicted, "as the decision made by this tribunal in the Dred Scott Case." But whereas the *Dred Scott* decision had aroused an uproar, no political leader used the egregiousness of this ruling to mobilize opposition as a political issue.

Many religious leaders did oppose segregation as "undemocratic." The American Missionary Association advocated "securing the full rights and privileges of citizenship of Negro Americans and their complete integration in American life." In 1896 the organization was successful in contesting a Florida law that prohibited integrated schools. This was the last political hurrah of the hardworking, well-meaning, sometime prejudiced, and usually paternalistic organization, even as it continued to concentrate on educational opportunities.

Lincoln's vision of a new birth of freedom was short-lived because both North and South widely and profoundly accepted racial hierarchy. In every section of the country virulent racism replaced memories of Lincoln's call for harmony. The madness went beyond legislative setbacks during Reconstruction. If African Americans were theoretically not good enough to vote and hold office, whites felt the need to exclude them from juries, from jobs, from schools, from neighborhoods. If African Americans were theoretically corrupt as a people, whites felt the need to isolate them, to deny them health care, even to kill them. Gradually a complete legal institutionalization of discrimination heralded a new era of race relations. The color line was nationally drawn as Jim Crow replaced slavery. Throughout the North and West, and mostly in the Midwest, towns that had welcomed African Americans during the more idealistic Civil War and Reconstruction years now turned them away. Moreover, whites often decided to instigate an exodus of their African American population by orchestrating attacks on the black community or a highly publicized lynching. These "sundown towns," in which no black person—or maybe Asian or Hispanic—was allowed after sundown, proliferated after 1890.

Throughout the country lynching kept the political, economic, and social system in place. Newspapers condoned mob action against accused African Americans, especially alleged rapists, calling the white lynchers "exponents of a law that is older than governments, and more venerable than the constitution of states." Lynching would be repeated beyond anything imaginable until even a look the wrong way or an accidental touch precipitated mob action. In South Carolina, Governor Ben Tillman proclaimed, "Governor as I am, I would lead a mob to lynch the negro who ravishes a white woman." One hundred nine African Americans were recorded as lynched in South Carolina from 1882 to 1903. Four hundred sixty-two African Americans were lynched in Mississippi between 1882 and 1930. Between 1890 and the 1920s Texans lynched 309 men, mostly African Americans. The North also perpetrated lynchings, not to keep African Americans in their place but to warn them to stay away. In the West lynching focused on Chinese workers. Nationwide the 1890s saw an average of 187 lynchings each year; likely a greater number went unrecorded.

During these many years of oppression, African Americans regularly sought to assert their civil and voting rights but found freedom stymied at all turns. Barred from many occupations, they were disparaged for not having good jobs. Not allowed to live in decent neighborhoods, they were condemned for living in slums. Not allowed to attend good schools, they were censured for not being well educated. Not allowed to see a doctor or enter hospitals, they were criticized for being sickly. The web of oppression was tightly interwoven.

The federal government failed to enforce its own laws or to protect the rights of African American citizens. But while the 1865 Freedmen's Bureau Act, the various Reconstruction Acts, Force Acts, and Civil Rights Acts, and the Fourteenth and Fifteenth amendments did not produce equality, African Americans made considerable gains that were to last them through the following years of trial. Landownership did increase. Learning and institutions of higher education continued to grow. If the outward effects of reform decreased, the inner spirit of the freedmen and -women continued to thrive. Political equality, economic opportunity, and the respect of white society could be, and were, taken away, but the knowledge of freedom and its potential could not be. Just as important, African Americans had created an interracial democracy, and that experience gave the community hope for the future even in the bitter nadir of race relations. Evidence in Reconstruction North Carolina, South Carolina, Louisiana, coastal Georgia, southern Mississippi, and Texas suggests the possibility of genuine interracial alliances between freedpeople and poorer whites. Local alliances, compromises, truces, and pragmatic deals might have functioned to link these two groups together politically—their cultural ties were always greater and more complex than either side allowed—had it not been for the political terrorism directed against Reconstruction efforts by the resurgent planter class.

In spite of the many disappointments in the years following Reconstruction, many in the African American community persevered. This hope for America's "better angels" was part and parcel of the Age of Lincoln. Continuing a millennial tradition, these hopeful people saw themselves as part of God's plan for history. Like the Israelites, they had been delivered from slavery, and also like the Israelites, they still had to face hunger and thirst in the desert, to walk through snakes, and ultimately to conquer giants before they could enter the Promised Land. Much as Lincoln understood that the United States was the last best hope of earth, they looked to the new millennium. The successes of Reconstruction had only hinted at the millennial promise in Revelation 5:9–10, which foresaw that every ethnicity and nation would one day live together in harmony and peace.

Thirteen

The New Colossus

ON OCTOBER 28, 1886, more than one million Americans, white and black, many of them immigrants newly arrived, lined New York's Fifth Avenue to share in a celebration of liberty. Marching in a grand parade to the city's teeming harborfront, citizens and dignitaries traveled by ferry to tiny Bedloe's Island to unveil a gigantic, gleaming copper statue, 150 feet tall, on a site selected by General William Tecumseh Sherman. *Liberty Enlightening the World* was a gift to the United States from France, which was recently vanquished by Bismarck's aristocratic Prussians, increasingly unconvinced of democracy's virtues, and riven by all manner of social and economic divisions. The gesture, financed by lotteries and sporting events, was as much a backhanded colonialist slap at Turkey for the marvel it hoped to plant at the mouth of the new Suez Canal, *Egypt Carrying the Light of Asia*, as it was a proud remembrance of an enduring republican ideal.

Imagined in 1865 as a symbol of the love of liberty as shared by France and America, the statue was the idea of Edouard-René Laboulaye, an ardent supporter of the Union at a time when the French monarchy unofficially supported the Confederacy. The *Times* of London cheekily wondered "why liberty should have been sent from France, which has too little, to America, which has too much." For some Frenchmen at least, such as Victor Hugo, the idea of liberty was an ideal to be constantly sought. The great French novelist never glimpsed how the emerging egalitarianism of the Age of Lincoln was being turned back, but in his awe upon seeing the Statue of Liberty's completion in France, Hugo pronounced, "The idea—it is everything."

In the two decades intervening between Laboulaye's imagined gesture of 1865 and its delivery of 1886, America itself seemed to slip far from the pinnacle of Lincoln's triumph. Then the nation's leaders had been upright religious men, idealistic abolitionists, egalitarian intellectuals, high-minded statesmen, and vigorous captains of industry. Now freedom's fortunes, such as they were, seemed bound up with the success of narrow-minded corporate leaders, chiseling lawyers, sneaking speculators, and political bagmen. The golden age of the millennium was nowhere in sight. Instead, America's greatest writer, Mark Twain, a man at once more sadly sentimental and more misanthropically cynical than any author before or since, sneered at life in "The Gilded Age," when men dreamed only of millions and—like his foolish, wayward schoolboy Tom Sawyer—had no inkling of what to do with such riches once gained. At century's end New York Tammany ward heeler George Washington Plunkitt could trumpet his success as a champion of "honest graft" as a positive good. Even as he helped loot the city's treasury—on a minor scale, certainly—he made sure to share his windfall with local constituents, creating jobs, doling out rewards, and greasing palms. "I seen my opportunities and I took 'em," he pronounced. More than one immigrant who passed through Ellis Island in these years must have imagined that those words were in fact the legend inscribed at the base of the Statue of Liberty that welcomed them to the New Jerusalem of the Almighty Dollar.

The pulsating belief in an imminent millennium that dynamized antebellum culture was not so much defeated by the slaughter of civil war and Reconstruction as it was secularized. In the years after Appomattox, northern white Protestants, horrified by the cost of restoring the Union and abolishing slavery, cast off their grand expectation of Christian perfection and abandoned the task of bringing on God's Kingdom. A growing middle class determined instead to protect their earthly possessions. Newcomers arriving by the shipload also sought to cash in on American economic opportunity. They did not come to empty their lives of sin, but to fill it with material blessings. Many were not Protestants, but Catholics and Jews. No longer would the northern ecclesiastic community speak of millennial longings in near concert, hereafter restricting themselves instead to the more incrementalist need to uphold a stricter reliance on law and order.

By 1886 America had passed from the hands of its politicians, with dreams of civil service reform, fair tariffs, and sound monetary policy, into the hands of ruthless new men of action and ambition—Andrew Carnegie, John D. Rockefeller, Cornelius Vanderbilt, Leland Stanford, and Tom Scott. At the end of the century men such as these, meshing corporate leadership, criminal violence, and political corruption, were the new "robber barons" who shaped the nation, hand-picked its presidents, charted its economic course, and condemned millions to lives of poverty and toil. Freedom in this new age was bound up irretrievably with the pursuit of wealth through technological progress, and along with wealth came a liberty from restraint that many thought could only end in libertinism, vice, and cultural chaos.

France's monumental gift needed a pricey pedestal, to the cost of $100,000. Raising those funds seemed unattainable—the rich simply sat on their hands—until the publisher of the *New York World*, Joseph Pulitzer, commenced patriotic advertising to encourage ordinary people to donate funds: "We want the Pedestal built with the dimes of the people, not with the dollars of the rich few." Between May and August 1885 his appeals helped raise the money as well as boost subscriptions to his paper. Upon meeting the financial goal, he congratulated "the toiling millions" and their "faith, no less than the self-sacrifice, which makes Republics possible."

To interpret the monument, builders turned to a recent sonnet by Emma Lazarus, a sickly New York girl of Sephardic Jewish parentage, whose cousin, Benjamin Cardozo, would go on to serve as a Supreme Court justice in 1932. Outraged by the plight of eastern Europe's Jewry, she dreamed of a homeland where the oppressed and downtrodden might build a new Holy City. Lazarus died in 1887 of Hodgkin's disease before either her activism or her art could reach full flower, but the vision she expressed in her poem, "The New Colossus," expressed millennial hopes for a new century. Inscribed on the pedestal of the Statue of Liberty, her vision offered powerful words of greeting to those traditionally considered the least of mankind:

Give me your tired, your poor,
Your huddled masses yearning to breathe free,
The wretched refuse of your teeming shore.
Send these, the homeless, tempest-tost to me.

Seldom in poetry, never in politics, was such a defiant boast offered. At a time when all the world was mad for notions of Wagnerian *völkisch* purity, social Darwinism, and racial superiority, America called not for the best the world offered but for its worst—the lowest, the most despised, the ones who understood most keenly what freedom pointed toward because they had scarcely glimpsed it. These, at least, would know how to fight for what they wanted. The statue welcomed immigrants to a land of freedom and opportunity, and that appeal, rooted in the Age of Lincoln, drew millions, but in the 1880s and 1890s they had to be tough enough to handle it.

Americans at that time hardly held forth the hand of fellowship. Immigration swelled America's population in 1890 to almost sixty-three million people, double that of 1860, despite the more than six hundred thousand Civil War deaths. The rising tide, many natives feared, would dilute national strength, sap economic vitality, and weaken the foundations of family, church, and community. From every land immigrants brought seemingly odd habits and a clannishness that repelled many of the native born. Increasingly natives leaned on the old prejudices of the Know-Nothings and their sort. And while Europe's "refuse" still managed to flood in ever greater numbers through New York, Philadelphia, Baltimore, and New Orleans, the nation as a whole, but particularly the West Coast, turned back the "Yellow Peril" of Chinese immigrants. By vastly restricting the flow of temporary workers and settlers from China, Japan, and elsewhere, white Americans, even as they violently established colonies in the Philippines and trading settlements on the Asian mainland, kept wages high on the Pacific Coast, and maintained the culture "pure" of racial mixing. Most of this was the work of ordinary men fearful of where the future was leading and dreading the collapse of their local communities besieged by strange, alien outsiders.

One of the orators at the Statue of Liberty's unveiling, railroad lawyer Chauncy Depew, warned of the growing difficulties of change and assimilation, of "the problems of labor and capital, of social regeneration and moral growth, of property and poverty." He recommended "the benign influences of enlightened law-making and law-abiding liberty" without recourse to "anarchists and bombs," such as had exploded in Chicago that summer. Freedom, as Lincoln understood it and as Americans were increasingly aware, was at every moment inextricably intertwined with the preservation of order.

The end of the Civil War could not return the nation to its antebellum culture. In its aftermath some Americans wondered how much of their way of life had been lost. Simplicity, mutuality, and trust seemed gone. In 1871, when a disillusioned Walt Whitman published *Democratic Vistas*, he lamented that democracy had failed in the United States and predicted that it would continue to fail unless American citizens made a radical recommitment to personal integrity and brotherhood. "Never was there, perhaps, more hollowness of heart than at present," he wrote. "Genuine belief seems to have left us." The rapid expanse of secular culture and the ethos of money-grubbing left the country with "little or no soul," Whitman believed. The shallow hurrahs of reunion and the heedless pursuit of dollars masked a total failure of the millennialist impulse.

As northern communities grew in size and local life became more complex, neighborhoods lost a feeling of independence. What autonomy could one citizen have amid business amalgamation and the concentration of government power? Abraham Lincoln had stubbornly refused to allow a government "of the people" to disintegrate, but Lincoln's millennial, providential assumptions, his view of equal opportunity, were contested nationwide—not just in the South.

The monstrous symbol of changed times was the locomotive. After the war, railroad building trussed together the shattered nation that Lincoln's war had won, and hundreds of millions of dollars of capital flowed into the coffers of nearly four hundred booming enterprises. Civil War generals became railroad executives and developers, and sturdy young veterans by the thousands revisited the long marches and outdoor life of military service by enlisting in the boisterous construction gangs that pushed trackage westward. Five years after Appomattox more nonfarming Americans were "working on the railroad" than in any other occupation. For most it seemed a harsh and dangerous life, mingling the low wages of capitalism with the gang labor and endless toil likened to slavery itself. To some, it seemed, servitude had been not so much vanquished by civil war as simply transformed. Cartoons depicted the railroad as Mary Shelley's man-made Frankenstein monster. Increasingly, men spoke of the "octopus" of capitalist domination, of railroad lines that promised liberation but too often served to ensnare and devour them.

For those who directed corporations like the Baltimore and Ohio (B&O), the Pennsylvania, or the Atchison, Topeka, and Santa Fe Railroad, trains promised wealth, high social status, and unrivaled political power. Thomas Alexander Scott, a twenty-seven-year-old station agent, rose to become general superintendent of the Pennsylvania Railroad through eight years of hard toil and careful study. Scott drove himself ruthlessly upward and had little compunction about pushing aside less ambitious men. By the time the Civil War broke out, Scott had become an expert on assembling, regulating, and coordinating dozens of trains, and his knowhow propelled him first to the company vice-presidency and then to a crucial role in mobilizing the nation's railroads behind the Union military effort. Under his management, federal troops and supplies had moved with speed and efficiency from point to point, gaining an element of disciplined regularity that the Confederates never matched. At war's end, Scott applied his business acumen and political connections to transforming the company he headed. In the space of a decade the Pennsylvania Railroad went from a local concern, stretching a mere four hundred miles, to the largest single corporation in the world, spanning fifteen states and swallowing up one-eighth of the total revenues of the railroad industry. Private credit reports described Scott: "The R R King of this country . . . has millions of money at his command & exerts a greater corporative influence than any man in the U.S."

Just as local ward heelers prospered by filching from city coffers and doling out graft to a broad circle of friends and supporters, Scott and his railroad grew by driving rival firms to the wall by cost-cutting, swallowing them up, then raising prices to compensate for the expense of his buccaneering schemes. To facilitate these maneuvers and put a respectable public face on plundering, Scott appointed state and national luminaries such as John Sherman and Samuel Tilden to the railroad's board of directors, paying handsome salaries for their support. Scott used new trust laws (pioneered by John D. Rockefeller for his oil companies) to organize his enterprises vertically and to protect them from taxes. More important, Scott prodded the Pennsylvania legislature to write new laws allowing the creation of the holding company—a wholly new, and to many contemporaries, alarming entity: a business concern that produced nothing, bought and sold nothing, and had no human share-holders or assets of its own. The general population understood little of what trusts or holding companies were or what they meant for the cor-poratization of America.

Through the deft use of this legislation, Scott used the resources of the Pennsylvania Railroad to absorb rival lines, then gathered the reins of power in these firms into his own hands, to rule or ruin them as he saw fit. Thus Scott snatched up the Union Pacific Railroad, served as president for one tumultuous year, then cashed out his holdings at a tidy profit. These he used to capture the Texas and Pacific Railroad; other tentacles reached out to purchase newspapers and magazines, to bribe government officials, and to invest in banks, steel mills, and other con-cerns. In 1873, when Scott threw a dinner party in Harrisburg, he was able to assemble in one room a large share of the wealth and power of the entire nation, and that little circle of Carnegies and Pullmans, Cookes and Goulds, was eager to call the former station agent their friend and mentor. In a real sense, it was America itself that had been railroaded.

The railroad boom went hand in hand with a transformation in American agriculture that still ripples down to the modern era. Whereas in 1820 more than 90 percent of Americans worked in agriculture, by 1870 that figure was just over 50 percent, and by 1890 for the first time the cen-sus noted that a majority of gainfully employed persons were working in nonagricultural pursuits. Prior to the Civil War the self-sufficient family farm had been the emblem of freedom and independence, and landown-ership was an essential ingredient in the Republican political philosophy of both Jefferson and Lincoln alike. Between 1850 and 1870 the number of household heads with property remained at between 50 and 56 per-cent. After 1870 the number began to fall until in 1901 only 19 percent of U.S. families owned their own homes.

As some were losing land, others made good use of the railroads to in-crease their economic situation. From the Midwest to California railroads offered farmers a commercial outlet, encouraging cash crops, raising land values, and contributing to the consolidation of land in fewer hands. For larger holdings, farmers wanted more equipment, fertilizer, and pesticides, bought on credit. Tons of bird droppings excavated from the coastline of Peru and Ecuador revitalized the cotton lands of Georgia and South Carolina—and lined the pockets of venturesome New England shipping companies and local merchants. With these and similar developments farmers grew ever more dependent on national and international markets. Chicago shipped midwestern grain to the East Coast, where it was sent to Europe. By the early 1870s the development of refrigerated railroad cars gave rise to vast stockyards and slaughterhouses. In Chicago the Union Stockyards killed and processed more than a million hogs a year. There and in St. Louis, Cincinnati, and elsewhere such endeavors provided jobs as well as made meat affordable and available to a broad range of city dwellers.

Railroad standardization and the expansion of new trackage by more than thirty-five thousand miles between 1865 and 1873 transformed the culture of the West and the nation. In the 1870s 190 million new acres were put under cultivation. Kansas, Nebraska, the Dakotas, and Texas filled out at boom-time tempo. By 1880 the frontier line was jutting irregular fingers into the semiarid plains. Between 1889 and 1893 much of the Indian territory of Oklahoma was taken by white settlers in a wild melee of "Boomers" and "Sooners." Nine new states came into the Union between 1865 and 1890, and Secretary of State William Seward engineered the purchase of Alaska in anticipation of acquiring Canadian British Columbia. It was not would-be farmers, cowboys, and miners who spilled out of the burgeoning cities to settle the West. Most craftsmen and tradesmen remained too tied to local networks to risk the move; the unskilled simply lacked the means. It was, rather, bank tellers, junior clerks, assistant editors, pencil-pushers of every kind, the budding, grasping lower middle class and the newly arrived immigrants— the sort typified by William Faulkner's keen-eyed Snopes family or the pioneers of Willa Cather—who led the march to distant territory. Also moving west after the Civil War were about twenty-five thousand African Americans, making their homes in both rural and urban areas.

Western cities like Denver, Salt Lake City, and Portland grew to be great urban centers. San Francisco, with a population over two hundred thousand by 1870, was the fifteenth largest city in the United States. The "rugged individualism" of western settlers, outlaws, and near-outlaws who became fabulously wealthy went hand in hand with the intervention of the federal government's land grants and railroad subsidies. The U.S. military was the single largest employer in the Dakotas, Utah, Arizona, and New Mexico during this period. Few men or women succeeded out west by the strength of personal effort alone.

With government land grants and direct aid, railroads were given welfare allotments more grand than anything ever planned, let alone offered, to help newly freed slaves. Any objections went unheard as land grant policy forked over much of the acreage of the West to railroads. Railroad officials often played crucial roles in state political parties, selecting nominees, sponsoring events, and funding political races. Governments in turn did the railroads' bidding, confiscating property as needed, passing legislation limiting workers' compensation, using courts and troops to keep labor pliant and toiling. In the South railroad companies even coordinated with Ku Klux Klan leaders to ensure that their black construction crews would be able to work without interference.

In the West, railroads supported the new cattle industry that had fed vast armies. In Texas, Richard King amassed a ranching empire larger than the state of Rhode Island, and not through grit and stubbornness alone. In a setting where vertical integration of industry was both dubious and risky, he succeeded by making his trail bosses the owners of his herds at the beginning of the hundred-day drive to market each year. Thus segmenting the production process, he both transferred the burden of economic uncertainty to other shoulders and created a network of loyal clients and allies he could call upon for favors and support.

In the North, structures and infrastructures were changing dynamically. Speed, opportunity, knowledge, and choice seemed to grow beyond all imagining. A great symbol of this revolution was the fabulous transatlantic cable. Attempted on the eve of the Civil War, it took four failures before a successful message was finally transmitted between England and Canada on August 16, 1858: "Glory to God in the highest, and on earth, peace, good will to men." The cable ceased working shortly thereafter. A successful attempt in July 1866 meant financial messages could flash between New York and London by Morse code in real time, removing all manner of uncertainty and irregularity in transactions between Old World and New. Along every railroad line moving westward, telegraph wires snaked through cities and hamlets, passing news and inquiries faster than the swiftest locomotive. By the American centennial virtually the whole nation, England, and much of continental Europe had been linked by wire and rail into a single network of finance and communication. More distant sites in Asia, Africa, and Australia were still connected to the rest of the world only by ship, but the development of massive, steam-driven screw propeller vessels and the digging of the Suez Canal, completed in 1869, greatly reduced the uncertainty of long-distance voyages and the passage of information from port to port. In the same way the transit of political news and social information of all sorts multiplied in speed and volume. News of the Prussian victory over the French at Sedan, Henry Stanley's meeting with David Livingstone in the jungles of Africa, and the collapse of the Taiping Rebellion in far-off China became the stuff of dinner-table conversation within days, even hours of their occurrence. Even where Americans still dwelt in narrow, self-contained "island communities," these rapid changes gave them a firmer sense of where they stood and a clearer picture of where they were headed. Even as they maintained the independence of separateness, most citizens were joined to a common, progressive, transnational enterprise as never before.

Simpler shifts produced more impressive changes at the local level. For women of the northern urban working class, world news was interesting, especially if it involved a home country, but it was the grueling toil of domestic labor that dominated their consciousness: distances to be trudged through filthy, dangerous streets to do the daily shopping, the tedious hours of carrying water, bucket by bucket, up narrow stairs to do the washing and cooking each day, and the difficulty of locating safe, cheap supplies of food, wood, and coal and of continually cleaning the soot and grime that caked everything, spreading disease and attracting rats and roaches. And yet all saw improvements as basic structural changes after the Civil War transformed urban life. Cleaner, better maintained, gas-lit streets made venturing outdoors a more pleasant experience, and better policing made it safer, too. New waterworks and sewage plants brought fresh, clean water right into the household—or at least to more conveniently located public pumps—and carried away domestic waste. Inside the home, running water, gas lighting, free deliveries of food and fuel, and

the installation of bathrooms transformed the very meaning of domesticity for most and vastly enriched the quality of family life. For ordinary
men and women, such basic structural changes represented a transformation of everyday life, a comprehensive, government-driven emancipation
less profound than what Lincoln proclaimed but arguably more thoroughgoing. That it was a by-product of other priorities was not lost on most
Americans.

During and after the war the pattern of government help for corporations continued, and the expansion of public responsibilities increased
the amount of money handled. Almost inevitably, preferential government support divided winners from losers in the new postwar regime as
corporations vied for benefits of state aid and tariff protection. As communities bargained against one another to bring in business, widespread
corruption flourished. The Democratic Party's Tweed Ring in New
York, for example, oversaw the construction of the New York County
Courthouse, stipulated to cost no more than $250,000. In the first year
of construction alone, however, the city appropriated $1 million, much
of which went to Tweed's organization. Final costs topped $13 million.

Bill Tweed, Jay Gould, and their ilk seemed meritorious when
weighed against the example of more desperate men like Daniel Drew and
the reckless "Diamond Jim" Fisk. In the latter cases individualism and
selfishness had simply run amok. Born in upstate New York in 1797, Dan
Drew imbibed little of the millennial spirit that vitalized that region in
the antebellum era. When others were concerned with education and
reform, Drew kept his eye on personal financial uplift, parlaying a cattle-
driving business into a successful steamship line, then turning to broker-
age and stock speculation. Across a long and rapacious life, Drew never
progressed beyond the simplest capitalist dictates—buying cheap and
selling dear—and he never learned to moderate his appetites. By 1857 he
had become obsessed with the possibility of turning quick profits by ma-
nipulating railroad stock, a plan he pursued by craft, insider trading, and
simple fraud over the next two decades. Others, younger and more ruthless, allied with him and conspired against him, and stock prices reared
and plunged in consequence. The savings and livelihoods of tens of
thousands of ordinary workers and citizens hung on the outcome of these
raids, and ultimately Drew himself went from scheming millionaire to

friendless bankrupt, a king's ransom having trickled through his hands. His penniless death in 1879 was the last exclamation point to a deeply cautionary tale.

More instructive still was the fate of Big Jim Fisk, the Vermont boy who ran away to join the circus in the early 1840s. A further apprenticeship as a peddler and salesman prepared him for sharp dealing in government contracts during the Civil War, cotton smuggling, and speculating on stocks of the riskiest sort. "Jubilee Jim" soon became Drew's ablest assistant, passing on into alliance with the still more ambitious Jay Gould and Bill Tweed as the prospects for profit shifted. Individualistic, striving men who had risen up, Lincoln-like, from rural poverty to great wealth and national stature, they believed, like Whigs of old, that government should aid and support their efforts, vital as they were to reconstructing the nation and driving the economy forward. But whereas Lincoln understood that the rule of law had to direct man's obligations to man, these new financiers embraced a dog-eat-dog mentality of modern life and felt no such obligation or constraint. Fisk and Gould triggered a fiscal crisis in September 1869 with their bid to corner the gold market. When Grant learned of their scheme, he thwarted it, but Fisk was not worried. While smaller investors in gold lost their all, Fisk and Gould managed to sell their gold for a large profit. Fisk simply went looking for other sheep to fleece. As opposed to penny-pinchers like Rockefeller, Fisk treated economic enterprise as a grand and rambunctious celebration, an opportunity for living large and spending freely. If money flowed like water around him, more tended to flow toward than away from him, and that was all the calculus that capitalism required. To cooler heads like Cornelius Vanderbilt and even hard-bitten Tom Scott, however, it was clear that plungers like Fisk gambled too wildly to last long. When a business partner finally shot Diamond Jim over some hanky-panky with a Broadway showgirl, most were surprised only that he had lasted to the ripe old age of thirty-eight.

During the Civil War laborers fought for a republic of free labor, one in which they could be economically independent, but the very world that had made such an ideology possible was passing away forever. Many urban workingmen noticed that defeating the slaveocracy had not brought them greater freedom but had only fostered a new industrial aristocracy. The very war measures that Lincoln promoted to bring about Union victory served to accelerate the social changes that made the Republican dream of propertied independence more difficult to obtain. Before the Civil War working people had toiled to meet their needs and yield a small measure of comfort once their labors were ended. The measure of freedom for most working people was the degree of skill they possessed. Journeymen generally set their own pace on shop floors, divided the work as they saw fit, and trained and disciplined underlings by their own standards. In many cases workers provided their own tools and played important roles in design, prerogatives that employers appreciated. Now large and unskilled work crews, facing little hope of advancement, proved apt to stop for a smoke, go off to the local saloon for a pick-me-up, or call it quits on a hot day. When bosses stuck their noses in, workers sent up an almighty squawk. What employers called steadiness, workers called slavery. What seemed like independent manhood to the toiler looked like impudent rebellion to the boss. There was no middle ground because the issue was not hours and wages and conditions alone—it was also freedom and masculine identity, matters on which any compromise amounted to total collapse. One labor newspaper questioned whether workers enjoyed independence at all, for "capital has now the same control over us that the aristocracy of England had at the time of the Revolution." By 1880, as farm ownership in the North and Midwest spiraled downward and young men and women entered urban stores, factories, and workshops, laboring for the benefit of another—increasingly, a corporate other—in return for a monetary reward measured in pieces of commodities produced or pieces of time yielded up had become a lifelong prospect for many. Indeed, as unemployment mounted and immigrants poured in from distant lands, many were happy to have a chance to gain "steady work."

In some ways the Civil War solidified the northern white working class. Germans, Irish, English, the native-born, and others had fought together in the contest, and this shared experience helped ease ethnic tensions. Many labor unions spawned during the Civil War cut across ethnic lines but not racial. In the North and South, especially in urban areas, white laborers used their whiteness to inform class identity, and discrimination and exclusion of blacks and Asians from trade unions became the rule. Women were also not welcome in most labor unions. They were competition for men, worked for lower wages, and interfered with a white man's right to a higher "family wage." Women's pursuit of individual freedom clashed with community values of order and the manly independence of the breadwinner. Almost universally, in northern and southern cities, employers and managers successfully divided the workplace along racial, gender, and occupational lines. Among all workers, regardless of whether they were children or adults, men or women, white or black, capitalists looked for the lowest wage and the minimum obligation.

Capitalists were only too happy to leave workers to their own devices once they walked out the factory gate. How they fed and sheltered themselves with the wages they earned, whether they rested or caroused, whether they took ill or died, was none of the boss's concern. One of the principal economic reasons for the triumph of capitalism in the New World was precisely its refusal to worry itself with the well-being of any except those who did a day's work—and then only for the term of that day. Bosses bought an individual's labor-power for a given period of time, expecting to wring as much production out of it as they could. During the war northern bosses offered patriotic justifications for the "stretch-out" and the "speed-up" of the labor process itself.

At the war's conclusion, bosses continued to take more control. Traditionally ordinary citizens had contested that control, defining their freedom by the labor of their own hands. American postwar workers increasingly, however, yielded up that ground, defining work as a species of unfreedom, something to suffer through. As never before in American life, ordinary people came to focus their attention on leisure as a strategy of identity and self-worth. Freedom became profoundly connected with the time one spent away from work, pursuing private concerns in the few hours left over after work and sleep. Certainly to a workingman of the Jacksonian era, or to Abraham Lincoln himself, such a change would have seemed bizarre if not utterly monstrous.

Not all working people yielded up workplace control so easily. Skilled workers continued to defend their control over work processes. Neither did workers abandon the link between labor and political citizenship so readily. In the West, Dennis Kearney's Workingmen's Party focused on protecting labor's rights by attacking Asian "coolies," accused of driving down wages and conditions. Just as Klansmen believed that social peace depended on pushing African Americans toward a servitude similar to slavery, California workingmen claimed that, if class war was to be averted, "the Chinese must go!" In northeastern Pennsylvania, worker cohesion catalyzed the Ancient Order of Hibernians (AOH), which opposed Civil War conscription and sheltered Irish coal miners who organized as the Molly Maguires. Just as the Mollies had done for decades with English landlords in Ireland, they waged in Pennsylvania's coal country a course of intimidation and murder for more than two decades. When Irish miners considered that management had made an unfair decision in terms of hiring or payment, they sent an anonymous threatening note, seeking rectification. Lacking a timely response, members met, decided on a course of action, and meted out rough justice, up to assassination.

By the 1860s the unity and militancy of the Mollies had migrated from the mines to the ballot box. Through intimidation and violence, Irish miners' advocates, usually AOH men, "won" election to key sheriffs' positions, judgeships, and other local offices. Now when workers struck, coal bosses could not call on the law, as they had previously, to send the men back underground. Eventually coal and railroad companies broke workers' control by infiltrating the secret society with Pinkerton spies. In a series of trials promoted and argued by company lawyers and executives, dozens of Irish miners were prosecuted for murders dating back a decade and more. Ultimately nearly forty Molly Maguires were hanged before corporate dominance was established in the late 1870s.

Some argued that the failure of working-class resistance lay in the local scope of its politics. In the early 1870s, aging idealists like William Lloyd Garrison, Wendell Phillips, and Charles Sumner clung to Lincoln's call for harmony between capital and labor and hoped that the growing conflict could be defused by education, moral uplift, and honest dialogue. Others saw little use in such measures. Hard-bitten conservatives like John D. Rockefeller and laissez-faire liberal intellectuals like E. L. Godkin of *The Nation* united in a belief that support for capitalist development would raise all boats on a rising economic tide. By this standard, clean government, sound money, and common sense offered the best course for boss and worker alike. Common sense, needless to say, meant that working people would put their shoulder to the wheel and be grateful. With luck and pluck even the poorest might rise up. The penniless Scots boy Andrew Carnegie, after all, parlayed hard work into boundless corporate wealth. Even a rail splitter, with hard work and self-learning, had become the president.

Carnegie may have been the richest man in America, but he was not alone in being one of the new wealthy. In 1860, 41 millionaires, most of them southern planters, lived in the United States. In 1870, 545 millionaires lived mostly in the Northeast. By 1897 the estimate was about 3,000 millionaires, and by 1922 the number was 5,904. Wealth was also more concentrated. In 1860 the wealthiest 10 percent owned 73 percent of the wealth; by 1912 the wealthiest 10 percent owned 90 percent. Carnegie gave much of his wealth to philanthropy, libraries in particular. Other wealthy people gave to higher education, fostering a new birth of educational opportunities in America. Even middle classes gave to the arts, to museums, to theaters, to symphonies, and as a consequence city life became more interesting.

On the other side, American workingmen grew somewhat doubtful of the possibilities of individual self-improvement. In the decade after the Civil War skilled laborers clustered into a host of new unions—the Order of the Knights of St. Crispin (shoemakers), the Brotherhood of Locomotive Engineers, the Amalgamated Association of Iron and Steel Workers, and dozens more. Although most groups remained focused on particular crafts, they realized from the first that the only way to resist capital's encroachments was through a "big tent" approach. Founded in 1866, the National Labor Union (NLU) sought to draw all craft workers under its banner, championing the cause of an eight-hour workday: "The first and great necessity of the present to free labour of this country from capitalist slavery, is the passing of a law by which eight hours shall be the normal working day in all States of the American Union." At its height nearly 650,000 Americans claimed membership, including those united in a segregated affiliate for "colored" workers. By 1872, however, the NLU had imploded over the leadership's insistence on using political activism in place of direct action in the workplace to win its goals. Many disaffected NLU members moved over to the rival Knights of Labor, a broadly inclusive group that admitted blacks, women, and immigrants but not Asians and that excepted only bankers, liquor manufacturers, lawyers, and gamblers from the list of "productive" occupations worthy of membership. Here, too, however, although union members argued for the eight-hour day, the abolition of child labor, and equal pay for equal work, they were loath to confront capital's power directly. In this view—not so much conservative as simply realistic—government-sponsored arbitration held a better chance for success than going on strike.

To a still more radical minority, such well-mannered combinations served only to betray the interests of the working class and delay the mighty conflict between capital and labor that was sure to come. Since the late 1840s socialist and Marxist immigrants like Joseph Weydemeyer and Wilhelm Weitling had propounded the doctrine of class struggle, first in opposition to slavery's regime, then in response to capitalism's startling hegemony. Their numbers remained few, especially outside the ranks of German and French immigrants, and their influence in the labor movement was minuscule. But to men of property they seemed like the mustard seed of biblical prophecy—small and insignificant, but with potential to spread rapidly and almost impossible to control. Those who scoffed at their tiny numbers were quickly reminded of the monster rallies of the Chartists and the Land Leaguers that shook Britain in the 1840s and 1850s, the "red '48ers" who had almost set the European continent aflame with their views of socialism, or the militants of the Paris Commune who in 1871 had raised the red flag in support of the redress of debts, the separation of church and state, and women's suffrage. A fear of foreign fanatics led Americans to overlook the still more frightening fact that communitarianism, socialism, and democratic commonwealth were all profoundly native beliefs, deep-rooted in their own history and culture. What, after all, had Lincoln appealed for in his call for "a new birth of freedom" if not that a "government of the people, by the people, for the people" would not allow self-interest and individualism to trample the rights of Americans as a whole?

In 1876 an obscure meeting in Newark, New Jersey, drew together leftists, egalitarians, and oddballs—mostly native-born Americans—into a loose national confederation called the Workingmen's Party of America, rechristened the Socialist Labor Party the following year. Before Daniel De Leon took the reins fourteen years later, the party's Marxist orientation remained vague and undirected; from the beginning, however, the party made its purpose clear. Like the abolitionists, their cause was not to mend the breach they found between capital and labor. That was a hopeless, pointless task. They were revolutionists bent on overthrowing a new system of "wage" slavery, whether by the means of Lincoln or of John Brown.

Such extreme measures seemed doubly necessary in the rocky years after 1873. That spring the industrialized world slipped into a long depression, beginning with the collapse of the Vienna stock exchange, which curtailed credit, threw millions of men out of work, and raised an economic storm around the globe that lasted into the 1890s. In America the effects of European financial reverses were sharp and sudden, as credit-driven railroads, banks, and other industries found their loans abruptly demanded for payment. By 1876 fully one-quarter of American railroads and more than eighteen thousand factories and financial institutions had gone bankrupt, turning tens of thousands of skilled laborers into penniless tramps. As men roamed the countryside begging for work at any wage, those who still had homes and jobs watched them fearfully. As unemployment nudged 15 percent, those who had been productive workers, household heads, and citizens a few months earlier were now seen as dangerous outcasts, shabby aliens, lurking villains. Sales of handguns, for men and women both, soared as householders' dread fantasies of invasion and robbery ran wild. Such fears were exacerbated by the railroads themselves, who sought to secure their own survival by cutting wages and swallowing up their weakest competitors. Pay packets shrank by almost half at the same time that even the most saving and thrifty of working people discovered that banks like Jay Cooke's booming concern had actually squandered their careful deposits on speculative ventures. It was one thing for the careless and the profligate to suffer when hard times hit—that was the way of the world; but for thousands of Americans who had toiled and scrimped to save for a small home or education for their children, the ethical moorings of the national enterprise seemed to have suddenly disintegrated.

In 1876 disintegration, defeat, and depression were pushed aside in the grand celebration of the nation's hundredth birthday. Frederick Douglass was invited to give an oration at the unveiling of the Freedmen's Monument in Washington, D.C. Douglass did not shy away from Lincoln's prejudice but put it into context because of his accomplishments. Under Lincoln's presidency, African Americans "saw ourselves gradually lifted from the depths of slavery to the heights of liberty and manhood." They saw prejudice fade away as two hundred thousand African American soldiers fought for "liberty and union under the national flag." They saw full recognition of "the black republic of Hayti, the special object of slaveholding aversion and horror." The Haitian minister, "a colored gentleman," was "duly received here in the city of Washington." "Though Mr. Lincoln shared the prejudices of his white fellow-countrymen against the Negro," Douglass approved of Lincoln's administration: "It is hardly necessary to say that in his heart of hearts he loathed and hated slavery."

In nearby Philadelphia in May of that same year, President Grant and Emperor Dom Pedro of Brazil opened the grand international exhibition at the American Centennial Celebration. The one-hundredth birthday party for the democracy showed no hesitation in celebrating America's new destiny, now one of power and technology. Self-congratulation that May of 1876 took no notice of either rampant northern unemployment and unrest or of the racial violence taking place throughout the southern states. White organizers kept African Americans off planning committees and construction crews. The Emancipation Proclamation did receive some notice in the Art Gallery of the Centennial where a sculpture by Italian Francesco Pezzicar attracted interest. "The Freed Slave" stood proudly, gazing into the future, one hand outstretched with manacle broken, the other holding the famous proclamation. Viewers enjoyed a sculpture by African American Edmonia Lewis, "The Death of Cleopatra," and African American painter Edward Bannister won an award for his "Under the Oaks." None of the actual exhibits featured African American culture. Only one display hired African Americans— a "Southern Restaurant" with music by "old-time plantation darkies." Neither were they hired as security guards; that job went to unemployed white members of the Grand Army of the Republic, an organization of white and black Union veterans in mostly segregated units.

Between eight and ten million visitors were amazed at the various exhibits: telephones, typewriters, electric lights, a "new floor-cloth called linoleum." Despite worry over economic depression, despite all the talk of graft and corruption that littered the public press, there seemed little doubt that the nation was speeding forward to unimagined prosperity and power. The most popular exhibit was the Corliss machine, the seven-hundred-ton, forty-foot-high, fourteen-hundred-horsepower steam engine that supplied power to eight thousand presses, pumps, gins, mills, and lathes in Machinery Hall.

Some said that such machinery robbed America of its soul and its freedom. In the Age of Lincoln, they believed, the nation had gone terribly, perhaps fatally, wrong. Others demurred. According to essayist and novelist William Dean Howells, "It is in these things of iron and steel that the national genius most freely speaks."

The centennial planning committee was adamant that Native Indians, as opposed to African Americans, be included in the American story. Objects from the cultures of the southwestern Navaho and Apache and from the northwestern Tlingit and Haida included baskets and weapons, canoes and totem poles. Yet in the midst of this celebration, the federal government was active in removing Native Americans from the land that railroads wanted. Whereas in 1862 Lincoln had carefully studied the Indian uprising in Minnesota to separate the guilty from the innocent, his Civil War generals, Sherman and Sheridan, did not carry on that legacy. In 1866 Sherman proclaimed, "We must act with vindictive earnestness against the Sioux, even to their extermination, men, women, children." In 1873 Phil Sheridan used his Civil War experience to justify slaughter: "During the war did anyone hesitate to attack a village or town occupied by the enemy because women or children were in its limits? Did we cease to throw shells into Vicksburg and Atlanta because women and children were there?" Many white rural westerners agreed with Sherman and Sheridan and rejected the Republican policy of removal onto reservations.

In late 1875, when Sioux and Cheyenne Indians fought whites who, against the rule of law, invaded the sacred lands in the Black Hills, Hunkpapa Sioux spiritual leader Sitting Bull said, "No white man controls our footsteps. If we must die, we die defending our rights." The death in 1876 of popular Civil War hero George Custer during the Native American victory at the Battle of Little Bighorn outraged the public on the eve of the centennial. In retaliation, the United States redrew the boundary of the reservation so the Black Hills were open to white settlement.

In 1876, as the centennial celebration closed down, the organizers were well pleased with the exhibits and the attendance. Congress authorized the new National Museum to house the exhibits and "Americana" artifacts. Outside museum walls, however, the nation was in turmoil. For the past three years the economic situation of industrial workers had grown more desperate as the depression of 1873 showed no sign of abatement. Working-class northerners, the traditional base of the Democratic Party, seethed with anger and frustration against the economic and political corruption they saw all around them. When bosses on the Baltimore and Ohio Railroad announced the second wage cut in less than a year on July 14, 1877, the fuse was lit.

Termed the Great Railroad Strike of 1877, the explosion touched off that day in Martinsburg, West Virginia, was much more than a strike, and it passed far beyond railroads. Indeed, it may be that the uprising—which spread from the Appalachian foothills to the cities of the eastern seaboard to the railheads of the Mississippi to the Pacific Coast—was the closest thing to a social revolution Americans have seen. The tumult raised a host of questions that had long dominated the Age of Lincoln: the rule of law; the proper relation of labor, capital, and the state; the rights of the individual versus those of the community; and the role of race, gender, ethnicity, and class in American political and social life. In the end the lords of capital prevailed once more—thanks to the bullets and bayonets of the federal government—but their victory was won at a grievous cost.

The strike began when West Virginia trainmen refused to move their engines until the latest wage cut was rolled back. At that time the B&O Line was locked in a death struggle with Tom Scott's Pennsylvania Railroad, a conflict that turned on the ability of each to cut costs and restrict its rival's access to valuable markets. In the beginning the strike was as much a war between corporate rivals, mortgaged to the hilt, operating on razor-thin margins of profitability, as it was a dispute over wages between bosses and workers. For both companies time was of the essence: while hundreds of workers threatened control of the railroads themselves, trains that did not move represented thousands of dollars of lost profits. Responding to corporate demands, Democratic governor John J. Jacob dispatched the state militia to Martinsburg to get freight moving again. Once they were on the scene, however, West Virginia's citizen-soldiers refused to march against the strikers. That mutiny caused railroad executives to lean on newly installed Republican president Rutherford B. Hayes, whom they helped elect, and he called in federal troops.

During the next week strikers battled soldiers, and even when trains began rolling again, this only served to pass the news up and down the railroad lines that the bosses and government had conspired to usurp the democratic rights of American workingmen. By July 20, riots had broken out all over Baltimore, as laboring men and women marched on the railroad yards. Attempting to restore order, Maryland militiamen shot down nine demonstrators. This further angered the crowd, and federal troops were called out once more. They killed eleven more strike supporters and wounded forty others. The next day, news of the Baltimore massacre spread to Pittsburgh, where thousands of wage-earners staged a spontaneous sympathy strike, seizing control of the streets and immobilizing rail transport. While major newspapers despaired over this reenactment of the Paris Commune, the bosses never blinked. Tom Scott suggested that the state put strikers on "a rifle diet and see how they like that kind of bread." More reasonable businessmen also called for a show of government force. After all, they argued, everything moved over the rails—mail, medicine, food, and supplies. People could starve without the trains.

When Pittsburgh police refused to wade in against the thousands of strikers who had paralyzed commerce in the city, state militiamen were sent in once more. Marching straight off an express train from Philadelphia, they opened fire on the crowd, killing twenty and wounding twenty-nine. Instead of breaking and running, as expected, the strikers stood their ground. Enraged by the casualties they had suffered, they chased the militia into a nearby roundhouse and set it ablaze. By morning, the conflagration had spread across thirty-nine buildings, incinerating twelve hundred railroad cars and destroying a hundred locomotives.

In contrast to common depictions of "riotous" behavior, the crowd limited the damage it caused strictly to corporate property. This was no insensate mob, bent on mindless destruction: it was politically aware, tactically restrained, and scrupulously accurate. The same could not be said for the militiamen. When they blasted their way out of the roundhouse on the morning of July 22, they killed another twenty strikers, setting off more rioting across the city and the nation. By nightfall, word of the Pittsburgh battle had traveled back to Philadelphia, where outraged workingmen put the torch to large sections of corporate property. Farther afield, in East St. Louis, Illinois, biracial crowds took control of the city, shutting down railroad traffic and appointing their own provisional government. Civil War veterans donned their old uniforms once more, parading alongside railroaders, freedmen, and immigrants, announcing the triumph of democratic principles in their city. During the next week the uprising in East St. Louis spread across most of Illinois, shutting off railway traffic, closing down commerce, and drawing out coal miners from a wide range of pits in the southern part of the state. In Chicago, the Workingmen's Party called twenty thousand strikers out into the streets, and police, national guard, and federal troops battled them for almost a week. Scores were wounded in pitched battles that raged up and down Halsted and Canal Streets; at least twenty were killed. A headline in the *Chicago Times* in 1877 expressed fear of mob rule: "Terrors Reign, The Streets of Chicago Given Over to Howling Mobs of Thieves and Cutthroats."

All told, hundreds of thousands of American working people rose up, from Vermont to California, as one militiaman attested, "to break down the power of the corporations." That they failed, after a struggle lasting nearly two months, was testimony to the power of capital to command the military power of the nation-state. President Hayes sent federal troops literally from city to city, shutting down one by one the confused attempts at economic democracy that strikers initiated.

The most aggressive leaders, men like De Leon and Eugene V. Debs, saw the defeat of the strikers of 1877 as a great moral failure and spent the balance of their careers striving to right what they believed to have been a monstrous wrong. For De Leon, that meant decades of sectarian scribbling and political marginalization, a course of action that touched Vladimir Lenin, who studied his writings. For Debs, the course twisted through strikes and political rallies that seemed more like religious revivals, to antiwar and presidential campaigns, to prison and beyond. For Debs as for Lincoln, politics was finally an act of faith. That the regime he challenged sneered at him, marginalized him, called him a traitor and a criminal, and finally jailed him shows how the corporatism that Lincoln sponsored ultimately subverted the fairness that Lincoln himself stood for.

With the end of the 1877 chaos in northern urban areas, many Americans seemed convinced that the country was awash in confusion—political, social, economic, and cultural. Northern Republicans had eliminated slavery but never expected or knew how to apply concepts of freedom and independence to a changing world where African Americans and factory workers demanded rights. As northern industrial workers grew more strident and as southern African American agricultural workers grew adamant about their political rights, leading businessmen within the Republican Party saw their freedom threatened on many fronts. Controlling a hungry and angry labor force took precedence over concern for democratic government. The idea of mob rule terrified all alike. Middle-class sensibilities allowed only one response: maintain order at any price. If militia and federal troops trampled the legal rights of workingmen and women, so be it. If white vigilantes murdered and terrified African American voters, so be it. The goal was order first and foremost. And within an orderly society, a new business class began to define liberty as laissez-faire capitalism.

After the Civil War, the Democratic Party had been trying to broaden its appeal in the North by a denunciation of capitalism and especially monopolies in addition to its platform of white supremacy. Not until the election of 1884, however, did Democrats win back the White House. The Republican nominee was former speaker of the House and U.S. senator James G. Blaine, who had failed to receive the Republican nomination in 1876 and 1880 because of corruption (he stood accused of selling his influence in Congress to obtain a federal land grant for the Little Rock and Fort Smith Railroad for a personal remuneration of $110,150). The Democratic nominee was New York governor Grover Cleveland, known as "Grover the Good" for his integrity and reform efforts in cleaning up Tammany Hall. But on July 21, 1884, a Buffalo newspaper reported that Cleveland had in an orphan home an illegitimate son (whom Cleveland then acknowledged). The campaign slung mud. Democrats mocked, "Blaine, Blaine, James G. Blaine, / The Continental Liar from the State of Maine." Republicans reciprocated with "Ma! Ma! Where's my Pa? / Gone to the White House, / Ha, ha, ha."

On October 29, 1884, one hundred eighty financiers wined and dined with Blaine, among them Jay Gould, John Jacob Astor, William H. Vanderbilt, and Russell Sage. Reporters were barred from attending the dinner, but Joseph Pulitzer, new owner of the *New York World*, sent cartoonist Walt McDougall. Pulitzer was also interested in a chance remark that one of his reporters heard at a meeting of Blaine and a group of Protestant ministers. The front page of the *World* the next morning announced to this city of five hundred thousand Irish, German, and Italian Catholics that Republicans thought Catholic Democrats stood for "rum, Romanism, and rebellion." Across half the front page was a drawing by McDougall, based on the biblical Babylonian feast: "The Royal Feast of Belshazzar Blaine and the Money Kings." In the foreground, an unemployed workman and his wife and child beg for table scraps while Blaine and the tycoons enjoy "Lobby Pudding" and "Monopoly Soup."

Grover Cleveland won New York by only 1,149 votes, and New York was the pivotal state. On November 7, 1884, the flag at New York's Union Club flew at half-mast. For the first time since 1856, a Democrat was elected president.

Party affiliation mattered little on the issue of Native Americans in the West. Whereas whites in the South wanted no interference from Congress in southern race relations, and African Americans desperately sought help that never came, whites in the West did want federal help with the Native American population, and the Native population could trust neither local whites nor the federal government. In 1887 Congress passed the Dawes Act. The act was ostensibly a chance for assimilation by granting U.S. citizenship to Native Americans and settling them on their own personal allotment of land. To receive an allotment, Native Americans had to "anglicize" their names. The name changes allowed government agents to slip the names of their relatives and friends onto the Dawes rolls and thus reap acres of land for cronies. Senator Henry Dawes, Republican senator from Massachusetts, thought that private property instead of communal land on reservations would have a civilizing influence. To be civilized, he once claimed, was to "cultivate the ground, live in houses, ride in Studebaker wagons, send children to school, drink whiskey, own property."

Private property, however, actually took away the traditional communal way of life and weakened the cohesion of Native American communities. The Dawes Act affected individualistic lifestyle and cultural perspectives on wealth also. In some Native American cultures, status depended on how much one gave away or shared; the new emphasis was supposed to be on how much surplus an individual could accumulate. Further, the goal of making Indians behave more like white Americans, i.e., in nuclear families with a male head, contrasted with many Native groups' traditional gender roles where women had significant property rights.

In truth, the Indians did not receive the benefits of U.S. citizenship, the protection of federal authorities, or the promised assistance that would have enabled them to make their individual landholdings productive. Moreover, tribal lands not used for allotments were declared "surplus" and eligible for sale to non-Indians. As a consequence of this Dawes Act, more than 90 million acres of the tribes' collectively held 150 million acres passed out of Indian ownership. Summarized by Republican Senator Henry Teller of Colorado, formerly the Secretary of the Interior, the purpose of the act was "to get at the Indians land and open it up for resettlement."

Now considered one of the most grievous atrocities in U.S. history, the massacre at Wounded Knee took place on December 29, 1890. Five hundred U.S. soldiers, supported with artillery, surrounded a Lakota encampment with orders to take them to the railroad for transport to Omaha, Nebraska. In the process of disarming Native Americans of their guns, knives, tools, and more, a shot went off and the U.S. soldiers went on a killing spree. One estimate placed the Native American death toll at nearly three hundred men, women, and children, some shot in the back while running away, some, having escaped into the wilderness, frozen to death. Public reaction to the battle at the time was generally favorable, and Congress awarded eighteen Medals of Honor.

Far from any repercussions of what the railroad industry wrought for Native Americans, George Pullman founded the Pullman Palace Car Company, manufacturing luxury railroad cars. One of Tom Scott's most dedicated lieutenants, Pullman thought the callous approach of the 1870s and 1880s was responsible for most of the labor violence that dominated that era. Different tactics would yield a different result, he argued. Pullman preferred a paternalistic approach to labor relations, and he built the model village of Pullman, Illinois, some eight miles outside of Chicago. The adult population worked for the Pullman Company, their families lived in attractive houses rented to them by George Pullman, shopped at his stores, ate in his restaurants (all nonalcoholic), read the books he stocked in the local library, worshiped in his churches, and walked the streets he swept and lit and policed. He paid decent wages and provided fair benefits. He offered clean housing, indoor plumbing, and modern gas lighting, all in a safe, friendly, harmonious community.

It was, in many senses, the idyllic plantation of which Edmund Ruffin and his kind had dreamed, except there were no black people.

In the spring of 1886, Pullman was surprised to learn that his very own workforce had voted to support the general strike for an eight-hour workday. He was even more surprised on May 1, when 340,000 union members from across the country participated in an "eight-hour" work stoppage. These developments were worrisome, he wrote on May 4; because of "the excesses of our turbulent population, so many are uttering doubts just now as to whether democracy has been a triumph in America." Later that very day Chicagoans read about such excesses when the *Chicago Daily Tribune* reported that a bomb had exploded in Haymarket Square as policemen were dispersing the remainders of a workers' rally. Seven policemen and four workers died; sixty-seven policemen and fifty laborers were wounded. The new business and middle classes avidly followed sensationalized news stories under headlines of a "Hellish Deed" and "A Night of Terror," wherein newspaper editors deliberately confused the rally for an eight-hour day with anarchism, Marxism, and free love.

Even after Haymarket, Pullman did not expect such demonstrations from his workers. He presumed them to be grateful for their blessings. His workers, however, saw things differently. Although Pullman provided nice homes, his rents and utilities fees were 10 to 25 percent higher than the going rates. In the Depression of 1893, Pullman laid off most of his workers and then rehired them at 20 to 25 percent less than they had made previously. His workers asked for a cut in rent to go along with the pay cuts, and he refused—while the company had a $25 million surplus after having paid out more than $2.5 million in dividends. When a workers' committee came to discuss the conditions, Pullman told them, "We have nothing to arbitrate," and fired them on the spot. In his opinion, "the workers have nothing to do with the amount of wages they should receive." Pullman was simply agreeing with other businessmen who defined freedom in industrial America as the "liberty of contract." Laborers were not forced to work, their theory propounded, but agreed to work for specified pay. If a worker did not like his work arrangement, he was free to move on and find another job but was not free to negotiate wages or to go on strike.

In May 1894, not granted the respite, fifty thousand of his workers folded their arms and walked off the job. In July, at nearby buildings left after the International Columbian Exposition of 1893, a massive fire (blamed perhaps accurately on the strikers) engulfed the exhibition's "court of honor," erasing structures dedicated to manufacturing, electricity, machinery, and railroads. Although federal troops broke up the strike at the cost of seventy killed or wounded, the final tally was greater still. Pullman and his class were stunned by the labor rebellion; the working class, it seemed to them, did not appreciate kindness.

But they did understand that when hard economic times hit, the working class was squeezed between lower wages and higher costs. They also knew that all the amenities that the Pullman Company offered came at a simple, ultimately impossible cost. For all they gained in clean conditions and order and security, Pullman's workers were required to surrender their freedom. They could not buy or sell as they wished; they could not read the books they chose, they could not argue ideas in public without fear of consequence, or drink or dance or worship as the spirit rather than the company instructed them. So it was that citizens rose up in Pullman—as they would in other places and other times.

The 1880s and '90s saw a dismantling of the democratic, egalitarian vision of America that Abraham Lincoln had championed. Although working people resisted capital's control over the terms of their labor, bosses increasingly gained the upper hand. American capitalism garnered control of industrial production. The Age of Lincoln had finalized one contest of the meaning of freedom, but his vision of a level playing field never came to pass.

A century and a half earlier, when the Pennsylvania Assembly commissioned a mighty bell for their statehouse steeple to commemorate the fiftieth anniversary of its colonial charter, the new bell held a Biblical injunction: "Proclaim LIBERTY throughout all the land unto all the inhabitants thereof." The reference to Leviticus 25:10 called for God's pronouncement of freedom from slavery and freedom from debt: "It shall be a jubilee unto you; and ye shall return every man unto his possession, and ye shall return every man unto his family." By the end of the nineteenth century, however, the vision of America as a land of freedom that would no longer tolerate slavery was still a land very much possessed of the unfreedom of debt.

Fourteen

A Cross of Gold

ON APRIL 30, 1894, the Commonwealth of Christ came at last to Washington, D.C. Its representatives were politicos and workingmen—not angels, to be sure—and their numbers were as unimpressive as their peculiar vision of millennial harmony. But in many ways their naïve faith and simple, sweeping demands brought the nation full circle to the Millerite believers of a half-century earlier and the millennial spirit that did so much to shape the Age of Lincoln. Led by "General" Jacob Coxey, a small-time Ohio politician, the five hundred–odd marchers who constituted "Coxey's Army"—newspapers derided them as tramps and crackpots—called upon Congress to end unemployment, vanquish social strife, and regenerate rural communities and idle factories. By an action both plain and radical, they set out on foot across the American heartland from Massillon, Ohio, in late March, preaching a gospel of national salvation through public works and full employment. The press focused its ridicule on his monetary theory: the printing and circulating of vast amounts of paper money. Backed by pledges of redemption from the federal government—covenants of the sort that had underwritten military victory in 1865 and shored up egalitarian efforts during Reconstruction—Americans would literally purchase their way into utopia, buying and selling goods, creating jobs, building bonds of property and custom. The acme of statesmanship, the zenith of public service, and the chief duty of citizenship, it turned out, was to promote and facilitate consumption in the marketplace. Governance and worship both, for Coxey and his followers, had mutated into little more than esoteric forms of shopping. The City Upon a Hill had become Vanity Fair.

In its broad principles, the program of government-sponsored economic recovery and social reform that Coxey promoted foreshadowed the deficit-finance schemes that reshaped American capitalism forty years down the road. But Coxey (who named his first son Legal Tender) managed to tangle up notions of free enterprise, government activism, and conservative moral reform in a theoretical stew that smelled pungently socialist to some. The upshot was political farce. Marching up Capitol Hill to declare his principles to the nation at the end of a five-week trek, Coxey was arrested for walking on the grass. His corporal's guard of supporters scattered, and the spotlight faded.

Frank Baum, a ruined South Dakota storekeeper turned Chicago journalist, witnessed the failure of "Coxey's Army" up close. Baum knew many farm families whose few years of contact with the market economy had run athwart of drought or rain or pests or low prices or sickness or something else. Susan Orcutt from western Kansas wrote to Governor Lorenzo Lewelling in 1894 after hail destroyed her crops and garden, "I take my Pen in hand to tell you that we are Starving to death. It is pretty hard to do without anything to Eat hear in this God for saken country." How were the common farmers to cope, she wondered, when eastern capital and harsh western nature conspired to wreck their fortunes?

Baum's answer came in the form of a parable, an allegory on the election of 1896. The children's book he penned as a follow-up to his 1899 bestseller *Father Goose* transposed elements of personal experience and political philosophy into a manifesto disguised as whimsical fiction. *The Wonderful Wizard of Oz* (1900) traces the trials of everygirl Dorothy (the syllables of whose name, reversed, read *Theodore*, after Republican reformer Theodore Roosevelt) as she attempts to return to the tranquil farm life from which she has been separated by a powerful cyclone. Dorothy is assisted by a scarecrow who has his own problem: "If my head stays stuffed with straw instead of with brains, as yours is, how am I ever to know anything?" Even without the brains he so desires, the scarecrow is as uncommonly sensible as many unschooled farmers. Another companion is a tin woodman. Having had to work harder and faster, he accidentally chopped off pieces of himself that were then replaced by tin, and like too many industrial workers, he became bit by bit part of the machine. The tin woodman thinks he is lacking a heart, but he is actually a devoted and sentimental friend. Dorothy and these constituent elements of the farmer-labor coalition are joined by an ineffectual cowardly lion, laughably obvious to all as the Democratic champion, pacifist William Jennings Bryan. The group travels through a land where color defines section. On their way Dorothy and her companions travel on a road paved with bricks the color of gold. Along their journey they encounter yellow, hardworking Winkies (immigrant Asians) and the Winged Monkeys, a group of once "free people" whose lands have been taken from them (Native Americans). The foursome do not meet anyone representing disfranchised African Americans, replicating their near invisibility in the press at the time.

Dorothy wears silver (not ruby) slippers, and Americans who had endured the financial debates of the 1890s understood that such colorful rigmarole represented working-class wisdom of the day: a currency based on both gold and silver was solid and advantageous to ordinary Americans. The "greenback" philosophy of Coxey, however, was simply wishful thinking, attributing value where there was none, just as the residents of Oz imagine that their city is richly bejeweled because they view it through green spectacles. The Wizard (the president) as it turns out has no power, but the story's four protagonists working together, with the support of the Munchkin "little people," can defeat the Wicked Witches of political abuse and environmental disasters. Ultimately, Dorothy discovers, the power to return to the home she remembers so fondly has been with her all the time—if only she wishes hard enough. Frank Baum's allegory became an instant classic. The People's Party did not fare so well.

The Populists were the last of Lincoln's people, the last whose concerns for racial justice and millennial perfection were based on faith in the goodness of the common man. Ironically, just as the United States was becoming an urban nation, yeoman farmers arose to challenge the worst abuses of the personal freedom unleashed with the Civil War. Populism emerged from a wave of agrarian protest that had begun in the late 1860s in the West and then the South. Farmers' Alliance leaders, often rural preachers, black and white, spread the Alliance message with traveling lecturers and camp meetings akin to religious revivals. Their message itself was religious. A magazine in Georgia, the *Social Gospel*, proclaimed that their work would bring to fruition "a divinely ordered society, to be realized on earth. It is the application of Christ's Golden Rule and Law of Love to all the business and affairs of life." Another spokesman declared, "Christ himself was the author and President of the first Farmers' Alliance." The Alliance in Limestone County, Texas, worked toward creating a just society until the day when "God carried His work to its final consummation."

In 1890 Farmers' Alliances won elections throughout the South and West. In Georgia they chose the governor and the platform and named 75 percent of the senators and 80 percent of the representatives. Battling lawyer Thomas E. Watson, son of a planter who lost his slaves with emancipation, won a seat in the U.S. House of Representatives. Watson believed that newspapers did not report the needs of the working farmer, so he started the *People's Party Paper*. Dedicated "to educate our people upon governmental questions; to assail official corruption, to oppose class-rule, legislative favoritism, and the centralized tendencies manifest in both old parties," the paper would champion "the common people—their grievances, their hopes, their rights."

Bringing together many of the Alliance members, as well as labor organizations, and greenback advocates—people who took the side of debtors over creditors—was the People's Party, which held its first national convention in Omaha in 1892. According to Watson, Populists were the "sworn foes" of the "monopoly of power, of place, of privilege, of wealth, of progress." Never espousing the end of private property, Populists wanted to enlarge ownership, to make sure that opportunity was open to "the poorest, the weakest, the humblest." Sounding very much like Abraham Lincoln, Watson declared the need for a new policy "whose purpose is to allay the passions and prejudices of race conflict, and which makes its appeal to the sober sense and honest judgment of the citizen regardless of his color." It was important to make sure the "contest" was "fair." Watson concentrated his efforts on the importance of a fair vote for all citizens black and white, as "every citizen shall have his constitutional right to the free exercise of his electoral choice."

Populists denounced the widening gap between rich and poor as inimical to American freedom and republicanism, yet they shrank from examining its implications. The Civil War had left too many casualties, the South devastated, and the nation transformed. What awful misfortunes would a class war bring? The year 1877 had seen a bloody foretaste. No populist leader wanted more to drink from that dreadful cup. When Minnesota reformer Ignatius Donnelly penned the party preamble, he evoked godly zeal under a banner of high purpose. Donnelly argued the need "to restrain the extortions of aggregated capital, to drive the money changers out of the temple." "Raise less corn and more hell," shouted Mary Lease of Kansas, but what form such hell-raising might take to be truly effective remained uncertain. Outgunned by the state and by the forces of capital, Populists both South and West argued that the law and the vote offered the best way to bring on the millennium. "So the populists of today represent a demand for the enactment into law of the truths taught by Jesus," Lease argued, "the truths which must prevail before Christ's kingdom can be established, and the earth made a fit abode for man."

The Populist presidential candidate in 1892 was James Weaver of Iowa, who had become a staunch abolitionist after reading *Uncle Tom's Cabin* and who had fought for the Union at Shiloh. He turned away from the Republican Party when it turned away from equal rights for African Americans. While many Populists held racist and xenophobic attitudes common to the general white population in the United States, Weaver worked with the Colored Farmers' Alliance and called for policies where all classes and races could share in the economic wealth of America. After considering Tom Watson as a vice-presidential candidate, the convention went instead for former Confederate General James G. Field of Virginia, a nod to the need for Union and Confederate balance on the ticket.

The Populist Party combined antiprivilege sentiments with support for an active government. Populists campaigned on their belief in a small inexpensive government resting on the franchise of family farmers, but at the same time they favored the contradictory position that government should act on behalf of the needy and the poor. Farmers wanted equal access to success. Increasing government power to regulate would ensure that all citizens benefited from economic resources. In 1892 Populists won elections to state and federal legislatures, and Weaver garnered a million popular and 22 electoral votes. The success of the third-party Populists was higher than that of any other third-party movement up to that time. It did not last. In the election of 1896 the Populists forsook their millennial message and instead fought the battle on the capitalists' playing field, allowing the crusade to be a monetary one rather than a social or moral one.

That year the Republican national convention was held in St. Louis, where not one hotel would rent rooms to African American delegates. Racial justice was not an issue; monetary policy dominated the campaign. The Republicans chose William McKinley and the gold standard. In Chicago that summer Democrats nominated the young Nebraska orator William Jennings Bryan as their candidate. Bryan denounced the Republican Party's sole issue of the gold standard to aid bankers and industrialists, chiding "the idle holders of idle capital." Although the Democrats' sole issue was also money, silver in this instance, this "Great Commoner" spoke, as he believed, "in defence of a cause as holy as the cause of liberty." Bryan's powerful rhetoric invoked the millennial ideal of antebellum reform: "Having behind us the producing masses of this nation and the world, supported by the commercial interests, the laboring interests and the toilers everywhere, we will answer their demand for a gold standard by saying to them: You shall not press down upon the brow of labor this crown of thorns, you shall not crucify mankind upon a cross of gold."

Amid searching questions about the benefits and drawbacks of fusion with the Democrats, the Populists also nominated Bryan as their presidential candidate. Choosing Bryan meant giving up on all issues of interracial cooperation and voting rights, concentrating almost exclusively on the silver issue. The Populists chose Tom Watson for their vice-presidential candidate, having been utterly betrayed by the Democrats' choice of Arthur Sewall. Democrats hoped Sewall from Maine would attract eastern voters, but the wealthy shipbuilding owner, director of the Maine Central Railroad and president of the Bath National Bank for years, was anathema to the Populists. Nevertheless, without a candidate of their own, Populists supported Bryan over McKinley. A Populist newspaper in 1896 anticipated a Bryan victory with an allusion to slavery: "Cheer up, for the day is already dawning when you rightly hope to be something more than a corporate slave." Bryan never spoke to Watson and never reached out to the Populists.

With the failure of the Populists to offer a viable candidate, someone with the vision and political instinct of a Lincoln, the election of 1896 turned to sectional politics. Union veterans in the North voted Republican, and Confederate veterans voted Democrat.

Southern Democrats feared the Populist rhetoric of equal opportunity. As Democratic leader Patrick Walsh said, "We know the farmers of the South are impoverished and discontented," but "better, a thousand times better, suffer the ills of the present, suffer poverty, rather than . . . division and separation from the Democratic party." The argument against independent political movements in the South was always a cry against "Negro domination" and the need to maintain white supremacy. Indeed some southern Populists did want to include African Americans in a democratic government. Watson tried to make that point to farmers in 1892: "The accident of color can make no difference in the interests of farmers, croppers, and laborers," he said. "You are kept apart that you may be separately fleeced of your earnings . . . you are deceived and blinded that you may not see how this race antagonism perpetuates a monetary system with beggars both." Other southern Populists were as opposed to African American participation as were the southern Democrats. Western Populists had other issues to worry about and ignored the plight of African American farmers. In the South, the Democrats had already disfranchised most African Americans so even the more egalitarian white Populists, willing to vote for economic self-interest rather than along the color line, did not have a bloc of African American voters to support their efforts.

In the few localities where African Americans still exercised voting rights in the 1890s, Populists continued to win elections on the county level. Republicans and African Americans joined forces with different interest groups and especially the Populists to leverage the best deals they could in the increasingly Jim Crow South. In 1894 in North Carolina the Republican Party and the Populists fused, and the biracial coalition won state elections. They won again in the 1896 elections. And again, against such victories reaction set in. Borrowing from the terrorist campaigns in South Carolina, some even wearing the "Red Shirts" reminiscent of 1876, North Carolinian Democrats in 1898 waged an extraordinarily racist campaign. They invited Ben Tillman from neighboring South Carolina to stir up even more racial animosity.

White Democrats succeeded throughout the state except in one place.

North Carolina's largest city, Wilmington, had a black majority and an active biracial coalition of Republicans and Populists. Even against the violence, fraud, and intimidation, the Wilmington Populist Republican coalition prevailed. White Democrats then went on a two-day rampage. They ransacked Wilmington, murdered African Americans, destroyed a black newspaper that had challenged the Democratic accusations of "black bestiality," and installed themselves in the "elected" positions. Neither state nor federal forces intervened in this coup d'état.

Too many southern whites refused to address economic issues because all concerns took a back seat to racial hierarchy. And in spite of protestations to the contrary, after the disfranchisement of African Americans, and following the Populist revolt, many poor whites were also disfranchised in the South. White supremacy was victorious in the South; gold supremacy in the North. In the aftermath of the Populist debacle of 1896, Watson himself became a racist, anti-Catholic, and anti-Semitic demagogue. "Lynch law is a good sign," he wrote; "it shows that a sense of justice yet lives among the people."

The Populist Party never recovered from its endorsement of the Democratic Party, with its insistence that the most important single issue was the silver standard. Tom Watson believed that the 1898 Spanish American War, concomitant with a shift in American priorities to global concerns, finished off the Populist movement and also reform in America. War allowed politicians to bury "issues they dare not meet," he declared: "The blare of the bugle drowned the voice of the Reformer." The end of the Populists signaled the end of a yeoman class who sought to extend the personal, virtuous, face-to-face social relations they grew up with as rural, evangelical Protestants. With the party's demise went the hope of restructuring the American economic system along more egalitarian lines. Future reform efforts would take a less millennial approach. New reformers would not trust and encourage the spark of God in the spirit of the common man. Whether the Progressives of the early twentieth century or the New Dealers of the 1930s, reformers would seek to control and rein in both the masses and the magnates.

Divergent groups bore the legacy of Lincoln. Those favoring corporate development claimed his Whig mantle of advocating railroads, industrial growth, internal improvements, access to investment capital, and improved facilities for education. Those favoring open opportunity and a level playing field claimed his mantle of emancipation and justice in an egalitarian economy. Lincoln himself had complained in 1859 about those who considered "the *liberty* of one man to be absolutely nothing, when in conflict with another man's right of *property*." His Republican Party was "for both the *man* and the *dollar*, but in cases of conflict, the man *before* the dollar." The Populists were the last group to place the man before the dollar.

The Populists were also the last political party before the modern civil rights movement that centered much of its energy on questions of African American polity, one of the issues that defined the Age of Lincoln. The methods of moral suasion which had propelled Garrisonian abolitionism in the years after 1830 had succeeded by concentrating the attention of the wider reform community on a single, central, grievous wrong. Now those yet willing to lend their aid to the project of perfecting America found themselves assailed by a horde of profoundly dissonant Pied Pipers. By the end of the century, collateral projects like temperance and women's suffrage, which had taken a back seat to emancipation, reasserted their claims to an increasingly exhausted and divided audience of followers. Scattered reformers included legislators who focused on railroad freight rates, women's suffrage, adulterated food and drugs, and "white slavery" as causes worthy of Washington's attention. Activists like hatchet-wielding Carrie Nation and the fire-and-brimstone preacher Billy Sunday targeted drink as the nation's chief menace, challenging lawmakers to follow their all-or-nothing line or suffer the political consequences.

Reformer Frederick Winslow Taylor, an engineer at Massachusetts' Midvale Steel Company, set about bridging the divide between bosses and workers. Armed with stopwatch and clipboard, Taylor in 1881 promised soaring productivity and sumptuous dividends for investors, as well as snug homes and fat pay packets to the toiler. First he would prove his case with a single toiler, an immigrant pig-iron handler he named Schmidt. Closely supervising his every movement, instructing him when to rest and when to work, Taylor coached Schmidt to meet ever greater work targets in less time with less fatigue. Such a partnership of brain and brawn, Taylor argued, could not but revolutionize the nation, yielding greater profits for employers, and greater satisfactions—material and otherwise—to America's working class. Within a few years "Taylorism" in various forms had spread widely in American industry and education and into the home itself. That, under this new labor regime, men and women were expected to surrender control of the work process itself— indeed, to yield up control of their bodies in a way that slavery's foes had most feared—was scarcely noticed. Times had changed, and workers like Schmidt were content to enjoy what little measure of freedom they had after the last factory whistle blew, slowly conceding the battles that Nat Turner and John Brown, Abe Lincoln and Tom Watson had fought. Modern America was *the jungle*, the most honest of socialist novelists declared.

Every attempt to stamp out "evil" in its myriad forms only seemed to create new variants. When Georgia's Fulton County prohibited the sale of liquor in 1884, local druggist John Pemberton remixed his wine-based headache medicine into a remedy he called Coca-Cola, good for everything from morphine addiction to impotence. Jaded, perplexed, and wary, many turned toward incremental, bureaucratic, "progressive" models of reform. By century's end, "muckraking" writers like Lincoln Steffens, Frank Norris, and Upton Sinclair aroused anger against social conditions, while on the other end of the political spectrum, the jingoist propaganda of newspapers controlled by William Randolph Hearst stirred conservative nationalism. For native-born middle-class city dwellers especially, the best way to bring the nation toward Christian perfection seemed to involve soap and water and vigorous scrubbing, a stern education, wholesome food, modest clothes, regular exercise, hard work, and church on Sundays.

That local, state, and federal governments should play a leading role in advancing these measures seemed only simple common sense. Obviously the power that had saved the Union ought to be used to keep its citizens on the path of righteousness. Under the leadership of Anthony Comstock's New York Society for the Suppression of Vice, government lashed out against lotteries and birth-control pamphlets, commercial fraud and "pornography" of all sorts—including medical textbooks that treated human sexuality too openly.

Between 1865 and 1896, as Americans struggled to formulate a coherent response to the cultural challenges they perceived, the accent fell upon reining in baser passions—of the lawgivers as well as the lawbreakers. Deportations and lawful executions would replace riots. The great inventor Thomas Edison worked hard to rationalize the elimination of wrongdoers in the same way Dr. Joseph Guillotin had done a century earlier. By harnessing his competitor George Westinghouse's alternating current mechanism to the device he called an electric chair, Edison's company promised to dispatch hatchet murderer William Kemmler in 1890 both quickly and humanely. Promise outran performance. "They would have done better using an axe," an angry Westinghouse declared; yet such coolly orchestrated, relentlessly mechanized processes marked for most a long step forward from the macabre public executions and hangings of bygone years. As with this and other bewilderingly wonderful inventions that closed out the Age of Lincoln—barbed wire, dynamite, margarine, the cash register, the phonograph, the zipper, the bicycle—novelty seldom seemed an accurate indicator of social progress. Less than three generations hence, the regimes of mass production would converge with mass destruction, the sewing machine and the machine gun creating gendered spheres of wage labor focused on creating and killing at a pace none could have foreseen.

Henry Adams, for one, was appalled by how technology had stifled his nation and supplanted the genius of its citizenry. He was the son of the diplomat Charles Francis Adams, grandson of President John Quincy Adams, and great-grandson of Founding Father John Adams. While his forebears had made history, Henry was a mere history professor. While staring at a piece of immense machinery, he was mesmerized and repulsed by the soulless, whirring thing. In time gone by, he noted, men and women seeking the great source of power in this world had knelt before the Holy Virgin in the magnificent cathedrals that dotted Europe's towns and cities. Now those shrines were empty, the religious ideal forgotten. Science—nay, technology—had replaced faith, and factories had pushed aside churches. Instead of bending the knee, modern man lifted his fist in a salute to the machine he served as deity and as creator of value and abundance.

Writing in the third person, as was his custom, Adams recorded his reaction in 1900 to the massive steam engine:

> To Adams the dynamo became a symbol of infinity. As he grew accustomed to the great gallery of machines he began to feel the forty-foot dynamos as a moral force, much as the early Christians felt the Cross.

The planet itself seemed less impressive, in its old-fashioned, deliberate, annual or daily revolution, than this huge wheel, revolving within arm's length at some vertiginous speed, and barely murmuring—scarcely humming an audible warning to stand a hair's-breadth further for respect of power—while it would not wake a baby lying close against its frame. Before the end, one began to pray to it; inherited instinct taught the natural expression of man before silent and infinite force.

Others grew enamored of the possibilities of technological progress—or worried by its potential misuses. A growing number of writers penned portraits of utopian or dystopian futures to come. The most vivid of these, Edward Bellamy's *Looking Backward* (1886), posited a socialist, technological America of the year 2000, where want had been overcome. Exactly which technologies might promote such changes remained uncertain, but scores of Bellamy Clubs sprang up across the nation to lay the groundwork for the new world he envisioned. While much of late nineteenth-century utopian socialism put its faith in family, church, and local community values, Bellamy's perfectionist view of America requires no God. He writes instead a fable of unselfish abundance, scientific improvement, and group purpose wherein the state replaces the family and the highest national purpose is summed up in the hedonism of shopping. Bellamy's book, like a slew of lesser literature, redefined Americans as consumers, not producers, recipients of the state's benefits, not creators. For the People of Plenty imagined here, freedom meant little more than the freedom to amass and enjoy, to exchange and consume material objects of ever more wondrous variety.

More ominous for America's future was a different reliance on the use of law to bring about a reformation of man and society. Reformers looking to cultural perfection and technologies of social control mixed genetics and evolutionary theory with garden-variety racism and a host of class-based prejudices; a powerful lobby of American intellectuals including inventor and entrepreneur Alexander Graham Bell and Yale professor of political science William Graham Sumner mourned "the forgotten man," and championed the new "science" of eugenics, a self-satisfying discipline that promised to perfect Americans as a people by eliminating those sorts and traits deemed backward or unpalatable. The creation of a purer, higher strain of human being offered a seemingly sensible rationale for restricting marriage across lines of race, class, and ethnicity, institutionalizing sexual "inverts" and "perverts," "delinquents," and "morons," and advocating more desperate measures still. The desire to elevate and cleanse the nation in these years led to such disparate measures as immigration restriction, the passage of the Pure Food and Drug Act, enforced sterilization of those deemed physically or mentally "unfit" to reproduce, and the flowering of a host of female beauty pageants. In the name of scientific progress and the national interest, Jews, Asians, Hispanics, African Americans, and Native Americans were systematically segregated, ghettoized, and demonized as "pariah groups." Where the state fell down in the pursuit of social hygiene, local communities applied more down-home remedies: all-white sundown towns, refusing housing, jobs, and social services to those deemed unfit, rioting in and burning down minority neighborhoods, and terrorizing, defaming, and lynching those who challenged local norms and prejudices.

Denying Lincoln's belief in a system of individualism and private property but using his vision of government action and power to enforce law, future prophets would concentrate on class struggle on a global scale. Watching the world-fixers from his barstool in a Southside Chicago tavern, Finley Peter Dunne's fictional Irish American, Mr. Dooley, had little time for the extremists who had populated and driven the Age of Lincoln. "A fanatic is a man who does what he thinks the Lord would do," Dooley opined, "if He knew the facts of the case."

When Henry David Thoreau crowed about the limitless perfectability of man in the closing lines of *Walden*, when Frederick Douglass called upon government to eradicate the evil in its midst and raise up the slave by virtue of his social merit, when Abraham Lincoln linked constitutional law to a program of social regeneration, they little imagined the dread and crooked pathways along which Americans would later carry their ideas.

The world of mass politics was changing. Barbecues, parades, and rallies for the whole community, where speakers educated, entertained, and established a personal bond with their electorate, passed from the scene of American life. Whereas Lincoln addressed his audiences as one concerned citizen to another, politics became more professional. Government became more businesslike and bureaucratic. Money and monopoly issues were entrusted to regulatory agencies, namely the Federal Reserve

Board and Federal Trade Commission. The Republican federal administration enormously enlarged its own powers and expanded the ranks of administrators, clerks, and officials at all levels of government, in keeping with their activist and ameliorative vision. A new civil service brought efficiency, and inertia, to a growing bureaucracy. Government clerks everywhere, men and women, pounded on typewriters and communicated on telephones, 53,000 government employees in 1871 and 166,000 ten years later.

Americans seemed increasingly content to leave government to the legislators, morality to the churches, and education to the new "universities" that had been popping up across the nation after 1876. As social problems grew ever more complex, public officials and private citizens grew to rely upon a range of new professional organizations for information, guidance, regulation, and policy. Even as thousands of ordinary Americans flocked to rural summer "chatauquas" in search of education and community, the age of the amateur reformer was drawing to a close. The lobbyist, the pitch-man, the pundit, and the expert-for-hire were waiting in the wings. They were well suited to promoting reform, certainly, but not reformation.

As a new faith in science and experts replaced millennial idealism, aims centered on protecting freedom and voting rights for the African American and all citizens lost out to expanding the interests of corporations and trusts. With the acquiescence of the three branches of the national government, discriminatory legislation extended, solidified, and rigidified a racial segregation that in most of the late nineteenth century had been evident only in local patches. Although not all at once, a complete legal institutionalization of discrimination heralded a new era of race relations. Within the African American community were divisions over the best way to handle diminishing freedom. For Booker T. Washington, coping with the parameters of the social sphere to which whites assigned him, the political and social course was clear. If African Americans were required to remain, for the most part, in the South, if they were expected to stay tethered to the soil, cultivating cotton and tobacco, Washington wanted them to develop themselves as artisans and scientific farmers, growing bigger and better crops than neighboring whites, cooperating and supporting one another, accumulating property, and building strong institutions.

At his Atlanta Exposition Address in 1895 Washington spoke for the benefit of whites: "The opportunity to earn a dollar in a factory just now is worth infinitely more than the opportunity to spend a dollar in an opera house." Lying to himself about the endemic problem of white racist attacks on African Americans who were improving their economic lot, Washington believed that traditional prejudices and cultural objections would die out, slowly but surely. "The wisest among my race understand that the agitation of questions of social equality is the extremist folly, and that progress in the enjoyment of all the privileges that will come to us must be the result of severe and constant struggle rather than of artificial forcing." The task for African Americans was to erect a strong material foundation for themselves and wait for the scales to fall from the eyes of the whites who held them down. Washington agreed with Bryan and Coxey—the color line that truly mattered in America was not white or black or yellow, but gold and silver and green.

Booker T. Washington spoke out against lynching and worked tirelessly to make "separate" facilities more "equal." He had the ear of some white authorities for suggestions on appointments and policies, and he became one of the few African Americans with political power. But how limited that power was. He had to walk a careful line and follow segregation rules, and even then white supremacists railed against him. When Washington was invited to dine at the White House, U.S. senator Benjamin Tillman of South Carolina exclaimed, "The action of President Roosevelt in entertaining that nigger will necessitate our killing a thousand niggers in the South before they will learn their place again."

Washington, like most advocates of rural and laboring Americans, calculated human worth in quantitative, material terms. Asked what it was American working people finally wanted, the white labor leader Samuel Gompers explained simply: "More." For Washington, likewise, the successful African American was a man of property, possessed of a family (the black woman was always, in his vision, subordinated to husband or father or brother), a plot of land, a strong back, a good name, and the goodwill of those who lived around him. With the passage of time, he would surely gain this, his dearest dreams—or draw nearer unto them, at any rate. To Washington, the African American was like one of the Chosen, still wandering in the wilderness, enduring a time of preparation and cleansing, destined like those around him, one and all, for a richer reward—if they remained true to the covenant they had made. Washington invoked the role model of Lincoln for patience and obedience to law, "while being ambitious we shall at the same time be patient, law-abiding and self-controlled as Lincoln was." Ultimately with labor, prayer, and patience, the chosen people would surely be revealed.

The countrified Booker Washington had a brilliant aristocratic antagonist, William Edward Burghardt Du Bois, the first black graduate of Harvard's doctoral program. Du Bois viewed the notions of Washington with imperious contempt.

Washington had been born a slave in southwestern Virginia and predicated his politics on guiding his people, materially, culturally, and psychologically, *Up From Slavery* (1901), as he phrased the title of his bestselling autobiography. Du Bois was born in 1868, after slavery, after civil war, after the passage of the Fourteenth Amendment. Growing up in Massachusetts with his mother, having no contact with his freeborn Haitian father, Du Bois found no kinship with the mass of impoverished rural freedpeople living in the ex-Confederacy.

In his timeless classic, *The Souls of Black Folk* (1903), Du Bois worried about the changing millennial aspirations within the black community; "in all our Nation's striving is not the Gospel of Work befouled by the Gospel of Pay? So common is this that one-half think it normal; so unquestioned, that we almost fear to question if the end of racing is not gold, if the aim of man is not rightly to be rich." Speaking for African Americans but also for all Americans at the end of the nineteenth century, Du Bois asked, "What if the Negro people be wooed from a strife for righteousness, from a love of knowing, to regard dollars as be-all and end-all of life?" W.E.B. Du Bois questioned how the pursuit of money changed the meaning of freedom, "Must this, and that fair flower of Freedom which despite jeers of latter-day striplings, sprung from our fathers' blood, must that too degenerate into a dusty quest of gold."

Raised to regard himself as equal to all with whom he mingled—the cream of African American society at Nashville's Fisk University, the white intelligentsia of Harvard, the best minds of Europe at the University of Berlin—Du Bois had no intention of toadying before the likes of a figure so coarse and common, so aggravatingly patient and disgustingly humble, as the so-called "Wizard of Tuskegee" (after the agricultural college Washington founded in Alabama).

Neither did Du Bois toady before the memory of Lincoln. His respect for Lincoln had nothing to do with putting him on a pedestal, and Du Bois had to defend himself from the outrage of African Americans who wanted no criticism of Lincoln. Du Bois's admiration for Lincoln drew on Lincoln's flaws, "so that at the crisis he was big enough to be inconsistent—cruel, merciful; peace-loving, a fighter; despising Negroes and letting them fight and vote; protecting slavery and freeing slaves. He was a man—a big, inconsistent, brave man."

While strongly agreeing with Washington that African Americans should be judged as individuals, Du Bois knew that he himself belonged to the select—and self-selecting—group that the ancient Puritans called the "Elect of God." Du Bois believed that talented African Americans, "the Talented Tenth," were the equal of any white and deserved a decent education, including college. Du Bois believed this educated ten percent of African Americans would become the civil rights leaders of their communities. A race riot in Lincoln's hometown of Springfield, Illinois, in 1908 inspired Du Bois and other African Americans, including antilynching crusader Ida Wells Barnett, to assemble in New York to discuss solutions to problematic race relations. Concerned whites, some of them children and grandchildren of abolitionists, at least one of them, William English Walling, the son of slaveholders, were equal participants at the assemblage. This meeting led to the establishment of the National Association for the Advancement of Colored People (NAACP). Du Bois became the editor of the NAACP's influential newspaper, *The Crisis*.

As the nineteenth century drew to a close, the fortunes of African Americans hardly registered with most of those who had worn the Blue or the Gray or their descendants. Perhaps it was only simple realism, but the mass of ordinary Americans quietly folded up their hopes of social perfection at the end of the nineteenth century and filed them away at the back of some great national sock-drawer, too precious to discard, too foolish to leave out for public display. The brilliant short stories of William Sydney Porter—two-bit drugstore clerk, embezzler, runaway husband, jailbird, drunkard, southerner—captured perfectly the mood of cynicism, failure, and loss that pervaded the passing of the Age of

Lincoln. Under the pen name O. Henry, he wrote "The Cop and the Anthem," about a New York hobo who tries all manner of minor crime in hopes of being thrown into a warm jail cell for the winter. Only when he resolves, in a moment of heartfelt Christian repentance, to get a job and rebuild his life is the final irony revealed. The tramp is arrested for loitering; his personal millennium is forestalled, perhaps forever. With that characteristic twist O. Henry told the story of modern America. Hope was the most savage and fruitless delusion; modern men and women were not meant for such fine feelings.

The history of the United States during the nineteenth century concentrates on sectional conflict, civil war, and Reconstruction. As the meaning and expansion of freedom and of citizenship rights galvanized the age, Lincoln was the fulcrum. Prior to the Civil War, America was in the frenzy of a millennial age. Millennialism permeated antebellum political debate, undergirded the presumption of Manifest Destiny, and buttressed the understanding of honor. Righteous men knew God's plan. Extremes eroded any middle ground as powerful constituencies rallied to intransigent positions. For such fanatics, the purpose and promise of America lay in protecting their right to hold those positions. Contravening them was Abraham Lincoln and his particular sense of southern honor. Lincoln recast America's purpose, and his call for a new birth of freedom came to fruition in new amendments to the Constitution, none of which was inevitable, all of which promised to embrace an equality of opportunity that transcended any particular and exclusionary right. Under rulings that touted "separate but equal," the U.S. Supreme Court put to rest those millennial schemes of equality; nevertheless the Thirteenth, Fourteenth, and Fifteenth amendments would continue to promise freedom from slavery, equal protection under the law, and the right to vote. Even as the darkness of the nadir began to settle over the land, a handful of believing blacks, and a smaller number still of trusting whites, put their faith in the law and continued to work on redrawing freedom's boundaries.

In the passing of the age, Americans gave up old dreams of heavenly perfection and enshrined new hopes of material progress—incremental, tangible, calculable in dollars and dimes, full bellies and fine clothes. In place of noble statesmen and great leaders, they trumpeted clean hands and efficient administration. In place of pure hearts, gentle spirits, and feminized consciences, they held up manly toil, stoic endurance, and the virtue of struggling self-interest. But in the American mind, the Civil War itself never truly ended. It was transmuted to a romantic memory, the stuff of elaborate weekend rituals of bloodless battles during which no contraband crossed enemy lines at risk of life. It flowered into a national pastime for vacationing families that took in the emotional majesty of Little Round Top and Cemetery Ridge without making sure to wrestle likewise with untold lynchings across America. Whether found in the shock of a geneticist discovering slaves in one's family or in the wastes of New Orleans's devastated Ninth Ward, the war is with us still, as myth and reality both. Just as in the Age of Lincoln, moral choice, democratic citizenship, and equality still mingle. "Determine that the thing can and shall be done," wrote Lincoln, "and then we shall find the way."

Bibliographical Essay

Notes for *The Age of Lincoln* are available online in a fully searchable format at TheAgeofLincoln.com. *The Age of Lincoln* is the culmination of a scholarly lifetime of research and teaching. To distill every resource consulted into a single bibliography would be impossible. Each study is listed only once, though often it would fit under several categories. This bibliographical essay lists the studies upon which I most relied in developing my interpretations or arguing against others. Specific citations are in the notes at TheAgeofLincoln.com. Those interested may wish to print out the notes to read along with the text.

The scholarly literature dealing with the sectional crisis, the Civil War, Reconstruction, and its aftermath is compelling, complex, and enormous. A still larger and fascinating body of original documents—many of them in published form, many more available online—are open to further research in the matchless treasure houses of local, state, and federal archives and research libraries. If the arguments and interpretations in *The Age of Lincoln* have succeeded in sparking further interest in this remarkable era—or disagreement with the ideas expressed here—I hope readers will take up the challenge of pursuing it. Search out other scholarship, plunge into the sources, and pick up your own pen or keyboard. Those willing to wrestle with various explanations should definitely examine the sources included in this bibliography for a range of lively and perceptive interpretations. Reading one such analysis is only the first step toward understanding history, and understanding history is essential to defending moral government and cultivating democratic citizenship. That is why Lincoln went to Gettysburg, after all.

We are extraordinarily lucky to have a brilliant synthesis on the Civil War, James M. McPherson's *Battle Cry of Freedom: The Civil War Era* (1988). This masterpiece of scholarly research and clear, cogent writing has inspired a generation of Civil War literature since its publication. A synthesis by Eric Foner, *Reconstruction: America's Unfinished Revolution, 1863–1877* (1988), is likewise incredibly thorough and an excellent and reliable explanation of a complicated period. Every serious student of the period needs to read these award-winning books. McPherson provides a seventeen-page bibliographical note on "Sectional Conflict and Civil War"; Foner also has a useful "Selected Bibliography."

For Lincoln, I began with the magisterial David Herbert Donald, *Lincoln* (1995), whose eighty-six-page "Sources and Notes" is the model that I have tried to follow for my notes at TheAgeofLincoln.com. As Donald explains, to cite all the literature written on Lincoln alone would require a book twice the size of his monumental 714-page biography. On Lincoln, two of the best interpretative studies are Phillip Shaw Paludan, *The Presidency of Abraham Lincoln* (1994), and James McPherson, *Abraham Lincoln and the Second American Revolution* (1990); see also McPherson, ed., *"We Cannot Escape History": Lincoln and the Last Best Hope of Earth* (1995). On the politics of his administration, and its larger meanings, see Benjamin P. Thomas, *Abraham Lincoln: A Biography* (1952); David Donald, *Lincoln Reconsidered* (1956); Don E. Fehrenbacher, *Prelude to Greatness: Lincoln in the 1850s* (1962); Gabor S. Boritt, *Lincoln and the Economics of the American Dream* (1978); LaWanda F. Cox, *Lincoln and Black Freedom: A Study in Presidential Leadership* (1981); Allen G. Bogue, *The Earnest Men: Republicans of the Civil War Senate* (1989); Mark E. Neely, Jr., *The Fate of Liberty: Abraham Lincoln and Civil Liberties* (1991) and *The Last Best Hope of Earth: Abraham Lincoln and the Promise of America* (1993); Garry Wills, *Lincoln at Gettysburg: The Words That Remade America* (1992); Douglas L. Wilson, *Honor's Voice: The Transformation of Abraham Lincoln* (1998); Allen C. Guelzo, *Abraham Lincoln: Redeemer President* (1999); Richard J. Carwardine, *Lincoln: A Life of Purpose and Power* (2006); Daniel Epstein, *Lincoln and Whitman: Parallel Lives in Civil War Washington* (2004); Stewart Winger, *Lincoln, Religion, and Romantic Cultural Politics* (2003); Doris K. Goodwin, *Team of Rivals: The Political Genius of Abraham Lincoln* (2005); Adam I. P. Smith, *No Party Now: Politics in the Civil War North* (2006); James Oakes, *The Radical and the Republican: Frederick Douglass, Abraham Lincoln, and the Triumph of Antislavery Politics* (2006); William C. Harris, *With Charity for All: Lincoln and the Restoration of the Union* (1997). Two excellent works on Lincoln's Emancipation Proclamation are John Hope Franklin, *The Emancipation Proclamation* (1995), and Harold Holzer et al., *The Emancipation Proclamation: Three Views* (2006).

For broad interpretations of this era, a place to start is the classic *Civil War and Reconstruction* (2004). Written by James G. Randall in 1937, it has been revised, enriched, and thoroughly rewritten under the editorship of David H. Donald, Jean H. Baker, and Michael F. Holt (orig. 2001). The best overview of the middle decades of the century remains James McPherson, *Ordeal by Fire: The Civil War and Reconstruction* (1982, 3rd ed. 2002), again with a great bibliography. For narrative achievement, Allan Nevins, *The Ordeal of the Union* (1947–71) remains unsurpassed, carrying readers from the Mexican War to Appomattox in eight wonderfully readable volumes.

On the Civil War era, there are many fine books, including textbooks with suggested readings. Peter J. Parrish, *The American Civil War* (1975), and Charles P. Roland, *An American Iliad: The Story of the Civil War* (1990, 2nd ed. 2002), are good histories. Michael Fellman, Lesley J. Gordon, and Daniel J. Sutherland, *This Terrible War: The Civil War and Its Aftermath* (2003), draws upon more recent literature and, like *The Age of Lincoln,* carries Reconstruction past the traditional withdrawal of troops from the South. James Loewen, *Lies My Teacher Told Me: Everything Your American History Textbook Got Wrong* (1995), is a unique and insightful critique of high school textbooks that has wonderful insights for the Age of Lincoln. A good introduction to Civil War literature is James M. McPherson and William J. Cooper, eds., *Writing the Civil War: The Quest to Understand* (1998); for an annotated bibliography see also David J. Eicher, *The Civil War in Books: An Analytical Bibliography* (1997). Other excellent syntheses, bibliographical references, and historiographical collections are available from the Heath Major Problems series, particularly Michael Perman, *Major Problems in the Civil War and Reconstruction: Documents and Essays* (1998), and Paul D. Escott and David R. Goldfield, *Major Problems in the History of the American South,* 2 vols. (1990, rev. 1999). The Blackwell Companions to American History series contains invaluable historiographical essays of recent literature: William L. Barney, ed., *A Companion to Nineteenth Century America* (2001); Lacy K. Ford, ed., *A Companion to the Civil War and Reconstruction* (2005), and relevant essays in John B. Boles, ed., *A Companion to the American South* (2002). In addition, the relevant historiographical essays in the now somewhat dated Arthur S. Link and Rembert W. Patrick, *Writing Southern History: Essays in Honor of Fletcher M. Green* (1965), and John Boles and Ellen Nolan, eds., *Interpreting Southern History: Historiographical Essays in Honor of Sanford W. Higginbotham* (1987), place the literature within scholarly arguments and debates. For a group of British historians' perspectives, see Susan-Mary Grant and Brian Holden Reid, eds., *The American Civil War: Explorations and Reconsiderations* (2000). In addition, a number of topical scholarly edited encyclopedias are useful. For example, see Richard N. Current, ed., *Encyclopedia of the Confederacy* (1993); Mary Kupiec Cayton, Elliot J. Gorn, and Peter W. Williams, eds, *Encyclopedia of American Social History* (1993, with revisions on CD-ROM 1998); Jack Salzman et al., eds, *Encyclopedia of African American Culture and History* (1996, rev. ed. and CD-ROM 2000); Paul Finkelman, ed., *Encyclopedia of the United States in the Nineteenth Century* (2001); and Richard Zuczek, ed., *Encyclopedia of the Reconstruction Era* (2006). For individuals, see John A. Garraty and Mark C. Carnes, eds., *American National Biography* (1999).

Important works that examine the period through a theme include Richard Hofstadter, *The American Political Tradition and the Men Who Made It* (1948); Louis Hacker, *The Triumph of American Capitalism: The Development of Forces in American History to the Beginning of the Twentieth Century* (1965); Herbert G. Gutman, *Work, Culture, and Society in Industrializing America: Essays in American Working-Class and Social History* (1976); Paul S. Boyer, *Urban Masses and Moral Order in America, 1820–1920* (1978); Sacvan Bercovitch, *The American Jeremiad* (1978); George B. Forgie, *Patricide in the House Divided: A Psychological Interpretation of Lincoln and His Age* (1979); Melvin Stokes and Stephen Conway, eds., *The Market Revolution in America: Social, Political, and Religious Expressions, 1800–1880* (1996); and Alexander Keyssar, *The Right to Vote: The Contested History of Democracy in the United States* (2000). David Roediger, *The Wages of Whiteness: Race and the Making of the American Working Class* (1991) and *Working Toward Whiteness: How America's Immigrants Became White* (2005), is pioneering the development of critical race theory for historians by developing how and why laborers and immigrants used "whiteness" to benefit in American society. For a libertarian interpretation see Jeffrey Hummel, *Emancipating Slaves, Enslaving Free Men: A History of the American Civil War* (1996).

Arthur Schlesinger, Jr., *The Age of Jackson* (1942), brilliantly examines the period 1828–48; this interpretation has been recently extended by Sean Wilentz, *The Rise of American Democracy: Jefferson to Lincoln* (2005). An important synthesis recently updated and containing a bibliographical essay is Harry L. Watson, *Liberty and Power: The Politics of Jacksonian America* (1990, 2006). David Potter, *The Impending Crisis, 1848–1861* (1976) is the standard study of the sectional crisis. Bruce Levine has brought this argument up to date in *Half Slave and Half Free: The Roots of Civil War* (1992, 2005), which has an excellent revised bibliography. These studies all combine powerful interpretations with great readability. The largest meanings of the war and Reconstruction are best examined in the luminous collaborations of the Freedman and Southern Society Project (first led by Ira Berlin, now directed by Leslie S. Rowland), *Freedom: A Documentary History of Emancipation* (1982–). For perceptive explorations of the Age of Lincoln in the context of global capitalism, see Eric J. Hobsbawm, *The Age of Capital, 1848–1875* (1979); Eugene D. Genovese and Elizabeth Fox-Genovese, *Fruits of Merchant Capital: Slavery and Bourgeois Property in the Rise and Expansion of Capitalism* (1983); and Philip M. Katz, *From Appomattox to Montmartre: Americans and the Paris Commune* (1998).

Within a broad theme of liberty and freedom in the Age of Lincoln, many works have bearing. The starting point is Isaiah Berlin, *Four Essays on Liberty* (1969); David Hackett Fischer, *Liberty and Freedom: A Visual History of America's Founding Ideas* (2005) has a superb discussion of the important works. Especially meaningful were Daniel T. Rodgers, *Contested Truths: Keywords in American Politics Since Independence* (1987); Sheldon Hackney, *Magnolias Without Moonlight: The American South from Regional Confederacy to National Integration*, esp. chap. 10, "Shades of Freedom in America" (2005); and most of Eric Foner's books, especially his *The Story of American Freedom* (1998).

Many studies that attempt to grasp this era focus on local communities. These local studies not only tell us about daily lives and ordinary men and women and what their community and place meant to them, they also provide other useful information, such as mobility and social advancement or decline. See, for example, Don Harrison Doyle, *The Social Order of a Frontier Community* (1983) and *Faulkner's County: The Historical Roots of Yoknapatawpha* (2001); Peter R. Decker, *Fortunes and Failures: White Collar Mobility in Nineteenth-Century San Francisco* (1978); John Mack Faragher, *Sugar Creek: Life on the Illinois Prairie* (1986); Randolph B. Campbell, *A Southern Community in*

Crisis: Harrison County, 1850–1880 (1983); Steven H. Hahn, *The Roots of Southern Populism: Yeoman Farmers and the Transformation of the Georgia Upcountry, 1850–1880* (1983); Orville Vernon Burton, *In My Father's House Are Many Mansions: Family and Community in Edgefield, South Carolina* (1985); Paul D. Escott, *Many Excellent People: Power and Privilege in North Carolina, 1850–1900* (1985); John S. Gilkeson, Jr., *Middle-Class Providence, 1820–1940* (1986); Robert C. Kenzer, *Kinship and Neighborhood in a Southern Community: Orange County, North Carolina, 1850–1900* (1987); Peter R. Knights, *Yankee Destinies: The Lives of Ordinary Bostonians* (1991); Daniel E. Sutherland, *Seasons of War: The Ordeal of a Confederate Community, 1861–1865* (1995); Christopher Morris, *Becoming Southern: The Evolution of a Way of Life, Warren County and Vicksburg, Mississippi, 1770–1860* (1995); J. William Harris, *Plain Folk and Gentry in a Slave Society: White Liberty and Black Slavery in Augusta's Hinterlands* (1985); Frederick F. Siegel, *The Roots of Southern Distinctiveness: Tobacco and Society in Danville, Virginia, 1780–1865* (1987); Wayne K. Durrill, *War of Another Kind: A Southern Community in the Great Rebellion* (1990); Joseph P. Reidy, *From Slavery to Agrarian Capitalism in the Cotton Plantation South: Central Georgia, 1800–1880* (1992); Edward E. Baptist, *Creating an Old South: Middle Florida's Plantation Frontier Before the Civil War* (2002); Stephan Thernstrom, *The Other Bostonians: Poverty and Progress: Social Mobility in a Nineteenth-Century City* (1973); Edward L. Ayers, *In the Presence of Mine Enemies: The Civil War in the Heart of America, 1859–1863* (2003); and Jonathan M. Bryant, *How Curious a Land: Conflict and Change in Greene County, Georgia, 1850–1885* (1996).

On religion in the Age of Lincoln, see Mark A. Noll, *America's God: From Jonathan Edwards to Abraham Lincoln* (2002) and *The Civil War as a Theological Crisis* (2006); Randall M. Miller et al., eds., *Religion and the American Civil War* (1998); and Harry S. Stout, *Upon the Altar of the Nation: A Moral History of the Civil War* (2006). On antebellum religion, see Albert Post, *Popular Freethought in America, 1825–1850* (1943); Madeleine H. Rice, *American Catholic Opinion in the Slavery Controversy* (1944); Charles C. Cole, *The Social Ideas of the Northern Evangelists, 1826–1860* (1954); Charles A. Johnson, *The Frontier Camp Meeting: Religion's Harvest Time* (1955); Timothy B. Smith, *Revivalism and Social Reform: American Protestantism on the Eve of the Civil War* (1957): Donald G. Mathews, *Slavery and Methodism: A Chapter in American Morality, 1780–1845* (1965); Ernest L. Tuveson, *Redeemer Nation: The Idea of America's Millennial Role* (1968); Sidney Ahlstrom, *A Religious History of the American People* (1972); John Boles, *The Great Revival: The Origins of the Southern Evangelical Mind* (1972); Carol C. V. George, *Segregated Sabbaths: Richard Allen and the Emergence of Independent Black Churches, 1760–1840* (1973); Dickson D. Bruce, Jr., *And They All Sang Hallelujah: Plain-Folk Camp-Meeting Religion, 1800–1845* (1974); E. Brooks Holifield, *The Gentlemen Theologians: American Theology in Southern Culture, 1795–1860* (1978); William McLoughlin, *Revivals, Awakenings, and Reform* (1978); Richard J. Carwardine, *Trans-Atlantic Revivalism: Popular Evangelicalism in Britain and America, 1790–1865* (1978) and *Evangelicals and Politics in Antebellum America* (1997); Albert J. Raboteau, *Slave Religion: The "Invisible Institution" in the Antebellum South* (1978); Mechal Sobel, *Trabelin' On: The Slave Journey to an Afro-Baptist Faith* (1979); Anne C. Loveland, *Southern Evangelicals and the Social Order, 1800–1860* (1980); Margaret W.

Creel, *"A Peculiar People": Slave Religion and Community-Culture among the Gullahs* (1988); John Boles, ed., *Masters and Slaves in the House of the Lord: Race and Religion in the American South, 1740–1870* (1988); Nathan O. Hatch, *The Democratization of American Christianity* (1989); Curtis D. Johnson, *Islands of Holiness: Rural Religion in Upstate New York, 1790–1860* (1989) and *Redeeming America: Evangelicals and the Road to Civil War* (1993); Paul K. Conkin, *Cane Ridge: America's Pentecost* (1990); W. Reginald Ward, *The Protestant Evangelical Awakening* (1992); Mitchell Snay, *Gospel of Disunion: Religion and Separatism in the Antebellum South* (1993); A. Gregory Schneider, *The Way of the Cross Leads Home: The Domestication of American Methodism* (1993); Paul E. Johnson and Sean Wilentz, *The Kingdom of Matthias: A Story of Sex and Salvation in Nineteenth-Century America* (1994); Randy J. Sparks, *On Jordan's Stormy Banks: Evangelicalism in Mississippi, 1773–1876* (1994); Jama Lazerow, *Religion and the Working Class in Antebellum America* (1995); Christine L. Heyrman, *Southern Cross: The Beginnings of the Bible Belt* (1998); William R. Sutton, *Journeymen for Jesus: Evangelical Artisans Confront Capitalism in Jacksonian Baltimore* (1998); Ellen Eslinger, *Citizens of Zion: The Social Origins of Camp Meeting Revivalism* (1999); James O. Farmer, *The Metaphysical Confederacy: James Henley Thornwell and the Synthesis of Southern Values* (1999); Mark S. Schantz, *Piety in Providence: Class Dimensions of Religious Experience in Antebellum Rhode Island* (2000); John P. Daly, *When Slavery Was Called Freedom: Evangelicalism, Proslavery, and the Causes of the Civil War* (2002); Marianne Perciaccante, *Calling Down Fire: Charles Grandison Finney and Revivalism in Jefferson County, New York, 1800–1840* (2003); and John T. McGreevy, *Catholicism and American Freedom: A History* (2003).

On intellectual, religious, and cultural changes, especially in the postwar era, one needs to start with George Frederickson, *The Inner Civil War: Northern Intellectuals and the Crisis of the Union* (1965). See also Leo F. Marx, *The Machine in the Garden: Technology and the Pastoral Idea in America* (1964); David F. Noble, *America by Design: Science, Technology, and the Rise of Corporate Capitalism* (1978); John F. Kasson, *Amusing the Million: Coney Island at the Turn of the Century* (1978); George M. Marsden, *Fundamentalism and American Culture: The Shaping of Twentieth-Century Evangelicalism, 1870–1925* (1980); Burton J. Bledstein, *The Culture of Professionalism: The Middle Class and the Development of Higher Education in America* (1976); T. J. Jackson Lears, *No Place of Grace: Antimodernism and the Transformation of American Culture, 1880–1920* (1981); John P. Diggins, *The Lost Soul of American Politics: Virtue, Self-Interest, and the Foundations of Liberalism* (1984); David E. Shi, *The Simple Life: Plain Living and High Thinking in American Culture* (1985); Ken Fones-Wolf, *Trade Union Gospel: Christianity and Labor in Industrial Philadelphia, 1865–1910* (1989); Charles R. Wilson, *Baptized in Blood: The Religion of the Lost Cause, 1880–1920* (1990); Gaines Foster, *Moral Reconstruction: Christian Lobbyists and the Federal Legislation of Morality, 1865–1920* (2002); Daniel Stowell, *Rebuilding Zion: The Religious Reconstruction of the South, 1863–1877* (1998); Loren Baritz, *The Good Life: The Meaning of Success for the American Middle Class* (1989); Wilfred M. McClay, *Masterless: Self and Society in Modern America* (1994); Peter Karsten, *Heart versus Head: Judge-Made Law in Nineteenth-Century America* (1997); Beth B. Schweiger, *Gospel Working Up: Progress and the Pulpit in Nineteenth-Century America* (2000); David W. Blight, *Race and Reunion: The Civil*

War in American Memory (2001); and Louis Menand, *The Metaphysical Club: A Story of Ideas in America* (2001).

For Lincoln, the law was nearly sacred, especially the Constitution. On comparative legal developments, see Michael S. Hindus, *Prison and Plantation: Crime, Justice, and Authority in Massachusetts and South Carolina, 1767–1878*. On legal developments before the Civil War, see Morton J. Horwitz, *The Transformation of American Law, 1780–1860* (1977); Mark V. Tushnet, *The American Law of Slavery, 1810–1860* (1981); Norma Basch, *In the Eyes of the Law: Women, Marriage, and Property in Nineteenth-Century New York* (1982); Michael Grossberg, *Governing the Hearth: Law and the Family in Nineteenth-Century America* (1986); Daniel J. Flanigan, *The Criminal Law of Slavery and Freedom, 1800–1868* (1987); Philip Schwarz, *Twice Condemned: Slaves and the Criminal Laws of Virginia, 1705–1865* (1988); William E. Forbath, *Law and the Shaping of the American Labor Movement* (1992); Christopher L. Tomlins, *Law, Labor and Ideology in the Early American Republic* (1993); Andrew Fede, *People Without Rights: An Interpretation of the Fundamentals of the Law of Slavery in the U.S. South* (1992); Judith K. Schafer, *Slavery, The Civil Law, and the Supreme Court of Louisiana* (1997); and Ariela J. Gross, *Double Character: Slavery and Mastery in the Antebellum Southern Courtroom* (2000). More specifically on legal changes in the postwar era, see Harold Hyman, *A More Perfect Union: The Impact of the Civil War and Reconstruction on the Constitution* (1973); Herman Belz, *Abraham Lincoln, Constitutionalism, and Equal Rights in the Civil War Era* (1998); Edward L. Ayers, *Vengeance and Justice: Crime and Punishment in the Nineteenth-Century American South* (1984); James D. Schmidt, *Free to Work: Labor Law, Emancipation, and Reconstruction, 1815–1880* (1998); Harold D. Woodman, *New South—New Law: The Legal Foundations of Credit and Labor Relations in the Postbellum Agricultural South* (1995); Amy Dru Stanley, *From Bondage to Contract: Wage Labor, Marriage, and the Market in the Age of Emancipation* (1998); Robert J. Steinfeld, *Coercion, Contract, and Free Labor in the Nineteenth Century* (2001); Keith Weldon Medley, *We as Freemen: Plessy v. Ferguson* (2003); and Christopher Waldrep and Donald G. Nieman, eds., *Local Matters: Race, Crime, and Justice in the Nineteenth-Century South* (2001). One of the most careful and creative legal historians is Christopher Waldrep; see his *Roots of Disorder: Race and Criminal Justice in the American South, 1817–80* (1998) and *The Many Faces of Judge Lynch: Extralegal Violence and Punishment in America* (2002).

The economic history of this period is complicated and controversial; see Stanley Lebergott, *The Americans: An Economic Record* (1984). For the antebellum North, see Norman S. Ware, *The Industrial Worker, 1840–1860: The Reaction of American Industrial Society to the Advance of the Industrial Revolution* (1924); Reginald C. McGrane, *The Panic of 1837* (1924); Victor S. Clark, *A History of Manufactures in the United States*, vol. 1, *1607–1860* (1929); Robert G. Albion, *The Rise of New York Port, 1815–1860* (1939); Percy W. Bidwell and John I. Falconer, *A History of Agriculture in the Northern United States, 1620–1860* (1941); Joseph Dorfman, *The Economic Mind in American Civilization, 1606–1865* (1946); Bray Hammond, *Banks and Politics in America from the Revolution to the Civil War* (1957); Robert P. Sharkey, *Money, Class and Party: An Economic Study of Civil War and Reconstruction* (1959); Paul W. Gates, *The Farmer's Age: Agriculture, 1815–1860*

(1960); Douglass C. North, *The Economic Growth of the United States, 1790–1860* (1961); Edward Pessen, *Most Uncommon Jacksonians: The Radical Leaders of the Early Labor Movement* (1967) and *Riches, Class and Power Before the Civil War* (1973); Stuart Bruchey, *The Roots of American Economic Growth, 1607–1861* (1968); Clarence Danhof, *Change in Agriculture: The Northern United States, 1820–1870* (1969); Peter J. Coleman, *Debtors and Creditors in America: Insolvency, Imprisonment for Debt, and Bankruptcy, 1607–1900* (1974); David E. Schob, *Hired Hands and Plowboys: Farm Labor in the Midwest, 1815–60* (1975); Alan Dawley, *Class and Community: The Industrial Revolution in Lynn* (1976); Susan Hirsch, *Roots of the American Working Class: The Industrialization of Crafts in Newark, 1800–1860* (1978); Anthony F. C. Wallace, *Rockdale: The Growth of an American Village in the Early Industrial Revolution* (1978); Thomas Dublin, *Women and Work: The Transformation of Work and Community in Lowell, Massachusetts, 1826–1860* (1979) and *Transforming Women's Work: New England Lives in the Industrial Revolution* (1995); Bruce Laurie, *Working People of Philadelphia, 1800–1850* (1980) and *Artisans into Workers: Labor in Nineteenth-Century America* (1997); Daniel E. Sutherland, *Americans and Their Servants: Domestic Service from 1800 to 1920* (1981); Paul Faler, *Mechanics and Manufacturers in the Early Industrial Revolution: Lynn, Massachusetts, 1780–1860* (1981); Sean Wilentz, *Chants Democratic: New York City and the Rise of the American Working Class, 1788–1850* (1981); Jonathan Prude, *The Coming of Industrial Order: Town and Factory Life in Rural Massachusetts, 1810–1860* (1983); Philip Scranton, *Proprietary Capitalism: The Textile Manufacture at Philadelphia, 1810–1885* (1983); Hal S. Barron, *Those Who Stayed Behind: Rural Society in Nineteenth-Century New England* (1984); David A. Hounshell, *From the American System to Mass Production, 1800–1932: The Development of Manufacturing Technology in the United States* (1984); Barbara Tucker, *Samuel Slater and the Origins of the American Textile Industry, 1790–1860* (1984); Jeremy Atack, *Estimation of Economics of Scale in Nineteenth Century United States Manufacturing* (1985) and, with Fred Bateman, *To Their Own Soil: American Agriculture in the Antebellum North* (1987); Steven H. Hahn and Jonathan Prude, eds., *The Countryside in the Age of Capitalist Transformation: Essays in the Social History of Rural America* (1985); David Bensman, *The Practice of Solidarity: American Hat Finishers in the Nineteenth Century* (1985); Steven J. Ross, *Workers on the Edge: Work, Leisure, and Politics in Industrializing Cincinnati, 1788–1890* (1985); John M. Faragher, *Sugar Creek: Life on the Illinois Prairie* (1986); Graham R. Hodges, *New York City Cartmen, 1667–1850* (1986); William J. Rorabaugh, *The Craft Apprentice: From Franklin to the Machine Age in America* (1986); Mary H. Blewett, *Men, Women, and Work: Class, Gender, and Protest in the New England Shoe Industry, 1780–1910* (1988) and *Constant Turmoil: The Politics of Industrial Life in Nineteenth-Century New England* (2000); Christopher Clark, *The Roots of Rural Capitalism: Western Massachusetts, 1780–1860* (1990); David A. Zonderman, *Agitations and Anxieties: New England Workers and the Mechanized Factory System, 1815–1850* (1992); Winifred Rothenberg, *From Market-Places to a Market Economy: The Transformation of Rural Massachusetts, 1750–1850* (1992); Peter J. Way, *Common Labour: Workers and the Digging of North American Canals, 1780–1860* (1993); Daniel Vickers, *Farmers and Fishermen: Two Centuries of Work in Essex County, Massachusetts, 1630–1850* (1994); Tony A. Freyer,

Producers Versus Capitalists: Constitutional Conflict in Antebellum America (1994); Martin J. Burke, *The Conundrum of Class: Public Discourse on the Social Order in America* (1995); Jamie L. Bronstein, *Land Reform and Working-Class Experience in Britain and the United States, 1800–1862* (1999); Donna J. Rilling, *Making Houses, Crafting Capitalism: Master Builders in Early Philadelphia, 1790–1850* (2000); Robert A. Margo, *Wages and Labor Markets in the United States, 1820–1860* (2000); Edward J. Balleisen, *Navigating Failure: Bankruptcy and Commercial Society in Antebellum America* (2000); Jonathan M. Glickstein, *American Exceptionalism, American Anxiety: Wages, Competition, and Degraded Labor in the Antebellum United States* (2002); Martin Bruegel, *Farm, Shop, Landing: The Rise of a Market Society in the Hudson Valley, 1780–1860* (2002); and Kim M. Gruenwald, *River of Enterprise: The Commercial Origins of Regional Identity in the Ohio Valley, 1790–1850* (2002).

For the economic history of the antebellum South, see Ulrich B. Phillips, *A History of Transportation in the Eastern Cotton Belt to 1860* (1908); James C. Ballagh, *Southern Economic History* (1909); Broadus Mitchell, *William Gregg, Factory Master of the Old South* (1928); Lewis C. Gray, *History of Agriculture in the Southern United States of 1860* (1932); Harold D. Woodman, *King Cotton and His Retainers: Financing and Marketing the Cotton Crop of the South, 1800–1925* (1968); Ernest M. Lander, *The Textile Industry in Antebellum South Carolina* (1969); Robert S. Starobin, *Industrial Slavery in the Old South* (1970); Fred Bateman and Thomas Weiss, *A Deplorable Scarcity: The Failure of Industrialization in the Slave Economy* (1981); Kenneth W. Noe, *Southwest Virginia's Railroad: Modernization and the Sectional Crisis* (1994); Bess Beatty, *Alamance: The Holt Family and Industrialization in a North Carolina County, 1837–1900* (1999); John Majewski, *A House Dividing: Economic Development in Pennsylvania and Virginia Before the Civil War* (2000); Michele Gillespie, *Free Labor in an Unfree World: White Artisans in Lowcountry Georgia, 1750–1860* (2000); Curtis J. Evans, *The Conquest of Labor: Daniel Pratt and Southern Industrialization* (2001); and Frank J. Byrne, *Becoming Bourgeois: Merchant Culture in the South, 1820–1865* (2006). Peter A. Coclanis, *The Shadow of a Dream: Economic Life and Death in the South Carolina Low Country, 1670–1925* (1989), explains the era through a strongly argued central theme. On economic change in the postwar South, see Roger Ransom and Richard Sutch, *One Kind of Freedom: The Economic Consequences of Emancipation* (1977); Michael Wayne, *The Reshaping of Plantation Society: The Natchez District, 1860–1880* (1983); and Thavolia Glymph and John J. Kushma, eds., *Essays on the Postbellum Southern Economy* (1985).

On the triumph of capitalism in the postwar era, see Alfred D. Chandler, *The Visible Hand: The Managerial Revolution in American Business* (1977); Daniel T. Rodgers, *The Work Ethic in Industrial America, 1850–1920* (1978); Alan Trachtenberg, *The Incorporation of America: Culture and Society in the Gilded Age* (1982, 2007); Mark W. Summers, *Railroads, Reconstruction, and the Gospel of Prosperity: Aid Under the Radical Republicans, 1865–1877* (1984); Martin J. Sklar, *The Corporate Reconstruction of Capitalism, 1890–1916* (1987) and *The Market, the Law, and Politics* (1987); Olivier Zunz, *Making America Corporate, 1870–1920* (1990); William Leach, *Land of Desire: Merchants, Power, and the Rise of a New American Culture* (1993); David Montgomery, *Citizen Worker: The Experience of*

Workers in the United States with Democracy and the Free Market During the Nineteenth Century (1993); and Heather Cox Richardson, *The Greatest Nation of the Earth: Republican Economic Policies During the Civil War* (1997). On the wartime roots of these changes, see three studies, Harold S. Wilson, *Confederate Industry: Manufacturers and Quartermasters in the Civil War* (2002); Mark R. Wilson, *The Business of Civil War: Military Mobilization and the State, 1861–1865* (2006); and Richard T. Bensel, *The Political Economy of American Industrialism, 1877–1900* (2000).

On the conflict between capital and wage labor in the postwar era, see Jonathan Grossman, *William Sylvis: Pioneer of American Labor During the Era of the Civil War* (1945); David Brody, *Steelworkers in America: The Nonunion Era* (1960); Gerald N. Grob, *Workers and Utopia: A Study of Ideological Conflict in the American Labor Movement, 1865–1900* (1961); Stanley Buder, *Pullman: An Experiment in Industrial Order and Community Planning, 1880–1930* (1967); Lloyd Ulman, *The Rise of the National Trade Union* (1968); David Montgomery, *Beyond Equality: Labor and the Radical Republicans, 1862–1872* (1972), *Workers' Control in America* (1979), and *The Fall of the House of Labor: The Workplace, the State, and American Labor Activism, 1865–1925* (1987); Melton McLaurin, *The Knights of Labor in the South* (1978); Daniel J. Walkowitz, *Worker City, Company Town: Iron and Cotton-Worker Protest in Troy and Cohoes, New York, 1855–1884* (1978); Leon Fink, *Workingmen's Democracy: The Knights of Labor and American Politics* (1985); David Roediger and Philip S. Foner, *Our Own Time: A History of American Labor and the Working Day* (1989); Kim Voss, *The Making of American Exceptionalism: The Knights of Labor and Class Formation in the Nineteenth Century* (1994); Alexander Saxton, *The Indispensable Enemy: Labor and the Anti-Chinese Movement in California* (1994); David O. Stowell, *Streets, Railroads, and the Great Strike of 1877* (1999); Craig Phelan, *Grand Master Workman: Terence Powderly and the Knights of Labor* (2000); and Robert E. Weir, *Knights Unhorsed: Internal Conflict in a Gilded Age Social Movement* (2001).

Lincoln was a student of political ideology as well as a politician and he studied the political culture. On political ideology, see Eric Foner, *Free Soil, Free Labor, Free Men: The Ideology of the Republican Party Before the Civil War* (1970) and *Politics and Ideology in the Age of the Civil War* (1981); Fletcher M. Green, *Constitutional Development in the South Atlantic States, 1776–1860* (1930); William E. Dodd, *The Old South Struggles for Democracy* (1937); Chilton Williamson, *American Suffrage: From Property to Democracy, 1760–1860* (1960); Daniel W. Howe, *The Political Culture of the American Whigs* (1979); Allen Kaufman, *Capitalism, Slavery, and Republican Values: Antebellum Political Economists* (1982); John Ashworth, *"Agrarians" and "Aristocrats": Party Political Ideology in the United States, 1837–1846* (1983); William J. Cooper, Jr., *Liberty and Slavery: Southern Politics to 1860* (1983); Kenneth S. Greenberg, *Masters and Statesmen: The Political Culture of American Slavery* (1985); Steven Watts, *The Republican Reborn: War and the Making of Liberal America, 1790–1820* (1987); Joyce Appleby, *Liberalism and Republicanism in the Historical Imagination* (1992); Daniel Feller, *The Jacksonian Promise: America, 1815–1840* (1995); James Simeone, *Democracy and Slavery in Frontier Illinois: The Bottomland Republic* (2000); Glenn C. Altschuler and Stuart M. Blumin, *Rude Republic: Americans and Their Politics in the Nineteenth Century* (2000); Wallace Hettle, *The Peculiar Democracy: Southern Demo-*

crats in Peace and War (2001). On antebellum political culture, see Ray A. Billington, *The Protestant Crusade, 1800–1860: A Study of the Origins of American Nativism* (1938); William D. Overdyke, *The Know-Nothing Party in the South* (1950); Louis B. Hartz, *The Liberal Tradition in America: An Interpretation of American Political Thought Since the Revolution* (1955); Marvin Meyers, *The Jacksonian Persuasion: Politics and Belief* (1957); Lee Benson, *The Concept of Jacksonian Democracy: New York as a Test Case* (1961); Michael F. Holt, *Forging a Majority: The Formation of the Republican Party in Pittsburgh, 1848–1860* (1969) and *The Rise and Fall of the American Whig Party: Jacksonian Politics and the Onset of the Civil War* (1999); James R. Sharp, *The Jacksonians Versus the Banks: Politics in the States After the Panic of 1837* (1970); Ronald P. Formisano, *The Birth of Mass Political Parties: Michigan, 1827–1861* (1971) and *The Transformation of Political Culture: Massachusetts Parties, 1790s–1840s* (1983); Daniel W. Howe, *The Political Culture of the American Whigs* (1979); Robert Kelley, *The Cultural Pattern in American Politics: The First Century* (1979); Paul Kleppner, *The Third Electoral System, 1853–1892: Parties, Voters, and Political Cultures* (1979); Stephen L. Hansen, *The Making of the Third Party System: Voters and Parties in Illinois, 1850–1876* (1980); Harry Watson, *Jacksonian Politics and Community Conflict: The Emergence of the Second American Party System in Cumberland County, North Carolina* (1981); Jean H. Baker, *Affairs of Party: The Political Culture of Northern Democrats in the Mid-Nineteenth Century* (1983); Stephen E. Maizlish, *The Triumph of Sectionalism: The Transformation of Ohio Politics, 1844–1856* (1983); and, ed., *Essays on American Antebellum Politics, 1840–1860* (1982); Amy Bridges, *A City in the Republic: Antebellum New York and the Origins of Machine Politics* (1984); Dale Baum, *The Civil War Party System: The Case of Massachusetts, 1848–1876* (1984); Elisabeth Griffith, *In Her Own Right: The Life of Elizabeth Cady Stanton* (1984); Thomas Brown, *Politics and Statesmanship: Essays on the American Whig Party* (1985); Joel H. Silbey, *The Partisan Imperative: The Dynamics of American Politics Before the Civil War* (1985); William E. Gienapp, *The Origins of the Republican Party, 1852–1856* (1987); Tyler Anbinder, *Nativism and Slavery: The Northern Know-Nothings and the Politics of the 1850s* (1992); William G. Shade, *Democratizing the Old Dominion: Virginia and the Second Party System, 1824–1861* (1996); Reeve Huston, *Land and Freedom: Rural Society, Popular Protest, and Party Politics in Antebellum New York* (2000); Harold D. Tallant, *Evil Necessity: Slavery and Political Culture in Antebellum Kentucky* (2003); Peter B. Knupfer, *The Union As It Is: Constitutional Unionism and Sectional Compromise, 1787–1861* (1991); and Richard T. Bensel, *The American Ballot Box in the Mid-Nineteenth Century* (2004).

There are fine biographies for nearly all principal political actors during the Age of Lincoln, and although no one rivals Lincoln for the number of biographies, many have several. For example, for Chief Justice Taney, see Carl Brent Swisher, *Roger B. Taney* (1935); Charles W. Smith, Jr., *Roger B. Taney: Jacksonian Jurist* (1936); and Walker Lewis, *Without Fear or Favor: A Biography of Chief Justice Roger Brooke Taney* (1965). See Avery O. Craven, *Edmund Ruffin, Southerner: A Study in Secession* (1932); William M. Mayhew, *Edmund Ruffin and the Crisis of Slavery in the Old South: The Failure of Agricultural Reform* (1988); and Betty L. Mitchell, *Edmund Ruffin: A Biography* (1981). See Merrill D. Peterson, *The Great Triumvirate: Webster, Clay, and Calhoun* (1987);

Richard N. Current, *Daniel Webster and the Rise of National Conservatism* (1955); Irving H. Bartlett, *Daniel Webster* (1978); Maurice G. Baxter, *One and Inseparable: Daniel Webster and the Union* (1984); Glyndon G. Van Deusen, *The Life of Henry Clay* (1937); Robert Remini, *Henry Clay: Statesman for the Union* (1991); Charles M. Wiltse, *John C. Calhoun* (1944); Gerald M. Capers, *John C. Calhoun—Opportunist: A Reappraisal* (1960) and *Stephen A. Douglas: Defender of the Union* (1959); Robert W. Johannsen, *Stephen A. Douglas* (1973); Fawn Brodie, *Thaddeus Stevens: Scourge of the South* (1959); David H. Donald, *Charles Sumner and the Coming of the Civil War* (1960) and *Charles Sumner and the Rights of Man* (1970); Martin Duberman, *James Russell Lowell* (1966) and *Charles Francis Adams, 1807–1886* (1968); Wendell Glick's edited *Henry D. Thoreau: Reform Papers* (1973); Alvy M. King, *Louis T. Wigfall: Southern Fire-Eater* (1970); Drew G. Faust, *James Henry Hammond and the Old South: A Design for Mastery* (1982); William B. McCash, *Thomas R. R. Cobb: The Making of a Southern Nationalist* (1983); Craig M. Simpson, *A Good Southerner: The Life of Henry A. Wise of Virginia* (1985); John B. Edmunds, Jr., *Francis W. Pickens and the Politics of Destruction* (1986); Frederick J. Blue, *Salmon P. Chase: A Life in Politics* (1987) and *Charles Sumner and the Conscience of the North* (1994); Nell I. Painter, *Sojourner Truth: A Life, A Symbol* (1996); Thomas E. Schott, *Alexander Stephens of Georgia: A Biography* (1988); William C. Davis, *Rhett: The Turbulent Life and Times of a Fire-Eater* (2001); Eric H. Walther, *William Lowndes Yancey and the Coming of the Civil War* (2006); Michael A. Ross, *Justice of Shattered Dreams: Samuel Freeman Miller and the Supreme Court during the Civil War Era* (2003); Debby Applegate, *The Most Famous Man in America: The Biography of Henry Ward Beecher* (2006); Edward A. Miller, Jr., *Gullah Statesman: Robert Smalls from Slavery to Congress, 1839–1915* (1995); Okon Edet Uya, *From Slavery to Public Service: Robert Smalls, 1839–1915* (1971); James Pickett Jones, *Black Jack: John A. Logan and Southern Illinois in the Civil War Era* (1967); Carl D. Cottingham, *General John A. Logan: His Life and Times* (1989); Russell Duncan, *Freedom's Shore: Tunis Campbell and the Georgia Freedmen* (1986); David Brown, *Southern Outcast: Hinton Rowan Helper and the Impending Crisis of the South* (2006); Louis R. Harlan, *Booker T. Washington*, 2 vols. (1972, 1983); David Levering Lewis, *W.E.B. DuBois: Biography of a Race, 1868–1919* (1993); C. Vann Woodward, *Tom Watson: Agrarian Rebel* (1938); and Michael Kazin, *A Godly Hero: The Life of William Jennings Bryan* (2006).

Social and cultural history have exploded in the last few decades. On the development of social relations in the antebellum North, see Robert Ernst, *Immigrant Life in New York City: 1825–1863* (1949); Roland W. Berthoff, *British Immigrants in Industrial America, 1790–1950* (1953); Oscar Handlin, *Boston's Immigrants, 1790–1880: A Study in Acculturation* (1959); Allen F. Davis and Mark H. Haller, eds., *The Peoples of Philadelphia: A History of Ethnic Groups and Lower-Class Life, 1790–1940* (1973); Kathleen N. Conzen, *Immigrant Milwaukee, 1836–1860: Accommodation and Community in a Frontier City* (1976); Clyde Griffen and Sally Griffen, *Natives and Newcomers: The Ordering of Opportunity in Mid-Nineteenth Century Poughkeepsie* (1978); Paul E. Johnson, *A Shopkeeper's Millennium: Society and Revivals in Rochester, New York, 1815–1837* (1978); Frederic C. Jaher, *The Urban Es-*

tablishment: Upper Strata in Boston, New York, Charleston, Chicago, and Los Angeles (1982); Kerby A. Miller, *Emigrants and Exiles: Ireland and the Irish Exodus to North America* (1985); Susan G. Davis, *Parades and Power: Street Theatre in Nineteenth-Century Philadelphia* (1986); Stuart M. Blumin, *The Emergence of the Middle Class: Social Experience in the American City, 1760–1900* (1989); Richard B. Stott, *Workers in the Metropolis: Class, Ethnicity, and Youth in Antebellum New York City* (1990); Stanley Nadel, *Little Germany: Ethnicity, Religion, and Class in New York City, 1845–80* (1990); Bruce Levine, *In the Spirit of 1848: German Immigrants, Labor Protest, and the Coming of the Civil War* (1992); Dorothee Schneider, *Trade Unions and Community* (1994); and Amy S. Greenberg, *Cause for Alarm: The Volunteer Fire Department in the Nineteenth-Century City* (1998). On cultural developments in the antebellum North, see David S. Grimsted, *Melodrama Unveiled: American Theater and Culture, 1800–1850* (1968); John Higham, *From Boundlessness to Consolidation: The Transformation of American Culture, 1848–1860* (1969); Stow Persons, *The Decline of American Gentility* (1973); Neil Harris, *Humbug: The Art of P. T. Barnum* (1973); Robert C. Toll, *Blacking Up: The Minstrel Show in Nineteenth-Century America* (1977); Barbara Novak, *Nature and Culture: American Landscape and Painting, 1825–1875* (1980); Karen Halttunen, *Confidence Men and Painted Women: A Study of Middle-Class Culture in America, 1830–1870* (1982); Jane H. Pease and William H. Pease, *The Web of Progress: Private Values and Public Styles in Boston and Charleston, 1828–1843* (1985); John F. Kasson, *Rudeness and Civility: Manners in Nineteenth-Century Urban America* (1990); Eric Lott, *Love and Theft: Blackface Minstrelsy and the American Working Class* (1993); Lewis Perry, *Boats Against the Current: American Culture Between Revolution and Modernity, 1820–1860* (1993); C. Dallett Hemphill, *Bowing to Necessities: A History of Manners in America, 1620–1860* (1999); James W. Cook, *The Arts of Deception: Playing with Fraud in the Age of Barnum* (2001); and Michael Zakim, *Ready-Made Democracy: A History of Men's Dress in the American Republic, 1760–1860* (2003). On social relations in the North after the Civil War, see Sam B. Warner, *Streetcar Suburbs: The Process of Growth in Boston, 1870–1900* (1962); Robert L. Wiebe, *The Search for Order, 1877–1920* (1967); Burton J. Bledstein and Robert D. Johnson, eds., *The Middling Sorts: Explorations in the History of the American Middle Class* (2001); Sven Beckert, *The Monied Metropolis: New York City and the Consolidation of the American Bourgeoisie, 1850–1896* (2001); Timothy J. Gilfoyle, *A Pickpocket's Tale: The Underworld of Nineteenth-Century New York* (2006); and Davison M. Douglas, *Jim Crow Moves North: The Battle Over Northern School Segregation, 1865–1954* (2006).

On social relations in the West and Midwest, see Allan G. Bogue, *From Prairie to Corn Belt: Farming on the Illinois and Iowa Prairies in the Nineteenth Century* (1963); Robert R. Dykstra, *The Cattle Towns* (1968) and *Bright Radical Star: Black Freedom and White Supremacy on the Hawkeye Frontier* (1993); Stephan Thernstrom, *The Growth of Los Angeles in Historical Perspective: Myth and Reality* (1970); Dee Brown, *Bury My Heart at Wounded Knee: An Indian History of the American West* (1972); Donald Worster, *Rivers of Empire: Water, Aridity, and the Growth of the American West* (1985); Patricia N. Limerick, *The Legacy of Conquest: The Unbroken Past of the American West* (1987); William Cronon, *Nature's Metropolis: Chicago and the Great West* (1991); Robert M. Utley, *Cavalier in Buckskin:*

George Armstrong Custer and the Western Military Tradition (2001); Robert M. Utley and Wilcomb E. Washburn, *The Indian Wars* (2002); and Jane E. Simonson, *Making Home Work: Domesticity and Native American Assimilation in the American West, 1860–1919* (2006).

On the development of social relations in the South, see Frank L. Owsley, *Plain Folk of the Old South* (1949); John Hope Franklin, *The Militant South, 1800–1861* (1956); Chalmers G. Davidson, *The Last Foray: The South Carolina Planters of 1860: A Sociological Study* (1971); John C. Inscoe, *Mountain Masters: Slavery and the Sectional Crisis in Western North Carolina* (1989); Bill Cecil-Fronsman, *Common Whites: Class and Culture in Antebellum North Carolina* (1992); Timothy J. Lockley, *Lines in the Sand: Race and Class in Lowcountry Georgia, 1750–1860* (2001); James D. Miller, *South by Southwest: Planter Emigration and Identity in the Slave South* (2001); and Jeff Forret, *Race Relations at the Margins: Slaves and Poor Whites in the Antebellum Southern Countryside* (2006). On the culture of the Old South, see Clement Eaton, *The Growth of Southern Civilization, 1790–1860* (1961); William R. Taylor, *Cavalier and Yankee: The Old South and American National Character* (1961); Dickson D. Bruce, *Violence and Culture in the Antebellum South* (1979); Bertram Wyatt-Brown, *Southern Honor: Ethics and Behavior in the Old South* (1982), *Yankee Saints and Southern Sinners* (1985), and *The Shaping of Southern Culture: Honor, Grace, and War, 1760s–1890s* (2001); Steven M. Stowe, *Intimacy and Power in the Old South: Ritual in the Lives of the Planters* (1987); Kenneth S. Greenberg, *Honor and Slavery* (1996); Nicolas W. Proctor, *Bathed in Blood: Hunting and Mastery in the Old South* (2002); and Martha Elizabeth Hodes, *White Women, Black Men: Illicit Sex in the Nineteenth-Century South* (1997). See also Joel Williamson, *The Crucible of Race: Black/White Relations in the American South Since Emancipation* (1984); Altina L. Waller, *Feud: Hatfields, McCoys and Social Change in Appalachia, 1860–1900* (1988); Don H. Doyle, *New Men, New Cities, New South: Atlanta, Nashville, Charleston, Mobile, 1860–1910* (1990); Edward L. Ayers, *The Promise of the New South: Life After Reconstruction* (1992); Leon F. Litwack, *Trouble in Mind: Black Southerners in the Age of Jim Crow* (1998); Stephen Cresswell, *Redeemers, Rednecks, and Race: Mississippi After Reconstruction, 1877–1917* (2006). On the development of a Southern white working class and its intersection with emancipated African Americans, see Roger W. Shugg, *Origins of Class Struggle in Louisiana: A Social History of White Farmers and Laborers During Slavery and After, 1840–1875* (1939); Frederick A. Bode and Donald E. Ginter, *Farm Tenancy and the Census in Antebellum Georgia* (1986); Robert T. McKenzie, *One South or Many?: Plantation Belt and Upcountry in Civil War–Era Tennessee* (1994); Eric Arnesen, *Waterfront Workers of New Orleans: Race, Class, and Politics, 1863–1923* (1994); Charles C. Bolton, *Poor Whites of the Antebellum South: Tenants and Laborers in Central North Carolina and Mississippi* (1994). Essential to understanding the postbellum South is J. William Harris, *Deep Souths: Delta, Piedmont, and Sea Island Society in the Age of Segregation* (2001).

The recent literature on women and gender has greatly modified our understanding of the Age of Lincoln. On sex and gender, especially in the antebellum North, see Allan S. Horlick, *Country Boys and Merchant Princes: The Social Control of Young Men in New York* (1975); Kathryn K. Sklar, *Catherine Beecher: A Study in American Domestic-*

ity (1976); G. J. Barker-Benfield, *The Horrors of the Half-Known Life: Male Attitudes Toward Women and Sexuality in Nineteenth-Century America* (1976); Nancy F. Cott, *The Bonds of Womanhood: "Woman's Sphere" in New England, 1780–1835* (1977); Ann Douglas, *The Feminization of American Culture* (1977); Ellen C. DuBois, *Feminism and Suffrage: The Emergence of an Independent Women's Movement in America, 1848–1869* (1978); Sylvia Hoffert, *When Hens Crow: The Woman's Rights Movement in Antebellum America* (1995); Barbara L. Berg, *The Remembered Gate: Origins of American Feminism: The Woman and the City, 1800–1860* (1978); Carl N. Degler, *At Odds: Women and the Family in America from the Revolution to the Present* (1980); Mary P. Ryan, *Cradle of the Middle Class: The Family in Oneida County, New York, 1790–1865* (1981); Nancy A. Hewitt, *Women's Activism and Social Change: Rochester, New York, 1822–1872* (1981); Barbara L. Epstein, *The Politics of Domesticity: Women, Evangelism, and Temperance in Nineteenth-Century America* (1981); Steven Mintz, *A Prison of Expectations: The Family in Victorian Culture* (1983); Nancy A. Hewitt, *Women's Activism and Social Change in Rochester, New York, 1822–1872* (1984); Carroll Smith-Rosenberg, *Disorderly Conduct: Visions of Gender in Victorian America* (1985); Christine Stansell, *City of Women: Sex and Class in New York, 1789–1860* (1987); John D'Emilio and Estelle B. Freedman, *Intimate Matters: A History of Sexuality in America* (1988); Karen Lystra, *Searching the Heart: Women, Men, and Romantic Love in Nineteenth-Century America* (1989); Lori D. Ginzberg, *Women and the Work of Benevolence: Morality, Politics, and Class in the Nineteenth-Century United States* (1992); Timothy J. Gilfoyle, *City of Eros: New York City, Prostitution, and the Commercialization of Sex, 1790–1920* (1992); Jeanne Boydston, *Home and Work: Housework, Wages, and the Ideology of Labor in the Early Republic* (1994); Nancy Isenberg, *Sex and Citizenship in Antebellum America* (1998); Catherine E. Kelly, *In the New England Fashion: Reshaping Women's Lives in the Nineteenth Century* (1999); Shawn Johansen, *Family Men: Middle-Class Fatherhood in Early Industrializing America* (2001); Bruce Dorsey, *Reforming Men and Women: Gender in the Antebellum City* (2002); Carole Shammas, *A History of Household Government in America* (2002); Anne M. Boylan, *The Origins of Women's Activism: New York and Boston, 1797–1840* (2002); Barbara Cutter, *Domestic Devils, Battlefield Angels: The Radicalism of American Womanhood, 1830–1865* (2003); and Jane Turner Censer, *The Reconstruction of White Southern Womanhood, 1865–1895* (2003).

On the experience of women, black and white, under the slave regime, see Anne F. Scott, *The Southern Lady: From Pedestal to Politics, 1830–1930* (1970); Catherine Clinton, *The Plantation Mistress: Women's World in the Old South* (1982); Suzanne Lebsock, *The Free Women of Petersburg: Status and Culture in a Southern Town, 1784–1860* (1984); Jean E. Friedman, *The Enclosed Garden: Women and Community in the Evangelical South, 1830–1900* (1985); Jacqueline Jones, *Labor of Love, Labor of Sorrow: Black Women, Work, and the Family from Slavery to the Present* (1985); Deborah G. White, *Ar'n't I a Woman?: Female Slaves in the Plantation South* (1985); Elizabeth Fox-Genovese, *Within the Plantation Household: Black and White Women of the Old South* (1988); D. Barry Gaspar and Darlene C. Hine, eds., *More Than Chattel: Black Women in the Americas* (1996); Marli F. Weiner, *Mistresses and Slaves: Plantation Women in South Carolina, 1830–1880* (1998); Susanna Delfino and Michele Gillespie, eds., *Neither Lady Nor Slave: Working Women of the Old South* (2002); Stephanie M. Camp, *Closer to Freedom: Enslaved Women and Everyday Resistance in the Plantation South* (2004); and Cynthia M. Kennedy, *Braided Relations, Entwined Lives: The Women of Charleston's Urban Slave Society* (2005).

On the ways slavery and race structured gender relations more generally, see Ernest M. Lander, *The Calhoun Family and Thomas Green Clemson: The Decline of a Southern Patriarchy* (1983); Jan Lewis, *The Pursuit of Happiness: Family and Values in Jefferson's Virginia* (1983); Jane T. Censer, *North Carolina Planters and Their Children, 1800–1860* (1984); Walter J. Fraser, R. Frank Saunders, Jr., and Jon L. Wakelyn, eds., *The Web of Southern Social Relations: Women, Family, and Education* (1985); Joan E. Cashin, *A Family Venture: Men and Women on the Southern Frontier* (1991); Carol Bleser, ed., *In Joy and Sorrow: Women, Family, and Marriage in the Victorian South, 1830–1900* (1991); Victoria E. Bynum, *Unruly Women: The Politics of Social and Sexual Control in the Old South* (1992); Peter W. Bardaglio, *Reconstructing the Household: Families, Sex, and the Law in the Nineteenth-Century South* (1995); Betty Wood, *Women's Work, Men's Work: The Informal Economics of Lowcountry Georgia* (1995); Stephanie McCurry, *Masters of Small Worlds: Yeoman Households, Gender Relations, and the Political Culture of the Antebellum South Carolina Low Country* (1995); Brenda E. Stevenson, *Life in Black and White: Family and Community in the Slave South* (1997); and Elizabeth R. Varon, *We Mean to Be Counted: White Women and Politics in Antebellum Virginia* (1998).

On gender relations in the Civil War, see George C. Rable, *Civil Wars: Women and the Crisis of Southern Nationalism* (1989); Catherine Clinton and Nina Silber, eds., *Divided Houses: Gender and the Civil War* (1992); Catherine Clinton, *The Other Civil War: American Women in the Nineteenth Century* (1999); Thomas P. Lowry, *The Story the Soldiers Wouldn't Tell: Sex in the Civil War* (1994); Elizabeth D. Leonard, *Yankee Women: Gender Battles in the Civil War* (1994); Lee Ann Whites, *The Civil War as a Crisis in Gender: Augusta, 1860–1890* (1995); Drew G. Faust, *Mothers of Invention: Women of the Slaveholding South in the Civil War* (1996); Jeannie Attie, *Patriotic Toil: Northern Women and the American Civil War* (1998); James Marten, *The Children's Civil War* (1998); and Nina Silber, *Daughters of the Union: Northern Women Fight the Civil War* (2005).

On gender relations in the postwar era, see Nelson M. Blake, *The Road to Reno: A History of Divorce in the United States* (1962); Eleanor Flexner, *Century of Struggle: The Woman's Rights Movement in the United States* (1959); Lois W. Banner, *Elizabeth Cady Stanton: A Radical for Women's Rights* (1980); Altina L. Waller, *Reverend Beecher and Mrs. Tilton: Sex and Class in Victorian America* (1982); Elliott J. Gorn, *The Manly Art: Bare-Knuckle Prize Fighting in America* (1986); Nancy Cott, *The Grounding of Modern Feminism* (1987) and *Public Vows: A History of Marriage and the Nation* (2000); Mark C. Carnes, *Secret Ritual and Manhood in Victorian America* (1989); Elaine S. Abelson, *When Ladies Go A-Thieving* (1989); Ted Ownby, *Subduing Satan: Religion, Recreation, and Manhood in the Rural South, 1865–1920* (1990); Mary H. Blewett, *Men, Women, and Work: Class, Gender, and Protest in the New England Shoe Industry, 1780–1910* (1990); Tera W. Hunter, *To 'Joy My Freedom: Southern Black Women's Lives and Labors after the Civil War* (1997); Leslie A. Schwalm, *A Hard Fight for We: Women's Transition from Slavery to Freedom in South Carolina* (1997); Laura F. Edwards, *Gendered Strife and Confusion: The Politics of Reconstruction*

(1997); Noralee Frankel, *Freedom's Women: Black Women and Families in Civil War Era Mississippi* (1999); Nancy D. Bercaw, *Gendered Freedoms: Race, Rights, and the Politics of Household in the Delta, 1861–1875* (2003); and Karin L. Zipf, *Labor of Innocents: Forced Apprenticeship in North Carolina, 1715–1919* (2005).

On antebellum reform and reaction to it, see Philip S. Foner, *Business and Slavery: The New York Merchants and the Irrepressible Conflict* (1941); Helene S. Zahler, *Eastern Workingmen and National Land Policy, 1829–1862* (1941); Alice F. Tyler, *Freedom's Ferment: Phases of American Social History from the Colonial Period to the Outbreak of the Civil War* (1944); Whitney R. Cross, *The Burned-Over District: The Social and Intellectual History of Enthusiastic Religion in Western New York, 1800–1850* (1950); Bernard Mandel, *Labor, Free and Slave: Workingmen and Anti-Slavery* (1955); Clifford S. Griffin, *Their Brothers' Keepers: Moral Stewardship in the United States* (1960); Lorman Ratner, *Powder Keg: Northern Opposition to the Antislavery Movement, 1831–1840* (1968); J.F.C. Harrison, *Quest for the New Moral World: Robert Owen and the Owenites in Britain and America* (1969); Leonard P. Richards, *"Gentlemen of Property and Standing": Anti-Abolition Mobs in Jacksonian America* (1970); Carl N. Degler, *The Other South: Southern Dissenters in the Nineteenth Century* (1974); Ronald W. Walters, *American Reformers, 1815–1860* (1978); George M. Thomas, *Revivalism and Cultural Change: Christianity, Nation-Building, and the Market in the Nineteenth-Century United States* (1989); Carl J. Guarneri, *The Utopian Alternative: Fourierism in Nineteenth-Century America* (1991); Barbara L. Bellows, *Benevolence Among Slaveholders: Assisting the Poor in Charleston, 1670–1860* (1993); Robert H. Abzug, *Cosmos Crumbling: American Reform and the Religious Imagination* (1994); Steven Mintz, *Moralists and Modernizers: America's Pre–Civil War Reformers* (1995); Leo P. Hirrel, *Children of Wrath: New School Calvinism and Antebellum Reform* (1998); Catherine M. Rokicky, *Creating a Perfect World: Religious and Secular Utopias in Nineteenth-Century Ohio* (2002); David S. Grimsted. *American Mobbing: Toward Civil War, 1828–1861* (2003); and Susan M. Ryan, *The Grammar of Good Intentions: Race and the Antebellum Culture of Benevolence* (2003).

On the abolitionist crusade, see W.E.B. Du Bois, *John Brown* (1919); Russel B. Nye, *William Lloyd Garrison and the Humanitarian Reformers* (1955); Louis Filler, *The Crusade Against Slavery, 1830–1860* (1960); Dwight L. Dumond, *Antislavery: The Crusade for Freedom in America* (1961); John J. Auer, *Antislavery and Disunion, 1858–1861: Studies in the Rhetoric of Compromise and Conflict* (1963); John L. Thomas, *The Liberator: William Lloyd Garrison* (1963); Martin Duberman, ed., *The Antislavery Vanguard: Essays on the Abolitionists* (1965); Gerda Lerner, *The Grimké Sisters from South Carolina* (1967); Alma Lutz, *Crusade for Freedom: Women of the Antislavery Movement* (1967); Staughton Lynd, *Intellectual Origins of American Radicalism* (1968); Benjamin Quarles, *Black Abolitionists* (1969) and *Allies for Freedom: Blacks and John Brown* (1974); Bertram Wyatt-Brown, *Lewis Tappan and the Evangelical War Against Slavery* (1969); James B. Stewart, *Joshua R. Giddings and the Tactics of Radical Politics* (1970); Aileen S. Kraditor, *Means and Ends in American Abolitionism: Garrison and His Critics on Strategy and Tactics, 1834–1850* (1970); Gerald Sorin, *The New York Abolitionists: A Case Study of Political Radicalism* (1971); Lewis Perry, *Radical Abolitionism, Anarchism, and the Government of God in Antislavery Thought* (1973) and *Childhood, Marriage, and Reform: Henry Clarke Wright, 1797–1870* (1980); Merton L. Dillon, *The Abolitionists: The Growth of a Dissenting Minority* (1974); James B. Stewart, *Holy Warriors: The Abolitionists and American Slavery* (1976) and *Wendell Phillips: Liberty's Hero* (1986); Ronald W. Walters, *The Antislavery Appeal: American Abolitionism after 1830* (1978); Peter F. Walker, *Moral Choices: Memory, Desire, and Imagination in Nineteenth-Century American Abolition* (1980); Robert H. Abzug, *Passionate Liberator: Theodore Dwight Weld and the Dilemma of Reform* (1980); Blanche G. Hersh, *The Slavery of Sex: Feminist Abolitionists in America* (1978); Lewis Perry and Michael Fellman, eds., *Antislavery Reconsidered: New Perspectives on the Abolitionists* (1979); John R. McKivigan, *The War Against Proslavery Religion, 1830–1865* (1984); Stephen B. Oates, *To Purge This Land with Blood: A Biography of John Brown* (1984); Edward Magdol, *The Antislavery Rank and File: A Social Profile of the Abolitionist Constituency* (1986); Richard H. Abbott, *Cotton and Capital: Boston Businessmen and Antislavery Reform, 1854–1868* (1991); William S. McFeely, *Frederick Douglass* (1991); Debra G. Hansen, *Strained Sisterhood: Gender and Class in the Boston Female Antislavery Society* (1993); Stanley Harrold, *The Abolitionists and the South, 1831–1861* (1995); Paul Finkelman, ed., *His Soul Goes Marching On: Responses to John Brown and the Harpers Ferry Road* (1995); Julie Roy Jeffrey, *The Great Silent Army of Abolitionism: Ordinary Women in the Antislavery Movement* (1998); Henry Mayer, *All on Fire: William Lloyd Garrison and the Abolition of Slavery* (1998); Paul Goodman, *Of One Blood: Abolitionism and the Origins of Racial Equality* (1998); Albert J. Von Frank, *The Trials of Anthony Burns: Freedom and Slavery in Emerson's Boston* (1998); Anna M. Speicher, *The Religious World of Antislavery Women: Spirituality in the Lives of Five Abolitionist Lecturers* (2000); Stacey M. Robertson, *Parker Pillsbury: Radical Abolitionist, Male Feminist* (2000); Catherine Clinton, *Fanny Kemble's Civil Wars* (2000) and *Harriet Tubman: The Road to Freedom* (2004); Milton C. Sernett, *North Star Country: Upstate New York and the Crusade for African American Freedom* (2002); Louis A. De Caro, Jr., *"Five from the Midst of You": A Religious Life of John Brown* (2002); Michael D. Pierson, *Free Hearts and Free Homes: Gender and American Antislavery Politics* (2003); Stanley Harrold, *Subversives: Antislavery Community in Washington, D.C., 1828–1865* (2003); Susan Zaeske, *Signatures of Citizenship: Petitioning, Antislavery, and Women's Political Identity* (2003); and Bruce Laurie, *Beyond Garrison: Antislavery and Social Reform* (2006).

The problem of slavery and its destruction dominates the historiography of the Age of Lincoln. Useful surveys of scholarly debates include Hugh Aitken, ed., *Did Slavery Pay?: Readings in the Economics of Black Slavery in the United States* (1989); John B. Boles, *Black Southerners, 1619–1869* (1983); Peter J. Parish, *Slavery: History and Historians* (1989); and Robert W. Fogel, *The Slavery Debates, 1952–1990: A Retrospective* (2003). An insightful treatment is Mark M. Smith, *Debating Slavery: Economy and Society in the Antebellum American South* (1998); see also his imaginative *Mastered by the Clock: Time, Slavery, and Freedom in the American South* (1997). Important overviews include Ulrich B. Phillips, *American Negro Slavery: A Survey of the Supply, Employment, and Control of Negro Labor as Determined by the Plantation Regime* (1918), *Life and Labor in the Old South* (1929), and *The Slave Economy of the Old South: Selected Essays in Economic and Social History*, ed. Eugene D. Genovese, (1968); John Hope Franklin, *From Slavery to Freedom: A History of Negro Americans* (1947, many editions since); Kenneth M. Stampp, *The Peculiar Institution:*

Slavery in the Antebellum South (1956); Stanley Elkins, *Slavery: A Problem in American Institutional and Intellectual Life* (1959); Robert McColley, *Slavery and Jeffersonian Virginia* (1964); Richard C. Wade, *Slavery in the Cities: The South, 1820–1860* (1964); Ann J. Lane, ed., *The Debate Over Slavery: Stanley Elkins and His Critics* (1971); George P. Rawick, *From Sundown to Sunup: The Making of the Black Community* (1972); Eugene D. Genovese, *In Red and Black: Marxian Explorations in Southern Life and Thought* (1972); and *Roll, Jordan, Roll: The World the Slaves Made* (1974); Robert W. Fogel and Stanley L. Engerman, *Time on the Cross: The Economics of American Negro Slavery* (1974); Herbert G. Gutman, *Slavery and the Numbers Game: A Critique of* Time on the Cross (1975) and *The Black Family in Slavery and Freedom, 1760–1925* (1975); Claudia D. Goldin, *Urban Slavery in the South, 1820–1860* (1976); Paul A. David, Herbert G. Gutman, Richard Sutch, Peter Temin, and Gavin Wright, *Reckoning with Slavery: A Critical Study of the Quantitative History of American Negro Slavery* (1976); Nathan Huggins, *Black Odyssey: The Afro-American Ordeal in Slavery* (1977); Lawrence W. Levine, *Black Culture and Black Consciousness: Afro-American Folk Thought from Slavery to Freedom* (1977); Gavin Wright, *The Political Economy of the Cotton South: Households, Markets, and Wealth in the Nineteenth Century* (1978); John W. Blassingame, *The Slave Community: Plantation Life in the Antebellum South* (1972, 1979); Paul D. Escott, *Slavery Remembered: A Record of Twentieth-Century Slave Narratives* (1979); Vincent Harding, *There Is a River: The Black Struggle for Freedom in America* (1981); Willie Lee Rose, *Slavery and Freedom* (1981); Charles Joyner, *Down by the Riverside: A South Carolina Slave Community* (1984); Saidiya V. Hartman, *Scenes of Subjection: Terror, Slavery, and Self-Making in Nineteenth-Century America* (1997); Michael Vorenberg, *Final Freedom: The Civil War, the Abolition of Slavery, and the Thirteenth Amendment* (2001); Sterling Stuckey, *Slave Culture: Nationalist Theory and the Foundations of Black America* (1987); and Robert W. Fogel, *Without Consent or Contract: The Rise and Fall of American Slavery* (1989). Peter Kolchin, *Unfree Labor: American Slavery and Russian Serfdom* (1987), suggested the fruits of comparative study; his *American Slavery, 1619–1877* (1993, 2003) has a superb bibliographical essay, and the tenth-anniversary issue has a new preface and afterword.

Recent studies have tended to focus on smaller themes or communities. See Norrece T. Jones, Jr., *Born a Child of Freedom, Yet a Slave: Mechanisms of Control and Strategies of Resistance in Antebellum South Carolina* (1990); Ann P. Malone, *Sweet Chariot: Slave Family and Household Structure in Nineteenth-Century Louisiana* (1992); Ira Berlin and Philip D. Morgan, eds., *Cultivation and Culture: Labor and the Shaping of Slave Life in the Americas* (1993); Charles B. Dew, *Bond of Iron: Master and Slave at Buffalo Forge* (1994); Larry E. Hudson, Jr., ed., *Working Toward Freedom: Slave Society and Domestic Economy in the American South* (1994); Wilma King, *Stolen Childhood: Slave Youth in Nineteenth-Century America* (1995); William Dusinberre, *Them Dark Days: Slavery in the American Rice Swamps* (1996); Larry E. Hudson, Jr., *To Have and to Hold: Slave Work and Family Life in Antebellum South Carolina* (1997); Midori Takagi, *"Rearing Wolves to Our Own Destruction": Slavery in Richmond, Virginia, 1782–1865* (1999); Michael A. Gomez, *Exchanging Our Country Marks: The Transformation of African Identities in the Colonial and Antebellum South* (2000); Sally E. Hadden, *Slave Patrols: Law and Violence in Virginia and the Carolinas*

(2001); Dylan C. Penningroth, *The Claims of Kinfolk: African American Property and Community in the Nineteenth-Century South* (2003); Emily West, *Chains of Love: Slave Couples in Antebellum South Carolina* (2004); Clayton E. Jewett and John O. Allen, *Slavery in the South: A State-by-State History* (2004); Eric Burin, *Slavery and the Peculiar Solution: A History of the American Colonization Society* (2005); and W. J. Megginson, *African American Life in South Carolina's Upper Piedmont, 1780–1900* (2006). Important recent broad interpretations include Ira Berlin, *Generations of Captivity: A History of African American Slaves* (2003); and Adam Rothman, *Slave Country: American Expansion and the Origins of the Deep South* (2005). A must-read for students of slavery and race relations is the Pulitzer Prize–winning evocative understanding of black culture and the search for home rule by Steven H. Hahn, *A Nation Under Our Feet: Black Political Struggles in the Rural South from Slavery to the Great Migration* (2003).

On the experiences of African Americans living beyond slavery's grasp in the antebellum era, see John Hope Franklin, *The Free Negro in North Carolina, 1790–1860* (1943); Leon F. Litwack, *North of Slavery: The Negro in the Free States, 1790–1860* (1961); Letitia W. Brown, *Free Negroes in the District of Columbia, 1790–1846* (1972); Jane H. Pease and William H. Pease, *They Who Would Be Free: Blacks' Search for Freedom, 1830–1861* (1974); Ira Berlin, *Slaves Without Masters: The Free Negro in the Antebellum South* (1974); James O. Horton and Lois E. Horton, *Black Bostonians: Family Life and Community Struggle in the Antebellum North* (1979) and *In Hope of Liberty: Culture, Community, and Protest Among Northern Free Blacks, 1700–1860* (1997); Leonard Curry, *The Free Black in Urban America, 1800–1850: The Shadow of the Dream* (1981); Barbara J. Fields, *Slavery and Freedom on the Middle Ground: Maryland During the Nineteenth Century* (1985); Gary B. Nash, *Forging Freedom: The Formation of Philadelphia's Black Community, 1720–1840* (1988); James O. Horton, *Free People of Color: Inside the African American Community* (1993); Tommy L. Bogger, *Free Blacks in Norfolk, Virginia, 1790–1860: The Darker Side of Freedom* (1997); Joanne P. Melish, *Disowning Slavery: Gradual Emancipation and "Race" in New England, 1780–1860* (1998); Graham R. Hodges, *Root and Branch: African Americans in New York and East Jersey, 1613–1863* (1999); Shane White, *Stories of Freedom in Black New York* (2002); and Leslie M. Harris, *In the Shadow of Slavery: African Americans in New York City, 1626–1863* (2003). On the complex question of black slaveholders, see Michael P. Johnson and James L. Roark, *Black Masters: A Free Family of Color in the Old South* (1984); and Larry Koger, *Black Slaveowners: Free Black Slave Masters in South Carolina, 1790–1860* (1985). Essential for both antebellum free blacks and economic development in the postwar era is Loren Schweninger, *Black Property Owners in the South, 1790–1915* (1990).

On the intersection of slavery and race, see Winthrop D. Jordan, *White Over Black: American Attitudes Toward the Negro, 1550–1812* (1968); Carl N. Degler, *Neither Black nor White: Slavery and Race Relations in Brazil and the United States* (1971); George W. Fredrickson, *The Black Image in the White Mind: The Debate on Afro-American Character and Destiny, 1817–1914* (1971).

On the slave trade, foreign and domestic, see W.E.B. Du Bois, *The Suppression of the African Slave Trade of the United States of America, 1638–1870* (1908); Frederic Bancroft, *Slave-trading in the Old South* (1931); Michael Tadman, *Speculators and Slaves: Masters, Traders, and Slaves in the Old South* (1989); Walter Johnson, *Soul by Soul: Life Inside the Antebellum Slave Market* (1999); Robert H. Gudmestad, *A Troublesome Commerce: The Transformation of the Interstate Slave Trade* (2003); Jonathan D. Martin, *Divided Mastery: Slave Hiring in the American South* (2004); and Steven Deyle, *Carry Me Back: The Domestic Slave Trade in American Life* (2005).

On slave resistance in the antebellum era, see Joseph C. Carroll, *Slave Insurrections in the United States, 1800–1865* (1938); Herbert W. Aptheker, *American Negro Slave Revolts* (1942); Robert S. Starobin, *Denmark Vesey: The Slave Conspiracy of 1822* (1970); Stephen Oates, *The Fires of Jubilee: Nat Turner's Fierce Rebellion* (1975); Eugene D. Genovese, *From Rebellion to Revolution: Afro-American Slave Revolts in the Making of the Modern World* (1979); Merton L. Dillon, *Slavery Attacked: Southern Slaves and Their Allies, 1619–1865* (1990); Sylvia Frey, *Water from the Rock: Black Resistance in a Revolutionary Age* (1991); Winthrop D. Jordan, *Tumult and Crisis at Second Creek: An Inquiry into a Civil War Slave Conspiracy* (1993); John Hope Franklin and Loren Schweninger, *Runaway Slaves: Rebels on the Plantation* (1999); Michael Wayne, *Death of an Overseer: Reopening a Murder Investigation from the Plantation South* (2001); Cassandra Pybus, *Epic Journeys of Freedom: Runaway Slaves of the American Revolution and Their Global Quest for Liberty* (2006); and Walter C. Rucker, *The River Flows On: Black Resistance, Culture, and Identity Formation in Early America* (2006).

On those who enslaved and owned African Americans, see Clement Eaton, *The Growth of Southern Civilization, 1790–1860* (1961); James Oakes, *The Ruling Race: A History of American Slaveholders* (1982); and *Slavery and Freedom: An Interpretation of the Old South* (1990); Laurence Shore, *Southern Capitalists: The Ideological Leadership of an Elite, 1832–1885* (1986); Drew G. Faust, *Southern Stories: Slaveholders in Peace and War* (1992); William K. Scarborough, *Masters of the Big House: Elite Slaveholders of the Mid-Nineteenth Century South* (2003); Richard J. Follett, *The Sugar Masters: Planters and Slaves in Louisiana's Cane World, 1820–1860* (2005); Daniel J. Kilbride, *An American Aristocracy: Southern Planters in Antebellum Philadelphia* (2006); Martha J. Brazy, *An American Planter: Stephen Duncan of Antebellum Natchez and New York* (2006). On proslavery thought, see William S. Jenkins, *Pro-Slavery Thought in the Old South* (1935); Harvey Wish, *George Fitzhugh: Propagandist of the Old South* (1941); Clement Eaton, *The Mind of the Old South* (1964); Eugene D. Genovese, *The World the Slaveholders Made: Two Essays in Interpretation* (1968) and *The Slaveholders' Dilemma: Freedom and Progress in Southern Conservative Thought, 1820–1860* (1992); Drew G. Faust, *A Sacred Circle: The Dilemma of the Intellectual in the Old South, 1840–1860* (1977); Donald Robinson, *Slavery in the Structure of American Politics, 1765–1820* (1979); George M. Fredrickson, *White Supremacy: A Comparative Study in American and South African History* (1981); Alison G. Freehling, *Drift Toward Dissolution: The Virginia Slavery Debate of 1831–1832* (1982); Larry E. Tise, *Proslavery: A History of the Defense of Slavery in America, 1701–1840* (1987); Paul Finkelman, *Slavery and the Founders: Race and Liberty in the Age of Jefferson* (1996); Michael O'Brien, *Conjectures of*

Order: Intellectual Life and the American South, 1810–1860 (2004); and Elizabeth Fox-Genovese and Eugene D. Genovese, *The Mind of the Master Class: History and Faith in the Southern Slaveholders' Worldview* (2005).

On nationalism and the growth of sectional conflict, see Arthur C. Cole, *The Irrepressible Conflict: 1850–1865* (1934); Glover Moore, *The Missouri Controversy, 1819–1821* (1937); Jesse T. Carpenter, *The South as a Conscious Minority, 1789–1861: A Study in Political Thought* (1931); Charles S. Sydnor, *The Development of Southern Sectionalism, 1819–1848* (1948); Roy F. Nichols, *The Disruption of American Democracy* (1948); Russel B. Nye, *Fettered Freedom: Civil Liberties and the Slavery Controversy, 1830–1860* (1949); Avery O. Craven, *The Growth of Southern Nationalism, 1848–1861* (1953); William W. Freehling, *Prelude to Civil War: The Nullification Controversy in South Carolina, 1816–1836* (1965) and especially his insightful development of secession, *The Road to Disunion: Secessonists at Bay, 1776–1854* (1990); Chaplain W. Morrison, *Democratic Politics and Sectionalism: The Wilmot Proviso Controversy* (1967); Eugene H. Berwanger, *The Frontier Against Slavery: Western Anti-Negro Prejudices and the Slavery Extension Controversy* (1967); Stanley W. Campbell, *The Slave Catchers: Enforcement of the Fugitive Slave Law, 1850–1860* (1968); James P. Rawley, *Race and Politics: "Bleeding Kansas" and the Coming of the Civil War* (1969); Joseph G. Rayback, *The Election of 1848* (1970); Frederick J. Blue, *The Free Soilers: Third Party Politics, 1848–54* (1973); Robert E. May, *The Southern Dream of a Caribbean Empire, 1854–1861* (1973) and *Manifest Destiny's Underworld: Filibustering in Antebellum America* (2002); Thomas D. Morris, *Free Men All: The Personal Liberty Laws of the North, 1780–1861* (1974); Richard H. Sewell, *Ballots for Freedom: Antislavery Politics in the United States, 1837–1860* (1976); Michael A. Morrison, *Slavery and the American West* (1977); William J. Cooper, *The South and the Politics of Slavery, 1826–1856* (1978); Don E. Fehrenbacher, *The Dred Scott Case: Its Significance in American Law and Politics* (1978) and *Slavery, Law and Politics: The Dred Scott Case in Historical Perspective* (1981); J. Mills Thornton III, *Politics and Power in a Slave Society: Alabama, 1800–1860* (1978); Gerald W. Wolff, *The Kansas-Nebraska Bill: Party, Section, and the Coming of the Civil War* (1978); Michael F. Holt, *The Political Crisis of the 1850s* (1978) and *The Fate of Their Country: Politicians, Slavery Extension, and the Coming of the Civil War* (2004); Thelma Jennings, *The Nashville Convention: Southern Movement for Unity, 1848–1851* (1980); Ernest M. Lander, Jr., *Reluctant Imperialists: Calhoun, the South Carolinians, and the Mexican War* (1980); Kenneth M. Stampp, *The Imperiled Union: Essays on the Background of the Civil War* (1980); and *America in 1857: A Nation on the Brink* (1990); John M. McCardell, *The Idea of a Southern Nation: Southern Nationalists and Southern Nationalism, 1830–1860* (1981); John Barnwell, *Love of Order: South Carolina's First Secession Crisis* (1982); Robert W. Johannsen, *To the Halls of the Montezumas: The Mexican War in the American Imagination* (1985); Richard Ellis, *The Union at Risk: Jacksonian Democracy, States' Rights, and the Nullification Controversy* (1987); Eric H. Walther, *The Fire-Eaters* (1992); John Ashworth, *Slavery, Capitalism, and Politics in the Antebellum Republic* (1995); Brian Holden Reid, *The Origins of the American Civil War* (1996); Mark J. Stegmeier, *Texas, New Mexico, and the Compromise of 1850: Boundary Dispute and Sectional Crisis* (1996); Harry V. Jaffa, *New Birth of Freedom: Abraham Lincoln and the Coming of the Civil War* (2000); Leonard L. Richards, *The Slave*

Power: The Free North and Southern Domination, 1780–1860 (2000); Manisha Sinha, *The Counterrevolution of Slavery: Politics and Ideology in Antebellum South Carolina* (2000); Susan-Mary Grant, *North Over South: Northern Nationalism and American Identity in the Antebellum Era* (2000); Paul Foos, *A Short, Offhand, Killing Affair: Soldiers and Social Conflict During the Mexican-American War* (2002); Jon Kukla, *A Wilderness So Immense: The Louisiana Purchase and the Destiny of America* (2003); Roger G. Kennedy, *Mr. Jefferson's Lost Cause: Land, Farmers, Slavery, and the Louisiana Purchase* (2003); and Nicole Etcheson, *Bleeding Kansas: Contested Liberty in the Civil War Era* (2004). An especially useful study of the Brooks-Sumner affair is T. Lloyd Benson, *The Caning of Senator Sumner* (2003). Along with Lee Soltow, *Men and Wealth in the United States, 1850–1870* (1975), the works by James L. Huston, *The Panic of 1857 and the Coming of the Civil War* (1987), *Securing the Fruits of Labor: The American Concept of Wealth Distribution, 1765–1900* (1998), and *Calculating the Value of the Union: Slavery, Property Rights, and the Economic Origins of the Civil War* (2003), are indispensable for understanding the economy and social mobility in nineteenth-century America.

Important studies of the secession crisis include Dwight L. Dumond, *The Secession Movement, 1860–1861* (1931); David M. Potter, *Lincoln and His Party in the Secession Crisis* (1943); Kenneth M. Stampp, *And the War Came: The North and the Secession Crisis, 1860–61* (1950); Steven A. Channing, *Crisis of Fear: Secession in South Carolina* (1970); William L. Barney, *The Secessionist Impulse: Alabama and Mississippi in 1860* (1974) and *The Road to Secession: A New Perspective on the Old South* (1972); Michael P. Johnson, *Toward a Patriarchal Republic: The Secession of Georgia* (1977); Walter L. Buenger, *Secession and the Union in Texas* (1984); Daniel W. Crofts, *Reluctant Confederates: Upper South Unionists in the Secession Crisis* (1989); Dale Baum, *The Shattering of Texas Unionism: Politics in the Lone Star State During the Civil War Era* (1998); Christopher J. Olsen, *Political Culture and Secession in Mississippi: Masculinity, Honor, and the Antiparty Tradition, 1830–1860* (2000); Charles B. Dew, *Apostles of Disunion: Southern Secession Commissioners and the Causes of the Civil War* (2001); and William A. Link, *Roots of Secession: Slavery and Politics in Antebellum Virginia* (2003).

The military history of the Civil War is enormous and increasingly sophisticated. Good overviews of central dynamics include David Donald, ed., *Why the North Won the Civil War* (1960, rev. 1996); Herman Hattaway and Archer Jones, *How the North Won: A Military History of the Civil War* (1983); Richard E. Beringer, Herman Hattaway, Archer Jones, and William Still, Jr., *Why the South Lost the Civil War* (1991); Gabor S. Boritt, ed., *Why the Confederacy Lost* (1992); and Gary W. Gallagher, *The Confederate War* (1997). Charles Royster, *The Destructive War: William Tecumseh Sherman, Stonewall Jackson, and the Americans* (1993) is especially important; it covers the military dimension of the conflict but also argues that the civilian populations, North and South, demanded a costly war to confirm their superiority and overawe the enemy. See also Fred A. Shannon, *The Organization and Administration of the Union Army, 1861–1865* (1928); B. H. Liddell Hart, *Sherman: Soldier, Realist, American* (1929); J.F.C. Fuller, *Grant and Lee: A Study in Personality and Generalship* (1933); Douglas S. Freeman, *R. E. Lee: A Biography* (1934) and *Lee's Lieutenants: A Study in Command* (1943); Kenneth

P. Williams, *Lincoln Finds a General* (1949–59); T. Harry Williams, *Lincoln and His Generals* (1952); Earl S. Miers, *The Web of Victory: Grant at Vicksburg* (1955); Archer Jones, *Confederate Strategy from Shiloh to Vicksburg* (1961); James G. Barrett, *Sherman's March Through the Carolinas* (1961); Clifford Dowdey, *The Seven Days: The Emergence of Lee* (1964); Thomas L. Connelly, *Army of the Heartland: The Army of Tennessee, 1861–1862* (1967) and *Autumn of Glory: The Army of Tennessee, 1862–1865* (1971); Thomas L. Connelly and Archer Jones, *The Politics of Command: Factions and Ideas in Confederate Strategy* (1973); Edwin B. Coddington, *The Gettysburg Campaign: A Study in Command* (1968); Eugene C. Murdock, *Patriotism Limited, 1862–1865: The Civil War Draft and the Bounty System* (1967) and *One Million Men: The Civil War Draft in the North* (1971); Richard D. Goff, *Confederate Supply* (1969); E. Milby Burton, *The Siege of Charleston, 1861–1865* (1970); Robert G. Tanner, *Stonewall in the Valley: Thomas J. "Stonewall" Jackson's Shenandoah Valley Campaign, Spring 1862* (1976); James Lee McDonough, *Shiloh: In Hell Before Night* (1977); Grady McWhiney and Perry D. Jamieson, *Attack and Die: Civil War Tactics and the Southern Heritage* (1982); Steven V. Sears, *Landscape Turned Red: The Battle of Antietam* (1983); James Lee McDonough, *Chattanooga: A Death Grip on the Confederacy* (1984); Joseph T. Glatthaar, *The March to the Sea and Beyond: Sherman's Troops in the Savannah and Carolinas Campaign* (1985); Harry W. Pfanz, *Gettysburg: The Second Day* (1987), *Gettysburg: Culp's Hill and Cemetery Hill* (1993); and *Gettysburg: The First Day* (2001); Jeffrey D. Wert, *From Winchester to Cedar Creek: The Shenandoah Campaign of 1864* (1987); Edward Hagerman, *The American Civil War and the Origins of Modern Warfare: Ideas, Organizations, and Field Command* (1988); Richard M. McMurry, *Two Great Rebel Armies: An Essay in Confederate Military History* (1989); John Henessy, *The First Battle of Manassas: An End to Innocence, July 18–21, 1861* (1989); John M. Priest, *Antietam: The Soldier's Battle* (1989); Michael A. Cavanaugh and William Marvel, *The Petersburg Campaign: The Battle of the Crater: "The Horrid Pit," June 25–August 6, 1864* (1989); Peter Cozzens, *No Better Place to Die: The Battle of Stones River* (1990); Steven E. Woodworth, *Jefferson Davis and His Generals: The Failure of Confederate Command in the West* (1990), *Beneath a Northern Sky: A Short History of the Gettysburg Campaign* (2003), and *Nothing But Victory: The Army of the Tennessee, 1861–1865* (2005); Grady McWhiney and Judith Lee Hallock, *Braxton Bragg and Confederate Defeat* (1991); Steven W. Sears, *To the Gates of Richmond: The Peninsular Campaign* (1992); Albert Castel, *Decision in the West: The Atlanta Campaign of 1864* (1992); Peter Cozzens, *This Terrible Sound: The Battle of Chickamauga* (1992); Ernest B. Furgerson, *Chancellorsville 1863: The Souls of the Brave* (1992); Archer Jones, *Civil War Command and Strategy: The Process of Victory and Defeat* (1992); Wiley Sword, *Embrace an Angry Wind: The Confederacy's Last Hurrah: Spring Hill, Franklin, and Nashville* (1992); Michael C. C. Adams, *Fighting for Defeat: Union Military Failure in the East, 1861–1865* (1993); John F. Marszalek, *Sherman: A Soldier's Passion for Order* (1993); John J. Hennessy, *Return to Bull Run: The Campaign and Battle of Second Manassas* (1993); James Lee McDonough, *War in Kentucky: From Shiloh to Perryville* (1994); Gordon C. Rhea, *The Battle of the Wilderness, May 5–6, 1864* (1994); Mark Grimsley, *The Hard Hand of War: Union Military Policy Toward Southern Civilians, 1861–1865* (1995); Ernest B. Furgurson, *Not War But Murder: Cold Harbor 1864* (2000); Paddy Griffith, *Battle Tactics of the Civil*

War (2001); William B. Holbertson, *Homeward Bound: The Demobilization of the Union and Confederate Armies, 1865–1866* (2001); Jay Winik, *April 1865: The Month that Saved America* (2001); George C. Rable, *Fredericksburg! Fredericksburg!* (2002); Ethan S. Rafuse, *A Single Grand Victory: The First Campaign of Manassas* (2002); James M. McPherson, *Crossroads of Freedom: Antietam* (2002); and Brent Nosworthy, *The Bloody Crucible of Courage: Fighting Methods and Combat Experience of the Civil War* (2003).

For those wishing greater detail still, the superb battle guides published by the Army War College bring the terms of combat alive. See Jay Luvaas and Harold W. Nelson, eds., *The U.S. Army War College Guide to the Battle of Antietam: The Maryland Campaign of 1862* (1987); Jay Luvaas and Harold Nelson, eds., *The U.S. Army War College Guide to the Battles of Chancellorsville and Fredericksburg* (1988); Matt Spruill, ed., *The U.S. Army War College Guide to the Battle of Chickamauga* (1993); Jay Luvaas, Steven Bowman, and Leonard Fullenkamp, eds., *The U.S. Army War College Guide to the Battle of Shiloh* (1996) and *The U.S. Army War College Guide to the Vicksburg Campaign* (1998).

There is an interesting and growing literature on soldiers during the Civil War. Among the most valuable works on this subject are James Robertson, *Soldiers Blue and Gray* (1998); Albert B. Moore, *Conscription and Conflict in the Confederacy* (1924); Ella Lonn, *Desertion During the Civil War* (1928); Bessie Martin, *Desertion of Alabama Troops from the Confederate Army: A Study in Sectionalism* (1932); Georgia Lee Tatum, *Disloyalty in the Confederacy* (1934); Bell I. Wiley, *The Life of Johnny Reb: The Common Soldier of the Confederacy* (1943) and *The Life of Billy Yank: The Common Soldier of the Union* (1952); Charles W. Wills, *Army Life of an Illinois Soldier* (1906); Jennifer Cain Bohrnstedt, ed., *Soldiering with Sherman: The Civil War Letters of George F. Cram* (2000); Gerald F. Linderman, *Embattled Courage: The Experience of Combat in the American Civil War* (1987); Earl J. Hess, *Liberty, Virtue, and Progress: Northerners and Their War for the Union* (1988) and *The Union Soldier in Battle: Enduring the Ordeal of Combat* (1997); Reid Mitchell, *Civil War Soldiers: Their Expectations and Their Experiences* (1988); James W. Geary, *We Need Men: The Union Draft in the Civil War* (1991); Larry J. Daniel, *Soldiering in the Army of Tennessee: A Portrait of Life in a Confederate Army* (1991); James M. McPherson, *What They Fought For, 1861–1865* (1995) and *For Cause and Comrades: Why Men Fought in the Civil War* (1997); William L. Burton, *Melting Pot Soldiers: The Union's Ethnic Regiments* (1998); Judith McArthur and Orville Vernon Burton, *A Gentleman and an Officer: A Military and Social History of James B. Griffin's Civil War* (1996); J. Tracy Power, *Lee's Miserables: Life in the Army of Northern Virginia from the Wilderness to Appomattox* (1998); David Williams, *Rich Man's War: Class, Caste, and Confederate Defeat in the Lower Chattahoochee Valley* (1998); Mark A. Weitz, *A Higher Duty: Desertion among Georgia Troops during the Civil War* (2000); Gerald Prokopowicz, *All for the Regiment: The Army of the Ohio, 1861–1862* (2001); David Carlson, *Plain Folk in a Rich Man's War: Class and Dissent in Confederate Georgia* (2002); Joseph A. Frank and George A. Reaves, *"Seeing the Elephant": Raw Recruits at the Battle of Shiloh* (2003); G. Ward Hubbs, *Guarding Greensboro: A Confederate Company in the Making of a Southern Community* (2003); Russell L. Johnson, *Warriors into Workers: The Civil War and the Formation of Urban-Industrial Society in a Northern City* (2003); and David Rankin, ed., *Diary of a Christian Soldier: Rufus Kinsley and the Civil War* (2004).

On the black military experience in the Civil War, see Benjamin Quarles, *The Negro in the Civil War* (1953); James M. McPherson, *The Negro's Civil War: How American Blacks Felt and Acted During the War for the Union* (1965); Dudley T. Cornish, *The Sable Arm: Black Troops in the Union Army, 1861–1865* (1966); Joseph T. Glatthaar, *Forged in Battle: The Civil War Alliance of Black Soldiers and White Officers* (1990); and Edward A. Miller, Jr., *The Black Civil War Soldiers of Illinois: The Story of the Twenty-ninth U.S. Colored Infantry* (1998).

For the debate on Confederate nationalism and popular will, see, for example, Emory M. Thomas, *The Confederate Nation: 1861–1865* (1979) and *The Confederacy as Revolutionary Experience* (1971); Paul D. Escott, *After Secession: Jefferson Davis and the Failure of Confederate Nationalism* (1978); Richard E. Beringer et al., *Why the South Lost the Civil War* (1986); George C. Rable, *The Confederate Republic: A Revolution Against Politics* (1994); Gary W. Gallagher, *The Confederate War: How Popular Will, Nationalism, and Military Strategy Could Not Stave Off Defeat* (1997); William W. Freehling, *The South vs. the South: How Anti-Confederate Southerners Shaped the Course of the Civil War* (2001); Robert E. Bonner, *Colors and Blood: Flag Passions of the Confederate South* (2002); and Clayton E. Jewett, *Texas in the Confederacy: An Experiment in Nation Building* (1992). The dissonance between the experience of the people and the promises and duties of the government has been thoroughly examined by Peter Wallenstein, *From the Slave South to New South: Public Policy in Nineteenth Century Georgia* (1987) and William A. Blair, *Virginia's Private War: Feeding Body and Soul in the Confederacy* (1998). On the Southern Confederacy, see Frank L. Owsley, *State Rights in the Confederacy* (1925); Charles H. Wesley, *The Collapse of the Confederacy* (1937); E. Merton Coulter, *The Confederate States of America, 1861–1865* (1950); Clement Eaton, *A History of the Southern Confederacy* (1954) and *Jefferson Davis* (1977); Charles P. Roland, *The Confederacy* (1960); Harry P. Owens and James Cooke, eds., *The Old South in the Crucible of War* (1983); Drew G. Faust, *The Creation of Confederate Nationalism: Ideology and Identity in the Civil War South* (1988); Eugene D. Genovese, *A Consuming Fire: The Fall of the Confederacy in the Mind of the White Christian South* (1998); Roger L. Ransom, *The Confederate States of America: What Might Have Been* (2005); Joan E. Cashin, *First Lady of the Confederacy: Varina Davis's Civil War* (2006); and William C. Davis, *"A Government of Our Own": The Creation of the Confederacy* (1997).

On the Civil War as a struggle of southerners against southerners and the southern home front, see Steve Channing, *Confederate Ordeal: The Southern Home Front* (1989); Philip S. Paludan, *Victims: A True Story of the Civil War* (1981); Malcolm C. McMillan, *The Disintegration of a Confederate State: Three Governors and Alabama's Home Front, 1861–1865* (1986); Steven A. Ash, *Middle Tennessee Society Transformed, 1860–1870: War and Peace in the Upper South* (1988) and *When the Yankees Came: Conflict and Chaos in the Occupied South, 1861–1865* (1995); Michael Fellman, *Inside War: The Guerrilla Conflict in Missouri During the American Civil War* (1989); Noel C. Fisher, *War at Every Door: Partisan Politics and Guerrilla Violence in East Tennessee, 1860–1869* (1997); Thomas G. Dyer, *Secret Yankees: The Union Circle in Confederate Atlanta* (1999); Martin Crawford, *Ashe County's Civil War: Community and Society in the Appalachian South* (2001); John D. Sarris, *A Separate Civil War: Communities in Conflict in the Mountain South* (2006); and Robert Tracy McKenzie, *Lincolnites and Rebels: A Divided Town in the American Civil War* (2006).

The best study of the northern home front is Philip S. Paludan, *"A [
test": The Union and the Civil War, 1861–1865* (1988). See also V. Jacque Voeg[
Not Equal: The Midwest and the Negro During the Civil War (1967); and J. Matth[
man, *Mastering Wartime: A Social History of Philadelphia During the Civil War* (20[
The North Fights the Civil War: The Home Front (1994). For other studies of the no[
home front, on topics including nationalism and conflict in the North, see Jo[
Silbey, *A Respectable Minority: The Democrat Party in the Civil War Era, 1860–1868* (19[
Frank L. Klement, *Dark Lanterns: Secret Political Societies, Conspiracies, and Treason Tri[
in the Civil War* (1984), *The Copperheads in the Middle West* (1960), and *The Limits of Dis-*
sent: Clement Vallandigham and the Civil War (1970); Grace Palladino, *Another Civil War:*
Labor, Capital and the State in the Anthracite Regions of Pennsylvania, 1840–1868 (1990); Iver
Bernstein, *The New York City Draft Riots: Their Significance for American Society and Politics*
in the Age of the Civil War (1995); Melinda Lawson, *Patriot Fires: Forging a New American*
Nationalism in the Civil War North (2002); and Jennifer L. Weber, *Copperheads: The Rise*
and Fall of Lincoln's Opponents in the North (2006).

On the social and cultural history of the Civil War, see John K. Betterworth,
Confederate Mississippi: The People and Policies of a Cotton State in Wartime (1943); Bell I.
Wiley, *The Plain People of the Confederacy* (1943); Charles W. Ramsdell, *Behind the Lines*
in the Southern Confederacy (1944); Mary E. Massey, *Refugee Life in the Confederacy* (1964);
William Dusinberre, *Civil War Issues in Philadelphia, 1856–1865* (1965); Randall C.
Jimerson, *The Private Civil War: Popular Thought During the Sectional Conflict* (1988); Maris
A. Vinovskis, ed., *Toward A Social History of the American Civil War: Exploratory Essays*
(1991); Anne C. Rose, *Victorian America and the Civil War* (1992); Reid Mitchell, *The Va-*
cant Chair: The Northern Soldier Leaves Home (1993); Alice Fahs, *The Imagined Civil War:*
Popular Literature of the North & South (2001); and Cheryl A. Wells, *Civil War Time: Tem-*
porality and Identity in America, 1861–1865 (2005).

On the destruction of slavery, see Herman Schlüter, *Lincoln, Labor, and Slavery:*
A Chapter from the Social History of America (1924); Willie Lee Rose, *Rehearsal for Recon-*
struction: The Port Royal Experiment (1964); Peter Kolchin, *First Freedom: The Response of*
Alabama's Blacks to Emancipation and Reconstruction (1972); Louis Gerteis, *From Contraband*
to Freedman: Federal Policy Toward Southern Blacks, 1861–1865 (1973); C. Peter Ripley,
Slaves and Freedmen in Civil War Louisiana (1976); James L. Roark, *Masters Without Slaves:*
Southern Planters in the Civil War and Reconstruction (1977); Edward Magdol, *A Right to the*
Land: Essays on the Freedman's Community (1977); Peyton McCrary, *Abraham Lincoln and*
Reconstruction: The Louisiana Experiment (1978); Claude F. Oubré, *Forty Acres and a Mule:*
The Freedman's Bureau and Black Landownership (1978); Robert F. Engs, *Freedom's First*
Generation: Black Hampton, Virginia, 1861–1890 (1979); Leon F. Litwack, *Been in the Storm*
So Long: The Aftermath of Slavery (1979); Janet S. Herman, *The Pursuit of a Dream* (1981);
Ronald F. Davis, *Good and Faithful Labor: From Slavery to Sharecropping in the Natchez Dis-*
trict, 1860–1880 (1982); Eric Foner, *Nothing But Freedom: Emancipation and Its Legacy*
(1983); John Cimprich, *Slavery's End in Tennessee, 1861–1865* (1985); Gerald D. Jaynes,
Branches Without Roots: Genesis of the Black Working Class in the American South, 1862–1882
(1986); Clarence L. Mohr, *On the Threshold of Freedom: Masters and Slaves in Civil War*

Essay

People's Con-

...li, Free But

...ew Gall-

...o) and

...thern

...l H.

...7);

...s

397

of *Reconstruction: From Slave to Wage Laborer in* \
...da J. Morgan, *Emancipation in Virginia's Tobacco* \
...gue, *Reconstruction in the Cane Fields: From Slavery* \
...s, *1862–1880* (2001); Armstead Robinson, *Bitter* \
...*ry and the Collapse of the Confederacy, 1861–1865* \
...*Freedom: Louisiana and Cuba After Slavery* (2005); \
...*: Race, Labor, and Sugar in the Age of Emancipation* (2006); \
...*te Emancipation: Southern Plans to Free and Arm Slaves During* \
...*e* of the few state studies to treat both the antebellum and \
...is Carl H. Moneyhon, *The Impact of the Civil War and Reconstruc-* \
Persistence in the Midst of Ruin (1994).

...onstruction there is also a wealth of insights yet to be mined in W.E.B. \
...*, Black Reconstruction in America, 1860–1880* (1935). See also the revisionist \
...s of John Hope Franklin, *Reconstruction: After the Civil War* (1961), and Kenneth \
Stampp, *The Era of Reconstruction, 1865–1877* (1996). Early white interpretations of Reconstruction include racist and socially conservative content that mars a good deal of political and economic insight in the traditional "tragedy of Reconstruction" school. For example, see William A. Dunning, *Essays on the Civil War and Reconstruction and Related Topics* (1897) and *Reconstruction, Political and Economic, 1865–1877* (1933); James W. Garner, *Reconstruction in Mississippi* (1901); Walter L. Fleming, *Civil War and Reconstruction in Alabama* (1911); and Ella Lonn, *Reconstruction in Louisiana After 1868* (1918), among many others. Much better are Francis B. Simkins and Robert H. Woody, *South Carolina During Reconstruction* (1932); Alrutheus A. Taylor, *The Negro in South Carolina During the Reconstruction* (1924) and *The Negro in Tennessee, 1865–1880* (1941); Henry C. Warmoth, *War, Politics, and Reconstruction: Stormy Days in Louisiana* (1930); James W. Patton, *Unionism and Reconstruction in Tennessee, 1860–1869* (1934); Vernon L. Wharton, *The Negro in Mississippi, 1865–1890* (1947); and Thomas B. Alexander, *Political Reconstruction in Tennessee* (1950). See also Leonard D. White, *The Republican Era: A Study in Administrative History, 1869–1901* (1958); Eric L. McKitrick, *Andrew Johnson and Reconstruction* (1960); LaWanda Cox and John H. Cox, *Politics, Principle, and Prejudice, 1865–1866: The Dilemma of Reconstruction America* (1963); Joel R. Williamson, *After Slavery: The Negro in South Carolina During Reconstruction, 1861–1877* (1965); James E. Sefton, *The United States Army and Reconstruction, 1865–1877* (1967); Martin Abbott, *The Freedmen's Bureau in South Carolina, 1865–1872* (1967); Carol K. R. Bleser, *The Promised Land: The History of the South Carolina Land Commission, 1869–1890* (1969); Hans L. Trefousse, *The Radical Republicans: Lincoln's Vanguard for Racial Justice* (1969); John W. Blassingame, *Black New Orleans, 1860–1880* (1973); Peggy Lamson, *Glorious Failure: Black Congressman Robert Brown Elliott and the Reconstruction in South Carolina* (1973); Joe Gray Taylor, *Louisiana Reconstructed, 1863–1877* (1974); Charles P. Vincent, *Black Legislators in Louisiana During Reconstruction* (1976); Thomas Holt, *Black Over White: Negro Political Leadership in South Carolina During Reconstruction* (1977); Howard N. Rabinowitz, *Race Relations in the Urban South, 1865–1890* (1978); Claude F. Oubre, *Forty Acres and a Mule: The Freedmen's Bureau and Black Land Ownership* (1978); William C.

Harris, *The Day of the Carpetbagger: Republican Reconstruction in Mississippi* (1979); Lawrence N. Powell, *New Masters: Northern Planters During the Civil War and Reconstruction* (1980); Elizabeth R. Bethel, *Promiseland: A Century of Life in a Negro Community* (1981); Eugene Berwanger, *The West and Reconstruction* (1981); LaWanda F. Cox, *Lincoln and Black Freedom: A Study in Presidential Leadership* (1981); Gilles Vandal, *The New Orleans Riot of 1866: Anatomy of a Tragedy* (1983); Ted Tunnell, *Crucible of Reconstruction: War, Radicalism, and Race in Louisiana, 1862–1877* (1984); C. Vann Woodward, *Reunion and Reaction: The Compromise of 1877 and the End of Reconstruction* (1951); Michael Perman, *Reunion Without Compromise: The South and Reconstruction, 1865–1868* (1973) and *The Road to Redemption: Southern Politics, 1869–1879* (1984); Dan T. Carter, *When the War Was Over: The Failure of Self-Reconstruction in the South, 1865–1867* (1985); Joe M. Richardson, *Christian Reconstruction: The American Missionary Association and Southern Blacks, 1861–1890* (1986); Michael Rosenthal, ed., *Centennial* (1986); Michael W. Fitzgerald, *The Union League Movement in the Deep South: Politics and Agricultural Change During Reconstruction* (1989); Peter J. Rachleff, *Black Labor in Richmond, 1865–1890* (1989); Bernard E. Powers, Jr., *Black Charlestonians: A Social History, 1822–1885* (1994); James D. Anderson, *The Education of Blacks in the South, 1860–1935* (1988); Lou Falkner Williams, *The Great Ku Klux Klan Trials* (1996); Richard Zuczek, *State of Rebellion: Reconstruction in South Carolina* (1996); Scott Reynolds Nelson, *Iron Confederacies, Southern Railways, Klan Violence, and Reconstruction* (1999); Wilbert L. Jenkins, *Seizing the New Day: African Americans in Post-Civil War Charleston* (1998); Allen W. Trelease, *White Terror: The Ku Klux Klan Conspiracy and Southern Reconstruction* (1971, 1999); Paul W. Rodman, *The Far West and the Great Plains in Transition: 1859–1900* (1988); Richard J. Jensen, *The Winning of the Midwest: Social and Political Conflict, 1888–96* (1991); Jane Dailey, *Before Jim Crow: The Politics of Race in Postemancipation Virginia* (2000); Akiko Ochiai, *Harvesting Freedom: African American Agrarianism in Civil War Era South Carolina* (2004); Charles W. Calhoun, *Conceiving a New Republic: The Republican Party and the Southern Question, 1869–1900* (2006); James D. Schmidt, *Free to Work: Labor Law, Emancipation, and Reconstruction, 1815–1880* (1998); Xi Wang, *The Trial of Democracy: Black Suffrage and Northern Republicans, 1860–1910* (1999); Keith Ian Polakoff, *The Politics of Inertia: The Election of 1876 and the End of Reconstruction* (1973); and Richard T. Bensel, *Yankee Leviathan: The Origins of Central State Authority in America, 1859–1877* (1991).

On white restoration and the counterrevolution against Reconstruction, see Theodore B. Wilson, *The Black Codes of the South* (1965); William J. Cooper, Jr., *The Conservative Regime: South Carolina, 1877–1890* (1968); William Gillette, *Retreat from Reconstruction, 1869–1879* (1979); Forrest G. Wood, *Black Scare: The Racist Response to Emancipation and Reconstruction* (1968); Nina Silber, *The Romance of Reunion: Northerners and the South, 1865–1900* (1993); George C. Rable, *But There Was No Peace: The Role of Violence in the Politics of Reconstruction* (1984); Gilles Vandal, *Rethinking Southern Violence: Homicides in Post–Civil War Louisiana, 1866–1884* (2000); Heather C. Richardson, *The Death of Reconstruction: Race, Labor, and Politics in the Post–Civil War North, 1865–1901* (2001); Charles J. Holden, *In the Great Maelstrom: Conservatives in Post–Civil War South Carolina* (2002); and James K. Hogue, *Uncivil War: Five New Orleans Street Battles and the*

Rise and Fall of Radical Reconstruction (2006). The classic study of disfranchisement is J. Morgan Kousser, *The Shaping of Southern Politics: Suffrage Restriction and the Establishment of the One-Party South, 1880–1910* (1974); see also Michael Perman, *Struggle for Mastery: Disfranchisement in the South, 1888–1908* (2001).

For the Populist revolt and thereafter, see my detailed historiographical essay on populism at TheAgeofLincoln.com. The best short synthesis, which also has the best bibliographical essay, is Robert C. McMath, Jr., *American Populism: A Social History, 1877–1898* (1990). For the Alliance, see McMath's *Populist Vanguard: A History of the Southern Farmers' Alliance* (1975). The standard work on the movement is Lawrence Goodwyn, *Democratic Promise: The Populist Moment in America* (1976). See also Bruce Palmer, *Man Over Money: The Southern Populist Critique of American Capitalism* (1980); and James R. Green, *Grass Roots Socialism: Radical Movements in the Southwest, 1895–1943* (1978). On the Greenback movement, see Mark A. Lause, *The Civil War's Last Campaign: James B. Weaver, the Greenback-Labor Party and the Politics of Race and Section* (2001). For religion and populism, see Connie L. Lester, *Up from the Mudsills of Hell: The Farmers' Alliance, Populism, and Progressive Agriculture in Tennessee, 1870–1915* (2006); and C. Vann Woodward, *The Strange Career of Jim Crow* (1966) and *Origins of the New South, 1877–1913* (1951).

Acknowledgments

I began thinking about this book when growing up in a segregated southern small town in the 1950s and '60s as the Second Reconstruction got under way. In 1967 I traveled from Ninety Six, South Carolina, to New York City under the auspices of the Harvard-Yale-Columbia Intensive Studies Program, and was challenged, in a lecture course on the Old South at Columbia University, by a then young professor of history, Eugene Genovese. The following summer I attended Yale University, where Bill McFeely and Joe Ellis directed my attention to the centrality of the Civil War and Reconstruction to American History. At Furman University my professors encouraged my interests in Civil War, Reconstruction, race relations, and the place of minorities in American society. Many of the ideas and ways of approaching the narrative I learned from professors at Princeton, most particularly the two best, my PhD advisers, James M. McPherson and Sheldon Hackney. A research paper on Robert Smalls in James McPherson's graduate class introduced me to research in this era, and the readings for his Civil War and Reconstruction graduate class became the beginnings of the secondary readings that form the basis of my arguments. As anyone who has written on the Civil War understands, James McPherson is the most supportive of scholars, even when he might disagree with interpretations, and I appreciate his taking time out of his own writing to once again read one of my manuscripts. I am always amazed at how much I learn from him, and count myself fortunate to be not only his student but his friend.

Having accomplished some microhistory to address large questions in small places, I decided to tackle large questions in a larger place. A fellowship in 1988–89 at the Woodrow Wilson International Center for Scholars afforded me the opportunity to research in the Library of Congress and National Archives, as well as time to get a lengthy draft (and visit Eastern battlefields); I was soon to learn that this was only a baby step on this road. A fellowship in 1994–95 at the National Humanities Center gave me time to do original research in the marvelous collections in the area. To the staff at those incredible havens for scholars, thank you. A Pew Foundation fellowship in 1996 provided the opportunity to study and incorporate religion into my interpretation of the nineteenth century. I have benefited from the help of numerous librarians in libraries and archives across the country. Libraries are the historians' laboratory and we could not survive without archivists and librarians; my collective thanks to you all. John Hoffmann, curator of the Illinois History and Lincoln Collections at the University of Illinois, deserves special recognition for his many courtesies.

All of my students throughout my years as a southerner teaching in the Land of Lincoln, and especially that wonderful "family" of my graduate students, have contributed in many ways to my thinking and the shaping of this book. As the Pew-Lilly Foundation Graduate Professor at Notre Dame in 2001, I taught a graduate course, "American Crisis: Identity and Race in the Civil War Era," for a very special group of Christian graduate students selected from various universities, and subjected these students to my ideas and writing. The University of Illinois Research Board has provided generous support for research assistants. Especially for the last six years, graduate students have worked for me on this book project: Simon Appleford, Masatomo Ayabe, Ian Binnington, Phil Carpenter, Matthew Cheney, Nick Gaffney, Stephen Hageman, Kevin Hales, Kwame Holmes, Kalev Leetaru, Brandon Mills, Ben Murphy, Kerry Pimblott, Troy Smith, and Kris DuRocher Wilson. In finalizing this book I owe very much to my current graduate research assistant and PhD student Larry McDonnell. I want to thank him for challenging my interpretation, as well as for his diligence and willingness to work my schedule of very late nights and early mornings. Several of my graduate students who were not research assistants also made specific contributions: Frank Freemon, David Herr, and Stacy McDermott. Dawn Owens-Nicholson provided statistical advice and assistance and helped with the huge IPUMS data sets.

Scholars willing to take time to read another's manuscript and offer suggestions and corrections truly give definition and meaning to the term "academic community."

My colleagues at the University of Illinois, and the Southern History Reading Group that has met for more than fifteen years in my living room, were subjected to ideas and portions of this book over the years. In particular, my friends and colleagues Max Edelson and David Roediger read specific chapters; Fred Jaher, Bruce Levine, Robert McColley, and Larry Ratner read the entire manuscript. Several scholars and friends also read and improved the manuscript: James Huston, Charles Irons, Clayton Jewett, Tracy McKenzie, Lewie Reece, Heather Cox Richardson, Ben Severance, Jim Simeone, Jon Wakelyn, Chris Waldrep. Several others read selected chapters or portions: Ray Arsenault, Lloyd Benson (who also provided a Brooks-Sumner illustration), Bert Wyatt-Brown, Lewis Burke, Jane Turner Censer, Luke Harlow, Bill Harris, Charles Joyner, James Loewen, Mike Marty, John Mayfield, David Moltke-Hansen, Phil Paludan, Thomas Schwartz, David G. Smith, Mitch Snay, and Peter Wallenstein. All made invaluable comments and suggestions. I would also like to thank special friends Mike Marlow and Mary Timmons for their very close read and edits. On a number of different occasions, I turned to experts on particular issues for specific questions and received good advice and recommended sources. For example, John Giggie provided an African American millennial railroad illustration. In spite of all these folks' best efforts, I am certain that there are areas of contention, and of course, I, and I alone, am responsible for the interpretation and any errors.

While reading my essay "Sectional Conflict, Civil War, and Reconstruction," my publisher, Thomas LeBien, saw in it the kernel of a book. He has proven the ultimate patient professional, caring deeply about this book and about me and my family. I appreciate his careful readings, comments, and suggestions; but, more important, I appreciate his friendship. Assistant editor June Kim and production editor Wah-Ming Chang were models of gracious efficacy.

My family lived with this book as I have over the years. All my children— Joanna, Maya, Morgan, Beatrice, and Alice—have had to travel across the country for research and have lived so many years with this book that now I have grandchildren—Katie, Toby, Piper, Alex, Aurora, and Charlotte—all of whom provide great joy in my life. I would like to thank my daughter Morgan Johnston for her help with the photos and my son-in-law Will Johnston for his work on the website, TheAgeofLincoln.com. Georganne Burton has also devoted her time and energy to this project, and I want to thank her for all her editing help. Her talent has benefited every chapter, if not every paragraph. She believes in thesis statements and topic sentences, and as you can see, she did not win every discussion. An exemplar of Proverbs 31, she is the love of my life. This book is dedicated to her.

Index